MW01194124

RK

Scale, inches

Contour interval 80 feet. Datum is mean sea level
Road/railroad indicates that elevations
on this map should be decreased by 6 feet.

Topography by Francois E. Matthes and Richard T. Evans
Surveyed in 1902-1923

Polyconic projection. To place on North American datum
move projection lines 470 feet south and 280 feet west
5000 yard grid based upon U. S. zone system F

Edition of 1927
reprinted 1948

D E S E R T

BOUNDARY RIDGE

Trail

BALLARD

RRY McDONALD
T O'RILEY
McCORMICK

CANYON

DESERT FACADE

COCONINO PLATEAU

PAINTED DESERT

NAVAJO

Stopping for
1510 to
8130 for
trip from 8
Ti. Can to
mouth

Rope descent to
river bank; driftwood ladder

Blue
Ta

Rope

Rope

Rope

Rope

Pt. H.B.

BEALIES
1872

Pt. W.B.

Temple Rock

Temple Butte

STILL

Chuan Butte

Amatzul Crest

Gunther Castle

(Davis)

VISHNU TEMPLE

Kachina Shrine

TEAT FALLS

Lava Butte

VOTTEU LAKTIE!
STE

Cedar Mtn

Straight Canyon

Cedar Canyon

GRAND OBSESSION

GRAND OBSESSION

HARVEY BUTCHART
and the
EXPLORATION OF GRAND CANYON

Harvey Butchart in Oak Creek Canyon, 1946. *Courtesy Chuck Pullen*

GRAND OBSESSION

HARVEY BUTCHART
and the
EXPLORATION OF GRAND CANYON

ELIAS BUTLER
AND
TOM MYERS

PUMA PRESS
FLAGSTAFF

Copyright ©2007 Elias Butler and Thomas Myers.
Printed and bound in the United States of America. All rights reserved. No
part of this book may be reproduced or transmitted in any form or by any
means, electronic or mechanical, including photocopying, recording or by an
information storage or retrieval system—except by a reviewer who may quote
brief passages in a review to be printed in a magazine or newspaper—without
permission in writing from the publisher. For information, please contact
Puma Press, P.O. Box 30998, Flagstaff, AZ 86003 USA.

Although the authors and publisher have made every effort to ensure the
accuracy and completeness of the information contained in this book, we
assume no responsibility for errors, inaccuracies, omissions or any other inconsistency herein. Any slights of people, places, companies, or organizations are
unintentional.

FIRST EDITION / FIRST PRINTING

ISBN: 978-0-9700973-5-4 (Hardcover)
ISBN: 978-0-9700973-4-7 (Paperback)
LCCN: 2007925744

Front cover photographs: Harvey Butchart at Enfilade Point (1968) by
    Walter Maeyers Edwards. Inset of Harvey Butchart (1981) by Scott Baxter.
Rear cover photograph: Harvey Butchart near Palisades Creek (1958)
    by Allyn Cureton.
Inside cover maps: Harvey Butchart's East (front) and West (back) Matthes-
    Evans maps.
Book Jacket and cover design by Bronze Black
Book design and production by Mary Williams and Katherine Spillman
Edited by Michael Ghiglieri

For every hopeless Grand Canyon addict

Contents

AUTHORS'S NOTE

THE IDEA CAME in Tom Myers's garage. It's a good place to talk, amidst piles of books, rafting equipment, and greasy tools. On this day in 2002, we were discussing a pet fascination with flash floods when a dusty cardboard box labeled "HARVEY" in a corner of that dim space caught Elias Butler's attention.

In Grand Canyon hiking circles, the name "Harvey" summons to mind only one person: Harvey Butchart (pronounced "butt´-chart"), Grand Canyon's hiking legend. It doesn't matter if you never met the man. Most everyone calls him Harvey, as if we were all his friends.

Tom explained that in 1993, he decided to write a biography of Harvey. Harvey was initially receptive to the idea and gave Tom multiple interviews throughout the 1990s, both in person and by mail. But like flash floods, the inspiration came and went. Harvey's wife Roma was not supportive, and the deeper Tom dug, the more he understood the reasons why. Rather than create more strife in the twilight of a marriage nearly seven decades old, Tom stuffed Harvey and Roma's story into that cardboard box. It would be best to leave some things untold until they passed away.

Fast-forward to that day in the garage. Harvey and Roma had recently died after living long lives. Elias was intrigued with the thought of reading more about this well-known but enigmatic explorer, and began rummaging through the box. The two of us parted ways that afternoon with a simple handshake, resolving to resurrect the biography and see it through to its end. Over the next five years it grew by fits and starts into the book you now hold in your hands.

How to write a life? In Harvey's case, it seemed a nearly impossible task, at first. We encountered a problem that most biographers would envy—too much information. One glance at Harvey's thick-as-mud logbooks, finely decorated maps, hundreds of letters, and thousands of slides, and it became exceedingly clear *what* Harvey had done and *when*, at least in Grand Canyon. Missing from that mountain of information, however, was *why*. An astounding lack of reflection inhabits Harvey's writing. His story was somewhere in all that stuff, we were sure, but sometimes we felt like we needed to blast it out with dynamite.

Although Harvey willingly participated in this biography, it was not without reservations. Queries about how his obsession with Grand Canyon affected his personal life provoked unease, sometimes to the point where he announced that he was withdrawing his support. "I wouldn't care for the public to read the sort of thing that you seem to want," Harvey responded in one letter. Ultimately, however, Harvey provided detailed answers to all of Tom's questions.

For reasons explained in the text, we decided to commit a serious breach of biography etiquette by occasionally placing ourselves within the narrative. Each of us will at times be doing the "talking," and we have done our best to make clear who is doing so. If our story should help to develop a better sense of the demands of Grand Canyon route finding, Harvey's unique personality, and why he got so wrapped up in Canyon exploration, then our gamble will have paid off. We thus ask you, our reader, to proceed as you would along the exposed edge of a Redwall cliff—at your own risk.

In researching and writing *Grand Obsession*, several questions came to the fore. How to explain the incredible pull the Grand Canyon wilderness exerts on certain fanatical souls? What fueled the likes of Harvey Butchart, who willingly sacrificed much that most of us hold dear in order to attach his name to Grand Canyon? And is greatness in the ever-shrinking field of geographical exploration worth attaining at any price?

We leave the answers for you to discover, by trekking through the pages of this book.

Elias Butler
Tom Myers

Flagstaff, 2007

The best explorers are seldom as brilliant as they appear years after their death. In the earthly excursions that established their fame, they often stumbled, miscalculated distances, encountered unheard-of diseases, and sometimes suffered the ridicule of those who had stayed at home with the dog, the pipe and the afghan.

But for most of these adventurous souls, there were other rewards, the deepest of which remain vague to this day: it is the joy of discovery. It is not only the discovery of the palpable world, but the invisible hand that stays beyond it, beckoning the traveler from the beaten path to the trackless wild.

Sam Negri,
Earth's Mystical Grand Canyons

Harvey Butchart rediscovered an Anasazi Indian route in this Redwall
Limestone break below Enfilade Point. *J. Harvey Butchart, courtesy NAU
Special Collections*

Prologue

IN HARVEY'S FOOTSTEPS
2004

"THIS PLACE STARTLED ME," wrote John Harvey Butchart in *Grand Canyon Treks III*, his compact, eccentric guidebook to off-trail routes in Arizona's master gorge. We laugh when we read this. Harvey's rendering of the sheer cliff at our feet is a typically succinct statement from the five-foot, seven-inch professor of mathematics, summing up in four prosaic words his reaction to an untested and terrific drop.

The description is not only succinct but modest as well. In April 1971, Harvey had no idea if this particular route to the Colorado River was possible or not. The ripe 63-year-old was testing it, improvising where necessary, carefully probing as a surgeon might for the correct passage. When he found the solution to the route's most onerous problem—this drop over the massive Redwall Limestone cliff—he needed to face down some weighty fears.

Alone amidst the wilderness, fantastically detached from civilization, Harvey may have been startled but he was at home. The most compulsive and accomplished explorer in Grand Canyon's modern history welcomed danger where it touched discovery.

"Ay Chihuahua! Holy smokes! I'm not going down there!"

Tom Myers recoils from the sharp line of rock that divides canyon and sky, unwilling to accept that Harvey's route has just dropped several hundred feet down a near-vertical limestone gutter, a passage well suited for spiders, maybe, or perhaps sure-footed rams. We exhibit none of Harvey's reserve and freely swear obscenities at the stunning drop. Nausea swirls lazily in my stomach. I sit heavily to think or stop, knowing full well that we will not stop, not because we love the challenge of negotiating unprotected walls of brittle sedimentary rock, but because the ghost we hunt has gone down here ahead of us.

1

We left our ropes and rappelling devices at home, on purpose. According to Harvey this route requires only fingers and boots to negotiate. As we inspect more closely, it still looks impossible, But we do notice what attracted him to such an unlikely spot. The winding, perpendicular escarpment we've been following wears a collapsed look below, the work of a geologic fault. It's as if a massive fingernail has scratched the cliff face, roughening and breaking it just enough to provide a breach through an otherwise 600-foot vertical wall. There can be no question. This is our route.

While we contemplate this reality, we notice a telltale cairn nearby that not only suggests direction but also encourages descent, as if someone had anticipated our doubt. Against the usual pile of stones leans a long, flat sandstone slab that points unmistakably toward the steep and unsavory drop. The unusual rock bears a resemblance that Tom recognizes.

"That looks like a tombstone."

Tom is a doctor who has spent over a decade working at the small clinic at the South Rim. He has seen his share of bodies hauled out of the gorge, knows with intimacy what can happen when flesh and bone meets rock. Tom co-wrote a book (with Michael Ghiglieri) called *Over the Edge: Death in Grand Canyon*, which details all the recorded deaths that have occurred in the national park. Coming from Tom, the word "tombstone" carries more weight than I would like.

Atop the Redwall cliff along the Enfilade Point Route. *Elias Butler*

2

I close my eyes and gulp my imported tap water. The water is good but does nothing for my queasiness. I'm feeling a sudden fatigue from the continuous focusing and quick pace we've set. An uncertain sensation inside threatens to unsteady my mind and sabotage the concentration I'll need for climbing. I bring up my hand and find it trembling.

Yet our arrival here does not carry the frightful weight of uncertainty. We know a human being has made it down this cliff in one piece, so our minds are permitted to deal with the routine questions of *how* instead of *if*. Peering below at Tom, who is busy trying the first pair of holds in the rock, I can imagine the heart-racing fear (and yes, thrill) that would accompany this place if we had no idea whether or not it would go.

Discovery within North America—or most anywhere else in the twenty-first century—is an experience that few modern day explorers enjoy, unless he or she wishes to disregard all that has been published in the last 100 years. Such a self-imposed ignorance might be the answer for adventurers seeking a frontier in today's teeming West. Tom and I do not feel as if our excitement at this crack is tainted by not being first to tackle it, but only because we, as Americans who came along too late in the game for true geographic discovery, have seldom found a blank spot without a map to accompany it.

Our momentum comes from the flip side of being born in the age of certainty, one of digital maps, global-positioning satellite systems, commercialization of the wilderness, the information free-for-all. We seek relief from such products of our culture, from civilization itself. And as Harvey himself once wrote, only half jokingly, "You aren't really living if you don't risk your life once every six months."

Tom has decided the climb can be done. He silently slips into an airy passage adjacent to the cliff. I undo a short hand line to offer him a belay, listening to the soft report of flesh on rock that rises from below. Pebbles and flakes glissade into space as he attaches himself to the wall. He steps cautiously as a cat on shifting, loose holds, deliberating, descending, feeling the rock with his feet, his body tensed for sudden reaction. I locate a relatively solid piece of cliff, wedge into it as firmly as possible and toss the line to him. I catch myself wondering how much he weighs.

"Don't need it," Tom grunts without looking up. "But there's a better route—you should go down over there next to that chockstone. That looks easier." He nods at a boulder the size of five refrigerators trapped in the chute. The wall below it is pocked with holes perfectly sized for a human hand. It looks bad from here but I don't want to stall and think too much. I take his word and traverse a few feet, fasten my pack over my shoulders and carefully step off the edge.

I place my hands into the sharp gray rock, which feels cold and reassuringly solid. Bulges, concavities and thin edges present themselves in a beautiful pattern that allows a swift descent of the crux. It turns out to be easier than it first looked. When I arrive on solid ground a couple minutes later, Tom and I gaze up at the bad spot and shake our heads. The success or failure of a route in Grand Canyon often comes down to the existence of such places, thin avenues in the rock where the Canyon says "yes." We savor a small rush of relief and continue down toward the river, lowering ourselves off more chockstones and edges.

Of course, to claim such a thing as discovery in America, pioneering European-Americans had to brush aside the annoying reality that Indians had known the land long before them. Grand Canyon was no exception. The previous afternoon, combing the rim above while looking for the head of this route, Tom and I came across a tower of rock separated from the main cliff, a natural sentinel that had been fashioned into a rough keep by Anasazi Indians perhaps 900 years ago.

These people had placed a continuous wall of limestone blocks along the perimeter of the narrow, elongated platform, forming an impressive defense against attack either from the rim or from below. Easily capable of holding 100 warriors, it was the perfect rocky aerie from which to direct a sweeping line of fire at encroaching enemies—thus the mapmakers found the name "Enfilade Point" appropriate for the lookout. Its purpose remains debatable, a defensive post or a nice place to live, but everyone agrees the site does not lack for drama. Beyond the ruin lies an unbroken view to the east, where the Colorado River draws a silvery line beneath a thrilling expanse of nude cliffs and isolated buttes.

Despite the aesthetics and military advantages, however, there was one potential flaw to this dwelling: Water. There was none at the rim, none to be found nearby. The river, 4,000 feet below, or perhaps a waterhole hidden in the labyrinth of rock along the way, would have had to provide. The Anasazi needed a way down.

As Tom and I lumber the last few hundred feet to the Colorado, we come to a place where stones have been piled as a step. It breaks a 10-foot wall into a manageable drop. Just beyond this climbing aid, tucked beneath the protective shelter of an overhang, final proof of the old route appears: A semi-circular arrangement of low, decayed walls, a sprinkling of broken pottery pieces, grinding stones and metates lying in the dirt. To reach this spot through nearly a mile of cliff, we have had to conform our bodies to the shape of the Canyon where others long ago first learned how to do the same.

After the route had been used for the last time by the Anasazi, then later rediscovered and abandoned once more by the Havasupai Indians, it would again lie fallow until the arrival of a startled math professor in 1971.

A FRIEND ONCE POINTED OUT a head-and-shoulders photo on the back cover of one of Harvey's *Grand Canyon Treks* guidebooks. The yellow booklet appeared to be cheaply printed. The text was absolutely utilitarian in scope. I found it hard to understand, having little familiarity with Grand Canyon's routes at the time. I looked again at the photo, at Harvey's unruly, short-cropped haircut and proud expression. The face staring back exuded unmistakable self-assurance. Who *was* this man?

Among his Grand Canyon disciples, Harvey achieved legendary status long before his death due to natural causes in May 2002. Ever since the 1950s, his name had been synonymous with mastery of the wild and Byzantine Grand Canyon backcountry. Here was someone who routinely stood at the rim of this mile-deep gorge and decided to find his own way to the bottom. Writer Colin Fletcher even invented a word in his classic adventure book *The Man Who Walked Through Time* to describe the act of Harvey-style route finding: *Butcharting.*

Yet Harvey did not fit very well the profile of a rugged outdoorsman. Diminutive, weighing a trim 135 pounds, the bespectacled husband, father, and Northern Arizona University mathematics professor was never mistaken for someone capable of extraordinary feats of endurance. He looked like the archetypal bookworm, an armchair adventurer at best who wore tucked-in, collared shirts while out for a hike.

Make no mistake though. Harvey was the human version of what muscle car aficionados call a sleeper: A supercharged hot rod masquerading as Grandpa's sedan. Many who shared the Canyon

Harvey Butchart's portrait from *Grand Canyon Treks.* Bill Belknap, *courtesy Loie Belknap-Evans*

with Harvey admitted that when it came to negotiating steep, boulder-and-cacti-strewn canyons, few could keep up. "It was like he was made out of piano wire," said friend and long-distance runner Bob Packard.

Unlike many other athletic endeavors, Grand Canyon-style canyoneering favors those who are slightly built. Walking in and out of this mile-deep chasm, where extra muscle means extra weight and therefore more work, the ideal body is light and wiry.

Harvey might have been made for the place. He spent a good deal of his childhood living upon a mountain in Asia where hiking and climbing formed the main diversions for children. Within his lithe frame coursed the high-metabolic voltage necessary for frequent dips into an uncooperative landscape like Grand Canyon. It was a point of pride. Until he was in his mid-70s he could keep up a brisk pace for 10 to 12 hours a day for days on end. He never drank, never smoked. Harvey took full advantage of his natural gifts and rarely wavered in the fulfillment that they promised.

True to his appearance, Harvey did have an intellectual bent, a reserved and shy nature befitting a professor of mathematics. When he wasn't hiking, he could often be found locked in a quiet game of chess or Scrabble, his mind humming with variables and potential solutions. He indulged in calculus for fun. He was soft-spoken and sensitive, a lover of classical music and classic literature, by all accounts generous and kind.

He was also ferociously competitive, and definitely obsessed when it came to Grand Canyon.

"There are two reasons for me to do something," he once explained in his bemused way. "The first is that someone has already done it. The other is that no one has done it, which is even better." To those who knew him, Harvey possessed a discernible edge underneath his gentlemanly disposition. He thrived on the thought of being the first to crack open Grand Canyon's outback, but he very rarely said as much out loud. Instead, his determination expressed itself in his speedy, purposeful stride. This was a man who knew exactly where he was going, and the quicker he arrived the better.

Harvey became keenly aware of other explorers who came before or after him, and just where he stood in comparison. Clarence Dutton, a renowned geologist and writer who worked with John Wesley Powell, and one of the first scientists to study the Grand Canyon in detail, proclaimed in his 1882 masterpiece, *The Tertiary History of the Grand Canyon District*, that a total of four routes from rim to river existed within the gorge. Dutton was a Yale-educated army captain, a man skilled in words and topography. It seemed a safe estimation—how could it be possible to penetrate such a forbidding region on foot in more than a few places?

"Dutton had much to learn," Harvey wrote in 1976 after notching 84 rim-to-river routes in the Canyon. Harvey eventually raised this total to 116 by the time he made his last hike in the 1980s. Much to learn, indeed.

These routes formed Harvey's most coveted goals in the Canyon. Trails bored him. He instead preferred the thrill of figuring out for himself just where

the Indians might have accessed the gorge, or even where wildlife dared to follow slim ledges above nasty drop-offs. This was dangerous and fun, and if he succeeded in reaching the Colorado, he could notch another victorious hashmark
in his boots. "I once told him that he must know the inner Canyon's fastness as
well as the native bighorn sheep or wild burros did," wrote Francois Leydet in
the 1964 anti-dam Sierra Club picture book *Time and the River Flowing.* "But
when he showed me his topographic maps crisscrossed in ink with the routes of
his favorite hikes, I realized I had underestimated him. No individual bighorn
or burro ever had traveled so much of the Grand Canyon."

From the beginning Harvey found himself locked in a relatively short race
with time, for he was 38 when he first arived in Arizona and took his first hike
down the Kaibab Trail. Remarkably, throughout the next 42 years of devotion to
the gorge, he worked a full-time job and raised a family, relying on short weekend
forays or school breaks to establish himself as a backcountry expert. He compul-
sively planned his free time around an ever-expanding list of objectives—a butte
to summit, a route to discover, some mystery to unravel, his feats to make known.

Harvey had that peculiar, inspired, arrow-straight approach to life that often
marks the person of genius. Such single-mindedness is required for great accomplishment, but it is also a quality that tends to make it difficult to balance the
obligations of being a good father and husband. Obsessions carry price tags and
Harvey's was no exception. His wife Roma endured many a lonely day and night
because of his frequent absences, even frightening nights when Harvey suffered
broken bones or accidents and failed to return as promised. He was at least part-
ly aware of the anguish he caused. Still he kept going. Though he avoided major
injury himself, his intense, even blinding drive directly contributed to the death
of his favorite hiking and climbing partner, a remorse that haunted him for the
remainder of his days.

Yet none of this could douse Harvey's need for Grand Canyon and what it
gave him. Had he simply been a pioneering explorer, he no doubt would have
left his mark, but his greatest legacy was what he created for others—1,079
typewritten pages in which he carefully recorded his treks—a massive document that represents the fruits of nearly three years's worth of days spent inde-
fatigably striding through the Canyon's unknown regions. Typed in a dense,
meticulous voice, each page of Harvey's logbooks reveals a sharpened mind
capable of photographically memorizing the minutiae of each side canyon,
every turn in the Canyon's great form, each route he had found through its
cliffs. Eventually Harvey's inveterate chronicling would become the basis for
the first-ever Grand Canyon backcountry guidebooks: *Grand Canyon Treks*
(1970), *Grand Canyon Treks II* (1975), and *Grand Canyon Treks III* (1984).

These spare publications gave birth to canyoneering, that now-popular hybrid activity that combines elements of mountaineering, such as rappelling and rock climbing with backpacking, whitewater navigation, and route finding. Although a few others preceded Harvey in exploring the Canyon, he brought a combination of energy, writing skills, and astonishing longevity that inspired fellow guidebook author John Annerino to name him the "father of canyoneering." His feats would eventually give rise to a legion of followers, some of whom would perish trying to repeat his accomplishments.

These days, we cannot truly fathom the opportunity Harvey stumbled upon in mid-life: A vast and vastly beautiful crevasse in the lower 48 states that lay unexplored in modern times. After his arrival and subsequent decades of trailblazing, something ended in the West, for he perhaps deciphered its last truly difficult landscape. Yet what made Harvey's discoveries so unusual is that they did not lead to the typical consumerism and development. Physically and culturally, the impact has been slight. Grand Canyon is a rough place after all. But knowing that someone spent more than 40 years there without seeing everything only reinforces its importance to a society increasingly beleaguered by its own weight. Here is a wilderness with enough space to consume a lifetime of trips.

Rarely has one person been so singly associated with opening such an immense landform. Harvey Butchart did it by covering 12,000 miles in this last great unknown: The vertical mile between the Colorado River and the Canyon's two rims, and the 277 serpentine river miles between Glen Canyon upstream and the Grand Wash Cliffs downstream. It is a big place compared to something as small as a man. Yet Harvey spent much of his life proving that a small man could live by the biggest ambitions.

Harvey posing in his canyoneering outfit in Flagstaff, 1957. *Fronske Studio, courtesy Anne Madariaga*

FOUR HOURS AFTER LEAVING the river, Tom and I are thrashed by the massive effort it takes to ascend the steep talus slopes below Enfilade Point. Looking toward the ruined Anasazi fortress above, I realize we are now in its once-real line of fire. The builders would have found us easy pickings. An enfilade of sorts does come as Tom struggles just ahead on the steep slope. He crawls badger-like on all fours for traction, raining down a small volley of dirt, loose rock, and pinyon pine needles. Yet I'm doing no better, breathlessly crashing through the dense undergrowth.

We had heard that following Harvey at his pace would leave most people gasping, even to the point of vomiting. Scott Baxter, a climber and writer who spent considerable time bushwhacking with Harvey, said, "The main thing I think that people were in awe of about Harvey was that he'd take you down there and he'd grind you to a pulp. That's why he had this incredible turnover of partners, 'cause people just couldn't keep up with him. And that was part of his play, taking people in there and burning them off, and he admitted that. He made no bones about it. He was competitive down in there. To do more things and do them quicker than other people who were spending time in the Canyon."

Harvey no doubt enjoyed his superior abilities, but speed was necessary here. Pioneering routes through such a landscape, one would need to move fast to get anywhere.

Feeling like pulp, we finally reach the rim and stagger into camp. Tom and I try to dissect what we have learned over cans of beer and rehydrated enchiladas. We find that while we have walked a short distance in Harvey's footsteps, we haven't come much closer to understanding the depth and demands of his obsession with Grand Canyon. His essence remains an enigma. It eventually dawns on us that what we seek lies still further in the gorge—perhaps in some side canyon, or on the summit of a remote butte, or along the Colorado River where he once floated on his lightweight air mattress. We discuss these possibilities as we rattle over dirt roads toward home, the desert's flora rushing past like white gasps in the headlights.

Closer to Grand Canyon Village, we pass a yellow sign emblazoned with a large black "X": Railroad crossing ahead.

We begin Harvey's story here.

Laying track for the Grand Canyon Railroad, 1901. *Courtesy NAU Special Collections*

Chapter One
TO THE TITAN OF CHASMS
1901–1906

Twenty Yosemites might lie unperceived anywhere below. Niagara, that
Mecca of marvel seekers, would not here possess the dignity of a trout stream.

C. A. Higgins,
The Titan of Chasms (1896)

ON SEPTEMBER 11, 1901, workers dropped the last tie into place, laid the final
rails on top and pounded iron spikes into the assembly with sledgehammer
blows. The Arizona sun threw down its flat heat. A strip of cleared land led
south through ponderosas and sagebrush where the men had advanced. With
sweaty backs and brows, they raised their voices en masse, as men do after collectively reaching a longtime goal: All 64 miles of track, done.

The Grand Canyon Railroad made its inagural run one week later. Starting
from the town of Williams at the Santa Fe main line, well-dressed citizens, jour-
nalists, and Aitchison, Topeka, and Santa Fe Railway executives rode shining
cars north over the rolling Coconino Plateau, which lay green and dotted with
red Indian paintbrush from recent monsoon rains. Passengers were amazed to
average a brisk 15 miles per hour. Already, word was reverberating across the
country: The well-heeled tourist no longer needed to pay $20 for an uncomfort-
able, all-day, horse-drawn carriage from Flagstaff or Williams to see the "mighty
miracle." A one-way ride on a luxurious Pullman car cost only $3.95 and prom-
ised a considerably more accommodating journey in a mere three or four hours.
This was a great victory for America. Industrial tourism had finally penetrated
one of the most remote and mysterious regions in the country.

As it pulled into the crowded depot at the South Rim with a stout whistle
blast, the train unloaded not just human cargo but a hint of the future. Santa
Fe Railway president Edward Ripley had envisioned the Grand Canyon line as

the crown jewel in a series of Southwest attractions along the Santa Fe main line. Ripley could only guess how many would come now that he had defeated the major obstacle to Grand Canyon—a lack of reliable, speedy transportation. But there was one major hole in Ripley's plan. Across from the modest plank wood depot stood the Bright Angel Hotel. Plain, fashioned from cheap canvas and wood, sparsely furnished, lacking standard hotel services, the Bright Angel wore mule turds on its outside walls where cowboys regularly scraped their boots. Ripley knew that society's upper crust, everyone from foreign dignitaries to presidents, would soon be arriving by rail. This would not do. Obviously, he needed to build a first class hotel at the edge of the gorge, include a restaurant with a view, and make sure the menu offered delicacies such as fresh oysters and goose. He would spare no expense on construction and design.

The $250,000 El Tovar Hotel opened in January 1905. Named for a lieutenant El Tovar with the 1540 Coronado expedition—the first white man to see *El Canon Grande*—the new hotel epitomized luxury wilderness lodges in the West. Rooms sold out months in advance, a trend that has since continued.

Thirty-eight-year-old Louis Benton Akin could not count himself among the wealthy patrons of the El Tovar. The Corvallis, Oregon native tended a tiny studio in nearby Flagstaff where he lived a hand-to-mouth existence, there

Artist Louis Akin at Grand Canyon circa 1905-1906. *Courtesy Karl Moon Archives*

being little demand for his Western landscapes and Indian portraits. Akin did, however, land occasional jobs with the Santa Fe Railway. The company had hired him in 1903 to paint the Hopi Indians for an advertising campaign. Akin lived in the ancient Hopi town of Oraibi for close to a year as a result, where he was so well received that the Hopis invited him to join a secret ceremonial society. But the money had dried up after leaving Hopi. The artist thus jumped in 1905 when Santa Fe offered him another commission to advertise its new hotel and venerate the greatest canyon on Earth with oils, brush and canvas.

Akin's "El Tovar at Grand Canyon" would become an icon in western land-scape art just as its subject was in Western architecture. The chromolithograph depicted the hotel in its stark Canyon environment with unadorned realism. Akin had achieved that elusive balance in art, a piece with both commercial and artistic appeal.

After the painting left Akin's Flagstaff studio, Santa Fe's advertising division affixed it to countless pamphlets, postcards, and posters, which were then sent to all points of the compass. Thousands spread into California, a lesser number continued across the Pacific to the Asian coastal cities, and from there, at least one of Akin's renderings continued its purposeful trajectory farther west, where providence led it toward a range of misty mountains occupying the Middle Kingdom, otherwise known as China.

Hawk's Nest Pavilion, a lookout point at Mount Lushan. *Elias Butler*

Chapter Two

THE THATCH-HUT MOUNTAINS
1912

Sunlight steams purple mist off Incense Peak.
Far away, the waterfall is a long hanging river

Flying three thousand feet straight down,
Like the milky river of stars pouring from heaven.

Li Po (AD 701-762),
"Gazing at the Thatch-Hut Mountain Waterfall"

"I want to see the big trees! I want to see the big trees!"
From the beginning, it was the spectacles of nature that captivated John Harvey Butchart. He craved wilderness, and wished to test his body against whatever he found there. On this perfect summer day in 1912, that meant talking his father into letting him go to the Three Ancient Trees.

Dr. James Butchart had just announced that he and a friend were headed for this trio of arboreal giants, located within the mountain range called Mount Lushan (pronounced "loo-shawn") in southeastern China's Jiangxi ("shang-shee") Province. But James felt his ambitious five year-old son was too little for the three-and-a-half mile trek.

As an amateur naturalist, James usually encouraged his son's curiosity for the outdoors. He knew how Harvey loved to explore—his little legs were always moving him somewhere. James and his wife Nellie practically had to tie Harvey to a chair sometimes to keep him from wandering off. But the boy had a stubborn streak and often seemed oblivious to his own limits. This time Harvey would have to stay home.

Harvey protested, as any boy would. Although James was fair and open-minded, he could be stern, too. He gave Harvey a firm *no*.

James had been looking forward to a bit of a break today. He relished these summers at Mount Lushan, which offered time to recuperate from a solid 10-month grind of 80-100 hour workweeks in the city of Luchowfu (now known as Hefei). Between the demands of being a doctor, a preacher, a missionary, and a father and husband, James had few opportunities during the year to take even a simple walk. He knew exactly what would happen if he brought Harvey along. He would be spending his scarce leisure time piggybacking 40 pounds of little boy up a steep trail once Harvey got tired.

But James's friend was moved by the boy's pleas and suggested that they bring him along. James reconsidered, thinking perhaps his friend was right. Harvey deserved the chance to prove himself—or at least learn a good lesson. Dr. Butchart demanded honesty and morality from his children, just as he did of himself, and part of that meant keeping one's promises. James looked down at Harvey's face, so full of exaggerated hope, and gave his consent.

But on one condition, he told his son. Harvey could come as long as he walked the whole way—there and back—on his own. The boy jumped up and down, insisting he could make it. Thoughts of the woods, and the Three Ancient Trees hiding somewhere within them, flooded Harvey's mind to bursting. He was going on his first hike.

They stepped out of the neat, well-kept yard and into the cobblestone street the Western townspeople had named Central Avenue. Such a name reflected a world far removed from China, and indeed, this neighborhood could easily belong to rural New England. Tall pines and maples lined the sidewalks, casting welcome shade. A grassy park with wood benches, trimmed hedges, and rows of flowers brought America to mind. One block from the Butcharts's home stood a handsome Catholic Church. A tumbling brook ran beside Central Avenue, adding the murmur of flowing water to the general atmosphere of orderliness and cleanliness. Except for the occasional passing of a servant, one might never guess that all of this was China.

Harvey Butchart, circa 1910 in his hometown of Luchowfu, China.
Courtesy Anne Madariaga

16

The three hikers strolled past handsome brick villas set in generous yards. Their neighbors in Kuling all knew each other, united as they were by their status as foreigners. Most of them were enterprising men with families like James who migrated here each summer from the hot lowland cities of southeastern China. The Butcharts's annual escape from the city of Luchowfu in the subtropical Yangtze River valley was not a mere holiday, but a survival tactic. James had discovered the importance of a cooler summertime climate not long after first arriving in China in 1891. The Yangzte valley suffered from a withering combination of extreme humidity and unrelenting heat from May to September, and the surrounding lowlands offered no reprieve to Westerners unused to such conditions.

Many missionaries such as James and his wife Nellie found it difficult to even sleep in summer. Morale always took a corresponding nosedive. But the dangers went beyond the psychological. The Westerners's children became especially susceptible to an annual onslaught of diseases such as malaria and cholera.

Desperate for relief, and taking his cue from British soldiers who had faced the same problems in India, an English missionary-cum-land-speculator named Reverend Edward Selby Little established a resort town in the 1890s atop Mount Lushan. Reverend Little persuaded the Chinese authorities to lease land to foreigners and even conceived of the perfect name for his community: Kuling. It was a Chinese-like adaptation of the word

Advertisement for Kuling, circa 1920.

"cooling," which he realized would have an irresistible ring to it. Once word got out, missionaries and businessmen from the steaming cities got in line to drop $150 for a plot of their own in Kuling. It would be a foreigner's enclave, for the Chinese could not afford such a price. James was one of the first to lease land and built two cottages there by 1900.

Mount Lushan rises to nearly 5,000 feet between the Yangtze River and Lake Poyang, China's largest freshwater lake. The resulting surplus of moisture often conjures a picturesque "cloud sea" over the mountains, making for a pleasant town location. Kuling was drawn up within a 3,500-foot-high wooded valley atop Mount Lushan, where summer temperatures rarely climbed above 80 degrees. Insects were few. Many creeks and waterfalls splashed and tumbled nearby. In short, Kuling was everything a weary lowlander dreamed of. James had been going there for years when he met his wife Nellie, and together, they would eventually plan their childbirths around Mount Lushan. With the exception of Harvey, who arrived ahead of schedule on May 10, 1907 in Luchowfu, all four Butchart children were born in Kuling.

Although Kuling was new, Mount Lushan had been drawing a succession of itinerant Chinese pilgrims for thousands of years. Legends and tales of these hermits pervaded the range. One such myth held the origin of the mountain's name. In the eleventh century BC during the Zhou dynasty, seven brothers by the name of Kuang climbed the mountains to look for a place to build a home. They constructed a hut of clay and reeds and dwelt there happily. But when the next person came to Mount Lushan, it was discovered that all seven brothers had disappeared. Thinking them immortals, pilgrims began traveling to the hut to pay them homage. In time, the mountains came to be called Mount Kuang, and then, Mount Lushan, meaning "Thatch-Hut Mountains." In Chinese characters, Mount Lushan is 庐山, the first character resembling a roofed hut, the second symbolic of a peak, or "mount."

James, Harvey, and James's friend arrived at the end of Central Avenue and crossed the brook via an arched footbridge of carved stone. The path led them past the last of Kuling's homes, away from the brook and into the moist, sunbeam-filled forest. The small noises of town—the laughter of playing chil-

Kuling sits high atop Mount Lushan. *Courtesy China Travel & Tourism Press*

dren, the hacking cough of a Chinese servant, someone working away at a log with an axe—gave way to a conspicuous silence. Softer light fell in the woods, filtered as it was through transpiring fir trees and scraps of mist. Harvey detected the fine damp forest smells, the moss and soil and ferns. The air here had a crystalline quality to it, always fresh, cool and pure.

The trail that leads to the Three Ancient Trees. *Elias Butler*

James could never squeeze enough out of his few weeks at Mount Lushan. Too often during the year his lungs filled with the fetid respirations of one of his thousands of patients. In Luchowfu, forests and fresh air hardly existed. The Butcharts lived there amidst gray walls, the din of crowded streets, and often under an acrid pall of smoke from cooking fires or fields burned by farmers.

To be able to walk without any aim other than enjoyment, in clean mountain air, and in southeastern China's Jiangxi—*this* was why James brought the family each year to Mount Lushan. Little wonder then that Harvey, like his father, found the mountains enthralling. Tigers and wild boars lurked there. A wreath of cloud mist enveloped the range's 99 summits more often than not. A spring in the neighborhood provided sweet water by the bucketful.

Harvey had indeed inherited his father's love for nature. But there was more to it than that. He couldn't have known it, not yet, but that day, the wildness Harvey sensed at Mount Lushan began to exert a pull upon him, planting an urge that one day would become irresistible. As he moved deeper into the woods, his father plodding somewhere behind him, Harvey's feet carried him further into this new realm. He had taken the first step.

THE THREE ANCIENT TREES stood taller than any Harvey had ever seen. A Buddhist monk had planted the two cryptomerias 500 years earlier during the Ming Dynasty. At over 140 feet tall, they seemed to stretch into the sky forever. But the third tree, a 1,600 year-old gnarled gingko, presented an even more impressive visage. It absolutely dwarfed the three humans at its base. James

The Three Ancient Trees, in 2006. *Elias Butler*

explained that this giant was the last old-growth remnant of the once-majestic Mount Lushan forests that had been carelessly harvested and burned away in the distant past.

Adjacent to these giants lay Yellow Dragon Temple, a Buddhist shrine tended by a handful of monks. It had existed in one form or another for centuries and housed an unusual stone in its floor from which water flowed whenever the mountain mists were present. With its quiet men, incense smoke, bronze statues, and solemn bells and drums, the monastery lent the serene setting an atmosphere of the sacred.

After inspecting this handsome structure, James ushered Harvey back onto the trail. The hike so far had been deceptively easy, all downhill to the Three Ancient Trees. Now began the long, gradual return ascent to Kuling. Harvey started eagerly and kept up at first. But as James had anticipated, it was not long before Harvey revealed that he had nothing left in his five year-old legs. He started to drag. Finally, the boy stopped. James reminded Harvey of the promise he had made. But Harvey was tired and his feet hurt. No amount of guilt, or his father's consternation, could coax him any farther.

James stood firm and waited for Harvey to make good on his word. When it became clear that neither father nor son would budge, James's friend ended the stalemate. He offered to carry Harvey on his shoulders so that they might make it home in time for dinner. James agreed, knowing half his lesson remained intact: *He* was not the one carrying Harvey on his back.

When the trio returned to Kuling, James bade farewell to his friend, then admonished Harvey for breaking his promise. Next time Harvey would need to think more carefully about what he committed to. James gave his son a message that day that Harvey would hold dear in life: *Don't ever start something you don't mean to finish. Never, ever, give up.*

Harvey hated to disappoint his father, the man he idolized above all others.

They dusted themselves off and entered the house. Harvey's mother Nellie was in the kitchen, saying what Harvey's nose already told him, that dinner was almost ready. He flopped down on a sofa in the living room, letting his eyes come to rest on a large piece of artwork hanging on the opposite wall.

It was an artifact from America, a painting of some fantastic-looking place in that faraway dreamland. Nellie enjoyed decorating their homes with scenes from America to remind the children that they would be going there for good one day. This particular painting, Harvey later recalled, never failed to catch his eye.

In a way, the painting resembled Mount Lushan. A building similar to Hawk's Nest Pavilion stood atop a high vertical prominence while the land around it seemed to fall away into oblivion. But unlike Mount Lushan, the landscape in the painting did not appear lush and green and misty. It was rocky and jagged. Those monstrous forms in the distance could easily be the product of some overworked imagination. Oranges and reds and browns, buttresses, pinnacles, and mesas, all contrasted against a sky unlike any Harvey had seen in China. Even though it was only an illustration, such a preposterous void exerted an almost palpable pull on the senses. The unlikely union of that gaping immensity and the people walking so calmly at its edge—it suggested terror.

If Harvey had forgotten, he would have pointed to the image and asked, *"What's the name of that place in the painting, mama?"*

"That? That's the Grand Canyon, Harvey."

A copy of Louis Akin's "El Tovar and Grand Canyon" hung in the Butchart home in Kuling, China.

Chapter Three

FROM THE WARS OF GOD
1907–1912

If they had not gone as daring missionaries, they would have gone to gold fields or explored the poles or sailed on pirate ships. They would have ruled the natives of foreign lands in other ways of power if God had not caught their souls so young. They were proud and quarrelsome and brave and intolerant and passionate. They strode along the Chinese streets secure in their right to go about their business. No question ever assailed them, no doubt ever weakened them. They were right in all they did and they waged the wars of God, sure of victory.

Pearl Buck,
Fighting Angel (1937)

IT DID NOT TAKE LONG for the Grand Canyon to enter Harvey Butchart's life, nor for the path to be set that eventually brought the two together. He did not know that the subject of Louis Akin's lithograph, hanging like a portent in his parents's summer cottage, would one day become as familiar as his own reflection. What Harvey did know at five years of age was that he loved to see new places. The urge ran thick in his blood, for it was wanderlust that had lured his parents to the other side of the world, and to each other.

James Butchart and Nellie Daugherty came to China near the turn of the twentieth century as part of the influx of Christian missionaries from America, a tide of God's soldiers determined to convert the so-called "heathen" masses of the Middle Kingdom. It was an impossible job, extreme in scope, reserved for only the hardiest, tough-as-nails missionaries. James and Nellie left behind everything they had known in the West to live their best years on a diet of spiritual fulfillment and relative poverty. This was the stock Harvey came from.

The Butcharts formed a humble, well-respected family within the idealistic and tight-knit Christian community in Luchowfu. Religion was the foundation for everything in their lives, from work to play to relationships. If James and Nellie had journeyed to China because they believed God had called them there, then falling in love and raising a family must have been part of His plan, too.

James had grown up in Dorchester, Ontario, a tiny farming town halfway between Buffalo and Detroit, just north of Lake Erie. Born in 1866 to a Scottish immigrant named John Dick Butchart and his wife Christina Scott, James was baptized at 13 into the Disciples of Christ Church. Today known simply as the Christian Church, the Disciples of Christ was a new religion aimed at the idealistic and open-minded among the Christian faith. One of the largest spiritual movements to have originated in the United States (as of this writing, there are over 800,000 members), the Disciples formed in the early 1800s in Kentucky and Pennsylvania as an offshoot of the Presbyterian Church. It was a very tolerant version of Christianity that encouraged liberality at all levels—just the opposite of what the conservative Presbyterian leadership espoused at the time. The Disciples quickly gained popularity by virtue of its uncomplicated and limber philosophy, especially in Midwest America and Canada.

James distinguished himself both as a Disciple and in the secular world as a man of science. Self-educated in many fields including geology, botany and engineering, he ultimately sought a career in medicine, immigrating to the United States in 1886 where he was accepted at the University of Louisville at Kentucky. He graduated from medical school at the top of his class and then opened his first practice in Kentucky.

Word of James's impressive achievements spread in the Disciples community. The Foreign Christian Missionary Society decided that he was an ideal man for one of its most challenging goals: Spreading the Lord's message in China, a country whose borders had only just been forcibly opened by foreigners in the mid-1800s. China constituted a genuine blank spot on the map for most Americans, at once immense and alien. Who knew what waited there? The Disciples understood that converting a population steeped for 50 centuries in Eastern thought and religion would require people such as young and driven James Butchart.

At first, James refused the Disciples's request. He had no desire to perform poverty-level work in a strange country. After all, he was just gaining momentum as a physician in America. But James did thrive on a challenge, and foreign evangelism promised to be that and more. He also realized that he would be practicing medicine where his Western skills would not only be revolutionary, they would be in much greater demand than in America. James decided to leave as soon as he finished his training in New York City at the Postgraduate and Eye and Ear Hospitals.

In 1891, he crossed the Pacific on a transport steamer and arrived in the greasy seaport of Shanghai, taking a Chinese junk another 100 miles west on the Yangtze River to his first post in the city of Nanking (now called Nanjing). James had not just stuck his toe into China—he had jumped in with both feet. This 2,500 year-old city of 400,000 teemed nonstop with the loud chatter of Madarin. Its streets were chaotic veins of men pulling creaky wooden carts. Everywhere lay the aroma of smoke, offal, food, and sweat.

As the capital of Jiangsu Province, Nanking was the cultural hub of the vast east central Chinese lowlands. The Yangtze's prodigious load of silt created one of the richest arable regions in the world near Nanking, a fertile swath that covered only about 10 per cent of the country's total area, yet attracted a much higher percentage of its burgeoning population. The Yangtze basin thus made a prime target for evangelism, a fact that was not lost on the various Christian denominations that sent missionaries to the region by the hundreds.

James Butchart, circa 1895. *Courtesy Disciples of Christ Historical Society, Nashville, TN*

James got to work proselytizing and ministering to the Chinese at the University of Nanking Hospital. He brought a singleness of purpose to his task and quickly established a reputation as a competent physician. Within 12 months he was placed in charge of the hospital. James impressed his superiors so much that by 1897 they assigned him his greatest challenge yet: To establish a new mission and clinic in the city of Luchowfu, about 100 miles farther west.

This strategically important trade center in Anhui Province offered little to encourage a Christian missionary. Its populace consisted of Buddhists, Taoists, and Confucians, whose philosophies all predated Christ. Moreover, Luchowfu's residents were happily convinced of Chinese cultural and racial superiority. It is likely that none had ever seen a white man before, making James a bizarre novelty wherever he went. He learned to take the constant fascination and chiding in stride. James simply applied his intelligence and Herculean work ethic to the problem, learning the local dialect and welcoming Chinese patients and potential converts.

Most Chinese, however, remained suspicious of the "foreign devil" and his

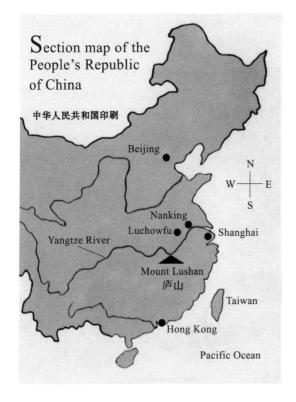

Section map of the People's Republic of China

中华人民共和国印刷

Beijing

N
W——E
S

Nanking
Luchowfu
Shanghai
Yangtze River

Mount Lushan
庐山

Taiwan

Hong Kong

Pacific Ocean

western medicine and strange deity. Gossip spread about what went on in his clinic. Some claimed he sewed boys's eyes shut with the wings of dragonflies, others gasped that he plucked out children's organs and ground them into remedies.

Finally, a single humanitarian act changed public opinion of the white doctor. Dr. Butchart performed an emergency appendectomy on a dying Chinese man who had been laid before him by a desperate family member. Afterward, the rescued patient wore his bloody gown with a hole where James had removed his appendix, thus becoming a walking advertisement for the doctor's services. Within days, townspeople flooded into the clinic.

Despite this show of support, James would have to flee Luchowfu in 1899 amidst what Westerners called the Boxer Rebellion, an anti-foreigner uprising that swept across China. James's escape from Luchowfu became legend in the missionary community and formed one of Harvey's favorite stories about his father.

The Boxer Rebellion had its roots in old resentments. China had suffered a string of military defeats to Western powers during the 1800s Opium Wars, and the ensuing arrival of foreigners was an embarrassing reminder of China's military ineptitude. But it was the drought of 1899 and widespread starvation that sparked the bloodshed. In desperation and anger, gangs of men across eastern China took up arms, seeking a scapegoat. They quickly directed their wrath toward foreigners—especially the Christian missionaries, whose alien ways, many Chinese believed, had upset the native deities who in turn had inflicted devastating famine.

The ruling Empress Dowager Tzu Hsi had long hated the Western presence in her country. She secretly encouraged these roving bands of peasants led by martial artists practitioners, collectively named "boxers" by the foreigners. As a result, hundreds of missionaries and Christian converts were murdered and tortured, often while the law looked the other way. Foreigners of all kinds became targets—including James, who fled just ahead of a mob intent on dragging him out of his clinic in Luchowfu. By dressing in peasant's clothes and yelling, "Stop thief!" in Mandarin as he pointed into the crowd, he diverted attention from himself and slipped away. James took refuge for several months under the cover of U.S. gunboats in Shanghai until an invading army that included the American, Japanese and Russian military crushed the rebellion in 1900. The allied governments demanded that China pass laws ensuring the safety of foreigners on her own soil, a humiliating blow with ramifications that have yet to be fully determined.

James returned to Luchowfu to find his clinic demolished. Yet with his usual optimism and tenacity he immediately announced plans to build a modern hospital, a much larger facility than his previous clinic. Within two years it was done. News of such a turnaround success immediately spread across the missionary community in China.

One person who heard of the young doctor's amazing triumphs was a 29 year-old teacher named Nellie Daugherty. Nellie had arrived as a Disciples missionary in Nanking a year earlier, in 1901. Born on January 7, 1872 in Bardolph, Illinois, Nellie was the daughter of a Pennsylvania carpenter named William Harvey Daugherty and his wife Sarah. Nellie followed her parents's lead and became a member of the Disciples of Christ in her teens, though she would prove a far more adventurous Disciple than either of them.

Nellie obtained an education degree from Eureka College in Illinois in 1894, becoming the first college-educated woman in her family. Teaching grade school for several years in Illinois, however, left her feeling unfulfilled. In 1901, while volunteering at church, she was reading a Disciples bulletin and noticed the

Luchowfu hospital dedication, December 1902. *Courtesy Jim Butchart*

Nellie Daugherty, circa 1897.
Courtesy Anne Madariaga

letters from overseas missionaries. Those exotic-sounding locales stirred something inside her, and she suddenly understood exactly what she wanted to do: She would go on an overseas mission herself. Though an uncommon vocation for women at the time, the Disciples had been ordaining women as missionaries for years, and Nellie was soon crossing the Pacific toward China.

Traveling alone to a country that had recently been hostile to foreigners gives a glimpse of Nellie's self-confidence. But she had no qualms about doing the Lord's work where it needed to be done. Nellie arrived in Nanking, immediately began her mission, and resumed her career as a teacher at the local Christian girls's school.

One day in Nanking in 1902, James stopped in at the Disciples headquarters and suddenly noticed the new face. James was 34 and had spent a decade working in China, always choosing to stay, never considering his work done, too busy perhaps to notice how alone he was. James and Nellie discovered their shared background: Both grew up a few hundred miles apart near the Great Lakes in rural North American farm country. Ironically, the two Westerners needed to sail halfway around the planet to get their romantic timing right. Following a brief courtship, they married in 1903.

"THE BOAT HAS EYES," explained Dr. Butchart after awakening his two sons, James Baird, seven, and John Harvey, five. They yawned and rubbed the sleep from their eyes, eager as always for this daily ceremony. The boys wanted to hear what was going to happen next to their father's imaginary vessel. James told them every morning how the boat traveled the world over, not to deliver a load of goods, but simply for the adventure. The boat with eyes never stopped exploring the oceans of the globe and always wanted to see what unexpected thing the next day might hold.

James could only spend 10 minutes with them in the morning before rushing off to work, but it was a time both he and the boys cherished. The youngsters knew they wouldn't see their father again until the following morning, for

James Butchart was a very, very busy man in 1912. As the only Western-trained doctor in the city, he found himself beseiged by many of Luchowfu's residents on any given day.

James looked in on his baby daughter, Helen, before kissing Nellie—who was pregnant with their fourth child—goodbye. Then he was gone, off to the hospital for another day of ministering Christianity and providing Western medicine to dozens, sometimes even over 100 patients.

As for Nellie, she refused to let the *amah* (nanny) take over all the motherly duties, as was conventional among most missionary wives. She insisted on changing Helen's diaper and rousing the boys from bed herself. Baird went to the local American school, or, if it was a Saturday, out to play in the spacious yard with Harvey (the boys went by their middle names, a common practice at the time). When confined inside by the weather, they enjoyed constructing forts in the attic out of furniture boxes. Together, the brothers could content themselves for hours.

Life in Luchowfu was not so different from life in America. At least, this is what James and Nellie often told their children. The kids would someday see for themselves when the family moved to America. Dr. Butchart planned to spend a few more years in China, but missionaries with families rarely stayed longer than 10 years at their posts. In the meantime, the Butcharts retained ties with the West by living within the culturally isolated compound in Luchowfu.

The walled-in island that the Butcharts called home was a city within a city, similar to the Chinatowns in New York or San Francisco. Behind barred gates, they enjoyed the security and familiarity of living with other Westerners who had for one reason or

Harvey Butchart, 1908. *Courtesy Anne Madariaga*

another been lured to Luchowfu. Christian missionaries of various denominations, foreign diplomats, and businessmen formed a tight community inside. The shops catered to Western tastes—toys from England were available, as well as French bread and American books. For the kids, the compound *was* America.

Dr. Butchart and his family lived a comfortable but somewhat humble existence in their spacious split-level home. The toilet consisted of a wood box with a hole in the top, and at the end of each day the box needed emptying. Staying clean was a constant struggle, as running water was an unknown luxury. Servants hauled water from the closest source 100 yards away, and it always had to be boiled first, for diseases to which the Chinese seemed immune were often deadly to foreigners. For illumination, they used oil lamps, for heat, small wood stoves saw them through the gray winter months. They were not rich by American standards, as James earned little compared to the salary he would have been making back in the States, yet the fact that they had servants did mark them as prosperous. Nellie, who came from a proud, hardworking family, never became accustomed to being waited upon. But with all the work of running a household, the help remained.

Beyond their servants, Harvey and his siblings had only occasional contact with the Chinese. On days when James or Nellie went into Luchowfu, however, Harvey could not have helped but notice the transformation that took place once outside the compound walls, for here was life in the raw. He heard the animated quarrels of business being conducted on the streets, smelled the freshly gutted fowl and looked into all those faces so different from his own. To him, home meant both the colorful humanity of Luchowfu and the distant shores of an almost mythical country he had never known. He belonged wholly to neither.

As the summer neared, everyone began to feel restless. Part of it was the growing heat, but much of it had to do with the nature of missionary work.

From left, Helen, Nellie, Harvey, James and Baird Butchart, circa 1911. *Courtesy Disciples of Christ Historical Society, Nashville, TN*

For all the Westerners's efforts, they converted relatively few Chinese. Even those who appeared to accept the gospel often represented false victories—the so-called "rice Christians." For example, many servants in the missionaries's homes were pragmatists who realized that by going to church services and feigning devotion, they could gain reliable employment and regular meals.

After enduring the daily indifference and occasional hostility of their unwilling subjects, even the most dedicated missionaries could buckle. Nervous breakdowns and severe depression were common risks of the profession. James and Nellie relied upon each other's determination to see them through the rough times, cheerfully pursuing their evangelistic goals and duties no matter how successful or dismal the results. Yet even the strong-willed must sometimes rest. By May of each year they had had it. With James working harder than ever at the hospital and church, and Nellie up to her elbows in kids and her own work, and with the smothering heat of that summer fast approaching, it was time to go to the mountains.

THE THREE-DAY journey from Luchowfu to Mount Lushan made a lively adventure in itself. With sweat running down their brows, the Butcharts boarded an English steamer on the Yangtze that was bound for the town of Kiukiang (now called Jiujiang) at the base of Mount Lushan, 180 river miles upstream. Harvey always looked forward to this annual river trip. It was almost like the "boat with eyes" his father was always telling him about. Best of all, it meant escaping the lowlands. As the Butcharts cruised upriver, the humidity hung in drab whiteness over the river valley while the world seemed to wilt underneath.

"At Kiukiang we changed to the Spartan life of sleeping on sagging beds with sagging springs," Harvey later wrote. "The rest house would furnish mosquito nets that sometimes had unwanted holes, good practice for camping in a tent in Colorado. I remember one night that was so hot where we were trying to sleep that Father hired a Chinese boatman to row us out into the Yangtze where we could get a light breeze from the air across the water."

The next morning, nine miles and 4,000 feet of elevation still separated them from Kuling. No roads existed, only a rugged trail that had been built hundreds of years earlier. This was a trek Harvey learned by heart, for he made it many times during his childhood. The men and boys would go on foot while the women rode in sedan chairs carried by Chinese load bearers.

Pearl S. Buck, the first woman to win the Nobel Prize for literature for her 1931 novel *The Good Earth*, spent several summers at Kuling as both a child and adult. She describes the trail from Kiukiang to Kuling in her memoir, *My Several Worlds:*

Now came, as always, the magical part of the journey...Up the mountain we climbed and soon the frothing bamboos changed to pines and dwarf chestnuts and oaks and we were on our way. The road wound around the rocky folds of the cliffs, and beneath us were gorges and rushing mountain rivers and falls. Higher and higher the road crawled, twisting so abruptly that sometimes our chairs swung clear over the precipices as the front bearers went on beyond the rear ones, still behind the bend.

Somewhere near the top of the mountain we turned a certain corner and were met, as I remembered, by a strong cold current of mountain air...The air of the plains had been hot and heavy, breathed in and out by millions of human lungs, but here on top of the mountain it was charged with fresh cold purity, and one breathed it in like lifesaving oxygen.

The trail from Kiukiang to Kuling, circa 1915. *Courtesy Methodist Church*

In addition to making his first real hike with his father that summer at Mount Lushan, Harvey took his first camping trip, too. "I remember the time Father took us to sleep at the foot of the Three Big Trees," Harvey wrote. "Baird and I were small enough so that we could sleep on one cot with our heads at opposite ends. Perhaps my enjoyment of wilderness and camping dates back to these short trips with Father."

For everyone, this was one of the best things about Mount Lushan: Spending precious time with James. Between his preaching and his work at the hospital,

James needed this time off to be with family and simply to stay sane. As far as Nellie was concerned, James had been working *too* hard. She had long recognized a dangerous single-mindedness in her husband when it came to serving the ill. Nellie wrote about her concerns in the following letter, which was published in the missionary newsletter, *The Christian Evangelist*:

"A Cheerful Letter From Lu Cheo Fu, China"
The medical work this year has surpassed all former records. In 11 months there have been 28,600 treatments and 1,035 out-visits. When the number for April is added to this, there will be over 30,000. Think of 315 in one day! Two days this spring the number went over 300. The daily average for the month of March was 177.
The hospital brings many callers to our home. The high class ladies are not willing to come to the clinics and mingle with the common people, so they come to our home. These, with many who come over from the clinic, and others who come only to call, make my work of entertaining very heavy. There have been 530 in less than six months.

Nellie closed with this somber presage:

The doctor is almost swamped with work and the demands are very heavy upon him. His strength is not equal to them.

Had she known her words were indeed prophecy, Nellie would have done everything in her power to thwart fate.

The Matthes-Evans team using the plane table. *Courtesy Grand Canyon National Park Museum Collection*

Chapter Four

THE MAPMAKERS
1902–1923

But the Colorado River? Well, it makes little difference whether there be water in the bottom of that mile-deep chasm or not. One might as well make a descent to the Styx for a cupful.

Francois Matthes,
Mapping the Grand Canyon (1905)

EL TOVAR HOTEL was not the only major development that the Grand Canyon Railroad precipitated upon its arrival in 1901. Now that that the world's most famous natural wonder could be visited so easily, it was inevitable that a few brave tourists would want to venture afoot into its depths. Some might even want to know where they were going.

Though topographers John H. Renshawe and S.H. Bodfish had drawn up a reconnaissance map of Grand Canyon under the direction of Major John Wesley Powell in the 1880s, it lacked the detail and thus usefulness that a modern map could provide. Such maps already existed for even the remotest parts of the West. For example, the last mountain range to be named in the lower 48 states, the Henry Mountains in Utah, had been mapped by 1892. But Grand Canyon thus far had proved too rugged—and too bereft of lucrative natural resources—to be forced onto paper.

Dr. Charles Walcott, director of the United States Geological Survey (USGS) in 1902, felt it wouldn't do to have the Canyon defined by outdated charts. In the months following the railroad's arrival, he hastily assembled an elite team of topographers in Washington, D.C. to correct the situation.

Realizing the difficulty that Grand Canyon would present, Walcott appointed the preeminent topographer of his time, Francois Emile Matthes, to conduct the expedition. Born in Holland in 1874, Matthes once confided to a friend, "I simply cannot be happy unless my work is conducted in country of inspirational beauty." Walcott's trust in the Dutchman would not be misplaced. Matthes had a passion for both hard work and the West's spectacular landforms. He would distinguish himself in his profession by mapping not only the Canyon but also the San Andreas Fault, Mount Rainier, and Yosemite, the latter of which he would consider far more challenging than what he confronted at Grand Canyon.

"The demands for a modern and detailed map became urgent," Matthes wrote, "from various quarters, for the most diverse purposes." Although he had

never been to the Canyon, Matthes did have experience with rough country. He had recently completed surveys in the Rocky and Bighorn Mountains, and was also no stranger to the arid topography of the Southwest. In 1901 he surveyed the Bradshaw Mountains quadrangle, and in 1902, the Jerome quadrangle, both of which lie in the rugged Basin and Range province of central Arizona.

Richard Evans was just beginning his career as a topographer. The 21-year-old Washington, D.C. native had assisted Matthes with the creation of the Jerome map. Matthes had been impressed with Evans's abilities, and did not hesitate to ask Evans to join him at Grand Canyon.

In March 1902 the two topographers, a rodman, a surveyor, a cook, and a team-

Francois Matthes. *Courtesy of the National Park Service, Yosemite National Park, Francois Matthes, I-201-01-0589*

ster arrived via the Grand Canyon Railroad at the South Rim. Matthes led them straightaway to have a look at their subject. With his usual zest for challenge and adventure, Matthes would later write that the Grand Canyon was, "the glorious forte-fortissimo finale to the thousand mile long rhapsody of gorges and canyons of the Colorado River."

Yet this was a dark, wintry day, and the effect was sobering:

> A dull-gray snow cloud hung over the landscape when we stepped out on the rim for a first peep at the great chasm. There it lay, a scene of sullen, stony grimness, overwhelming by its vastness, baffling with its chaotic profusion of

chiseled detail, but utterly devoid of charm. It did not capture our hearts, as the Rockies had done with their superb, snow-flecked peaks, mirrored in romantic forest-fringed lakes. To the topographer's mind this was the superlative of all Arizona box canyons, the biggest, deepest and most dreaded of them all. It promised trouble—heaps of it. Without a word we slunk severally back to our tent by the railroad track...

Matthes's unease did not last. The gorge would reveal its charm, not all at once, but in gradual doses as he became more intimate with its various moods. Bearing witness to the play of light in a theater such as Grand Canyon must have changed Matthes, for at the end of the fieldwork—during which time he would have carefully observed the Canyon at close range on a daily basis—a quite different opinion of that "stony grimness" emerged. "Little did we anticipate how its sublime power was to grow upon us," Matthes wrote, "until at the end of two years it seemed a hardship to leave it for the commonplace world of man."

Mapping the entirety of Grand Canyon, which stretched for 277 river miles, would have meant a lifelong project. Instead, the USGS instructed Matthes to limit his efforts to the 105 river miles that stretched between the "mouth of Marble Gorge to the mouth of Havasu Canyon," the "most important section of the Grand Canyon, that embracing its most superb beauty."

Before any measurements could be made, teams of men were sent to the tops of Bill Williams Mountain and Kendrick Peak near Flagstaff, both of which had defined benchmarks (a point with verified postiton and elevation). The men then communicated these positions via mirror flashes to their companions at Grand Canyon, who stood atop landmarks such as Red Butte and Cape Royal.

With these reference points thus established, the surveyors could begin to create benchmarks in the Canyon itself. They worked along the South Rim first, taking the spring and summer months to go from viewpoint to viewpoint. Operating without benefit of aerial photography, Matthes was forced to rely exclusively on the plane table method of map construction. Heretofore the plane table was relatively untested as a mapmaker's primary topographic instrument, but Matthes had a hunch it would prove ideal at Grand Canyon.

The mechanics of the plane table were simple. Using a line-of-sight device called an alidade, the surveyor focused on a distant location, such as a butte, and traced a corresponding line onto his map, which was tacked to the plane table. Taking multiple measurements of these positions from various points created intersecting lines that, through triangulation, defined precise locations and elevations.

Because the views were so sweeping, mapping from a single vista, such as at

Comanche or Grandview Points, easily consumed a week. But this was a map-maker's dream come true. As Matthes put it, "Thousands of intersections and hundreds of elevations from one instrument station—there is no other place on earth where it can be done."

As the topographers quickly learned, their main challenge would not be the mapping, but rather the transportation of the men, pack animals, and equipment to the various surveying stations. In this rugged country, which ranged from 8,000-foot alpine forests to a 2,000-foot desert, conditions frequently extended the very limits of the team's capabilities. Water had to be hauled daily from distant sources. Wagons were often useless in this landscape, and much of the burden was placed on mules and horses to supply the team. The temperature extremes could be especially debilitating. One of the surveyors, while trying to make an elevation reading at the foot of the Old Hance Trail in midsummer, found that the bubble in his leveling device became smaller as he descended into the withering heat. It ultimately disappeared altogether.

Reaching the North Rim proved exceptionally troublesome. Lee's Ferry, at the head of Grand Canyon, offered one roundabout route, although it meant a journey of some 250 circuitous miles to net a 10-mile distance. No bridges existed to walk the pack animals across the Colorado within the Canyon, and the only trails that met at opposite sides of the river were the North and South Bass Trails. "There was really not a single route by which the chasm might be traversed without hazard," Matthes wrote. "It is no exaggeration to say that the Grand Canyon, at that time, constituted a more impassable barrier than any mountain range in the United States."

Timing also proved critical. Winter buries the Kaibab Plateau in an expanse of deep snow. Though it was only late summer, the surveyors decided to save time and take the shorter and less certain Bass route, which tourist camp operator William Bass had developed from Indian routes in the 1880s. When the team arrived at Bass's camp on the South Rim, the friendly entrepreneur frowned on Matthes's plans. "No horses or mules, Mr. Bass advised the survey party, had ever been taken across the canyon by that route, and he strongly counseled against any attempt to do so," Matthes recalled. "However, as the surveyors seemed determined, he assured them that they might use his boat with which to cross the river."

When the team reached the foot of the trail, however, they found that Bass's boat was on the north side of the river. Only two members of the team knew how to swim. The two draftees decided to strike out for the far shore together. "Finding that the swirling flood had a pulsating movement, they timed their dash during an interval between two pulses and so got to the other side without being carried far downstream," Matthes wrote. "They soon returned triumphantly with the boat, which was of a curious home-made variety and required a good deal of bailing."

The question now arose as to what to do with the pack animals. Matthes explained:

> ...the chief of the party, while swimming, had discovered a very deep hole just off a flat rock platform. A plan at once suggested itself. Each animal in turn was invited to the edge of the platform to quench its thirst. Then, while still head down, it was given a vigorous push and sent heels over head into the water. As soon as its head again emerged, the long rope attached to the halter was tossed to the men in the boat, and they, tugging at the oars, towed the frantic animal across.

The plan worked. Soon the animals and gear stood on the north side. From here, however, they still needed to fight for two days to reach the North Rim via Bass's trail. In all it took over three days to make the laborious rim-to-rim trek. Echoing the sentiments of many a weary hiker who has since struggled along the same route, Matthes reveled in the succor offered by the cool Kaibab Plateau:

> It was nearly sunset when we emerged upon the flat surface of the plateau, and suddenly found ourselves in a glorious forest, where the thermometer ranged some 30 degrees lower than in the canyon, and where the grass grew as on a lawn. Half an hour through its idyllic shady aisles in the keen breezes of an altitude of eight thousand feet dissolved all memories of the toilsome furnace through which we had struggled for three days.

The surveyors continued working on the Kaibab Plateau through autumn, making measurements from vistas like Point Sublime, Tiyo Point, and Cape Royal. They lived off biscuits and all the venison they could eat, for the mule deer showed no fear of men and often crowded about the surveyors in a curious circle. The views and wild country fascinated Matthes. He was moved to impart his lofty taste in music upon the Canyon by naming features such as Wotan's Throne and the Walhalla Plateau, appellations culled from Richard Wagner's *The Ring of the Nibelung* operas.

By November 1902, with the first winter storm fast approaching, Matthes needed to get his team back to the South Rim. Instead of retreating down the known route, the distant Bass Trail, Matthes fixed his eyes on nearby Bright Angel Canyon. The North Kaibab Trail had not yet been constructed and the locals had assured them this side canyon was impassable. By chance though,

From left, William Forster and Herman Elliott pack a lightweight two-piece aluminum boat down the Bass Trail in February 1905.

while the team was checking out the route from above, two prospectors leading a burro emerged from Bright Angel. The miners reported that a boat was beached on their side of the river at the canyon's mouth. Buoyed by the good news, Matthes and his team started down with the pack animals and succeeded in reaching the Colorado via this new rim-to-river route, though they were forced to make 106 stream crossings while negotiating Bright Angel Creek.

Despite the months of fieldwork, the surveying was incomplete. The team returned each spring for the next three years to continue amassing data. The sprawling rim views meant that only toward the latter stages did they need to hike down to measure what was hidden from above. Matthes wrote that they became expert at negotiating the Canyon in the process:

> The party was distributed fairly all over the chasm, and its members had a way of emerging from it singly and at unexpected places, quite astonishing to their friends on the rim. Only seasoned men could have undertaken such bold movements.
>
> At one time two of the men were toying with the mighty river, descending its foaming rapids in a flimsy boat, while twenty miles away two others were creeping precariously along treacherous shaley ledges, intent on capturing a strategically located butte, with their instruments and maps on their backs.
>
> The tourist trails, traveled by many in awe and trembling under the surveillance of a strapping guide, were to us like highways, safe at any time of day or night.

After a substantial gap in time, during which Matthes took on other projects (such as mapping Yosemite), the easternmost section (bordered by Havasu Canyon) was finally surveyed in 1920 and 1921. With the fieldwork finally accomplished, the great task of finishing the maps commenced.

The original plan called for 15-minute quadrangles on the standard scale of 1:62,500—or about one mile to the inch—with 100-foot contour intervals. Yet Matthes noted that many significant cliffs were less than 100 feet high, which would be lost on a map with the standard interval. He decided to double the number of contour

The Matthes Evans team camping at Garnet Canyon.

lines by marking every 50 feet, and then enlarged the map to the greater field scale of 1:48,000—or 4,000 feet to the inch.

The USGS enthusiastically approved these modifications. Now there only remained the final step of inking and supervising the engraving. This proved so straining on Matthes, however, that it permanently disabled his eyesight. Yet when the Vishnu, Bright Angel, Shinumo, and Supai quadrangles were published in 1923, topographers celebrated them as perhaps the finest maps of their kind ever made (see inside covers). As a measure of the intractability of Matthes and Evans's subject, for all their efforts, the new map covered only about 55 per cent–or 1,127 square miles–of the Canyon's total area, from Nankoweap to Havasu Canyons. Even then, 32 per cent of the map is comprised of the relatively flat plateaus that form the Canyon's rims.

A portion of the great gorge had been committed to paper at last. Yet the enormity of what Matthes and Evans achieved did little to change the Canyon's accessibility. Because the surveying had largely taken place from the rims, it made for a unique situation. The existence of a detailed topographic map did not mean that the country had actually been explored. Instead, it only meant that the Canyon had been *seen* from remote points, thus leaving much of the charted terrain untrod.

"If the map shall prove a useful instrument in the hands of scientist or tourist," Matthes concluded, "the highest hopes of its authors will have been fulfilled." He would have doubtless been surprised to know that no one would find it more useful than a native of China, a young lad still finding his way in a world tainted by tragedy.

The first Kuling American School class photo, September 1916. Harvey sits on the stone pillar fifth from left, top row. Baird, Nellie, Ruth and Helen are below to his left. *Courtesy Walter Merwin Haskell*

Chapter Five

SEA CHANGE
1913–1920

After that I never cried again with any real conviction, nor expected much of anyone's God except indifference, nor loved deeply without fear that it would cost me dearly in pain. At the age of five I had become a skeptic and began to sense that any happiness that came my way might be the prelude to some grim cosmic joke.

Russell Baker,
Growing Up
On losing his father as a five year-old

ON A CHILLY FEBRUARY DAY in 1916, six young men who had been medical students of Dr. James Butchart lifted the casket upon their shoulders and commenced toward the foreign cemetery outside Nanking. They wore stark white, the color of mourning in China. Harvey, Nellie, Baird, Helen and Ruth plus dozens of missionaries and Chinese friends solemnly followed the pallbearers past fields that lay dead in winter brown. It was a rare honor for a foreigner to be given a funeral in the style of the emperors, which meant walking the casket three miles from Nanking's massive eastern gate towards Tze-ch'ing Shan, the Purple Mountain. In his short life, eight-year-old Harvey had never before confronted death. After watching his father be buried today, however, nothing would be the same.

The location of the foreign cemetery was a bitter irony. One of Harvey's favorite memories came from the time he and his father had camped at Purple Mountain. Now it would become a symbol of lost time, the fleeting days they had shared, and a future that suddenly threatened to spin out of control.

Purple Mountain's smooth-crested peak formed the most recognizable landmark in the landscape surrounding Nanking, where James had moved the

Butchart family three years earlier, in 1913, after proudly accepting an invitation to teach surgery at the University of Nanking. Not only had this appointment granted James the official Chinese approval he had spent his career working so tirelessly for, it was also evidence of the radical new chapter in Chinese history that had unfolded in recent months.

Nanking became the epicenter for the tumultuous Revolution of 1911, when rebels led by an American-trained physician and Christian convert named Sun Yat-Sen had succeeded in ousting the 2,000-year-old imperial Chinese government. During the violent months of this struggle, the Butcharts had fled Luchowfu to take refuge in Shanghai. Sun Yat-Sen helped establish a parliamentary government in Nanking, which was decreed the new capital of China—a country that would now begin to turn its back on tradition and embrace Western ideas and technology.[1]

James could not have failed to feel an immense pride and excitement at the prospect of playing a part in this reformation. As both doctor and missionary, he brought the very skills and philosophies China called for at this turning point in the country's trajectory.

Hence the Nanking that the Butcharts had moved to in 1913 was a different city than the one James and Nellie had known when they had met in 1902. An atmosphere of new possibilities pervaded its walls. Harvey may have felt sadness at leaving Luchowfu behind, but nearly 500 Westerners called Nanking home, many more than in Luchowfu. A lively social network, with frequent dinner parties and daily get-togethers and plenty of other children to play with, promised to make life in Nanking more like America than anything Harvey had yet seen.

As they had in Luchowfu, the Butcharts moved into Nanking's foreign compound, where a comfortable two-story house awaited them. If things had seemed busy in Luchowfu, life now became crazier than ever. Another child had been added to the household, Ruth Ann, who had been born in Kuling in 1912. Now that James was teaching in addition to continuing with his other duties, he became absolutely inundated with work. Nearly everyone in the foreign community knew him by virtue of his position as a doctor, and the social obligations also grew. Most days Nellie hosted one or another of Nanking's families for dinner or afternoon tea while servants rushed about trying to keep things

---

[1] To travel back in time to this era, watch the Oscar-winning film *The Last Emperor*, which documents the life of Pu Yi. Pu Yi was born a year before Harvey and gained the status of emperor of China at the age of two. He was forced to abdicate his throne in Beijing in 1912 following the revolution. The film provides not only an interesting look at Chinese history, but also the chance to imagine a young Harvey Butchart so close in age to Pu Yi, living and playing in a similar environment.

running smoothly.

Six-year-old Harvey began first grade in Nanking that year and enjoyed it from day one. The teachers told James and Nellie what they already knew, that Harvey showed great promise. In addition to his obvious smarts, Harvey had an especially impressive memory. He could recall in detail anything he had read or heard only once. Although he was shy, almost timid—which sometimes made it hard when he was around other kids—he excelled at his studies. Harvey would bury himself in books. Just like his father, who was an avid reader, the boy quickly developed a love for seeing the world through words.

"It amazes me when I think of all the boxes of books he had brought from America," Harvey remembered of his father. "There were shelves in his study with complete works of the great poets. I remember leafing through *Paradise Lost* [by John Milton] and admiring the pictures of fallen angels."

Harvey's abilities as a quick and clever thinker surfaced early. At six, he refused one day to go to his second floor bedroom alone after dark, protesting that a tiger lurked behind the stairs. Finally James took Harvey by the hand and brought a lamp to show that there was nothing there. Harvey indicated, however, that this was an *invisible* tiger.

Harvey could be insolent as well as charming. One evening when the Butcharts stopped at a friend's house, they stayed for a fried chicken dinner. After everyone had finished, Harvey asked for another piece of chicken. His father told him he had had enough. The boy then casually leaned back in his chair and yelled "I'm starving!" Once back home Harvey received a sound spanking from James for his outburst.

Yet for the most part, Harvey was a congenial child who presented few problems, especially when he could go to school. Hillcrest Day School operated just like a school in the States, with the missionary wives and mothers serving as instructors. With her teaching background, Nellie acted as a key figure. She made sure that classroom discussions and studies focused on the United States rather than on China.

Nellie in fact discouraged her children from interacting with the Chinese. She abhorred how some of the other missionaries's children adopted Mandarin as a second language. She made it a point to teach only the most basic Mandarin phrases that her students and children might need. One of the few sentences Harvey could utter was, "I don't understand your Chinese." The schoolbooks she used were English. Clothes, meals and games all were typically American or English style. And stories, unless introduced by a friendly servant, were the same stories kids in America heard. Nellie simply did not trust the non-Christian culture of the Middle Kingdom.

Dr. Butchart on the other hand was a capable Mandarin linguist who felt at ease amongst the Chinese. He encouraged his sons to experience the native culture on its own terms. When time allowed, he took Baird and Harvey into the hospital to show them around, and on Saturdays he brought them to Nanking's weekly market. And what colors and smells and sights there were! Crowded side by side on the narrow cobblestone streets the farmers, craftsmen, fishermen, and butchers displayed their goods. There were heaps of vegetables and fruit, baskets of walnuts and pumpkin seeds, oily piles of mutton glistening in the hazy gray light. James showed his sons how men unwound strands from silkworm cocoons and spun them into the finest silk fabrics. Together they strolled among the great din of shouting vendors where Harvey heard the outraged voices and laughter of commerce being conducted in the open. There was a kind of music to the market, a vigorous overture of lusty humanity, and James wanted his sons to hear it.

"He respected the Chinese workmen and didn't take the attitude of some foreigners, that if it was Chinese it must be inferior," Harvey recalled of his father. "Instead of ordering a set of silverware that he and Mother admired in a magazine advertisement, he showed the picture to a Chinese silversmith and gave the craftsman enough Mexican silver dollars to turn into the table settings. The silversmith was able to construct the molds and turn the Mexican silver into tableware that looked as fine as the picture showed them."

Nanking's outer wall. *Courtesy Barry Till*

James was also fond of taking the boys for walks atop Nanking's handsome outer wall. One of the city's most prominent features, the protective brick barrier had been built centuries earlier and measured almost 40 feet across, providing a pleasant walkway that offered commanding views of the beautiful countryside surrounding Nanking. One sight dominated the view from the wall: Purple Mountain, where tombs of the many Ming Emperors (the dynasty that ruled China from AD 1368-1644) lay hidden in the mountain's secret places. No one knew precisely where the emperors were buried. During the old Imperial funerals, nine identical processions, one from each of the nine gates of the city, would proceed to the mountain. Only one, however, would contain the emperor's body.

For Harvey the Purple Mountain was more than a mythic tomb, it also offered a great place to go camping. "One of my best memories concerned two camping trips that Father took us on," Harvey wrote. "He had a white wall tent and folding army cots. Chinese coolies [a name used by Westerners for Chinese laborers] carried the loads hanging from the ends of a carrying pole over the shoulder."

Despite such excursions, James's frenetic work pace continued to intensify while opportunities for relaxation grew sparse. He was apparently incapable of turning away patients who needed his services. As a result, he forsook his own interests, rarely indulging in pastimes or activities that he actually liked. "He had," Harvey said, "very little time for the family."

James's energy and devotion were indeed remarkable. Somehow he pushed himself in Nanking to satisfy his staggering load of responsibilities. No one knows what factors drive certain people to go beyond normal levels of performance in their chosen fields. James's quest for fulfillment manifested itself in a fixation with self-sacrifice, a notion rooted in his Christian mission, but one that was also very self-serving. In the process of giving his energy completely to his patients and students, he failed to apply the same level of concern to himself, and in the end, to his own family.

His demise began innocently, perhaps even unbelievably. In the winter of 1915-1916, while walking barefoot one night in the house, James stubbed his toe. The wound seemed minor. He ignored it, concentrating instead upon the multiple surgical cases he was working on at the time. Days went by without him noticing the infection beginning to spread.

"He was an M.D. but he didn't clean the crack between his toes that he made by stumbling into some furniture in the dark," Harvey said. "And then he went on wearing his shoes to all of his work and social engagements, and he realized he had an infection starting in. He tried to work on it but apparently something happened to his natural defenses, perhaps from breathing too much ether. My mother thought that he was performing a couple of operations without a mask, and that maybe something went wrong with his blood."

Dr. James Butchart fought his infection for weeks from a hospital bed. Nellie and the kids visited. James remained cheerful. But when gangrene set in he was confronted with the possible amputation of his foot, or else death from overwhelming infection.

Oddly, neither would transpire. While bedridden, his infected leg developed an internal blood clot. A nurse happened to be reading to him when part of the clot broke off and lodged in his lung, killing him quickly. He was 49 years old. James's death was mourned throughout both the Chinese and Western communities in Nanking, for his service had known no racial or class bounds. One of James's fellow missionaries wrote:

> James Butchart, doctor, preacher, teacher, pioneer, gentleman, friend, and Christian, has gone to the life eternal. Many believed him a god because of what he wrought. His was a great life, because talent, experience, and accomplishment were all for Christ, the Savior, in a land that knows him not.

"We were all devastated, especially my mother," Harvey recalled. Following the funeral, Nellie gathered herself together, then told her children they were leaving Nanking. Torn between returning to America and remaining in the only country her children had ever known, Nellie chose to retreat to Kuling, where a teaching job had been offered to her at the newly established Kuling American School. With World War I in full swing by then, it may not have been possible to secure transportation to America had she wanted to go.

During that move in September 1916, the Butcharts's loss hung over them like a bad dream, still fresh and raw. Nellie steadfastly relied on her faith and her will to see her children through. She dealt with her own pain by burying herself in the many tasks of organizing the new school and preparing to teach, which included gathering the students for the inaugural class photo. Nellie, Harvey, Baird, Helen and Ruth all dutifully posed in their formal school whites underneath the shade of trees lining North Field Road. In that moment, so soon after the shock of losing James, they all wear the unmistakable look of broken hearts.

MONEY WAS TIGHT. Nellie received help from the Disciples of Christ, but missions in China had always been a marginal exercise. She would do her best to fare on her own. There was the small salary she earned as teacher and supervisor of the new school, and, though she could not have liked it, the pity of Kuling's residents. Most had known James, had turned to him for help with medical matters of their own at one time or another. They were not about to let his family suffer this burden alone.

Harvey's predicament following his father's death was far from unusual in 1916, when millions of boys were rendered fatherless by World War I. Many young men were forced by circumstance to leave home and make their way in the world. But setting out on his own in China was unthinkable for Harvey.

The first breath of winter came to the mountain. As the leaves died and the streets froze, the schoolchildren huddled around the woodstove in the Butchart home. They listened as Nellie taught arithmetic and United States history. It was Harvey's first real winter. He had never seen snow or ice clinging to the eaves of the house. He watched the heavy storms sweep through and experienced

A lake at Mount Lushan in winter. *Elias Butler*

the brooding, silent world left in their wake. On days when clouds claimed the mountain, that is to say most days, the town turned gray and bitterly cold. This was not the Kuling that Harvey remembered.

Wintertime presented a challenge to the new school. Lacking a gym for a proper recess, the students needed an outlet for the animal energies, but what could they do? Without enough children of like ages for team sports, they had to go with some other kind of group activity. Surrounding town was an immense natural playground, 190 square miles of mountain range that contained enough physical challenge to absorb any bout of cabin fever. One of the teachers eventually suggested the obvious.

"We did a lot of hiking," Harvey said. "We had a half-day vacation on Wednesday and half-day on Saturday, school the rest of the time. But we got around over those mountains just about everyplace. I didn't realize that I began liking, permanently liking hiking at that time."

In addition to the hikes they took during school, Harvey and Baird also joined Kuling's Boy Scout troop. The scouts trekked to the more remote regions of Mount Lushan, went on campouts and backpack trips, swam and played games. And as thousands of scouts have since, they learned the rudiments of self-reliance in the outdoors: Compass and map reading skills, survival techniques, fire building, swimming, first aid, canoeing, etc. The scouts also provided Harvey with an introduction to downhill skiing. One day they constructed homemade skis out of barrel staves and loops of leather straps, then hit the slopes around town.

Over the next three years, from fourth to seventh grade, Harvey performed an apprenticeship of sorts at Mount Lushan. A great variety of terrain and climates existed within the immediate region. There were tall gray cliffs on which

One of many hiking trails at Mount Lushan. *Elias Butler*

to clamber about, caves to investigate, boulders to climb. Waterfalls coursed down secluded canyons into fine pools. Miles of quiet paths leading through the fog-drenched woods were ready to satisfy his boyhood wanderlust. And each time Nellie needed to go down the mountain to the larger town of Kiukiang, there was the 4,000-foot, nine-mile, seven-life-zone ramble to make. In short, Mount Lushan was a hiker's dream.

"We took it for granted," Harvey remembered. "It was run of the mill stuff to us, we didn't appreciate it quite as much as some of the people visiting there. They would tell us that we were living such a fine life and had such a wonderful chance to see what mountains were like in Utah and Colorado. We thought they were exaggerating. But it got under my skin."

As winter turned to spring and summer in 1917, Harvey entered his 10th year. He could make the hike to the Three Ancient Trees now without a hitch. And he had grown old enough that Nellie did not mind if he wanted to go exploring by himself. She felt that Kuling and its trails were safe, especially during summer when hundreds of missionary families would converge there. Sometimes Baird went hiking with Harvey, but if not, Harvey preferred solitude to the company of other kids. It felt good to be alone on the mountain.

And, there was something else that attracted him. It could be explained in part by singling out Mount Lushan's natural beauty—its mists, creeks, and soaring summits—but only in part. The rest of it was harder to pinpoint. A unique undercurrent pervaded the mountain, a feeling more than anything else; it hinted at something mysterious and fantastic without revealing anything.

Scores of solitude-seeking poets, landscape painters, philosophers and pilgrims had been drawn here throughout the centuries in order to steep their souls in this rare essence, to plumb the mountain for what it might inspire. At one time Mount Lushan had been the center of Buddhism and Taoism in all of China, and many of China's most famous poets composed odes to the Thatch-Hut Mountains.

Oddities occurred throughout the range, things guaranteed to catch the interest of a growing boy who liked to explore. For example, a phenomenon the

Chinese called "Buddha Light" could happen anytime the sun appeared on a foggy day. When standing on a high ridge, Harvey could look down hundreds of feet into the mists to see a rainbow encircling his perfectly cast shadow. Then there was the Immortal's Cavern, where a priest was said to have gained the secret to eternal life by meditating for years in the side of a cliff. Water dripped from a spring in the cave that contained such a high mineral content that a coin would float in a cup filled with this water.

Into this magical realm, Harvey wandered freely and in depth. He grew up a child of precipitous terrain, a mountain boy. The steepness of the trails and the altitude developed a strong pair of lungs in him and shaped his muscles for hiking.

The "cloud sea" at Mount Lushan. *Elias Butler*

There were places to sit and listen to water tumbling over a cliff, or to watch the sea of clouds gather around a peak, engulf it, and then reveal it once more. Places to escape to, where he could leave his peers behind in exchange for the raw drama of nature.

Danger existed here too, and Harvey learned to respect the mountain's sometimes-angry temperament. In summertime, when the scouts or a group of picnickers wanted to cool off with a swim, a couple of boys would always be detached to the tops of the canyon walls to watch for the threat of thunderstorms and flash floods. Harvey's neighbor Pearl Buck spent her honeymoon in Kuling in the summer of 1917. She wrote about Mount Lushan's flash floods in her autobiography *My Several Worlds:*

> One fearful aspect of those beautiful mountains of Lu was the flash floods. Springs at the top of the mountain had through the centuries cut deep gorges into the soil, and since the forests had long ago been destroyed, a cloudburst on top of the mountain could pour water into a gorge so suddenly that within minutes a great wall of water was built up, although below the sun might be shining. Every summer some lives were lost in these flash floods...The possibility of death always at hand lent an undertone of terror to the pleasantest summer day in Kuling.

Harvey stood beside the thundering floods and felt their power. He watched the muddy waters crest and then slowly recede until everything remained as it did before. Nature was his salve for the emotional impact of his father's death and he turned to it again and again. From the ages of nine to 13—a crucial time in the development of any young man, especially one who has been robbed of his father—he became expert at negotiating rugged country. Through the snows and spring flowers and summer thunderstorms he played and played, far removed from the rest of the world. The mountains were home.

But by the spring of 1920, Nellie was having other thoughts. As beautiful as this land was, the reminders of James were everywhere—in the house, in the neighbors's faces, on the trails. Ever since his death, Nellie had been keeping

A statue of Bai Juyi, a ninth-century Chinese philosopher. *Elias Butler*

her eyes fixed on America, waiting for the right time to leave China. She read the newspapers from Shanghai of her country's fate in World War I. Following the victory, she waited until June, 1920, when the school year ended. Just as the summer crowds were beginning to show up in Kuling, she sold her cottage, took her family and left. The Butcharts boarded a steamer in Shanghai a few days later and turned their backs forever on the Purple Mountain and Mount Lushan. What lay ahead none of them could predict.

It would be decades before Harvey got the chance to live near such mountains and canyons again. But he never forgot what it felt like to ramble through extraordinary country. The urge had been planted in his very core. He would bide his time, and when the opportunity finally returned, his built-up desire—both to challenge himself against the wilderness and to fulfill a vision of himself—would burst forth like a dam breaking.

Destiny was about to get thousands of miles closer.

Yellow Dragon Pool, where Harvey swam with Kuling's Boy Scouts. *Elias Butler*

The Mercersburg Spiders, 1920. Harvey is second from left, front row. *Courtesy Mercersburg Academy*

Chapter Six

HIGH GRADE POINTS AND
THE PRESIDENT'S DAUGHTER
1920–1929

I had gone with two or three girls but I was pretty bashful and backward about girls.

Harvey Butchart

I was painfully shy and feeling socially inadequate, boys never gave me a second glance. Of course, I always had a crush on some boy who didn't even know I existed.

Roma Wilson

HARVEY PLAYED SECOND-STRING on the Mercersburg Spiders junior varsity football squad in 1920, a position guaranteed to keep him a perennial bench warmer. But during one early season match the coach finally barked out his name. Harvey ran onto the field and lined up, an undersized kid in oversized pads pushing his helmet back so he could see. The ball snapped at the quarterback's sharp "Hut!" Before Harvey knew what was happening, a brute from the opposing team rushed and flattened Mercersburg's tiniest Spider, hitting Harvey so hard he saw stars. No further persuasion was necessary to convince Harvey he should look elsewhere for the athletic glory he craved. "I decided," he said, "I wouldn't be a football hero."

Mercersburg Academy was a far cry from Kuling. The prestigious boarding school's students placed hiking near the bottom of the list when it came to sports. Little wonder, there being a dearth of canyons or peaks to lure the adventurous in that gentle Pennsylvania landscape. No, what you did if you were going to Mercersburg was get on the football squad, or the hockey or baseball teams, and show your aggressiveness like any other red-blooded American teenager—out there on a flat surface with your teammates.

As much as he may have wanted to join, Harvey just did not have the body or personality for team sports. He measured five-foot-three and 95 pounds of shy and spindly bookworm who felt more comfortable off by himself in the wilderness than playing catch with the roughhousing boys. High school had just started for Harvey in the fall of 1920, and he was already having a hard time fitting in.

His transition from China to America had gone smoothly enough to that point. Two months earlier, Nellie and the children had arrived in San Francisco aboard the SS *Ecuador* after leaving Hong Kong. Harvey never forgot his first sight of America as they steamed into the famous bay following the three-week journey, the *Ecuador* sounding a powerful blast to announce their arrival.

At the smelly wharf, Harvey noticed that the dockworkers—the common laborers—spoke English. And they were *white*. It was stunning for someone who had grown up with Chinese servants in the house. Harvey's status as a minority member of a privileged class had just shifted, much to Nellie's satisfaction. For her, this initial image of America had already made their trip worth it. "Actually, she [Nellie] had a peculiar reason you might not think of [for moving to America]," Harvey said. "She wanted us to get used to doing some chores and not having the Chinese do everything for us. Over there, if you wanted your grass cut, you hired a Chinese for peanuts to do it. And we had a Chinese cook, a Chinese waiter for our table, a Chinese amah to clean the beds and dust. She wanted us to learn how to mow the lawn and tend the garden for ourselves, and that was the main reason she wanted to come back to America."

With what money Nellie had raised from the sale of the Kuling cottage, and a looming future that lacked pecuniary prospects, she did what many people would have done in her predicament: She went back home. Nellie ushered her family onto a train and headed 2,200 miles east to the small town of Vermont, Illinois, where relatives and the church could help get the Butcharts back on their feet.

The shock of entering a different culture—one they had been told all their lives that they belonged to—confronted Harvey and his siblings at every turn during that long train ride. Things that Americans took for granted were the strangest. Harvey flipped a switch to read by *electric* lights, flushed the toilet with *clean running water* and saw *automobiles* blur past the windows. He spoke English with everyone he met. In the dining car, cheeseburgers, grilled ham-and-cheese sandwiches and french fries tasted like heaven. It took less than a month to go from the third world to the first, from seeing people live in squalor to admiring the architectural marvel of a skyscraper. America had existed for so long as mere conjecture and simplified images. Now it revealed itself as a fascinating, ultra-modern complexity, at once familiar and supremely alien.

It was also frightening. There would have been plenty of reasons for Harvey and his siblings to feel different. They were fatherless, they were from China, they were poor. Yet because they looked like everyone else now, they were supposed to fit right in. Never mind that they had little in common with the native kids. Sure, Harvey might have heard of the Great War from afar, but he had held no stake in the matter. Same with baseball or what kind of toys kids played with. Even the government was baffled. Getting citizenship for the children proved problematic, as the family was a menagerie of birthrights by locale. Nellie had been born in America, James in Canada, the children in China. Nellie would go before the U.S. Immigration Board several times before her kids finally gained citizenship status.

In Illinois, grandparents and other relatives took in the broken family, doing their best to ease the children's awkwardness. The Daughertys had found a modest house for the newcomers in the neighborhood, which would provide just what Nellie wanted: A quick transition from Chinese servitude to American self-reliance. It was little more than a beat-up farmhouse, an aging structure in dire need of maintenance and repair. Finances being what they were made hired help out of the question.

"Mother didn't get a part time job teaching after coming back in 1920," Harvey said. "When she learned that she would have to take some courses in education before being allowed to teach, she tried to supplement her income in rather unpleasant ways. She tried selling cosmetics door to door."

Despite Nellie's satisfaction at finally seeing her children do their own chores, she was indeed looking down a hard road. There would be years of loneliness and struggle ahead that only a widow left to care for four hungry mouths midstream in life could know. Not that she was a stranger to adversity. Raised in a strict Christian home, Nellie had had an abrupt introduction to adult life. At 10, her own mother had died of illness, leaving her and her father in charge of a family of five. She had raised her three brothers as her own.

But that would have paled next to the challenge that she now faced. Money was going to be a problem. It literally gnawed at her guts, as she suffered from intermittent abdominal pains produced by stress, a condition that would worsen over the years into colitis. At night, in her private moments, she worried over how they would manage for the next month or two, much less her

Helen and Ruth Butchart in Illinois, 1920. *Courtesy Anne Madariaga* children's long-term future. The boys would need to go to college soon and where was the money for that? *Dear Lord, have mercy.*

Help arrived for Harvey and Baird's education by the end of the summer. Nellie managed to scare up funds by pleading her case to the United Christian Missionary Society, a non-profit aimed at helping missionary causes. Nellie wrote a grateful letter about her sons's good fortune that was published in the December 1920 Disciples of Christ periodical, *World Call:*

> I am counting my blessings. My dear boys are in school at Mercersburg, Pennsylvania, where the students give $2,000 a year for missions. I am able to keep them there, because of the missionary purpose of that school, for $150 each year instead of $800.

Harvey and Baird left Illinois that August for the highly regarded prep school. Nellie felt strongly about a good education and her boys would certainly get one at upper-crust Mercersburg. Located in southeast Pennsylvania near the Maryland border, the school boasts several distinguished alumni from the Roaring Twenties, such as Academy Award-winning actor Jimmy Stewart and prolific author David Lavender, whose works include *River Runners of the Grand Canyon*. Even Vice President (and eventual president) Calvin Coolidge's son, Calvin Jr., could be counted among the students at Mercersburg.

Separated from their mother and sisters, on their own at a new school in this strange country, Harvey and Baird relied upon each other. Harvey had it worse, for at 13, he should have been in eighth grade but tests showed him ready for

high school and he was advanced a year. Small to begin with, Harvey now found himself that much smaller than his classmates. Baird on the other hand was tough and big as well as intelligent. He could hold his own. As long as Baird was there, Harvey knew he would be all right.

But an older brother cannot be there all the time. The gangly, bookish, shy, pre-pubescent Harvey made a natural target for the school bullies. His high intellect could not have helped matters. In math class, Harvey solved problems the older students could not. His writing in English topped them also. Earning high marks made his mother proud but also invited the wrath of the very element he wished to avoid. "I was sort of a small boy,"

Baird Butchart's Mercersburg senior portrait, 1922. *Courtesy Mercersburg Academy*

Harvey said, "and my brother was getting into scraps. But he would defend me, keep me from getting beaten up or anything."

Harvey's bid for gridiron glory had flopped and he felt he didn't have a prayer on the basketball court because of his size. Still, he was searching, as adolescents are wont to do, for his place in an unfamiliar and hostile world. He had athletic gifts for mountain climbing and hiking but there was no way to show it at Mercersburg. Harvey eventually reacted by withdrawing to his studies, avoiding others when possible, and abandoning organized sports. The pressure of being the quiet, intellectual kid from China threatened to draw an introverted young man even further inward.

Then, as if to underscore his troubles, he actually flunked his math class that spring. Until now, anything less than above average had been scholastic no-man's-land for Harvey Butchart. Getting picked on was one thing. Harvey could not help that. But failing was quite another and he would not stand for it. As a result, he displayed what would become a defining, life-long trait: The will to make up for mistakes with determined and intelligent focus.

> After I'd been given a failing mark at the end of that semester, I went home to Illinois where my mother was living. And she had taught algebra. I took the same book I'd had at Mercersburg Academy and we started to review the book. I studied it to understand it, not just gloss over it. So I got my algebra straightened out there.

He would have to wait to prove his math skills at Mercersburg. Nellie moved the family again in the summer of 1922, this time 80 miles closer to Chicago to the tiny town of Eureka. The small Midwestern farming town was a slice of rural 1920s America, 1,600 people surrounded by miles and miles of alfalfa and cornfields.

It would be tough to find a region less amenable for a kid brought up on exploring rugged terrain. Nevertheless, Harvey took to the humble topography near Eureka, extracting from it what adventure he could. The Mackinaw and Illinois Rivers, as well as a local stream named Walnut Creek, meant good swimming. Harvey constructed homemade rafts and orange crate dinghies, scrounging junk piles for his materials. In a display of early endurance on land, Harvey bicycled 150 miles round trip to the scene of an historic Indian battle named Starved Rock State Park in Illinois.

Following Harvey's sophomore year at Eureka High, Nellie's alma mater, Harvey and Baird returned to Mercersburg as Nellie again found luck with the high tuition. This time Harvey did not fail algebra. He poured himself into what he realized by now counted as his natural strength: Academic achievement. Being the brain won him few friends, yet Harvey's teachers recognized and praised his impressive classroom performance. At the end of the school year, in June 1923, the weekly student newspaper, *The Mercersburg News*, printed the following in a summary of academic awards:

> Working Boy's Prize Scholarship: A prize of $20.00 given by a friend of the school to the working boy who maintains the highest scholarship during the year. Awarded to John Harvey Butchart, '25, Nanking, China.

Indeed, Harvey flourished at Mercersburg. Following his junior year, he earned enough credits to leave high school and begin college as a 17-year-old. He returned to Eureka to look into continuing his education at Eureka College, a small Disciples of Christ institution where Nellie had graduated with her teaching degree. Because Baird was leaving for Princeton to study medicine on a scholarship, Harvey wanted to stay close to home anyway to help his mother. He enrolled at Eureka in the fall of 1923 as an undeclared freshman.

Unlike Baird, who aspired to become a doctor, Harvey saw no obvious career path for himself through the maze of academic ivory towers. He briefly entertained thoughts of following his parents's lead. "When I was a freshman in college," Harvey said, "I was thinking I'd get ready and go back to be a missionary in China. I actually went to a group that was meeting once a week, preparing to go that way." For a while, he even contemplated the medical missionary field as his father had done. Nellie instantly quashed the notion. After watching her husband work himself to death, she had plenty of justified apprehensions about her son practicing medicine in a foreign land.

Nellie instead nudged Harvey toward a teaching career. At first Harvey ·questioned whether teaching matched his personality. His introversion clashed with visions of being forced to speak in front of people. Yet teaching did have this advantage: He would have summers off to do as he liked. Finally, the math professor at Eureka buttonholed Harvey and convinced him that he would make good grades. That settled it. Harvey declared himself a math major. In the eighth grade, it had been his scholastic nemesis but now Harvey attacked mathematics with everything he had. His grades went far beyond good. They were outstanding. Considering that Harvey later discovered he owned a genius-level I.Q., this was no surprise.

Amidst all his studies Harvey never lost his yearning to hike. He had long since exhausted any opportunities in Eureka and felt the need for *something* physical to test his athletic urges. "Back in the Middle West when I was growing up in high school and college," Harvey said, "I was interested in various things connected with camping and a little bit of hiking, but not much in the cornfield country there. We [Baird and I] went on camping trips up on the Illinois River—a rather pretty beauty spot. Still is pretty there. But I became more interested in tennis than anything else at that time."

Harvey had finally discovered a sport that catered to his unique strengths as an athlete. What he lacked in muscle mass mattered little in this game, which rewards strategy and finesse more than brute force. Harvey the loner found the one-on-one format to his liking. And he discovered perhaps for the first time a great satisfaction in the act of competing. Tennis allowed him to achieve victory as an *individual*—far more gratifying than sharing the spoils on a team. As he realized with growing confidence how good he was, he became eager to pit himself against his foes. Harvey could be unmerciful, for he had a bit of a chip on his shoulder from past humiliations. Nimble, intense, and able to put the ball where he wanted, Harvey earned a reputation as a tennis assassin. He excelled almost every time he played. With a few months of practice, he easily made Eureka's tennis team. Harvey had grown to a modest 5'7" and 125 lbs as a 20 year-old, but he had little trouble beating the best players from other schools. In a display of his dominant ability, Harvey won all his singles matches during his senior year in 1927 except for one—the championship match at the Illinois state finals.

Despite his prowess with a racquet, and the fact that he was Mr. Calculus on campus, Harvey did not exactly clear the net with girls. He was simply too shy to approach them and too quiet to garner much notice. But that was about to change. The final stamp of triumph on that senior year of college was not another academic accolade or a victory on the court. It was success in the one facet of his young life that had thus far eluded him—*romance*.

For three years now—ever since his freshman year at Eureka—Harvey had kept his eye on the same girl. She, however, had never so much as turned a fleeting glance his way. This small detail did not discourage his growing ardor. Perhaps the bigger issue with Roma Wilson was that her father happened to be the ultraconservative, fire-and-brimstone president of Eureka College. Everyone on campus knew Bert Wilson was not one to be trifled with, especially when it came to matters of student propriety. Harvey got a taste of Bert's dictator-like qualities at the beginning of his senior year during the compulsory back-to-school dance called "The Grind."

In the crowd that night, doubtless to her considerable regret, was self-conscious 21-year-old Roma, a brainy French Literature major. Being the president's daughter meant Roma was in a no-win situation. The other students treated her differently, her father meddled in her affairs and embarrassed her to no end, and as far

Roma Wilson, circa 1925 at age 19.
Courtesy Anne Madariaga

as she was concerned, it all helped to make college life the pits. She attended tedious school functions such as The Grind not because she wanted to—she had an overriding hatred of such rituals—but because her father expected it.

The dance began with the students arranging themselves under the watchful eyes of the school administration. They formed two large circles, one comprised of men, the other of women. Like two cogs, they then turned in opposite directions ("grinding" against one another) so that the students met conveyor-belt style. Harvey masked his excitement when he shook Roma's hand. He planned to make his intentions known later.

The undergrads sat down. Ahead lay an evening of polite ballroom music, speeches by the faculty and administration, and cookies and ice cream. Not all the students found such proceedings satisfactory for a back-to-school party. A few pranksters had bribed the orchestra. The music galloped suddenly. On cue, the students leapt from their seats and burst into the foxtrot. Bert Wilson stood in shock. He knew the work of the devil when he saw it. Bert was not the only devout Christian who feared what such dancing could precipitate. *The Cincinnati Catholic Telegraph* had published the following about the foxtrot soon after the dance began to gain in popularity in the mid-1920s:

> The music is sensuous, the embracing of partners—the female only half-dressed—is absolutely indecent; and the motions—they are such as may not be described, with any respect for propriety, in a family newspaper. Suffice it to say that there are certain houses appropriate for such dances; but those houses have been closed by law.

With a powerful bark, Bert commanded the orchestra to halt in midstream. Then, as Roma sank into her chair, Bert went apoplectic on the students. When the last of his condemnations echoed off the walls of the auditorium, the entire crowd sat silent. Roma was mortified beyond belief. Harvey perhaps swallowed hard. Everyone stared at the veins bulging from Bert's temples while he scanned the room for a challenger. None appeared. He finally nodded to the band, and the slow, docile strains of a proper waltz chased the last remnants of the devil— and fun—right out of the building.

The incident may have given Harvey pause. Bert's Puritanism made him a spectacularly unpopular president on campus, especially after he had instituted rules the previous year outlawing smoking and social dancing. Not that Harvey, a life-long Christian and teetotaler, had much at stake when it came to ciga- rettes and foxtrots. But how would it be to have such a staid and stuffy man as his father-in-law? Harvey had the rest of the school year to think about it, which is exactly what he did, as he waited until the spring semester to approach Roma, right before both would graduate.

Until then, Roma had all but given up hope that anyone would ever be interested in her. Her romantic life amounted to a series of frustrations going back to her childhood in the Midwest. She came from the corn country of Humboldt, Nebraska, and like Harvey, she was the second born, arriving on March 8, 1906, as one of Bert and Edith Wilson's eight daughters. Both her par- ents were pious Disciples of Christ churchgoers. Bert had started out as a pro- fessor of English for a Disciples institution, then moved on to preaching, mis- sionary work, and fundraising for the church before accepting the job as presi- dent of Eureka. He was the dominant disciplinary force in the domicile, tough on all his daughters. Bert would not tolerate inappropriate dress, language or conversation. He demanded virtue and moral perfection. The eight females in the house learned to fear his temper. Whenever he lost it, and sooner or later he always did, they would cower as if God himself was unleashing his fury.

In this atmosphere of anxiety, Roma grew up a terribly insecure girl. At an early age, her introversion was such that she hated to have her picture taken, even with family, as "she felt she was being put on display." Many childhood photos feature Roma wearing a scowl, which she would later regret. Her person- ality meant friends were scarce. The Wilsons were a peripatetic family with Bert going from job to job, and any friendships she did develop always dissipated. When the Wilsons moved to Eureka in 1923 on the eve of Roma's senior year in high school, it meant another year of loneliness ahead.

"High school days were a disaster for me," she would later admit. Dealing with teenage life threw her insecurities into sharp relief, the most maddening of which was her lack of confidence around boys. It was simply impossible for her to be at ease with the opposite sex. She was never the prettiest girl in her class, and coupled with her shyness, it meant the boys forgot she was there. Of course, she had her sisters whom she could rely on for support, but even they could compound rather than relieve her misery. Roma wrote, "I would have given everything to be just like [Roma's sister] Violet. Boys flocked to her like bees to honey because of her sunny personality. She was cute and funny and just naturally fit in anywhere, not just with boys."

Ironically, Roma failed to notice the one boy who did know she existed. Even with only 225 students in the entire school, the chameleon-like Harvey had somehow managed to remain below Roma's radar, all the more surprising when one considers how similar they were. Harvey did not see Roma's timidity as a flaw. He saw someone who could understand what it meant to be a social outcast. After all, he never dated a girl unless forced to. "I had gone with girls mostly in a little local fraternity," Harvey wrote, "at social functions where they had a picnic and you had to invite a girl. But I had this girl in mind since freshman year and I sat next to her in our Latin class, [which] had only about five members."

Yet when Harvey gathered up his courage and introduced himself to Roma, she was unimpressed. According to Roma's sister Elaine, Harvey had to pester Roma several times about going out with him before she finally conceded. Roma later explained, "Harvey was at Eureka all this time, but I wasn't even aware of him until our senior year. I think he sat next to me in a class. In our senior year many of my sorority sisters were getting engaged, and I didn't even have a boyfriend. We had very few formal dates as Harvey didn't have any money, but we began going about on campus together a bit. My dad called him 'high grade points' and preferred him to 'low grade points,' my other friends."

As demanded by custom, Harvey bravely met Bert Wilson on their first date—and came away unscathed. Harvey was easy for Bert to like: A polite, conservative, intelligent, God-fearing young man. Even if "high grade points" didn't have any money, he did seem to have a future. Whether Roma was as taken with Harvey is another matter. She resented her father's criticism of her "low grade points" friends. Indeed, if Bert approved of Harvey it may have been the biggest turn-off possible. She had plenty of reasons to feel that when her father got involved with her personal relationships, things were certain to end in utter frustration.

Bert Wilson, Eureka College president. *Courtesy Anne Madariaga*

For instance, Bert had told Roma to do something in college she absolutely despised—join a sorority. It was his way of encouraging her to become more comfortable around others. She hated the idea, thought it terribly unfair, but felt powerless to object.

Halfheartedly, and probably terrified, she somehow became a Phi Omega. Although Bert was pleased, Roma ran into the petty superficiality she feared when her sorority sisters mentioned that they did not approve of Roma's best friend, a girl named Ella whose father happened to be the school janitor. Roma remembered:

> Being the janitor's daughter, Ella was not rushed by any sorority. If she had been outstandingly beautiful or glamorous, she probably could have broken down the barriers, but being just the ordinary daughter of the janitor, she was not good enough for me, so my sorority sisters liked to imply. In the spring of my senior year, I withdrew from the sorority for this reason, but my father more or less forced me to reconsider, and I rejoined. At least I did try! All in all, I didn't see anything especially 'Christian' about this so-called Christian college.

That spring, fed up with the social scene, misunderstood, self-conscious and often depressed, Roma was at an all-time low when Harvey finally asked her out. Harvey had experienced the same kind of estrangement from the students at Eureka and offered his empathy. Despite her father's approval of Harvey and her initial lukewarm feelings, she began to see something in him. After all, he was the only one who had ever shown an interest in her, and that had to count for something. Harvey said that they got "hot and heavy" towards the end of their senior year. This was the first time either of them had ever shared feelings of love with another person.

On April 4, 1928 Harvey asked Roma to marry him. For Roma, high-grade-points-Harvey Butchart was no knight in shining armor. He did not sweep her off her feet, he did not take her breath away, and they did not fall madly into passionate love. But intellectually they were on the same level and, quite simply, he was available. "We hardly knew each other but didn't want to be left out of the socially accepted ritual of going together and getting engaged," she later admitted. While peer pressure may have forced the relationship, Harvey was still the shy man who had a thing for this shy woman. Roma said yes.

Harvey's Eureka College portrait, circa 1925. *Courtesy Eureka College Archives*

"With love to my sweetheart, Roma," circa 1928. *Courtesy Anne Madariaga*

If it sounds as if this courtship perhaps lacked passion, or even true love, it is probably all too true. Roma may have worried that she might never attract another suitor. In the 1920s, America expected its women to marry young. On the other hand, things had worked out for Harvey just as he had planned all along. Beginning in the spring semester of 1928, he had set three major goals for himself: Become the #1 tennis player on the college tennis team, make straight A's, and get engaged. He achieved all but the first—he ended up as the #2 tennis player.

That May, Harvey graduated at the top of his class with his degree in math. Roma earned hers in French Literature with a minor in Latin. Harvey learned that he had been awarded a prestigious scholarship to attend the University of Illinois at Urbana-Champaign, where he planned to pursue his master's degree in math. In the fall, he and Roma moved to Champaign, a couple of hours east of Eureka. As fiancées, they did not yet live together but Roma had escaped her father at least, and would study for her master's in French Literature while continuing her relationship with Harvey.

Meanwhile, Bert began to see serious repercussions of his heavy-handedness at Eureka. In the fall of 1928, a young man destined to end Bert's presidency enrolled as a freshman. This agent of fate from nearby Dixon, Illinois was named Ronald Reagan. "Dutch," as he was nicknamed, quickly became well known around campus, a handsome economics major who was both articulate and outgoing.

When Bert decided to lay off part of the faculty and impose other cuts at Eureka that fall, resentment spread across campus like a prairie fire. It meant many juniors and seniors would

Eureka College student Ronald Reagan, 1931. *Courtesy Eureka College Archives*

66

not be able to take classes they needed to graduate. The students seized upon Bert's cutback plan as the issue they could use to get rid of him and his outdated, fuddy-duddy restrictions. They immediately circulated a petition calling for Bert's resignation. And at the center of the loud protest was Reagan, whose clash with Bert would spark one of the most successful political careers in United States history.

In a 1967 *Los Angeles Times* article, Reagan explains:

> While I didn't play much football that fall, I did taste another type of combat—my first taste of politics. Giving that speech—my first—was as exciting as any I ever gave. For the first time in my life, I felt my words reach out and grab an audience, and it was exhilarating. A week after the strike began, the president resigned, the strike ended, and things returned to normal at Eureka College.

Reagan had won. By December 1928, classes resumed at Eureka with a new president. Despite Roma's reservations about her father, witnessing Reagan's rise to Hollywood stardom and political fame was difficult. Dutch never got a vote from Roma.

The next year, on July 29, 1929, Harvey and Roma married in Eureka. It was a modest ceremony in the Disciples church, followed by a reception in Nellie's backyard. Harvey was 22, Roma 23. They honeymooned at Starved Rock State Park 50 miles north on the Illinois River, where Harvey had once bicycled as a teenager. "Our honeymoon was Spartan," Harvey recalled. This was a fitting prelude to their lives over the next decade, as America would soon tumble into economic despair.

Although Harvey may have enjoyed the thought of getting out for a hike once in a while, this was no time for recreation. He was married now and needed to finish his education. His career lay ahead, as did a family and all the obligations any aspiring young man in the prime of his life faces. He spent his 20s and most of his 30s acting responsibly, working hard—and silently aching for someplace to get out and explore.

Harvey and Roma Butchart, newly-weds in 1929. *Courtesy Anne Madariaga*

TAKE ONE
THIS PUBLICATION IS FREE

Arizona

VISITORS
AND GREETERS
GUIDE

WHAT TO SEE
WHAT TO DO
WHERE TO GO
HOW TO GET THERE

MARCH

Chapter Seven

SOUTHWESTERN MEDICINE
1929–1945

ARIZONA
The Year-round State
Arizona is an all-year playground. It is a land of endless contrasts. Within a few hours you may stand in the midst of America's most primitive life or enjoy the more effete pleasures of modern civilization. Nowhere else can you find within the compass of one state's borders so many national parks and monuments. Historic and pre-historic spots abound. Our state is yours—to see and enjoy.

1939 Arizona Visitors and Greeters Guide

GAZING KEENLY AT HIS MAP of the western U.S. in the summer of 1945, Harvey located the small black dot that identified the mountain town and jabbed the sharp tip of his compass into its center. The pencil scratched softly while he traced a circle, its radius set at a precise distance equivalent to 500 miles. When he finished drawing, he studied the circle's contents. Everything inside it would be accessible within a day's drive. What names it held! Arches, Zion, Saguaro, Organ Pipe, Chaco Canyon and Death Valley; the Abajos, the San Juans, the Mogollon Rim, the Painted Desert, the Colorado River, Glen Canyon. And that was just what lay nearby. The potential for this new move looked endless. Flagstaff, Arizona was clearly the hub of a hiker's paradise.

Yet by far the most intriguing attraction was the large chasm closest to Flagstaff—the mythical Grand Canyon of his youth. If things panned out Harvey would soon be seeing it in person. Perhaps his daughter Anne's malady held a silver lining after all.

This was the real reason for moving, after all. He and Roma had been told that no treatment options remained. They were getting desperate. And as a father, he would do anything for his little girl. Harvey Butchart had to get this teaching job.

Flagstaff was home to Arizona State College, a small but growing school nestled in the high country of northern Arizona. ASC needed a mathematics professor. More importantly, Flagstaff also had an arid climate—the only cure for Anne's steadily worsening asthma and hay fever, according to their doctor.

If Harvey got this job, the Butcharts would make their fifth move in 13 years, which suited Harvey just fine. He would gladly leave Iowa in a heartbeat for the Southwest. Fortunately, with over a decade of teaching and a Ph.D. in mathematics under his belt, his resume looked better than ever. He had racked up an impressive record ever since college, paying his dues as both an itinerant math professor and a serious hiker stuck in America's flat breadbasket.

Harvey's extended stay in the Midwest had more to do with the Great Depression and his mother than with actually wanting to live there. He and Roma had been married exactly three months when Black Tuesday arrived on October 29, 1929. As unemployed students trying to earn their master's degrees, they had little to lose. Yet the Depression coincided with other unfortunate events. Nellie, who had been doing all she could to help provide for the education of each of her children, slid into poor health in the fall of 1929.

"My mother went through some hard times to get us through college and graduate school," Harvey wrote. "She kept on trying to help us even when her eyes were failing. And she had heart problems, in addition to the colitis." At 57, Nellie's health would not allow a regular job. Instead, she was forced to live exclusively on a small retirement income, while Harvey and his siblings did what they could to make ends meet.

But money woes were nothing compared to mourning a member of the family. It caught everyone by surprise that fall when Harvey's athletic, 19-year-old sister Helen fell suddenly ill. She had just begun her junior year at Eureka College and always enjoyed good health. Helen was an "A" student, a striking, curly-haired blonde many considered exceptionally beautiful, but she was quickly confined to a hospital bed after being diagnosed with acute leukemia. After struggling desperately for months, Helen died in July 1930. Harvey, Baird and Ruth buoyed their fragile mother the best they could. With all of them still stuck in school, it made the situation that much more agonizing. Not simply because they had lost their sister, but because none of them had any money to help Nellie. When Harvey and Roma left her in Eureka following the funeral, Harvey felt determined to apply himself to his studies as never before.

Not that he had much choice. Just before Helen's death, Harvey had graduated from the University of Illinois at Urbana with his master's in mathematics and a scholarship to continue there in pursuit of his doctorate. By the time he started that fall, he quickly found Ph.D. math to be such a challenge that he doubted whether he would pass without serious assistance. "I got more than the average amount of help in graduate school," Harvey said. "I did have the luck, though, to have as my advisor a young man who was only about five years older than I, and about 200 to 300 per cent smarter, and he gave me a lot of extra help, a lot of time in his office…he suggested the title for my Ph.D. thesis."

Harvey found the esoteric field of differential geometry to be his forte. His future students remembered that Harvey could simultaneously draw two perfect circles freehand on a chalkboard, though this was only the most obvious and superficial evidence of his talent. The thesis title that his advisor suggested became "Helices in Euclidean N-Space." Put simply, helices are three-dimensional spirals resembling coil springs that lie on the interior surface of a cylinder. What Harvey proposed to do was define their curvatures in n-space, meaning multi-dimensional space. The project quickly subsumed an enormous scope beyond Harvey's expectations, devouring his cognitive abilities like a black hole.

"I did a lot of work on that thesis," Harvey said. "Hard figuring. And I remember one time a single calculation was so lengthy that I had to get wrapping paper, about 20 feet long and 18 inches wide and chuck it over a table top—working over here, carrying it over there. It was a massive calculation. I had the pleasure though after getting a certain formula figured out, hammering and clawing, taking about four weeks to get something down on paper. And then another three weeks to find a mistake in the calculation, and work it out right. After that, I found a way that I could come to the same formula in just a few hours. I had sheets of 8 x 11 paper and I was working on 24 of them simultaneously. I had to keep working back and forth from sheet to sheet."

Harvey's affinity for the field of n-space may be explained in part by looking at one of his predecessors. Arthur Cayley was a nineteenth-century British mathematician who held the prestigious position of professor of pure mathematics at Cambridge as a 42-year-old in 1863. Often referred to as "a mathematician's mathematician," Cayley's voluminous body of published work ranks him as the third-most prolific writer in the history of mathematics. His study and development of n-space theory remains a significant contribution to that field. Although such a conjecture is impossible to prove, a surprising number of parallels link Cayley to Harvey, suggesting some intriguing possibilities as to what kind of personality might be drawn to n-space mathematics.

One of Cayley's pursuits outside the office included mountaineering and serious hiking. He once claimed that the reason he undertook mountain climbing was that the feeling of elation he achieved by conquering a peak was similar to what he experienced by solving a difficult mathematics problem. He considered mountain climbing the easier of the two. Cayley, like Harvey, also possessed a photographic memory, read voraciously, and was described as shy and single-minded. Put Cayley in Flagstaff and it might have been he who became obsessed with route finding in Grand Canyon.

For some reason, many "eggheads" such as n-space scholars like Cayley are attracted to risky outdoor pursuits. Numerous mathematicians of all kinds, engineers, and physicists happen to be rock climbers, mountaineers or serious hikers. The evidence implies that these apparently disparate activities appeal to those with a talent for pattern recognition, with a strong urge for discovery and achievement. Harvey exhibited these qualities in math, and later, in Arizona's deepest chasm.

Harvey also possessed a competitive spirit. Being the first to achieve breakthroughs as either a mathematician or outdoor adventurer brings personal reward and the chance for renown. Each of these pursuits also happens to constitute an endeavor lying at the periphery of society's mainstream, which often earns their practitioners adjectives such as "weird" or "zany" or "out there"— terms aimed at Harvey during his lifetime.

Within the onerous challenges of his graduate school subject, Harvey blossomed. The work forced him to employ both his intense focus and his genius. By the spring of 1932, Harvey earned his Ph.D. by completing and defending "Helices," which was published in the prestigious *American Journal of Mathematics.* Harvey would later write that he considered his thesis the greatest accomplishment of his life.

Unfortunately, the result of Harvey's toil was not a well-paying job. He had been able to student-teach part time during graduate school for a meager salary, but his entry into the workforce happened to coincide with the very depths of the Depression era. For nearly a year following graduation, the newest "doctor" in the Butchart family saw only one reward for his academic efforts: A standing place in the unemployment line.

Life for Harvey and Roma hit rock bottom when they came to the inescapable conclusion that they had to live with in-laws. They stayed with one of Roma's sisters, and then, Bert and Edith Wilson. "That was the time when Ph.D.'s would get a job selling gas at a gas station," Harvey said. "And I didn't even get that. I was living with my wife's relatives through the years and I was unemployed from '32 to '33. Possibly the influence of my wife's father [Bert Wilson], who was a fairly big guy in the denomination…Butler University was a church school that had been started by the Disciples of Christ, I guess he talked them into hiring me."

Missing from Harvey's explanation is what it was like to live with the tyrannical Wilson for a year without gainful employment. It was not uncommon for people to be living with in-laws during the Depression, however, as most were grateful for any roof over their head. And, there was this benefit to poverty: Both Harvey and Roma learned how to spend almost nothing to get by, a skill Harvey later applied habitually to his outdoor pursuits even when he had money.

Although Wilson landed Harvey a job at Butler University in Indianapolis, Indiana, it was not the faculty position Harvey envisioned. Consistent with a trend that continues at most universities to this day, Harvey was more valuable as a sports coach than as an academic instructor. As Butler University's tennis coach, he received a salary of $2,100 per year, or a little over $40 per week. "The reality was," Harvey remembered, "I felt more like a manager than coach, as the players were so good I couldn't tell them anything." Still, a short description of the tennis team that appears in the Butler University yearbook states, *"A stiff schedule has been arranged by Coach Butchart to test the skill and endurance of his athletes."*

Work was work, and Harvey was at least happy for the chance to get himself and Roma a home of their own. Shortly thereafter, he did get a "real job" teaching math and astronomy at Butler.

So began a series of relatively brief tenures for Harvey throughout the Depression decade. He

Coach Harvey Butchart of the 1932 Butler University tennis team. *Courtesy Butler University*

worked wherever he could in the Midwest, flitting from job to job as opportunities arose. He and Roma remained in Indianapolis for three years, from 1933 to 1936, during which time Roma gave birth to Beth Anne in June 1935. The Butcharts's luck continued to improve in 1936 when another church institution, Phillips College in Enid, Oklahoma, offered Harvey a full-time position and a better salary. There he stayed until 1939, when he applied for and landed a position at William Woods College in Fulton, Missouri. Roma again became pregnant and gave birth to James Douglas in June 1939. By then the Depression was finally ending, and for the first time in years, things for the Butcharts looked far less desperate, maybe even promising.

Throughout the 1930s, Harvey made it a point to help his mother however he could, sending her money if he had enough to spare, as did his pediatrician brother Baird, and by looking in on her with regular visits. She was nearly blind with glaucoma but had been holding up despite her frail health. In early 1940, however, she became seriously ill with cancer. In May, Nellie died at age 69 in Eureka. "She had been suffering from colitis for quite a while," Harvey later said. "One doctor we talked to said that probably colitis was due to her nerves, from the fact that her husband had died when she was 45, and then the oldest daughter, Helen, died when she [Nellie] was 58 years old. And between those two bereavements, my mother was pretty torn up." She never remarried following James's death, instead devoting her life to her children.

To Harvey, who followed in his mother's footsteps by becoming a teacher, Nellie was a hero, someone who sacrificed for her children and her beliefs. Throughout his life he would insist she remained his greatest inspiration.

FOLLOWING THE JAPANESE ATTACK on Pearl Harbor in 1941, Harvey found himself exempt from the draft. Instead of fighting overseas, he remained in Fulton, battling it out in the classroom. The following year Harvey was offered the opportunity to teach more advanced mathematics at Grinnell College in Iowa and he moved the family once again, though this was their last move within the Midwest.

By now Harvey had discovered a summertime remedy for the lack of Midwestern hiking opportunities. In 1938, he had finally been able to afford a decent car—a black 1934 Ford sedan he nicknamed "King Henry" (for Henry

Harvey, Roma and Anne enjoy a picnic in 1938. *Courtesy Anne Madariaga*

Ford). Mobile for the first time as an adult, Harvey quickly made good on an ambition that he had harbored since Mount Lushan days: To visit the Colorado Rockies.

These famous mountains form part of the North American Cordillera that stretches 3,000 miles from Alaska to northern Mexico. Harvey and Roma could easily reach Estes Park, one of the most spectacular parts of the range, within a day's drive from Iowa. This small mountain town adjacent to Rocky Mountain National Park inspired Harvey to follow in his father's footsteps by starting an annual family tradition. Every summer for the next decade, the Butcharts set up a tent in Estes Park for weeks, sometimes even months at a time.

Both he and Roma reveled in the majestic scenery and the kids seemed to love it too. They all enjoyed hiking. But when Harvey wanted a more severe physical challenge, he took off alone for the peaks that towered over the surrounding terrain. There was something about summits that beckoned to him—part of their allure was aesthetic, but they also constituted a set of specific objectives that could be tackled in a systematic fashion. Achieving a quantifiable measure of success—an inherent aspect of mountain climbing—appealed to Harvey's desire for orderly accomplishment.

"Many years ago when we were in Missouri and Iowa, we used to camp in Rocky Mtn. N.P.," Harvey wrote. "I climbed just about all the named summits from Longs Peak north and west." Longs Peak qualifies as one of Colorado's 54 Fourteeners, those peaks of special renown that rise to an altitude of at least 14,000 feet. It is Long's Peak in particular that deserves mention here, for Harvey met both a compelling future and a ghost of the past atop this 14,259-foot spire of ice and rock.

In his book *Beyond the Hundredth Meridian: John Wesley Powell and The Second Opening of The West*, author Wallace Stegner notes that when John Wesley Powell's party (including future Grand Canyon boatman Jack Sumner) made the first ascent of Long's Peak in 1868, Powell had met his destiny. The Colorado River begins on the western flanks of Long's Peak, and though Powell did not yet know it, he of course would find fame as an explorer by being the first to lead a river expedition through Grand Canyon in 1869. Harvey likewise looked unknowingly at his own future while atop Long's Peak in the late 1930s.

Yet climbing the occasional mountain such as Long's did not satisfy Harvey. He soon set his sights on all 54 of Colorado's Fourteeners, some of which happen to be demanding climbs that require technical skills and gear. With these targets now before him, he had found his first hiking obsession in the West.

"One of the books that made the greatest impression on me was titled *The Romance of Mountaineering*, by Irvine [sic–R.L.G. Irving]," Harvey explained. "I had found it in a library when I was a teenager. I have never seen it again, but I would surely enjoy reading it now." *The Romance* details notable climbs made by European and American mountaineers in the early 1900s. Stark photographs show classic peaks such as Mont Blanc and several in the Himalaya. The Rockies provided Harvey's first chance to finally climb mountains that resembled those in *The Romance,* and he took full advantage. Though by the time he climbed his last Fourteener in the 1980s he would end up eight short of his goal, mountaineering provided Harvey with just the kind of outdoor challenge that he craved—a combination of scrambling, long-distance hiking, and climbing amidst superb beauty.

Harvey began to show signs of the endurance and tenacity that would later characterize his energetic hikes and climbs in Grand Canyon. His Colorado treks became routine even when they consumed miles of gnarly terrain in a single gulp. "For a pleasant day with a feeling of achievement thrown in," wrote Harvey to a friend, "give me my memory of the time I went from Maroon Lake to Buckskin Pass and then along the ridge to the summits of the North and South Maroon Peaks [both are Fourteeners] and then on beyond until I could get back down the trail." Such a trek meant a class-III, 10-mile hike/scramble including a 4,000-foot off-trail ascent.

Each visit to Colorado's mountains further whetted Harvey's appetite for rugged country. In the spring of 1945, after three years in Iowa, he was itching

Camping in Colorado with "King Henry," Harvey's 1934 Ford sedan. *Roma Butchart courtesy Anne Madariaga*

for his next trip when bad news hit: Anne, who had been plagued by lung ailments since a toddler, was diagnosed with asthma.

Following the doctor's advice, Harvey began to look for a job out west. Only one possibility emerged, and a slim one at that, Arizona State College in Flagstaff, Arizona. Neither Harvey nor Roma had been to Arizona, much less heard of Arizona State College, home of the Lumberjacks. But from Harvey's preliminary research into the school and the community, it quickly emerged as an attractive option. The ASC position carried the more challenging rank of math department chairman and came with a $3,600 annual salary—25 per cent more than he made at Grinnell. Following his experiment with the compass and map, Harvey needed no further convincing. "I applied for the position with all the eloquence I could summon."

After receiving good recommendations regarding his teaching and experience, officials at ASC offered Harvey the job in June 1945. By August the Butcharts were headed for Arizona. Anne recalled VJ Day (Victory in Japan) and the end of World War II occurring while they crossed New Mexico. Every business was closed as the nation celebrated. The Butcharts kept driving until the silhouette of Flagstaff's landmark, the San Francisco Peaks, filled their windshield.

Flagstaff in the 1940s: ASC campus and San Francisco Peaks. *Courtesy NAU Special Collections*

The quiet mountain setting was a radical change for the family. Flagstaff occupied the southern edge of the Colorado Plateau, an arid, high tableland dissected by innumerable canyons, most of which eventually drain into the master stream, the Colorado River. Rich in beauty and in large tracts of bare rock wilderness, the Colorado Plateau remained one of the least inhabited areas in the country. Flagstaff was in one of the Plateau's wetter regions, where the largest ponderosa pine forest in the world sprawls over a 7,000-foot-high volcanic landscape of cinder cones and lava flows.

In 1945 about 5,000 people called Flagstaff home, most of them attracted by abundant jobs in the timber and ranching industries. Flagstaff bustled with constant motion. It marked a crossroads of Route 66 and the Senator Highway and formed a stop for the Santa Fe Railroad. The town also stood only 80 miles from the region's main draw, Grand Canyon, and sat close to numerous other national parks and monuments. All of this made tourism its new prime industry in 1945.

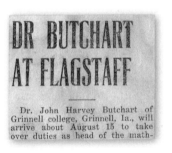

Dr. John Harvey Butchart of Grinnell college, Grinnell, Ia., will arrive about August 15 to take over duties as head of the math-

Prescott Courier, August 1945. Courtesy NAU Special Collections

Harvey was delighted to find that Flagstaff proved to be just what the doctor ordered. Locals boasted that it had the cleanest air in America. Anne's asthma improved dramatically almost upon arrival.

Harvey's new job looked promising as well. In the years prior to Harvey's arrival, the onset of World War II meant the departure of many of ASC's students. By the 1944–1945 academic year, only 161 students attended class on the Flagstaff campus. Room and board cost $37.50 per month and tuition was $9 per semester. Following the end of the war in 1945, however, the college saw a spike in enrollment as returning veterans sought to continue their education on the GI Bill. Harvey arrived just in time to help the school handle the surge.[1]

Right away, the administrators at ASC expected Harvey to make full use of his expansive knowledge of all mathematical fields. That first year, the new math department chairman taught Math for Elementary Teachers, Math for High School Teachers, College Algebra, Trigonometry, Analytic Geometry, Modern Geometry, Differential Calculus, Integral Calculus, Advanced Calculus, Differential Equations, Mechanics, Synthetic Projective Geometry, Theory of Equations, and several special classes. Harvey was not only chairman of the math department, for all practical purposes he *was* the math department.

---

[1] In 1966, ASC would become Northern Arizona University, the name it holds today.

Even with his demanding schedule, which included chair duties, teaching and conducting research, Harvey made it a point to hike the local mountains within a week of arriving. Fighting a bout of bronchitis, he nonetheless completed a 20-mile trek from the family home near the university to the 11,500' summit of Agassiz Peak (one of the San Francisco Peaks) and back in one long day.

When told the college had its own hiking club but lacked a sponsor, Harvey volunteered. He enjoyed leading trips and the camaraderie of the students, and decided it would be a fine way to kick-start his familiarity with the region. Soon he was taking students hiking nearly every weekend. The club was small and close-knit, made up of a very active group of six or seven members. Because few students owned cars, the ASC hikers sometimes had to hike just to reach their hikes, such as at Walnut Canyon National Monument a couple miles outside Flagstaff, or 12,633-foot Humprey's Peak.

A 1946 ASC bulletin carried this announcement:

> Since hiking is Dr. Butchart's hobby, he finds northern Arizona an ideal region in which to live. As sponsor of the Lumberjack Hikers, he is reported by members as being an enthusiastic and companionable hiker.

Harvey had finally moved to a region that matched his ambitions and desires, most of which had been repressed for decades. Of course, there was one nearby landscape in particular he wanted to see more than any other. The urge to visit Grand Canyon had slowly burned in him ever since childhood. Now it waited only a short drive away.

Enthusiastic hiker? They hadn't seen anything yet.

Elias Butler

Chapter Eight

THE CANYON NOBODY KNOWS

Although it was first seen by white men eighty years before the pilgrims landed from the Mayflower, and although prospectors swarmed over it for twenty years before 1900, for all practical purposes, it is still unknown territory.

Harvey Butchart,
"The Canyon Nobody Knows" (1964)

ON JUNE 26, 1944, a year before Harvey arrived in Arizona, 42-year-old Doctor of Theology Allan MacRae was enjoying his honeymoon backpack trip in Grand Canyon when a friend delivered some startling news: He had just spoken with park rangers, who told him they needed to talk to MacRae immediately. MacRae backtracked up the North Kaibab Trail, then opened a small door hiding an emergency telephone and lifted the receiver. His conversation with the assistant superintendent was brief. Men were trapped. One rescue effort had failed. Would MacRae be willing to forge a route down 3,000 feet of rock and rescue the stranded men himself? He would. Would MacRae be willing to do it without pay? "That is quite immaterial. I'd of course be only too glad to do anything I can to assist," he replied. MacRae hung up and quickly started back down the trail to tell his brand new wife Grace that their honeymoon was being postponed. They were hiking back to the rim, now.

The slight, bespectacled professor may have seemed, on paper, an odd choice to lead a dangerous search and rescue mission. But MacRae knew his way around Grand Canyon. This native of Michigan had a penchant for getting off the main trails and bushwhacking his way into

Professor Allan MacRae. *Courtesy Reformationart.com*

the wilderness. He had been hiking the Canyon on and off since 1922, 14 extended trips in all. Though MacRae taught at a seminary in Pennsylvania, he visited the Canyon often enough that by now the rangers knew him by name. If anyone could pull off a rescue, the Park Service figured, it was Professor MacRae.

While MacRae and his wife hoofed it up to the North Rim, Ranger Ed Laws was tending the tiny Park Service outpost at Tuweep, some 80 miles to the west. Located on the vast, unpopulated Uinkaret Plateau north of Grand Canyon, Tuweep was perhaps the most remote ranger station in the country. Sixty miles of dirt road separated it from the nearest paved highway. There was no telephone at Tuweep, not even a radio.

Most rangers in the Park Service had long since been drafted to fight overseas; Laws was the one ranger in the park who possessed backcountry rescue skills. He soon noticed a distant rooster-tail of dust approaching to the north. Laws's interest would have been roused. At Tuweep in 1944, this represented a major event. Someone was coming.

Later that day Laws and MacRae were quickly ushered to the North Rim headquarters and introduced. The pleasantries over with, they received their briefings: Three Air Force crewmembers had bailed out of a B-24 Liberator over Grand Canyon in the early morning of June 21. They had landed within a declivity known as Tuna Creek, an unfrequented abyss in the Hindu Amphitheater about 16 miles northwest of Grand Canyon Village. Their captain, fearing that his plane had suddenly suffered a mechanical failure when the engines died, had ordered his crew to bail out. Only after airmen Roy Embanks, Maurice Cruikshank and Charles Goldblum jumped did the captain realize that someone had accidentally turned off a fuel switch. The B-24 later landed in nearby Kingman without incident.

But the parachutists had now been stranded for four days, trapped by the Canyon's web of rock and heat. So far the best the government could do was drop supplies and notes instructing the airmen to sit tight. The lone Park Service rescue attempt had failed after rangers hiked a small boat down from the South Rim to the Colorado River at Hermit Rapids, only to turn back at seeing the river in flood. They said it would have been suicide to even attempt to cross in such a flimsy boat.

MacRae felt confident they could reach the men but admitted he did not know of a route. "I had made a trip through that area in 1924," he later wrote in a letter to Harvey Butchart, "but had not gone nearly as far as Tuna Creek."

The story quickly commanded front-page headlines and regular radio broadcasts, even though the invasion of Normandy had just taken place. That no rescue had yet succeeded spelled major embarrassment for the U.S. government. Many asked how it could be possible that a national park was so inaccessible. Neither the military nor the Park Service could offer any answers.

In fact, no one in 1944 knew how to get into Tuna Creek other than by parachute, much less how to get out of there. The same went for the majority of the Grand Canyon backcountry. It soon became clear to the frustrated government agencies that there was no reaching the three men except by foot (helicopters were not yet an option for search and rescue teams). Soldiers took positions on the rims and peered through their binoculars, but Tuna Creek was simply hemmed in by too much unbroken vertical rock. For a culture that had no experience in Grand Canyon route finding, trying to read the cliffs was like trying to decipher hieroglyphics. Unless Laws and MacRae could find a way into Tuna Creek, the airmen weren't going anywhere.

Knowledge of the sort that the rescuers needed had long since disappeared from the landscape of human consciousness. By 1944 the Grand Canyon had fallen into one of its cyclic spells of relative abandonment and was largely unknown to the latest crop of humans to settle the adjoining region. The place constituted a modern paradox. Compared with much of the West, where raw land had shrunk with the arrival of whites, the wilderness in Grand Canyon had actually expanded since the late 1800s.

This was nothing unusual for the place. It fit a pattern established over thousands of years by the comings and goings of various peoples. The Canyon could be likened to either a boomtown or ghost town, depending on the era. Familiarity with the Canyon's interior—its routes, springs, food sources and good places to camp—could only exist so long as people stayed. When the parachutists unwittingly dropped in, decades had passed since the last time anyone had rediscovered the old foot routes subtly threading the immense gorge.

Outside the handful of tourist trails and the Havasupai Indian village of Supai, only the river could be considered well known in 1944. John Wesley Powell and his men made the first descent of the Colorado three-quarters of a century earlier, and by the end of World War II, the river was even seeing occasional tourist trips. Yet the boatmen rarely explored beyond the Colorado, which was distraction enough, and contributed but a smattering of knowledge about the backcountry. At least two hundred people had floated through the Canyon by 1944, but the river parties, including Powell's first and second expeditions, changed little in terms of the Canyon's accessibility.

Those few who struck out for the rim often did so because of disagreements instead of the desire to forge new routes. When Seneca and Oramel Howland and William Dunn left the first Powell expedition to avoid running Separation Rapid, they pioneered a difficult river-to-rim route via the aptly named Separation Canyon. Yet the men failed to live long enough to communicate the details of their escape from Grand Canyon.

Of course, despite brief lulls in visitation during the world wars, thousands of people had been visiting the South Rim annually since the 1910s, which had given rise to a small metropolis called Grand Canyon Village during the busy summer months. Restaurants, shops and other amenities of modern civilization erased any notion of wilderness along this minute stretch of the Canyon's edge.

But the breadth of such a wound in the Earth is neither river, nor rim. Those two boundaries merely frame the vertical mile of rock that constitutes 99 per cent of this landscape. That a large number of people crowded about a few view-points *on top*, or whisked through *the bottom* on the Colorado only made its remoteness seem more confounding. "The canyon is less than a two-hour drive from Flagstaff, and yet the natural bridges, Indian ruins, caves and ropeless climbs seem as little known as if they were in some remote area of Alaska. Maps are unreliable concerning water. Some of the springs that are shown have gone dry…" Harvey warned in a 1964 essay titled "The Canyon Nobody Knows," 20 years after the parachutists became trapped.

By the fourth day of their ordeal, the parachutists (none of whom had visited Grand Canyon before) understood Harvey's assessment all too well. Just to the north of their makeshift camp in Tuna Creek stood what pioneer geologist Clarence Dutton named Point Sublime, a scenic vista accessible by car. But it was cut off from the airmen by 3,000 feet of rock.

For the rescuers, using Point Sublime as a starting point also looked impossible. The inner canyon sanctuary of Phantom Ranch lay just 10 miles to the

east of the parachutists, but no trails crossed the very deep and rugged side canyons blocking the way. Grand Canyon photographer and river runner Emery Kolb offered to help by rowing a boat down to Tuna Creek, but the Park Service seemed to think the 62-year-old would only add to their troubles.

Laws and MacRae began by studying the Matthes-Evans map and aerial photographs.

A successful rescue: From left, Ed Laws, Allan MacRae, and airmen Maurice Cruikshank, Roy Embanks, and Charles Goldblum. *Courtesy Grand Canyon National Park Museum Collection*

They decided that the likeliest-looking route into Tuna Creek began at an isolated promontory east of Point Sublime named Grama Point. The two men set out on June 27 and, as expected, found a break in the cliffs that allowed them to descend about 2,200 feet, as far as the bottom of the Supai Formation. But there they encountered 600 feet of underlying Redwall Limestone, about 150 feet of which blocked further progress. They walked laterally atop the Redwall to search for a break. Luck was with the rescuers, for they soon discovered a previously unknown spring and encouraging signs. "As we went," MacRae wrote, "we began to notice animal tracks, and the idea occurred that perhaps there was a way here by which animals would go to the foot of the canyon in winter."

It took another two days of bushwhacking and route finding, but MacRae and Laws finally managed to retrieve the stranded airmen. One of them, Flight Officer Cruikshank, had suffered a broken foot upon impact and was hobbling about with a makeshift cane. The group retreated along the route the two rescuers had found, with everyone helping Cruikshank up the rough stretches. MacRae later wrote:

> Within 10 or 15 minutes after reaching the top we were met by newsreel men, a large contingent of Army Aviation soldiers, and the Park Service men. The rest of the day was rather hectic, with radio broadcasts being made and considerable rivalry between the Park Service and the Air Force as to which would get the most credit for the rescue. I tried to maintain strict neutrality.

One of the airmen emerged with a bottle of whiskey he had received in an airdrop. A reporter asked why he hadn't drunk it in the Canyon. The airman replied that there was no ice in Tuna Creek.

LAWS AND MacRAE were celebrated as heroes. They demonstrated how individuals experienced in route finding could accomplish what an army of men unfamiliar with Grand Canyon could not. The pair understood the country, meaning that they knew what sort of eyes one needed to use in scanning the cliffs and canyons for signs of passage.

For the first-time visitor looking into 5,000 feet of space, it is easy to believe that reaching the Colorado is only possible using a trail; after all, the cliffs appear too continuous, the brush too thick, the rock too unstable. Yet for all its apparent impregnability, Grand Canyon does not lack for routes, the off-trail "trails." Its armor of vertical rock is in fact riddled with geologic faults, those underlying fractures that tend to grind cliffs to rubble. The resulting broken escarpments and talus slopes are the Canyon's entry/exit signs, where travel

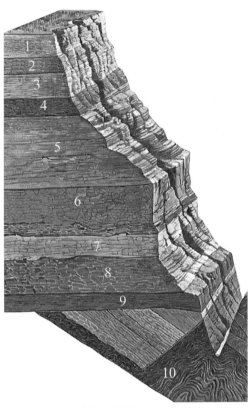

Geologic map of Grand Canyon. Rock layers are as follows: 1) Kaibab Limestone 2) Toroweap Formation 3) Coconino Sandstone 4) Hermit Shale 5) Supai Formation 6) Redwall Limestone 7) Muav Limestone 8) Bright Angel Shale 9) Tapeats Sandstone 10) Vishnu Metamorphic Complex *Courtesy Grand Canyon Association*

becomes possible from one rock layer and into the next.

With the help of faults to negotiate these layers, a rim-to-river route thus becomes a succession of distinct challenges. For example, descending the uppermost layer, the Kaibab Limestone, might mean a few cliffs to navigate. But the face of this 300-foot rim rock is often fractured, which sometimes makes it passable without a rope. Underneath the Kaibab is a crumbly white limestone/sandstone variation, the Toroweap Formation, which can be problematic—especially if attempting to climb it. Prone to breakage, the Toroweap has frightened away more than one canyoneer too distrusting of its brittle nature. More formidable than the Toroweap is the next layer, the Coconino Sandstone, the 350-foot cliff (its average height) that is easily seen stretching along the Canyon like a band of vanilla icing. The Coconino often erodes into vertical walls hundreds of feet high that can be cause for a long rappel or an exposed tip-toe along a narrow ridge; complete breaks in it tend to be harder to come by than in the overlying limestones.

But once through the Coconino, the going usually gets easy, if somewhat tedious. Soft ledges of red, sloping Hermit Shale present little problem when going up or down. Walking atop its gully-cut, unstable surface, however, will test any hiker's patience.

Although the next older layer is usually the thickest, the Supai Formation is actually a series of lesser cliffs and slopes. A single sheer façade, the Watahomigi Formation, can present a considerable obstacle. On the whole the Supai is nearly always impassable. But, in places, it can be negotiated on foot due to its lack of uniformity.

It is the next layer that is by far the most troublesome. When one peers at the Grand Canyon from the rim, the 340-million year-old Redwall Limestone clearly stands out by forming the thickest, most consistently vertical escarpment within the scene. This deposit of ancient seas often measures 600 feet thick within a single perpendicular cliff, thus making it the ultimate test for any rim-to-river route. Because of its barrier-like qualities, the Redwall might be likened to a deep moat between rim and river.

The Redwall's Paleozoic origin becomes believable when seeing this rock at close range. Its ancient surface dissolves through a chemical reaction with rainwater that leaves spiky edges, jagged cracks and something like shark's hide, making it hell on raw skin. Demolished sunset-red Supai rocks rest in picturesque fashion atop the Redwall throughout Grand Canyon. With this desert receiving perhaps six or 10 inches of rain each year, over the course of thousands of years it is enough to continually bleed a crimson Supai stain onto the vertical surface of the gray Redwall, hence the misnomer.

Everything of importance to a hiker takes place in this formation. As the main aquifer in Grand Canyon, the Redwall is the most common source of flowing water in the tributaries. Springs issue from its porous interior in great numbers; sometimes, even rivers can be seen blasting out it. Following a wet winter on the North Rim, a waterfall might appear one day from out of a cave, stick around for a few weeks, then recede when the Canyon's interior plumbing system can again handle the excess flow.

Once below the Redwall, the less ornery Temple Butte and Muav Limestones make their appearance. These offer easier travel than the Redwall, although they do tend to form sheer escarpments where they reach their greatest thickness in the western Grand Canyon. The underlying Bright Angel Shale, a soft, greenish mix of old mud and sand, can be up to 300 feet thick yet forms few problems. Hikers often tread the top of this rock because it creates the friendly Tonto bench, the relatively level platform that makes for an easy walkway in the eastern Grand Canyon.

Below the Bright Angel, route finders must face the Tapeats Sandstone. This coarse layer erodes into a series of overhanging ledges that often require significant breakage before becoming passable. At an average of 200 feet the Tapeats is not terribly thick, but it tends to force hikers to follow side canyons, where running water has had a chance to help clear the fault-shattered debris.

In stretches of Grand Canyon where it appears, the Vishnu Metamorphic Complex presents the final obstacle to the Colorado. Negotiating this black, 1,000-foot-thick combination of the Canyon's oldest rocks can be hazardous.

The schist erodes into near-vertical cliffs but lacks the orderliness of the younger sedimentary rocks up above, making it a chaotic horizon where guesswork is less dependable. As with the overlying Tapeats Sandstone, faults are nearly always a necessity for any chance of making it through this last barrier to the Colorado.

The importance of using faults to get through all this rock was not lost on Laws and MacRae—or on the first ones to travel into Grand Canyon. Their paleo-trails, beaten by hoof and paw, remain the best means of travel in the more remote areas. Every off-trail hiker has followed animal paths at one time or another. Seasonal migrations by deer, bighorn sheep, coyotes and mountain lions—and their mammalian predecessors like Harrington's mountain goat and giant ground sloths—have taken place between rim and river for untold eons. The animals established the most efficient, energy-saving routes in their quest to find water, locate prey, or evade predators.

The first humans to descend into the Canyon 10,000 or more years ago made use of these routes. So did the next known group of people, who arrived much later, perhaps around 6,000-2,500 BC. Little is known about these early canyoneers, other than that some were artists and hunters whose dreamlike imagery, expressed in colorful, surrealist paintings beneath remote rock overhangs, tells of a mystical connection to their surroundings. Presumably to ensure a good hunt, they placed animal figurines in isolated caves throughout Grand Canyon, always in the same limestone layer and with the same pattern of tidy arrangement. *Magic* is the word that comes to mind when confronting the art they left behind. Whoever they were, their desire for meat led them down the succession of cliffs where it yielded to careful hand and foot work.

Abstract pictographs of unknown origin, perhaps 2,500-3,500 years old. *Elias Butler*

Their ability to access the Canyon from above did not simplify things for later peoples who tried to do the same. After all, it has never been *easy* to locate complete routes. To understand the enormity of the problem—how to reach the river from the rim at any particular place—one need only step to the edge and look down. Although you might be lucky enough to be standing atop a break in the uppermost cliffs, very soon some grim obstacle such as a 500-foot drop will usually present itself. This is the first lesson the Canyon teaches route finders: Without some hint of where to start, all you have to hope for is dumb luck.

The first white explorers to reach Grand Canyon learned this right away. An exploratory party led by Don Garcia Lopez de Cardenas in 1540 arrived to investigate intriguing Indian reports of a great river west of present-day New Mexico. Hopi guides directed the Spaniards to the vicinity of the Palisades of the Desert in the eastern end of the Canyon, near present day Desert View. Cardenas's mission was to locate a river route back from whence they came in Mexico. He promptly sent a few men down from the rim to check out the Colorado, expecting a report by the end of the day. The party's recorder wrote down the details of the first Europeans to trek below the rim:

> ...the three lightest and most agile men, made an attempt to go down at the least difficult place, and went down until those who were above were unable to keep sight of them. They returned about four o'clock in the afternoon...because what seemed to be easy from above was not so, but instead very hard and difficult...

Harvey would come to know such complications well. He spelled them out in "The Canyon Nobody Knows":

> To see something new, you will have to submit to scratching by cat's claw, false sage and manzanita. You will find a lot of loose scree lodged perilously above sheer cliffs, and you may not appreciate following dry or wet streambeds over seemingly endless supplies of boulders. If you are really breaking trail you will have to expect the frustration of coming to the place where the bed drops away in an impossible fall forcing a detour that may take hours.

Cardenas quickly gave up Grand Canyon route finding. He had important business to attend to and no patience for cliffs. Perhaps he railed at the Canyon with a clenched fist, cursing the barrier it formed to north-south travel. And if so, it is not hard to imagine the Hopi guides snickering among themselves, for they knew better.

The Hopi belonged to this landscape. They migrated from Grand Canyon (among other places) to their mesas in the Painted Desert around AD 1200, and had long maintained their own rim-to-river route down the Little Colorado gorge, a route that was still seeing ceremonial use into the twentieth century. The Hopi believe that humankind emerged into this world from an unusual spring in this large tributary, and continue to hold a vigorous respect for the Grand Canyon.

Petroglyphs that perhaps date to AD 900-1150. *Elias Butler*

Both their mythology and familiarity with the Canyon's interior came directly from their ancestors, the Anasazi (a Navajo appellation), or, as the Hopi prefer, the *Hisatsinom*, or, according to the latest archeological terminology, the Ancestral Puebloans. Whatever we choose to call them, these highly adaptable pre-Columbian Indians, as well as their contemporaries known as the Cohonina, ranged over almost all parts of Grand Canyon for hundreds of years and were among the most successful at living off what is at best a tough, scanty land.

As resourceful hunters and farmers, the Anasazi developed a comprehensive network of travel routes throughout Grand Canyon, especially during their heyday between AD 950 and 1150. In fact, few places exist where their sign has not been found. By the end of his route-finding days, Harvey gained an intimate respect for these trekkers who preceded him by a millennium. From the epilogue of Harvey's *Grand Canyon Treks:*

> People have asked me if there is any part of the Grand Canyon…where a person could go and feel as if they were the first to be there. I would have to quickly respond by saying we might all be cautious in claiming a first because native people have been in the Canyon for at least 4,000 years and seem to have been everywhere. As hunters of bighorn sheep, gatherers of mescal, and farmers, they really got around.

The Indians's improvements along some non-climbing routes, such as log ladders positioned against cliffs, or small steps chiseled out of steeply pitched rock attest to a rate of foot traffic that probably exceeded what the same areas see today. The Anasazi also crossed the Colorado River from bank to bank at opportune spots. Perhaps they even constructed some means of floating the river, although this possibility still vexes anthropologists.

But when the Anasazi migrated elsewhere by the thirteenth century, they left behind mere traces and hints of their extensive routes. As time erased the well-beaten paths over the next 100 years, the wilderness again crept back to claim the Canyon.

Ancestors of the Hualapais, Havasupais, and Southern Paiutes were the next to settle, arriving around AD 1300. They rediscovered and recycled the best of the Anasazi footpaths. Before long, these newcomers traveled as freely throughout the Canyon as their unrelated predecessors. One by one they "catalogued" the best places to find water, forage, and game, and learned how to reach riverside farmlands from points on the rim. The Havasupai ranged from the Little Colorado River to Havasu Canyon, taking up seasonal residence atop the South Rim or down below near water sources. The Southern Paiutes meanwhile claimed their territory on the north side of the river and developed a network of footpaths that extended from the Kaibab to the Shivwits Plateaus. Once again, the Canyon was seeing human traffic. These people might still be using their routes today had whites not come along and changed everything.

By the nineteenth century, the tidal wave of European-American settlers included a few souls who either by design or fate ended up in Grand Canyon country. White desire for land and

An Anasazi cliff dwelling with a view. *Elias Butler*

wealth lured prospectors, Mormon farmers, missionaries, rustlers, bootleggers, trappers, gentiles, and members of governmental surveys. What followed their arrival in the mid-to-late 1800s was a predictable, sad pattern.

As Anglos encroached upon more and more of the Indians's land, they sometimes met opposition, such as in 1866 when the Hualapais carried on a three-year campaign of resistance. But this invited the wrath of the unmerciful U.S. military. Both settlers and soldiers pressured the various tribes to forfeit much, if not all, of their territories, and ultimately brushed Indian rights aside. Finally, Congress sent governmental surveys to establish tiny remnants of land called reservations in the 1880s for the Havasupais and Hualapais, and in 1903 for the Paiutes.

The Indians's time of roaming freely across Grand Canyon had ended. Under the new restrictions imposed by whites, the old routes between the side canyons and atop the high, forested plateaus began to fall into disuse, save for those few that were salvaged by settlers or preserved for ceremonial purposes. The miners in particular followed the old Indian paths where they could, dynamiting routes where they could not. A few of these trails remain in use to this day.

Seth Tanner was a Mormon pioneer and miner who developed one such route in the 1880s to reach the Colorado near present day Palisades Creek. Hikers using the Tanner Trail owe thanks to both him and the Indians. Another miner, John Hance, arrived around the same time as Tanner. He improved on a former Havasupai route that descended Hance Creek to access his asbestos mines, resulting in the Old Hance Trail.

Harvey would write about these hardscrabble characters in a 1962 article entitled "Old Trails in the Grand Canyon":

> Each had his mine somewhere in the inner canyon: copper, asbestos, and now and then a miner panned gold on the sandbars or hauled a sluice-box down some labyrinthine side canyon to the edge of the Colorado River. Each miner had laboriously pecked a trail to his mine over which the ore was packed out by mule and burro.

However, Grand Canyon's sedimentary rocks are the wrong type for precious metals. Once the miners realized that little could be gleaned from the Canyon but hard living, they were quick to depart. They took their knowledge of the trails with them. A handful such as William Wallace Bass and Ralph Cameron stayed to extract the far more reliable wealth offered by the increasing arrival of tourists, but even these operators faded with the arrival of the Santa Fe rail line and El Tovar Hotel. As the Canyon became more popular in the years following, the government decided to preserve the area to thwart more development and settlement. A significant stretch of Grand Canyon was named a national monument in 1908 and then a national park in 1919.

Throughout these changes, no one had bothered to write down anything about the old trails, leaving the Canyon, for all intents and purposes, once again unknown. Of course, Francois Matthes and Richard Evans had put a portion of it on the map by 1923. Prior to this achievement, in 1921, the National Park Service made the Canyon more accessible than ever by building a suspension bridge over the Colorado at Bright Angel Creek. This in turn led to the 1928 construction of a new trail that stretched 21 miles from rim to rim, the Kaibab Trail. Combined with the existing Bright Angel Trail, the Kaibab now focused hikers into a narrow corridor where they could enjoy the pleasures of venturing into the gorge.

Surrounding this busy little strip, however, the Canyon remained a wilderness, largely abandoned save for the village of Supai in Havasu Canyon. Backcountry exploration had never been a priority for the government. There simply was no incentive for it, beyond the occasional search for missing people such as honeymooners Glen and Bessie Hyde in 1928, or the trapped parachutists in 1944.

And now, in 1945, a new stage was set. Unlike all the previous periods of discovery, exploration this time around would not have much to do with rescue, mining, surveying, or hunting. It would be done for less obvious motives, for utter adventure, for the satisfaction of discovery. As Lawrence Leamer wrote in his fine book, *Ascent*, "To...nineteenth century Americans, experience was avoiding the mountains, not climbing them; getting through the desert, not journeying into it with breathless anticipation; cutting down the forests, not camping in them."

Yet in August of that year, the new math professor at Arizona State College had no Matthes-Evans map, had never looked at Anasazi petroglyphs, had only heard of Tuna Creek in the newspapers. Harvey Butchart was just another greenhorn tourist, about to see Grand Canyon for the first time.

ASC Math Professor Harvey Butchart in 1946.
Fronske Studio, courtesy Anne Madariaga

First photo of Harvey Butchart in Grand Canyon, Kaibab suspension bridge, 1946. *Roma Butchart, courtesy Anne Madariaga*

Chapter Nine
GETTING HIS LEGS
1945–1954

*At first glance the spectacle seems too strange to be real. Because one has
never seen anything like it, because one has nothing to compare it with, it
stuns the eye...The Canyon requires what we call in lingo of our day "a
double take." Only that way does its size, its antiquity or the grandiose-
ness of the forces that made it become real. Moreover, as I have learned
from many visits, the process has to be repeated every time. First there is
the impression of some sort of man-made diorama trying to fool the eye.
Only later comes the gradual acceptance of the unbelievable fact.*

Joseph Wood Krutch,
Grand Canyon Today and All Its Yesterdays

*Many writers have said that no words can describe what one sees from the
rim at Grand Canyon, and then they go on for pages doing what they have
just said is impossible.*

Harvey Butchart,
unpublished essay (1969)

IN AUGUST 1945, TWO WEEKS AFTER moving to Flagstaff, Harvey, Roma, Anne
and Jim boarded a college school bus loaded with ASC naval cadets and headed for the South Rim. At Grand Canyon, the bus stopped at one of the tourist
viewpoints to let everyone have a look.

Harvey never forgot the Louis Akin image of the Canyon he grew up with
in Kuling. "I'd seen that, day after day," Harvey said. "And it probably got under
my skin. Whenever I saw anybody's pictures, color slides for instance, people
who had toured in the summer, and showed slides back in the Middle West, I

was always fascinated by the Grand Canyon on the screen."

As it does to any newcomer, especially one who loves to hike, the actual spectacle took Harvey's breath away.

"*What hath God wrought!*" he recalled thinking to himself. The phrase echoed Samuel Morse's first words supposedly uttered over the telegraph in 1848, words that Morse had lifted from the bible.

The more Harvey looked, the more he began to feel something beyond astonishment those first few minutes. Before him unfurled the towering cliffs, snaking away into the distant haze, perhaps a hint of the mighty river sunk within the dark schist of the inner gorge a mile below, space exceeding anything he'd imagined. He could see himself scaling over the battlements, stretching his limbs to reach footholds as he'd learned to do in China. The Canyon's bold display of exposed rock triggered a spark of sharp longing.

He had been expecting a lot, but—*what a place for a hike!*

He went away "saturated with its grandeur" and returned two months later during Thanksgiving break to hike it for the first time. He brought the whole family, Roma, Anne, and Jim, but in a sign of things to come, at Harvey's suggestion, they took a different trail than he that day. They visited Indian Garden, about four or five miles down the Bright Angel Trail, while Harvey chose the much more ambitious South Kaibab-to Phantom Ranch-to Bright Angel loop, an 18.5-mile test of endurance. Today, prominent signs at both trailheads warn against attempting this in one day, as too many overly ambitious hikers have been rescued. Yet Harvey's speed was such that he caught up with his family while they were still hiking out. He even played hide-and-seek with Jim to coax him up the trail and carried him the last few miles to the rim.

The angular shapes and incredible views, the texture of the different rock layers, the utter physical challenge of falling and rising over 9,000 feet in a single hike — Harvey was enthralled. By making his first rim-to-river trek in the Canyon, he had performed a rite of passage of sorts. The act of descending from pine trees and junipers on

Classic view: Mather Point at sunrise. *Elias Butler*

the rim to a hot river environment felt familiar—it was just like the trek down and up Mount Lushan in China. Also, going through the various layers of rock was exciting in some strange way, like moving backwards through time.

Harvey especially enjoyed not slowing down for his family, being able to go as fast as he wanted to except at the end of the hike. At 38, he had the energy and stamina that most men experience only at 20. Harvey resolved to return for more.

As good as it had been, however, the Canyon did not immediately consume Harvey's interest. "I knew the Canyon was a great place for a hike, but I wasn't going to concentrate on it at first," Harvey later wrote. "The entire West was still my ambition. I was going back to Colorado and also other places in the West—California and Yosemite for instance, among others."

He also had much to discover near home with the ASC Hiking Club. After making an adventuresome ski-hike in March 1946, Harvey quickly received the community's blessing as club sponsor. From the Flagstaff newspaper, *The Coconino Sun:*

> Dr. Harvey Butchart, head of the mathematics department, proved his eligibility to be sponsor of the Hiking Club when on Saturday, February 23, he climbed the snow covered Agassiz Peak and skied down the northwest slope of the Snow Bowl. He had to wade waist deep drifts to reach the Agassiz summit. There he ate his lunch and walked down to the saddle of the San Francisco Peaks where he donned his skis and went by easy stages down to the ski lodge at Snow Bowl, arriving at 5:00 P.M. Two hours later he got to the road at the Fort Valley experiment station where he caught a ride back to Flagstaff.

Grand Canyon soon became a regular destination for the club. Harvey started taking students down the established trails for day hikes and the occasional backpack trip. "We didn't go into very remote or unusual areas," Harvey said. "Mostly down to the Phantom Ranch campground and over to Clear Creek, Hermit Creek, Hermit Trail and a few others. We kept to the main trails and didn't branch out too much in exploring in those days."

When Harvey visited the Canyon on his own time, it was usually to show friends or family around the park. Roma, Anne and Jim joined Harvey for several treks to the bottom. "Most of my trips were because of somebody visiting us in Flagstaff and then we [Roma and I] would take them to Grand Canyon," Harvey said. "And if they had teenage children I'd perhaps take them down and up, and it was more casual hiking without any very great ambition to become an expert and knowledgeable about the canyon—mostly just for the pleasure of hiking and showing guests the Grand Canyon."

ASC Hiking Club in 1949. Harvey is fourth from left, back row. *Courtesy Anne Madariaga*

To put these early forays into perspective, it must be remembered that hiking the trails was a much more adventurous undertaking in the 1940s than today. In the post-war years, the few tourists who went below the rim invariably stuck to the Kaibab and Bright Angel Trails. Harvey, however, made it a point to take the students down some of the more rugged and less used trails. This meant a bit of route finding here and there and a lack of other hikers to depend on in case of trouble. "There were these old abandoned prospector trails from the early days of the mines like the Tanner Trail or the Grandview Trail, which were seldom used," Harvey said. "You'd feel that, if you went down the Tanner Trail, you were sort of rediscovering country."

Yet Harvey quickly learned how even the roughest trail paled next to the dangers of hiking *off* trail. He ventured to Havasu Canyon with a small group of students in the spring of 1946 to visit the world famous waterfalls. After seeing the cascades, Harvey decided to continue exploring down the side canyon on his own. Although a good trail exists today that leads from Havasu Falls eight miles to the Colorado River, in 1946, this same stretch was a tangle of untracked brush.

Before he set off, one of his students mentioned she had once encountered seven rattlesnakes along this route. This gave Harvey pause. The desert newcomer later wrote in his logbook:

> I carried a big stick to defend myself. I wondered how I would ever see the rattlers under the tangle of growth. There were places where I tried going along the base of the cliff in order to pass the worst thickets...toward the river, I got rather high on the slope to get away from the vines and I slipped and came down with one hand on sharp limestone and the other on a barrel cactus. It took a long day of struggle to go from our camp near Havasu Falls to the Colorado River and back.

Harvey decided to avoid any more off-trail excursions in Grand Canyon

Harvey changes King Henry's flat on the way to an ASC Hiking Club Havasu Canyon outing, 1946. *Courtesy Doris Kirschvink*

during those early years in Arizona. Because each autumn meant a fresh crop of students who had never been to the chasm, he instead repeatedly hiked the same handful of park trails. He also continued to take Roma and the kids exploring elsewhere in the Southwest.

One early trip illustrates Harvey's yen for exploration, and his tendency to overestimate the abilities of his fellow hikers, including his own family. In April 1948, he brought Roma, 12-year-old Anne, and nine year-old Jim to the Navajo Reservation to hike to Rainbow Bridge, largest natural bridge in the world. This long trek into Glen Canyon entailed a round trip of 27 miles. Harvey decided they could do it in one day.

After reaching the remote bridge, they began the much more strenuous uphill return hike, which meant walking for miles over sandstone cobbles and then making a stiff 1,200-foot ascent. Harvey maintained a speedy pace, but Jim began to complain. Finally Roma demanded that they stop to allow the boy to rest. Darkness caught them miles from the car. Harvey built two large fires on the way back to keep them from freezing while Jim napped. By the time they returned after a 20-hour hike, everyone was done in.

Following this incident, the family tended to stay home whenever Harvey went hiking, while he became more adventurous. He took his first really remote Grand Canyon backpack trip on July 4, 1952. At the time, Thunder River was considered about the wildest trail hike a person could make in the Canyon. This massive spring gushes from an isolated cliff of Redwall Limestone far below the North Rim, miles

A family outing to Grand Canyon, 1946. From left, Jim and Anne Butchart, unidentified friend, and Harvey. *Roma Butchart, courtesy Anne Madariaga*

removed from the well-trodden Kaibab Trail.

As a measure of the utter desolation that characterized this corner of the Canyon, we can turn to the words of novelist Zane Grey. Grey tried to reach Thunder River in April 1908 during a research trip, but failed to find the route into Surprise Valley, the final obstacle. The best he could do was peer down from the Supai cliff that loomed above the voluminous spring. Grey was nonetheless moved to use the setting for the closing scene in his best-known novel *Riders of the Purple Sage*. Grey wrote this description of Thunder River to his wife Dolly:

> Mr. Rust [Grey's Mormon guide, David Rust] knows of a canyon where no man, except prehistoric, besides himself has ever put a foot. He reached it after a long, though not hard, climb over the marble walls below. This is a most beautiful place. There are great cottonwood trees, grass, and flowers, a great spring and stream, and deer and beaver.
>
> Think of it! All alone amidst the silence and grandeur of the canyon, far from the fretting world, and noise and distraction.

Thunder River's isolation had changed somewhat by the time Harvey arrived, for a stock trail had been built in the intervening years, but it was still wild country. He ventured there with friend Henry Hall, spending three scorching days exploring the area. Choosing to travel in the depressing midsummer heat did not deter him (it hardly ever did), though 45-year-old Harvey did complain that the younger Hall was "a weakling" who slowed him down.

Harvey at the Thunder River trailhead. *Courtesy Jorgen Visbak*

Even after experiencing Thunder River and seven years of hiking the maintained trails, Harvey still had found no reason to dedicate himself to the Canyon. There was just too much great country near Flagstaff he wanted to see. He had in fact arrived at the perfect time to explore Arizona, for it was still sparsely populated yet largely accessible by truck or jeep. Moreover, Harvey had not yet given up his fixation with the whole of the West or the Rockies. In the summer of 1953 he again took his family to Colorado, this time displaying remarkable drive by climbing 14 Fourteeners over the course of 15 days.

Gradually, however, his love affair with Grand Canyon began to bloom following all the casual dating. He was showing a renewed interest by the fall of 1953 when Roma was hired as a secretary at the Museum of Northern Arizona in Flagstaff. "I began to limit most of my efforts to the Grand Canyon after my wife took a job that held her in Flagstaff most of the summer," Harvey wrote. "I felt less guilty about leaving her behind if I weren't going so far away and seeing things like the Canadian Rockies while she worked in an office."

So, it was a matter of convenience, and a certain brand of consideration for his wife's feelings that narrowed his focus. Harvey started making more and more solo trips to the gorge. His level of intrigue rose. The established trails whetted his appetite for *something* more, but he wasn't sure what. Harvey always craved new knowledge, whether in the outdoors or mathematics, so he began by collecting information. "I read everything I could get my hands on about the Grand Canyon," Harvey said, "and talked to people, looked at the maps—especially the Matthes-Evans map."

Harvey bought a set of the topographic masterpieces, which were divided into east-half and west-half sections covering the national park. With the devotion a reverent preacher uses to study the good book, Harvey took full advantage of the map's exacting detail in the coming decades. They formed the single most important aid to his explorations, and remained the best available Grand Canyon maps until the 1960s. Harvey spent countless hours poring over their well-executed lines, and later used them as a canvases upon which to display his route-finding accomplishments. "This contour map," he wrote, "has been justly hailed as the equal of any on earth, and modern aerial photography can improve it little if any."

Harvey began noticing that his Matthes-Evans maps contained marching-ant lines that represented long disused tourist and miner trails, most of them unknown to park rangers. "Those maps showed a lot of trails, so I formed the ambition of getting everywhere where there'd ever been a trail," Harvey said. "Then I began to go places where there'd never been a trail."

Apart from his maps, however, Harvey did not have much information to work with. He summed up the scant literature available at the time in a 1962 *Appalachia* magazine article entitled "Old Trails in Grand Canyon":

> There are a number of other books about the Canyon, but they afford only incidental information about the trails. George Wharton James wrote two which told of travels on foot and by horse before 1900. His frequent hardships

make a good story, but they also indicate poor planning. Henry Van Dyke wrote a book interpreting the Canyon. Edwin Corle's *Listen Bright Angel* is most readable and contains secondhand information about some of the remote areas...The best summary of the trail possibilities appears in *Inverted Mountains*, by Weldon Heald, a former A.M.C. [American Mountaineering Club] member and able climber, and the geologist, Edwin D. McKee. McKee's chapter on the trails will at least suggest the questions one needs to ask.

Armed with this information, Harvey began stepping off-trail a bit more, but he did not yet realize that he could discover his own routes between rim and river, or that a huge chessboard of enticing problems waited just beyond the security of the paths. Such apperceptions would have to wait for the influence of others who had already made that leap.

For now, his fascination with Grand Canyon simply continued to grow. Harvey's single-mindedness allowed him to quickly amass data and experiences, but it also began to intrude on his time with the family. In the early 1950s, Roma was urging Harvey to show some interest in their son's baseball games. Jim was proving himself a talented athlete and Harvey had yet to see Jim play. Harvey finally decided to show his support. He took Jim's mitt, placed it on the porch, snapped a photo of it, then later gave the photo to Jim. He never did make it to one of Jim's games.

Meanwhile, Harvey's weekends were consumed more and more by Canyon treks with the ASC Hiking Club. Although no longer so interesting, these treks at least offered one benefit: They helped Harvey gauge his speed and endurance against people half his age. On many of these outings he was clearly the strongest hiker in the group. At some point it must have dawned on him that his unique athleticism made him superbly suited for Grand Canyon. His legs felt strong and tireless during each long hike to the rim, and most of the time, he had to reign himself in so that he did not leave his students in the dust.

Before long, Harvey was testing the waters by performing ever-more impressive feats of stamina and nerve. While hiking with two students up the untracked Phantom Canyon near Phantom Ranch, the trio came to a wall of sandstone that neither of the students was willing to try. "It's your turn Doc. Show us how to go on," one of them suggested. The math professor took a few steps back and then began free climbing the 30-foot wall, using tenuous holds to scale the obstacle. He looked back down but neither of the boys had developed a thirst to repeat his climb. Instead, they turned back.

These students had shown prudence in knowing when to say no to their adventurous leader. As sponsor of the club, Harvey was expected to use good judgment regarding the safety and welfare of his charges, but he was feeling more ambitious and confident than ever. Perhaps it was inevitable that his feeling of invulnerability would eventually cause trouble.

In January 1954, Harvey brought a student group of three women and two men for a day trip into the gorge. The women felt in the mood for something casual, and opted to make the relatively short in-and-out hike to Plateau Point, located at the end of a spur off the Bright Angel Trail. Harvey along with Boyd Moore and Robert Gardner would meanwhile undertake the much more challenging Grandview-to-New Hance loop. This 20-mile hike over poorly maintained trails constituted unknown territory for Harvey. He wanted to see something new.

Harvey dropped off the women at the Bright Angel trailhead, telling them he would be back to pick them up by dark. On the way to the Grandview trailhead, he quickly stopped at Park Service headquarters to get some orientation on the loop. Fortunately, the ranger working the desk that day, Frank Sylvester, had hiked the experts-only New Hance Trail. After learning that none of the three men had ever been there, he urged against Harvey's plan. "Too long. You could get to the river and back by way of the Hance Trail all right, but two days would be better for the loop. And be aware, on the Hance it might be hard to find the break in the Redwall."

Harvey politely thanked him then drove straight to the trailhead so they could get started. Sylvester's advice was sound—for an *average* hiker—but Harvey certainly did not lump himself in with the amateurs. "I felt in the mood for something ambitious," Harvey wrote, "and I figured that I had companions that were at least my peer in hiking, so I convinced them that we should go over the whole loop in one day."

Ignoring the advice of an informed ranger in favor of adventure did not strike Carlton Boyd Moore as strange. He and Harvey enjoyed pushing the limits when it came to exploring. Moore was 22, the president of the hiking club, and no one had made more treks with the math professor. The pair had long since developed the kind of close friendship that comes from sharing the same passions and abilities.

Moore came from Berrien Springs, Michigan, not far from Harvey's old stomping grounds in Illinois. Moore had arrived at ASC in 1950 as a similarly frustrated Midwesterner with an urge to hike his socks off in Arizona. When he joined the hiking club, he and Harvey liked each other immediately. Moore stood six feet, 165 pounds and could move fast in rough terrain, a talent that quickly set him apart from the other students. He was one of the few who could match Harvey step-for-step.

Moore also had what Harvey described as "nerves of steel." Yet it was Moore's intelligence, will, and calm demeanor that impressed Harvey most.

Moore never complained no matter how rough things got. Harvey prized this characteristic, for he had endured his share of whining students who could not hack the rigors of his intense style. "We were kindred spirits," Harvey wrote, "and he was my main hiking partner for the years he was in college."

The two enjoyed taking on risky projects that the other students would shy away from, such as climbing Courthouse Butte, a 600-foot sandstone protuberance near Sedona that required technical rock climbing skills. Harvey later wrote to a friend:

> You have now found out what my most skillful and daring climb is like, Courthouse Butte. Boyd Moore and I did that...I carried a light rope ahead with me but there was no thought of belaying the leader. At one place I recall shinnying up a column of rock as one might climb a fairly large pine. I braced and held the rope for Boyd to follow...I used to say that if I would do that two more times, I would kill myself at least once.

The pair of daredevils fled civilization almost every weekend during the school year, if not with other club members, then together on trips of their own. During Moore's time at ASC, including his junior and senior years when he served as hiking club president, the two men averaged 350 miles annually. For the most part, they trekked locally in places such as Oak Creek, Walnut Canyon and Sedona. They had had their share of adventures in Grand Canyon too, but nothing as ambitious as the Grandview-to-New Hance loop. It was this trek that would convince Harvey of Moore's ability to keep it together when things went wrong.

Lumberjack Hikers

The Hiking Club offers students an opportunity to participate in healthful outdoor activities of a social and recreational nature and provide a means of their visiting places of geological and historic interest. Officers were: Boyd Moore, president; Gwen McBride, secretary-treasurer, and the sponsor and the best hiker of the group Dr. J. H. Butchard.

Boyd Moore

Courtesy NAU Special Collections, 1953

Together with Robert Gardner, they scurried down from Grandview Point into the Canyon at the normal Harvey Butchart pace—a controlled trot. The hikers made good time over the well-marked Grandview Trail, but things slowed once they took a shortcut to the Tonto Trail via a rough route east of Horseshoe Mesa. Leaving the psychological security of the beaten path at this point gave Gardner pause.

"We got the first hint that Gardner might be a handicap," Harvey wrote. "He took a long time making up his mind to come over the way we had." Another sign of trouble came when the trio stopped for lunch. Harvey discovered that Gardner's food supply for the demanding trek amounted to one can of sardines and a box of Cheezits. Long before they reached the New Hance Trail, Gardner's bowels began to cramp. Their progress stalled on the Tonto Trail. By now, the prospect of completing the loop in one day was fading faster than the daylight.

Harvey *had* to meet his female students on time at the rim. With Gardner still stumbling along, Harvey decided to go ahead, alone. Moore agreed to stay with Gardner while Harvey hiked out. Harvey told Moore he would return the following day with more food, and that Boyd should stay with Gardner and wait. "I left them with the advice to get to Hance Rapids," Harvey wrote, "and try to keep a big fire going all night."

The pair of hikers watched as Dr. Butchart rambled off. Harvey had neglected to bring a map on this hike and carried only a crude sketch of the New Hance Trail. As a result, he was uncertain which side canyon contained the trail to the rim. He made his best guess, scrawled a message in the sand for the boys, and started up.

Harvey managed to find the trail and followed it up the Redwall and Supai formations just as darkness set in. But then he veered off course. After stumbling about in the dark, he eventually rediscovered the trail higher up in the Coconino and reached the rim. Not that he was done hiking—Harvey still had five miles of pavement to cover to reach his car. His thick Mackinaw jacket took the bite out of the winter chill that lingered here at 7,000 feet, but also left him with a twinge of guilt. He had considered giving the jacket to his lightly clad students, but had decided he would need it in the icy rim air. "It was a fairly long and cold walk," he wrote, "before I came to the car parked at Grandview."

Meanwhile, Boyd led his famished companion to the beach at Hance Rapids. They sprawled in the fine sand, sharing Moore's remaining food. The meal did not amount to much. Their stomachs growled as the cold air spilled down from the rims. There was nothing to do but bed down as instructed and wait out the night, but despite building a roaring driftwood fire, they never quite stayed warm enough to sleep. Overhead, the stars turned coldly in their sockets.

Harvey was meanwhile speeding toward Grand Canyon Village when an oncoming vehicle flashed its headlights. He braked and rolled down his window. It was Frank Sylvester, the ranger who had warned him about taking the loop hike. Sylvester had Harvey's three female students.

"Where are the boys?" they all asked.

"Still in the Canyon," Harvey confessed. He explained the boys's predicament. The ranger resisted embarrassing Harvey by saying "I told you so." Instead, Sylvester said that there was nothing they could do about it now, and that Harvey better get the girls back to Flagstaff.

Harvey returned them to town well after midnight then went home to rest. He set his alarm clock, allotting himself three and a half hours of sleep. Despite his exhaustion and the soft bed, thoughts of his two students down in the Canyon kept him on edge.

When the alarm went off, Harvey grabbed all the food that was handy and drove back to the South Rim. He hoped Gardner and Moore would find his message in the sand and choose the correct side canyon to ascend.

Harvey huffed small clouds of vapor in the pre-dawn chill as he jogged down the New Hance Trail. Even though he had been over this ground less than 12 hours earlier, he now lost the trail in the vertical maze of the Redwall cliff. It was noon before he made it to the river and so far, he had seen no sign of his students. Harvey eventually discovered Gardner and Moore's abandoned camp on the beach and the still-warm ashes of their fire. Now beginning to really worry, Harvey opted to search upstream. Just before he would have disappeared from view of the trail, he heard a call.

It was Robert Gardner, standing in a ravine above. The young man looked exhausted, disheveled, and very relieved. He wolfed down a can of soup Harvey brought while explaining what had happened. After a cold, sleepless night on the beach, he and Moore tried to hike out. But they had difficulty finding the New Hance Trail, and never saw Harvey's message in the sand. Rather than risk winging it, Moore decided it was best to return via the Grandview Trail. But Gardner had balked at making the long trek back the way they had come. So they, too, split up. And now Moore was on his own somewhere between here and the Grandview trailhead. The math professor figured he better get the disoriented young Gardner up to the rim while he could.

After a laborious return that ate up the rest of that short winter day, Harvey deposited the wasted Gardner onto the backseat of his car and drove to the Grandview Trail. He then hiked into the Canyon for the third time in 36 hours, again in the dark. The temperature had dropped sharply. Harvey hiked as fast as he could, gingerly skidding down the ice-covered path that was perilously exposed to sheer drop-offs. He was more worried about Boyd than himself. Harvey knew his young friend needed help—Moore was making a very strenuous 25-mile hike in two days on a single scanty meal.

Worse, there was no moon tonight. If Boyd lost the trail in the dark, which was a possibility in his fatigued state, any climbing or scrambling that he might try could prove deadly. Hypothermia was another threat. Harvey scurried down growing more anxious by the minute.

Finally, he noticed a faint light far below, a pinpoint amidst the black fathoms. The hiking club sponsor expelled a huge sigh of relief. An hour later it indeed proved to be Moore, weak but alive. Harvey would later state that spotting Moore's flashlight had been one of the most gratifying sights he ever beheld in Grand Canyon. The two finally made it to the rim by 1:00 A.M.

Harvey's overconfidence had nearly caused a catastrophe. Still, he was proud of Moore for keeping a level head throughout the ordeal. Boyd had chosen the safest plan to avoid further complications and came out none the worse for the wear. Indeed, the next month the two friends were at it again on yet another Canyon hike.

Moore's performance impressed Harvey so much that he would soon insist that Boyd join him for his most ambitious trip yet. Harvey had it in mind to finally go beyond the realm of trails and tourist-toting mules. But there would be a twist: He would explore the Canyon's nether regions via the free flowing, unpredictable Colorado River.

Looking upstream at Sockdolager Rapid in the Inner Gorge, 1957. *J. Harvey Butchart, courtesy NAU Special Collections*

Sizing up Wotan's Throne (at top center). Harvey's route follows Cottonwood Creek at right. *Elias Butler*

Chapter Ten

THE FIELDWORK
2004

IN DECIPHERING WHAT DRIVES a man to become obsessed with such a thing as route finding in Grand Canyon, it helps to have a bit of the monkey on one's own back, too. Tom Myers and I both qualify in this department. At times we've succumbed to an irrational, single-minded desire to drop off a lonesome stretch of rim into God-knows-what and hike our brains out down there. Admittedly, it's a strange thing to do, and no surprise that few people derive pleasure from an activity so certain to bring physical suffering.

Yet, for us—and others out there, many of whom show much less restraint than ourselves—there is no mystery. Route finding is about freedom of movement.

So it was with little regret that we realized early on the necessity of following in the footsteps of Harvey Butchart, model for all route finders in Grand Canyon. We even started calling it "fieldwork," which gave it a legitimate ring. Not that this was really necessary. We had spent days mining the 26 cubic feet of materials in the Harvey Butchart Collection at Northern Arizona University. Both of us had become experts at speed-reading, at digesting folders full of hand-scrawled notes, at transcribing interviews, all by the cold light of fluorescent lamps in sterile, climate-controlled rooms. We had videos to scrutinize, slides to inspect, interviews to conduct, voluminous logbooks to process. At some point, we knew we would have to leave the cerebral stuff behind—if nothing else than for the sake of our own sanity—and venture into the realm of cliff, rattlesnake and cactus.

It is said that Harvey enjoyed doing things that most others could or would not do. This appealed to us. We considered ourselves physically fit, experienced at hiking Grand Canyon. We felt up for a challenge. Tom and I wanted to do the routes that Harvey himself considered extraordinary. Harvey's Enfilade Point route gave us a taste, but Harvey also climbed buttes, floated the river on his air mattress, rappelled down and ascended cliffs—all aspects of canyoneer-ing we had yet to face while trailing him. We knew more fieldwork would be necessary. A vigorous interaction with the Canyon, we reasoned, would give us a true understanding of our subject.

There were other reasons. We wanted to judge the oft-assessed criticism that Harvey's guidebooks are too obscure, too opaque for the average hiker to follow. And perhaps most important, we wanted to know the source of Harvey's obses-sion with Grand Canyon. If such an understanding lay anywhere, we figured, it was in that sanctuary of rock Harvey so frequently gave himself to.

With maps spread out, we hatched our plan: Descend the South Rim's Grandview Trail, then veer off-trail to the Colorado via a route that Harvey describes in *Grand Canyon Treks*. After crossing the river, we would continue working our way north in a long tributary called Vishnu Creek where no trail exists. Reaching its head would put us in position to climb the high, wedge-like butte known as Wotan's Throne (pronounced "Voh-tawns"), arguably Harvey's most prized climb in the Canyon. And then, we'd retrace our tracks to the Colorado, cross back to the south side, and complete our loop by returning to the South Rim using yet another route of Harvey's up Grapevine Canyon.

We would let Harvey lead the way by following his guidebooks wherever possible. Completing this 40-plus-mile, 20,000-feet-of-elevation-change, off-trail trek in three days would be daunting, this much we understood. Yet Harvey had accomplished the bulk of his 12,000 miles during similarly challenging weekend forays. It seemed proper to emulate his down-and-out, run-and-gun philosophy. We would move with haste.

WHEN THE DAY ARRIVES, we pack our things carefully. Any unnecessary weight is judiciously left behind. Harvey backpacked with only the most basic necessities, rarely carrying a pack that weighed more than 28 pounds. We try to do the same but our possessions quickly add up. On top of our cam-eras, food, water, clothing, stove, cups, sleeping bags, notebooks, pens, maps, headlamps, cans of celebratory beer, and backcountry pass, we also each need to lug one 10-pound polypropylene inflatable raft complete with pair of plas-tic paddles. When we finally heave the packs onto our backs, with the bright yellow paddles snagging on low-hanging pine boughs, they seem like crazy loads to be hauling around the Canyon. We collect a few stares as we cross the parking lot.

At Grandview Point, the scope of our trek for the first time becomes real. Wotan's Throne looms across the shimmering distance that falls away from the rim, a mighty butte separated from us by no more than seven or eight miles as the bird flies. Yet we will have to negotiate at least 20 jagged miles on foot to reach it. Confronted by this view instead of a map, it suddenly seems a little far-fetched to think we'll be on top of Wotan's in less than 36 hours.

We turn to leave. But before we can start down the trail, a curious man who has been eyeing our odd-looking packs interrupts our departure.

"Where you going with the paddles?" he asks.

Considering the desert plainly visible below, it is a reasonable question. The man looks suspicious when we explain, and obviously does not believe our story, but he nods politely.

We take our cue and descend, taking advantage of the maintained trail that zigzags down the uppermost geological strata. At 7,400 feet, Grandview Point is the highest point along the entire South Rim and on this late March day it is pleasantly cool—perfect weather. As always, it feels good to enter the Canyon's interior with new territory directly ahead and a more complicated, frenzied world receding fast behind.

Soon we reach the abandoned copper mines atop Horseshoe Mesa. Feeling strong, we head without stopping down the west side of the mesa's flank through the Redwall Limestone and into the valley of Cottonwood Creek. We pass a group of hikers. "Is this the way to Lee's Ferry?" we demand before they have a chance to ask about the paddles. A silent chorus of raised eyebrows follows until we laugh and explain our real mission, which sounds less unlikely to this audience. When we point to Wotan's Throne they simply shake their heads.

Tom and I go on our way, telling ourselves that Harvey would not think us so strange, just...ambitious. As we thread among the graceful trees that give this creek its name, we are making good time, moving fast on fresh legs toward the relatively level Tonto Trail. It smells like spring in the desert down here.

The Tonto parallels the course of the Colorado, running lengthwise 1,200 feet above the river atop the dark metamorphic rocks of the inner gorge. This will be the easiest walking of the whole trip. After the Tonto, it can only become more difficult. I dig out Harvey's notes as we approach a brown gutter of shattered rock, an unnamed tributary to Cottonwood Creek that cuts into the distinct rock layer called Tapeats Sandstone.

I read Harvey's instructions aloud to Tom: "One can get through the [Tapeats] in the west arm where the Tonto Trail crosses."

That's it. Harvey has told us it can be done, which is enough. We hike a bit farther on the Tonto until we reach a likely looking spot. There's no cairn, nothing to mark the way, just low cliffs of coarse sandstone dotted with cacti, and below, a deepening canyon that leads out of sight: Harvey Butchart country. Our real trekking is about to begin.

ONCE WE STEP off the trail, Tom and I are immediately confronted by an array of small cliffs, boulders and cactus gardens. Sweat begins to trickle out of my forehead as we sidestep these obstacles, descending into hotter country now. Each step here demands greater concentration than along the Tonto. Our progress slows. The heavy packs expose our lack of balance on the uneven ground, sending us stumbling about as if we've had a couple of drinks. The weight of the boats wants to push us toward the bottom of Cottonwood Creek, where we can be neatly swept along—like everything else in the creek bed—toward the Colorado River by the next flash flood. A canyon is nothing if not an efficient mover of things, and we find ourselves subconsciously heeding its call.

Yet, according to Harvey, we don't want to do that. Instead, we need to stay on the slopes of this side canyon, not in the bottom. From *Grand Canyon Treks*:

> ...follow the base of the Tapeats along the west side of the canyon until near the slope down to the bed near the river. There are several impassable falls in the bed higher up...In the bed you can stand on the lip of a 60-foot fall and look down at the river. Backing away a few yards you can climb over a low wall and walk down a talus to the river.

I reread the skeletal passage, twice. Three times. Harvey's articulations, while definite, do require the ability to *visualize*. We wonder what "slope" he might have been referring to. Nothing of the sort lies in view. We shrug our shoulders, and agree that at least he has kept the suspense going. I fold the paper back into my pocket and we continue down the deepening tributary gorge.

Route finding calls for a different type of movement than hiking the trails. One must adjust both physically and psychologically to the terrain by becoming a part of it, while the opposite is true on a trail. There the way is smoothed, the Canyon having been made to adjust to the traveler. All you have to do is marshal the necessary physical energy to follow a clearly defined line. You can let your thoughts drift on a trail, and the eyes can also wander. Not so on a route. Any lack of focus on one's immediate surroundings can mean a calf full of cactus spines, a broken ankle, or a headlong fall into the void.

A patch of loose scree that I fail to notice sends me hard to the deck, reminding me of this fact. I pull up a bleeding palm, bits of rock sunk in the cuts. One cannot expect to jump into a place like this straight from the flat sidewalks of home and not experience some difficulty. As we drop deeper into the abyss, the burn in my hand makes me more acutely aware of the texture of the ground, the rhythm of my movement, and the ever-changing array of the canyon below.

Bushwhacking down the Vishnu Schist. *Elias Butler*

We cross a ridge that stands far above the canyon bed. The heat has grown intense, for not only have we lost elevation, but the colors surrounding us have grown black and gray as opposed to tan and white: We've entered the Archean formations of the inner gorge. The ancient metamorphic rocks are spiny, jagged and tend to erode nearly straight up and down, creating a 1,200-foot-high vertiginous landscape comprised of Zoroaster Granite and Vishnu Schist. Though it looks passable, the long drop before us is steep and carpeted with slivers of pulverized stone. There is no obvious route, so we simply slide and skid between outcroppings of the schist.

Yet the farther we descend, the clearer it becomes that others have passed this way. Faint markings—a short stretch of tamped ground, a tiny cairn here and there—begin to appear. While nothing close to a trail, the signs are helpful. We have little time to waste on detours or delays.

Just as quickly as the route appears, however, it vanishes down a steep drainage where the going looks impossible. We backtrack, searching for an alternative. After finding nothing easier, we decide on an exposed cornice that demands cautious hand and toe work. At one point I look down between my legs at several hundred feet of space, my weight supported by a cracked assemblage of brittle holds. I snap my head up and vow not to repeat this mistake.

Beyond the cliff, the route leads directly down into a patch of thorny catclaw acacia that rouses our choicest expletives. We pull spines out of our arms and legs, brush the dead leaves from our hair and gingerly continue slip-sliding into the maw of the gorge. When we finally skate down onto the bed of the canyon, riding a miniature avalanche of loose rock, it's apparent that we have just come down the "slope" Harvey mentions in *Treks*. Somehow we have made it simply by surrendering to the urgings of this gothic landscape, by default.

In the canyon bottom, where water has had a chance to saw a path through the hardened schist, the walking becomes easy. We step over clean, sand-polished bedrock that gleams with a metallic luster in the sun, our footsteps squeaking as if on glass. Everything not higher than 10 feet above the bed looks rounded, the edges and points filed down to curves, the irregularities reshaped into buxom swells by the occasional cloudbursts that fill the feeder canyons upstream. A few basins of greenish water appear, what Harvey called "pollywog soup," remnants of the last storm. Even though we won't need it, my mind loosens a bit—there are no thoughts of having to solely depend upon what little water we've brought. We could stay for a while, if we want, and live off these *tinajas*.

Tom crouches down before a pool and drinks straight from the ripe-looking water. As an instructor of wilderness medicine, he is always testing some theory or another in the outback. Water quality in Grand Canyon is one of his pet interests. He states that after years of research, a team of scientists concluded almost all of Grand Canyon's side stream waters are "relatively pristine," and that contrary to popular belief, they typically lack infectious microorganisms. To prove the point, Tom says he plans to drink only unfiltered water this trip, from as many sources as possible.

He slurps noisily for at least a minute before letting out a great gasping sigh. When he asks if I want some, his chin dribbling, he's smiling. *No thanks.* Tom knows that I *don't* drink unfiltered water, not since a bout of giardiasis a few years previous that forever changed my own once-liberal drinking habits. I reply in sign language and take a sip from my bottle.

Below us, the cracked and cacti-covered walls narrow. Canyon wrens whistle unseen from the cliffs. Steep plunges have begun to appear in the smooth, shiny bed. The first of these requires us to climb past on the canyon wall. But when we find ourselves atop a drop of at least 50 or 60 feet, with no apparent way to get around, we know we have come too far. Harvey did mention the presence of such a fall, and described how to circumvent it, but this one does not fit his description. We're stumped.

We backtrack a few meanders and find a cairn we had missed on the way down, signaling a bypass. Reluctantly, we hump over an adjacent ridge before rejoining the canyon a bit downstream. Exhausting work in the hot spring sun. But once on the other side we find no more obstructions. We continue scurrying along, always mindful of the clock ticking. Our focus is so consumed by the terrain and the time that it comes as a jolt when we suddenly find ourselves on the lip of a cliff, looking straight down at the silent Colorado. We stand in wonder for a moment before we remember why we are here.

With one more climb out of the bed of Cottonwood Creek, we slide precariously down a long talus that deposits us in a cloud of dust upon a beach of rippled sand. Finally, the act of hauling boats on our backs down some off-trail declivity in Grand Canyon does not seem so preposterous. We have come as far as we can by foot. It's time to blow these damn things up and get on the river.

At last, the Colorado River. *Elias Butler*

Harvey in his river running outfit (note Chuck Taylor shoes), Tanner Rapid, 1954. *Courtesy Dale Slocum*

Chapter Eleven
BACKPACKING THE COLORADO
1954

"We carried no life preservers. I admit, I was scared to death."

Bessie Hyde on running Sockdolager Rapid with husband
Glen Hyde shortly before they disappeared in 1928.

"I HAVE NEVER REALLY LOST my sense of wonder," Harvey wrote to a friend in 1954, "but one time when I was coming up to the top of the Bright Angel Trail, and was asked by a tourist whether the trip to the bottom was worth the effort, I was tempted to reply, 'It was better the first 25 times.'"

By the early 1950s Harvey was bored with hiking the Canyon's trails. Not that he wasn't intrigued with the gorge. Every time he opened up his Matthes-Evans map he felt absolutely beguiled by the possibilities: Over one hundred side canyons begged for exploration down there. But he had no idea how to reach most of these tributary gorges. Not by trail anyway. It was frustrating to realize that even if he hit every trail in the park he would only see a fraction of the Canyon. Even entire amphitheaters lay untracked, such as the Hindu with its fractured web of mysterious defiles. Like a true mathematician, Dr. Butchart put the dilemma in terms of numbers. "It seems unfortunate that Grand Canyon," he wrote, "with two-thirds the area of Glacier National Park, should have only one-thirtieth as many miles of unmaintained trails. The Teton Park, one-tenth the area of Grand Canyon, has three times as many miles of trails."

Even without trails, Harvey realized one of his greatest barriers to off-trail freedom was water—not a lack thereof, but *too much*. He often descended a trail only to stop and stare wistfully at the Colorado, eager to cross to the other side, or continue lengthwise along the bank. But to cross that short distance, he would need to drive hundreds of miles to the opposite rim and then try to bushwhack down. Such a journey might take days, not to mention lots more gasoline. As for hiking along the river, impassable cliffs always got in the way. Harvey had to concede that the mighty Colorado cordoned off the most intriguing parts of Grand Canyon—the unknown tributaries—while he was left on the outside, looking in.

He considered the problem. A boat would help, but he didn't want to fork out the cash and besides, he had no whitewater experience. Yet with a small, lightweight raft that fit into his backpack, he'd be able to float short stretches of river at a time. Where to find such a boat? Portable trail rafts were nonexistent in those days. An acquaintance of Harvey's once described floating Oregon's Rogue River on inner tubes, but Harvey felt that bringing a pump would mean too much weight. After mulling over the problem in the spring of 1954, Harvey was floating on an air mattress in Oak Creek during a picnic when an idea suddenly slapped him in the face like a cold wave.

An air mattress? It made perfect sense! It was light, inexpensive and he was already carrying it for use as a sleeping pad, so why not? Harvey's pulse quickened when he imagined himself cruising down the river, rapids pounding ahead, the Canyon drifting past without having to work too see it, especially on those roasting summer days in the inner-canyon heat. It would save hours, even days of circuitous travel, and best of all, all those tributaries on both sides of the river would be his.

The whole idea made him itch to get his feet wet in the Canyon. Even though he had never run a river like the Colorado, Harvey's penchant for water and watercraft had

Harvey on his air mattress in Oak Creek Canyon. *Courtesy Allyn Cureton*

been ingrained since childhood, from traveling the great Yangtze on Chinese junks to later floating the Illinois River on homemade dinghies. In the summer before he began college, Harvey and a friend fashioned a small rowboat from orange crates and fitted it with a crude mast and sails. They launched on the modest Mackinaw River south of Eureka, continued down the Illinois and then the Mississippi Rivers, sailing all the way to the Mississippi's confluence with the Missouri near St. Louis, a total of 165 miles in 12 days. The adventuresome teenagers's goal had been New Orleans, but sunburn and boredom took their toll, forcing the boys to abandon their Huck Finn-style craft at St. Louis. In

1947, Harvey constructed another vessel at Estes Park, Colorado. He carried a four-by-eight-foot, 35-pound orange crate contrivance atop his head for two miles up the trail to Loch Vale. All told, Harvey had built nearly a dozen such rowboats over the years.

Anne, Harvey and Jim in one of Harvey's homemade rowboats, Minnesota, 1944. *Roma Butchart, courtesy Anne Madariaga*

Riding an air mattress would be novel, but not so different from what other river rats had used in Grand Canyon. In June 1945, Georgie White Clark and Harry Aleson hiked 24 miles from the Hualapai Indian Reservation town of Peach Springs to Diamond Creek before floating the flooding Colorado wearing life preservers. Carrying candy in malt cans (which kept the contents somewhat dry) they swam and floated 60 miles to Lake Mead, almost drowning along the way in the river's powerful eddies.[1]

Undaunted by this experience, they returned the following year for more. This time they increased the challenge by hiking 130 grueling miles across the Shivwits Plateau from St. George to the mouth of Parashant Canyon, again in June during the spring flood. The river repeatedly slammed them into the canyon walls but they again reached Lake Mead. "People often asked me how I could have done something so foolish," Clark wrote. "Actually those two swims proved invaluable. I learned more about water and the Colorado River on those trips than I could probably have learned in 10 years any other way."

Another, similar undertaking took place in April 1951 when NPS rangers Kit Wing and Les Womack made the first partial descent by boat through the Little Colorado River gorge, the largest tributary to Grand Canyon. Wing and Womack had set their sights on running 60 miles from the Navajo Reservation town of Cameron to the confluence with the Colorado, and then the 10 miles downstream to the Tanner Trail. Instead, drought conditions forced them to shrink their plan to a 13-mile stretch of the Little Colorado starting at Blue

---

[1] An eddy is a river term that refers to a cycling mass of water that forms along the banks of a river. Eddies rotate water upstream, thus making for a pullout where boaters can halt downstream progress. By the same token, eddies can also be very difficult to escape.

Springs, a remote and reliable source of water for the *Colorado Chiquito*, accessible only by a rough hiking-climbing route.

The pair spent two days lowering 200 pounds of equipment 2,500 feet down the Blue Springs route to the river, making ample use of their climbing rope to descend the most exposed stretches. Their heaviest load consisted of a 60-pound rubber boat, which, ironically, they had chosen because of its feathery weight. From the pair's 1956 *Desert Magazine* article:

> The boat? Obviously it must fold into a back-pack, and must weigh as little as possible. We settled on a Navy four-man inflatable raft.
>
> The awkward package the folded boat made gave us many uncomfortable moments on the cliffside. Much of the time we could not wear the boat on our backs, but had to pass it from hand to hand down the rocks. The combination of anxiety and heavy loads had us into near exhaustion by the time we returned to the river-edge.

Wing and Womack found more difficulties once they launched on the river. Travertine dams form in great numbers on the Little Colorado, and the result was a series of shallow stair-step falls. These obstacles forced the men to unload the boat and laboriously drag it past each fall. Wing and Womack eventually made their goal, but the slog through shallow water had not been quite the trip they had hoped for.

Harvey meanwhile would be able to easily and safely hike his air mattress anywhere, unlike Wing and Womack's monster craft. But Harvey did not know how an air mattress would perform on the mighty Colorado. So, in August 1954, Harvey and fellow ASC professor Ellery Gibson toted mattresses down the Hermit Trail for a trial run.

Elmer Purtymun, a motel owner from Sedona whom Harvey knew, had given Harvey the idea to visit Granite Rapids. Earlier that year, Purtymun had decided to lead a river trip through the Canyon but then abandoned the Colorado out of fright at Hance Rapid, leaving the rest of his even less experienced group to fend for itself. The remaining river party managed to float as far as Granite Rapids at the mouth of Monument Creek before being scared out of the Canyon as well.

Harvey and Gibson decided to see for themselves what sort of monster rapid had shooed Purtymun's group from the river. The pair left the Hermit Trail at the Tonto Bench, continued to Monument Creek and descended to the Colorado. They arrived to find Purtymun's abandoned gear piled on the bank and instantly understood the decision to abort. With the river running so low, Granite Rapids looked ferocious, raging over and through the Monument

Creek debris fan against the wall on the right bank.

Just upstream, however, Harvey noticed a placid eddy beyond the cataract's reach. *Perfect.* He inflated his air mattress and climbed on then tried to maneuver in the fast backwater current. With a little practice, he got the hang of it and was soon paddling merrily about the eddy. "I could cross to the far wall," Harvey wrote, "and get back with no tendency to be swept into the rapid."

Meanwhile, Gibson found it difficult to keep his balance on the squishy and slippery inflatable. He stood four inches taller than the petite math professor and outweighed him by 20 pounds, which put him at a disadvantage. With Granite bellowing just downstream, Gibson became uneasy. "I don't feel secure in this, Harvey."

Gibson's anxiety stemmed from more than just the usual river-nerves. Neither man had brought a life jacket. Back in 1954, only heavy, bulky "Mae West" life jackets were available. Not only would one of these behemoths nearly fill a backpack by itself, they also tended to absorb water after several hours of use. Harvey hated carrying any unnecessary weight into the Canyon and had thus elected to forego the safety devices. He felt confident in his abilities as a swimmer and figured the air mattress would provide all the flotation he needed.

Harvey decided to further test his theory the next day by taking his mattress on its maiden voyage downstream. He wanted to ride the 1.6 miles of calm water between Hermit and Boucher Creeks. Gibson declined to join him and said he would meet Harvey at the rim.

Harvey put in below Hermit Rapid the next morning. He went light, leaving his rucksack behind to be picked up later, as he had no way to keep the contents dry. The float took only 45 minutes and went beautifully. He fairly skipped up the Boucher Trail as he made his way back. "That idea of going downriver on the air mattress, such an easy way to get from Hermit to Boucher, compared to going along the Tonto Trail," he wrote. "It was restful and fun."

HARVEY VOWED TO run a few rapids on his next trip, as long as he could find a willing partner. In September he talked a young Navy training school instructor named Ben Surwill into joining him. He barely knew Surwill, who was an acquaintance from the halls at ASC. Yet together they planned to run one of the Colorado's more feared stretches, from Hance Rapid to Bright Angel Creek.

Roma agreed to do shuttle duty. She dropped the men off at the New Hance Trail with plans to meet them that evening at the top of the Kaibab Trail. Harvey and Surwill quickly hiked down Red Canyon to the foot of Hance Rapid. While they inflated their mattresses, the Colorado crashed against boulders just upstream, an audible reminder of the river's immense power. From here the two would be committing themselves to 10 miles of infamous, violent water. Just downstream waited the inner gorge of Grand Canyon, part of what explorer John Wesley Powell had called the "Great Unknown." The inner gorge is the result of a stark change in geology. Instead of the orderly sedimentary rocks that frame the river corridor for the first 76 miles of Grand Canyon, the 1.8 billion year-old black and rust-red Vishnu Schist and Zoroaster Granite appear for the first time, making a much darker, narrower and more gothic chasm. These remolded guts of long-destroyed mountains have frightened many a river runner by appearance alone.

As it had been for Powell, this was unfamiliar territory for Harvey. He had long wondered what mysteries awaited him in the inner gorge. But unlike Powell, Harvey knew full well the hazards he would face. He heard that whirlpools arise unpredictably in the constricted current, that rafts had been known to capsize on ferocious eddy lines. He also knew it would be impossible to avoid two of the largest rapids on the entire river—Sockdolager and Grapevine. He and Surwill were taking a serious risk.

Yet Harvey chose to run this stretch not in spite of the danger, but for the very reason that it would determine whether his experimental method of travel was indeed viable. The way he figured it, "If I could do that part of it, I could do it all."

Just below the tail waves of Hance Rapid, amidst the roar of whitewater, Harvey stepped in. He felt the millions of tiny grains, the pulverized and ground-up sediment from hundreds of upstream tributaries slide greasily around his calves. This was the Colorado of the ancient world, a free running river that was still busily carving Grand Canyon from raw bedrock. He let the current pull him away from shore.

He assumed Surwill knew his way around rough water. He was a Navy man, wasn't he? Neither man wore a life jacket.

The reality of what they were doing began to sink in when they heard an approaching rumble downstream. There could be no turning back now. The two cautiously stayed close together, with Harvey paddling a little ahead to watch for hazards. He told Surwill he would signal when to pull over to scout the large rapids, the first of which would be Sockdolager, a class-IV cataract (or, 8–9 on the Colorado River rating scale of 1–10). As they drew closer, leaping rooster tails of water and spray showed above the horizon line where the river fell from view.

They paddled over to the left bank. After making a brief survey of Sockdolager, they cautiously scrambled downstream along the south bank as far as it would allow, trying to avoid as much of the big water as possible. Eventually they became cliffed out, as had happened to Powell's crew here in

1869. A series of standing waves, rhythmically swelling and crashing with explosive force just downstream, commanded their attention. Several long minutes passed before they made their decision.

"We got into water after about a third of the rapid," Harvey said, "and pushed off and got free of the bank and swished through…with the waves about four and a half feet high or so, with sheer fun." They kept the air mattresses tucked under their arms like wings and held them flat against their stomachs, which allowed the two to "stand" in the water, hips and legs dangling straight down.

They repeated this technique at Grapevine Rapid, which also went with surprising ease. Floating the Colorado was not proving as dangerous as Harvey had thought, especially compared to what hazards awaited them on shore. The smooth, polished metamorphic rocks of the inner gorge felt like greased glass under their wet sneakers. Once, when they were just standing and talking things over, Harvey lost his footing and fell hard. His bruised hip hurt for days. At another rapid the pair attempted to bypass the whitewater along a narrow ledge 30 feet above the river. In the midst of their traverse, they suddenly agreed they were more likely to kill themselves avoiding rapids rather than running them. They returned to the safety of the river.

Except for Harvey's aching hip, his experiment seemed to be working. But they were not out of the inner gorge yet. In between the attention-grabbing Grapevine and Sockdolager, none of the boatmen Harvey had talked to had bothered to mention 83-Mile Rapid. Perhaps in their highly maneuverable rafts, the boatmen simply did not consider this cataract much of a hazard. But Harvey and Surwill were not in a *boat*. As soon as Harvey heard the rapid's deep bellow, he began paddling for shore while hollering and signaling for Surwill to follow. Harvey was crawling out of the water when he heard Surwill yell from the middle of the river.

"I can't make it to the bank! Here I go!"

Surwill was funneling directly into the accelerating water of 83-Mile Rapid. Harvey watched in disbelief. The rapid drew the young veteran toward "about the steepest place in the river that I'd ever seen," as Harvey put it, where much of the Colorado's considerable volume spilled over a huge boulder into a hole of violent recycling waves. Surwill passed down the glassy tongue, glanced the boulder at about a 45-degree angle, then dropped five or six feet into the maw of the rapid. Seconds went by and Harvey saw no sign of him. Finally, Surwill's head popped up. He swam into an eddy and waved to Harvey that he was okay. Not interested in repeating Surwill's spooky run—which he considered an act of utter recklessness—Harvey climbed past the rapid before resuming his float.

Surwill had been lucky. But from Harvey's point of view, the scare had another upside: It proved that his air mattress idea was going to work. If Surwill could withstand being dumped into an ugly pack of Colorado River hydraulics without a life jacket and come out fine, then what was there to fear? Harvey wasn't going to start shooting the biggest rapids for the hell of it, but he felt satisfied with the results of his test.

He would, however, look for a more prudent companion for future float trips, especially after Surwill displayed a lack of endurance on the hike out. "I began to wish I had checked Surwill for hiking speed before bringing him," Harvey wrote. "He had no wind at all and needed six and a half hours to go from the river to the rim." They arrived six hours overdue, at 1:00 A.M. Roma had waited patiently most of the night, but finally gave up and drove home, leaving it up to Surwill's wife to come from Flagstaff for the spent men the next morning. "Roma was quite disgusted at the mismanagement at the tail end of this expedition," Harvey wrote, "and I don't blame her!"

Despite Roma's understandable worry and anger, Harvey had become instantly hooked on river running. In one trip he had seen more new country than he had during the last year of hiking.

Two weeks later he was back to run the seven-mile stretch immediately upstream, from Tanner to Hance Rapids. But things went awry from the moment he blurted out his river trip intentions during the initial fall hiking club meeting at ASC. Gary Hansen, a student from Winslow, begged to join him. "Hansen talked a pretty good line about his Canyon hiking know-how," Harvey said. The math professor took it for granted that young Mr. Hansen could manage the physical demands of hiking and floating the Canyon. Harvey, apparently, was a very trusting person.

Harvey invited another student, Dale Slocum, a 34-year-old journalism major and budding photographer. Slocum had both hiking and river experience in Grand Canyon, having been a member of the failed Purtymun expedition a couple of months earlier. Slocum said he would like to bring along a friend, 26-year-old Young Veazy, a student who had never been to Grand Canyon. Harvey again agreed.

In mid-September, Slocum drove the foursome to the Tanner trailhead at Lipan Point where they camped for the night. Trip leader Dr. Butchart outlined their plan before hitting the sack: Get an early start, make the 10-mile hike to Tanner Rapid by late morning, float to Hance Rapid and then hike out the New Hance Trail, all in one very long day.

Things went smoothly the next morning until the unmaintained Tanner Trail became faint and fragmented in the Redwall. After losing it completely, Harvey and Hansen decided to look for another way down the forbidding limestone cliff. Meanwhile, Slocum and Veazy opted for trying to make a difficult descent via the bottom of Tanner Wash. In short, they split up, which was not the ideal formula.

Harvey and Hansen eventually made it to the river. After they waited 20 minutes, their two companions still failed to arrive. Reluctantly, they hiked up Tanner Wash in the stifling heat to search for Slocum and Veazy. They found them slowly working their way down a dangerous dry fall in the Tapeats Sandstone. This same dicey cut would later claim the life of a lost Trappist priest who fell while trying to reach water in 1959.

After the latecomers clambered down, Harvey hurried everyone to the river.

Already this was shaping up to look like another late-night epic. Following a quick lunch they inflated their air mattresses, whereupon Harvey gave a hasty demonstration in an eddy. Harvey's young protégés each did their best Dr. Butchart impersonation by practicing maneuvers in the quiet water.

Unfortunately, the swift pace Harvey had set on the way down began to take its toll. Veazy was feeling the exertion and the heat. He vomited. He was in no shape to go on. But by this time Harvey's patience was gone. He wanted to get moving downriver and felt that because Veazy was Slocum's "guest," the sick man was Slocum's responsibility. Harvey asked Slocum to hike Veazy back to the rim on his own. Slocum was miffed at Harvey for continuing with plans to float but he reluctantly agreed. The foursome would be split up yet again—Harvey and Hansen would head downriver, Slocum and Veazy would trudge back up the roasting Tanner Trail. They planned to rendezvous on the rim that evening.

From left, Gary Hansen, Harvey Butchart and Young Veazy inflate their air mattresses at Tanner Rapid. *Courtesy Dale Slocum*

Before parting ways, Slocum made several photographs of the river runners on their mattresses. As interesting as the photos are for the era they capture—a silty, mild, pre-Glen Canyon Dam Colorado River—what is more astounding is how they depict Harvey's carefree approach to river running. Wearing a sizeable backpack and no life jacket, he smiles with unmistakable pleasure, seemingly unconcerned with the danger. True, it was September and the river was low. And both men had stuffed their pack's contents into plastic bags. But if they happened to be thrown into the river, any flotation the flimsy bags provided would be scant

Harvey and Gary Hansen prepare to launch at Tanner Rapid. *Courtesy Dale Slocum*

protection against the Colorado's powerful boils and whirlpools.

Harvey was glad to see Hansen quickly adapt to his air mattress. When a powerful wave upset the two of them, Harvey and Hansen had the same instinctive reaction: They let their feet hang down while lying crosswise over the middle of the mattress. This method worked fine for even the worst water. But if too many rocks poked the surface, Harvey preferred to walk around rather than risk injury.

During this third experimental run, the pair ran several riffles and modest Basalt Rapid while bypassing two large rapids, Unkar and 75-Mile (aka Nevills Rapid). Harvey had assumed this stretch would be easier than his inner gorge float. But the eddies seemed more powerful this time and regularly forced them back upstream. When they finally reached Hance Rapid at 3 P.M. they were whipped. They hit the trail a half hour later, with Harvey setting his usual uphill pace. Almost immediately, Hansen showed that he did not even have the little bit of wind that Surwill had demonstrated. Harvey had figured on making the rim in less than six hours, but it was 11 P.M., eight hours later, before they reached the trailhead. Hansen was done. "The boy was so sleepy," Harvey wrote, "that he took the two air mattresses for warmth and lay down in the gutter beside the highway."

But Slocum and Veazy were nowhere in sight. Something had obviously gone wrong. Harvey began to wonder whether the two had even made it out of the Canyon. He left his comatose companion and started walking along the East Rim Drive towards Lipan Point, six miles away. When he finally arrived there, the trunk of Slocum's car was locked and both Slocum and Veazy were absent.

Harvey decided the best he could do was wait out the night, try to get some sleep, and go for help in the morning. Yet it was too

Harvey floats the muddy Colorado. *Courtesy Dale Slocum*

Heading downstream from Tanner Rapid. *Courtesy Dale Slocum*

cold to sleep. Harvey walked toward Desert View, another two miles east, but he could not find a decent place to lie down there, either. The bathroom was chilly and the mechanic shed floor was oily. Harvey loaded up with water and lumbered back to Lipan Point, likely regretting all the while that he had given away his air mattress. All totaled, he walked over 11 road miles that night. Still, he could not rest. He was freezing. He built two fires and sat between them, putting his head down on his knees, ready for this night to end. He finally managed to doze for an hour in the warmth of the rising sun.

Meanwhile, Slocum and Veazy had never even made it above the Redwall on the Tanner Trail. After being caught by nightfall, they tried to sleep in the bed of Tanner Canyon. But like Harvey and Hansen they got little rest. Their only stroke of good luck was in stumbling across a cache of canned food left over from the search for a seasonal ranger, 22-year-old Ronald Berg, who had died falling off a cliff in July that year.

After a short rest, Harvey contemplated his missing students. He figured they would need food and water, so he walked back to Desert View and called on NPS District Ranger Joe Lynch. Yet according to Harvey, Lynch "couldn't let me have any food."

While Lynch couldn't spare a mouthful for lunch, he had no problem giving Harvey an earful about splitting up his party. He also lambasted him over the foolishness of floating the river, and said he didn't have time to help look for the students. Smarting from this reprimand, Harvey called Veazy's wife in Flagstaff to ask for food and help. Two hours later, she arrived with supplies. Harvey quickly started down the Tanner Trail.

Harvey soon encountered a dazed Veazy, gave him water, then continued until he reached Slocum, who was in even worse shape. After helping him to the rim, Harvey drove everyone back to the New Hance Trail where they finally collected Hansen from his ditch.

Harvey later wrote, "So ended another snafu!"

DESPITE A REPEAT of the debacle he had experienced with Surwill, Harvey took a great measure of confidence from the way he and Hansen had handled themselves on the river. He now knew he could float the entire length of Grand Canyon. Meanwhile, Slocum had written an article about Harvey's wild rides through Sockdolager and Grapevine Rapids for the *Arizona Republic*. When Slocum's story made it onto the Associated Press wire and radio, the mathematics professor who braved the Colorado on his air mattress became national news.

College Profs Spot Bighorn At Canyon

Sighting of a bighorn sheep, an animal not seen in the Grand Canyon area in many years, was a highlight of a one-day hiking-floating jaunt in the Canyon Saturday, Dr. H. Harvey Butchart, head of the college math department, said today.

From the *Arizona Republic*, 1954.
Courtesy Anne Madariaga

Not everyone was amused by the daredevil tale. Grand Canyon National Park Superintendent Preston Pat Patraw did not abide such hijinks in *his* park—especially when splashed all over the airwaves. Several days later, Harvey received a firm notice on government stationery. "If you ever wish to put a 'boat, canoe, raft, or other floating craft' on the river," Patraw admonished, "you need to get a permit first."

The superintendent wasn't the only one inspired to write Harvey that week. In Berkeley, California, Otis Marston's ears had pricked immediately during the radio broadcast. Marston tracked down Harvey through ASC and quickly fired off a letter of his own, initiating what would become a sprawling, 25-year correspondence.

October 22, 1954
Dear Dr. Butchart,

It seems you must be an unusual Professor of mathematics since you go into great canyons and travel the rivers in unorthodox fashion…
I am much interested in establishing a relatively complete file of the River record and would like the story of your trip.

Truly,
Otis Marston

Marston was a possessive, obsessed man when it came to the Colorado River and Grand Canyon, the two absolute centers of his universe. At any one time he was either planning his next river trip, talking about the Canyon, writing about the Canyon, or otherwise researching the area's human history for a definitive book he planned to write someday. He very much resembled the future Harvey Butchart in this regard, which explains why the two made natural friends.

Marston was 13 years Harvey's senior, a native of Berkeley with two engineering degrees and a successful career as an investment banker. His aggressive demeanor, high IQ, and considerable family wealth had brought him quick success. Yet by the time he hit middle age Marston felt that his life lacked adventure. In the summer of 1942, Marston and his teenage son Garth took a commercial river trip with pioneering outfitter Norman Nevills down the Green and Colorado Rivers. To say that the river had a profound impact upon Marston would be an understatement. Within five years he happily exchanged his previous existence as a corporate moneyman to become a full time river runner and historian, never looking back. He even acquired a new name to complete the transformation— "Dock," a playful sobriquet Nevills had given him based on his professorial appearance.

At five-foot-six, Marston and his fuzzy

Otis "Dock" Marston. *Bill Belknap, courtesy Loie Belknap-Evans*

white goatee and round glasses also brought to mind the character "Doc" from Disney's *Snow White and the Seven Dwarfs*. Yet in one sense, the appellation did not quite fit. Instead of the cute and lovable Doc, Marston would have been more aptly named after Grumpy. For Marston could be cranky, pompous, and outspoken, all at the same time. Most remember Marston the egomaniac, the insensitive and opinionated critic, the very definition of a curmudgeon. He made not a few enemies by virtue of his abrasive personality and penchant for bad-mouthing nearly everyone who had gained a modicum of notoriety on the river.

Bill Mooz, a metallurgic engineer from California who shared a 25-year friendship with Marston, explained:

> He was a son-of-a-bitch. He was tough, crusty and opinionated beyond belief. He could be as rude as hell. He knew it, too. On occasion, he even got on the outs with the very best of his friends. But he depended on a lot of friends to help in his endeavors. He used to send out correspondence with a cartoon skunk on his letterhead to represent how he was viewed by the Canyon and river running community.

Indeed, Marston took delight in his role as the burr under the river runners's collective saddle. Not only did he consider himself the last word on river history, he also felt compelled in some cases to rewrite that history as he saw fit, much to the annoyance of his peers in the small, competitive world of Colorado River boatmen. Some even considered him a homophobe after he accused several well-known boatmen of being gay.

Yet for all his contrariness, few could doubt the "skunk's" importance. Marston had dedicated himself to pouring thousands of hours into an ambitious dream: Researching and writing the ultimate Colorado River history book. He worked tirelessly to establish himself

Dock Marston's letterhead. *The Huntington Library, San Marino, California*

as the authority in this field. Yet he was no writer and never would produce the book he envisioned. Still, modern researchers consider his massive collection, housed at the Huntington Library in California, *the* source for Colorado River lore.

Harvey read Marston's letter with interest, for he had never heard of him. He passed the name by Dale Slocum and wrote a reply:

Oct. 26, 1954
Dear Dr. Marston,

Dale Slocum recognized you immediately. I have read a number of accounts of Colorado River voyages, but not much about recent experiences and I did not know that you are now the dean of that fraternity. It is an honor to hear from you. There are two sides to the publicity about my adventures. I got in touch with you…but I also got a fairly gentle but firm notice from the Grand Canyon Park superintendent…

I have been hiking the used and unused trails of the Grand Canyon for the past nine years since coming to Flagstaff…

Mostly for longer vacations I have gone to climb mountains in Colorado, the Tetons or California, but for now I am going to continue with the Colorado River in the Grand Canyon at least until I have been from Lee's Ferry to Lake Mead. I might even enter the race to see how many times one man has made it. I understand you have been through it nine times.

Best Wishes,
J. H. Butchart

Harvey's letter exhibits his trademark competitiveness, as well as proof that his focus had changed: No longer did he yearn to explore the West's great national parks. Harvey—like Marston—had become obsessed with the Colorado River. Marston sensed that here was a kindred soul, and sent his enthusiastic response:

October 30, 1954
Canyoneer Butchart,

The use of the River within the Grand Canyon for transport puts you into the group of CANYONEERS. May I welcome you? …

I think I commend your ambition to see the River course from Lee's Ferry to Lake Mead… My desire is to make some comprehensive chronicle of the River navigation. I also hope to work out some of the answers to a few of the technical problems of safe navigation. That is one of the chief interests in the use of air mattresses…

Good hunting,
Otis Marston

From the start, Marston dropped his grouchy demeanor when it came to Harvey. The two would share a mutual respect throughout their lengthy pen-pal relationship. Perhaps it was their common ground: Both were bright, high-ly educated, and first saw Grand Canyon as middle-aged men. Harvey was 38 when he took his first hike, Marston, 48 when he took his first river trip. As a result, they both approached the Canyon as though they could hear the clock ticking. They had places to go, things to see. There was history to be written—and *history to be made.*

Then again, maybe the key to their friendship was the ground that separat-ed them. Marston felt so ultra-possessive about the river that just about anyone who had anything to do with the Colorado would in effect be stepping on his toes. Harvey, on the other hand, was just a visitor to the river—he was obvious-ly much more of a hiker. Thus, he lay outside the river community, and present-ed less of a threat to Marston's delicate ego.

They were off. Harvey had finally met someone who was crazier about Grand Canyon than himself. The effect was almost immediate:

Dec. 4, 1954
Dear Dock,

Your long and friendly letter has whetted my interest in the Grand Canyon to a higher pitch than ever. I guess I am living so close to the Canyon that it didn't seem very glamorous. I considered it a good place for a two or three day excursion, but when I had a longer vacation coming up, I would feel that I had to range further from home. Now I am in the mood to stick to this area until I have the answers to a lot of questions and have a lot more places first hand. I clearly see that five years won't be too long to spend covering the side canyons and old trails.

P.S. It's quite an honor to be called a canyoneer!

In making perhaps the biggest understatement of his life, Harvey was cor-rected by Marston, who prophetically replied, "There is enough new area to cover in the Grand Canyon to last two lifetimes."

In between writing letters that month, Harvey also met with his pal Boyd Moore at the ASC Homecoming in Flagstaff. Twenty-three year-old Boyd had graduated the previous spring and now attended the University of Arizona in Tucson in pur-suit of a master's degree in geology, but he had a soft spot for returning to his alma mater. Harvey regaled him with stories of running Sockdolager and described how his river trip companions had done so poorly as hikers. Harvey then got to the point: He invited Boyd to run the length of the Canyon with him the following spring. "When do we start?" answered Boyd, a grin spreading across his face.

BY APRIL 1955, THE ANNUAL Grand Canyon flood began to take shape. From high in the glaciated Rocky Mountains of Colorado and Wyoming, snowmelt raced down the elaborate plumbing system formed by the hundreds of tributaries of the Green and Colorado Rivers. When the runoff began to reach Lee's Ferry, it had warmed along the lengthy journey to a frigid 55 degrees—only a bit warmer than the modern-day Colorado released from the black depths of Lake Powell.

On April 10, the two men yelped involuntarily when they stepped in. No one save a few close friends knew that insurance salesmen Bill Beer and John Daggett were attempting to make history by swimming Grand Canyon from beginning to end.

The pair of Californians had recently dreamed up their scheme during a party. Their only flotation would be lifejackets and gear bags, their only protection from the cold, cheap wetshirts and long underwear. Though both men were surfers experienced with rough water, they had not dared tell the Park Service what they were up to. Beer and Daggett knew their chances of success hinged on keeping things as quiet as possible. Tentatively, they waded into the cold river and allowed the current to take them downstream.[2]

Harvey, just like the rest of the Grand Canyon community, knew nothing of Beer and Daggett. Yet the notion of riding the Colorado without a boat must have been floating in the air. Four days later, Harvey typed the following letter to Superintendent Patraw, asking permission to do nearly the same thing as Beer and Daggett:

John Daggett and Bill Beer in their swimming gear, Grand Canyon, 1955. *Courtesy John Daggett*

[2] This tale was many years later recorded with gritty eloquence when Bill Beer wrote the classic *We Swam the Grand Canyon: The True Story of a Cheap Vacation that Got a Little Out of Hand.*

Dear Sir:

    I would like your permission to float
down the Colorado River with one or two companions towards the end of May and possibly
again in August.

    You may remember that I experimented with
floating on air matresses last September. I
am convinced that, unless the water is too cold,
this method of navigation has several advantages.
One avoids the labor and danger connected with
lining around the rapids, and there is no hazard
from the heat. I know I can carry enough food
and bedding in a waterproof knapsack. From reading
and firsthand experience, I know the escape routes
from the river if a retreat should be necessary.

    Since coming to Arizona in 1945, I have been
interested in exploring old trails in the Grand
Canyon, and as I have been corresponding with Otis
Marston this winter, I am more eager than ever to
become familiar with all its beauties and mysteries.
In particular I propose to make some rough measurements
of the bridge Barry Goldwater discovered. I would
also like to show that the river trip need not be
expensive and require elaborate equipment. As for the
danger of travel by air mattress, "Dock" Marston
tells me that it was tried successfully as early as
1940 by some dudes in a Nevills party.

    Even without permission to float through the Park
and Monument, I intend to go down Marble Canyon as
far as the Park boundary and then walk up to Goldwater's
bridge, and then out to Point Imperial by the old
Nancoweap trail, but I would like to have your consent
to continue as far as I have the time or inclination.

Sincerely,
J. H. Butchart

National Archives and Records Administration, Pacific Region.

Harvey's motivation came not only from his yearning to explore side canyons, but also his thriftiness—commercial float trips cost an arm and a leg. As for the permit, it certainly was not going to curtail Harvey's plans if Patraw refused to grant one. Harvey would do as he pleased, never mind what the government thought—at least outside the superintendent's jurisdiction. Still, since Patraw had rebuked Harvey the previous summer, Harvey knew he needed to at least make this formal request. He would play by the rules this time.

When the superintendent finally opened Harvey's letter several days later, he decided that he needed to think it over before giving an answer. But while

Patraw was pondering the unusual request, the news broke about Beer and Daggett. A worried friend had decided they were overdue and inadvertently tipped off the Park Service. The "frogmen" were actually fine, just making slower progress than they had estimated.

Unaware that they were now celebrities, Beer and Daggett interrupted their trip at Phantom Ranch, hoping to quietly load up on supplies at the South Rim. From reading a newspaper on their way to a store, they discovered that they had been presumed dead. But instead of keeping a low profile, their hunger got the best of them and they were soon gorging on fancy grub in the Bright Angel restaurant. When the chief ranger of the park happened to walk in, they were caught. The NPS immediately informed Beer and Daggett their trip was over and ordered them to hand in their flippers.

The government's position was understandable. Rangers had been conducting a costly and embarrassing search. The local paper had run dramatic headlines. But Beer and Daggett were not about to back down, not after the misery they had been through in the first 88 miles. They told park officials "they [NPS] wouldn't have a minute's peace until someone does swim down this river," with "literally hundreds if not thousands of guys trying to finish what they started just to get in the record books." Their argument was a stretch. But it worked. The Park Service agreed to look the other way, which would eventually result in the first swimming descent of the Colorado in Grand Canyon.

Superintendent Patraw intended to make sure it was the last one, too. While a flurry of copycats never did appear, there was at least one other hopeful with whom Patraw had to contend. A man who was politely knocking at the front door while Beer and Daggett had slipped through the backdoor.

Yet Harvey did not have the frogmen's kind of leverage now. His air mattress approach was novel, but the first run *without a boat* was already underway. In the fresh wake left by Beer and Daggett, the bureaucratic waters had suddenly become much more turbulent for other mavericks like Harvey Butchart.

Not that it mattered much to him. Harvey was determined to get on the river. The only question was whether Patraw would allow him to float through the park.

Early on, Harvey had written a defiant letter to Marston to explain his back-up plan, in case Patraw denied his permit:

April 2, 1955
Dear Dock,

    I am still planning to take to the river at Lee's Ferry and go down to Nankoweap, whether the park service gives me its approval or not...If the superintendent doesn't think much of my method of travel, I'll go out to Point Imperial by the old trail [Nankoweap]...If there is still time before summer school, I might go on to Lake Mead. I am using the singular, but a former hiking companion is counting on doing this sort of thing with me...

Sincerely yours,
Harvey Butchart

To avoid more late night epics with heavy-footed companions, the likes of which Harvey had suffered during his trial runs, he planned to team with that "former hiking companion," Boyd Moore. Boyd was indeed a hiker's hiker. But time and experience would soon show that Harvey, once again, had not made the wisest choice. What he really needed was a hiker who was not afraid of the water.

Boyd Moore. *Courtesy Anne Madariaga*

Chapter Twelve
BOYD
MAY 1955

I believe the first running of rapids with an air mattress was at Diamond Creek in 1940 when the dudes in Nevills' party rode thru the rapid with them. Nevills thot that no publicity should be given to this escapade since it might lead to lack of caution. Goldwater was in this party.

I suppose you have tried swim fins and found them troublesome or too heavy. With a pack like that, my guess would be that a life preserver, at least for the pack, might be worth considering.

Dock Marston,
Letter to Harvey Butchart (April 1955)

I found that a heavy heart is the worst load a person can carry up the trail.

Harvey Butchart (May 1955)

SUPERINTENDENT P.P. PATRAW was no boatman, but neither was he a stranger to the perils of the Colorado. In 1928 he participated in the search for missing honeymooners Glen and Bessie Hyde by running one of the roughest stretches, from Bright Angel Creek to Bass Rapid. An extreme cold spell made the already grueling job of portaging and lining the boat at the worst rapids even tougher. Patraw commented afterwards, "I'll tell you right now, I never worked harder than those days on the Colorado River."

So when he read Harvey's letter requesting permission to go down the river on his air mattress in late May—peak flood time—it set red flags flying. But Patraw did not immediately deny Harvey permission. He instead called to clarify a few points, ending the conversation by asking Harvey to send another letter that included his river trip itinerary. Patraw promised to think it over a bit more once he saw Harvey's plan in writing.

Harvey complied, dutifully typing an itinerary in which he noted safety precautions he planned to take (he conspicuously failed to mention life jackets) and confidently suggested that the risks were minimal. Further, he would float an estimated 20–25 river miles per day—a very optimistic figure:

May 4, 1955
Dear Mr. Patraw,

I am enclosing the requested information about my proposed trip. We will take no real chances. As I see it, the difficulties, if any, will likely be in the form of sunburn or possibly the cold temperature of the water. Last Sunday on the way home from Zion, I experimented some more for about four miles down from Lee's Ferry.

Sincerely,
J.H. Butchart

Proposed Itinerary

May 24: Lee's Ferry to Tanner Wash, 25 miles.
May 25: To Nankoweap Creek, 27 m.
May 26 and 27: Natural Bridge.
May 28: To Hance Rapids, 25 m.
May 29: To B.A. Trail and up to Indian Gardens.
May 30: To the rim for supplies, and then to Shinumo, 20 m. From here, if the going seems to be good, we will go on to Lake Mead as fast as possible. If we should be having any trouble keeping up to the above schedule, we will come out at Supai.

J.H. Butchart, 313 Summit, Flagstaff, Ariz.
Boyd Moore, 730 N. Warren, Tucson, Ariz.
Marvin Ratcliff, 812 W. Aspen, Flagstaff, Ariz.

Mrs. J.H. Butchart will be responsible for decisions as to rescue operations. It is suggested that nothing be done until Otis Marston goes through early in June.

Equipment

This trip is to be carried out by floating on air mattresses which will be carried past the rapids as far as possible. Light sleeping bags and concentrated food will be carried in knapsacks. Canteens will be used on trips away from the river. A first aid kit and a rubber patching kit will be taken. If necessary, a call for help will be given by building three fires in a row.

Yet by the time Harvey's letter reached Patraw, the superintendent had been answering too many calls from reporters asking about Bill Beer and John Daggett. Their story had become national news ever since the pair triumphantly ended their swim on May 5. In between interviews with the press, the beleaguered superintendent sent this reply to Harvey on May 16, a week before Harvey planned to get on the river:

Grand Canyon National Park
Grand Canyon, Arizona

May 16, 1955

Mr. J. H. Butchart
313 Summit Avenue
Flagstaff, Arizona

Dear Mr. Butchart:

    We have studied your application for a permit for a trip down the Colorado River, through Grand Canyon National Park, beginning May 23. After careful consideration we have found no alternative but to withhold issuance of the permit for this time.

    By late May, the River in the Canyon is normally close to its highest stage of spring run-off. At high stages the character of the rapids changes considerably. Some rapids disappear as such, and become greatly elongated stretches of very swift water, sometimes several miles in extent, and in some cases it would not be practicable to land, and even if it were, it would not be practicable to bypass the rapids by foot.

    I do not regard your float equipment as safe or adequate, particularly under the conditions expected to prevail at that time. We regard a rubber boat as the minimum safe equipment.

    If you insist upon continuing with your present plans, you will be doing so without the approval of this office.

Very truly yours,

P. P. Patraw
Superintendent

National Archives and Records Administration, Pacific Region

Despite Patraw's reasonable concerns, Harvey had no intention of canceling his trip. As he had promised Marston, he instead narrowed the scope of his plans. He and Boyd would only float outside the park boundaries, from Lee's Ferry to Nankoweap Canyon, a distance of about 50 miles. Once at Nankoweap they would hike to nearby Kolb Natural Bridge before making their way out via the Nankoweap Trail. Harvey told Boyd the trip was still on. They would begin the day after his daughter Anne's wedding, which was scheduled for May 22.

Boyd was in attendance that day when Anne married 1954 ASC graduate Sam Madariaga in the Butchart home in Flagstaff. Boyd gave the newlywed couple an ironing board (which, as of this writing, is still used by the Madariagas). As soon as the reception ended, Harvey was raring to get the river running adventure underway. He and Boyd began preparations to leave. But that evening, while listening to Harvey talk excitedly about their trip, Boyd made a tough confession. He told the math professor that he was a poor swimmer. In fact, Boyd said, he was "practically a non-swimmer." He wanted to back out.

Harvey encouraged Boyd not to throw in the towel. "I told him that swimming had very little to do with the case," Harvey said, "as we would merely be paddling over the sides of the mattress, or holding on and kicking with our feet when we got tipped over."

Harvey didn't know it, but his explanation did little to reassure Boyd. Yet Boyd did not press the issue. He told Harvey he would go and kept his growing sense of dread to himself.

The next day, May 23, Roma and her friend Wanda Euler shuttled Harvey and Boyd to Lee's Ferry, where they inflated their mattresses and laid out their gear. The weather had been warm and the Colorado was rising by the day, churning past at an impressive 28,000 cfs. Several large swells including the Paria riffle stirred within sight of the launch ramp. Combined with the river's low guttural roar, the scene offered sobering signs of the Colorado's power.

It was just what Harvey had been hoping for. He had fulfilled his professional obligations for another year and this adventure promised to be the antidote to all those quiet hours in the classroom. He quickly hopped aboard, paddled a bit downstream, then paused in a small eddy to wait for Boyd.

Now came the moment that Boyd had feared most. He warily stepped into the flood, dragging his mattress over the dirt-brown snowmelt. The two women watched from shore. Boyd positioned himself by his mattress and tried mightily to act brave. It took a monumental effort for him to lie down, but he did. Because he was 30 pounds heavier than Harvey, he and his mattress sank deeper into the water. Boyd felt the current's terrifying, insistent tug. After a moment during which he tried to ignore his shrieking internal alarm, he stiffly pushed off.

His jerky movements made for an awkward sight. Boyd floated as long as he could stand it—about a minute or two, until he was out of view of Roma and Wanda—before heading for shore. When he stepped out of the river, he told Harvey he was done.

"In the short distance from the boat landing to the mouth of Paria Creek," Harvey wrote, "Boyd decided that it was not for him." Even though Harvey was confused about this sudden about-face, he gained a clue to the extent of Boyd's fright when they paddled across a small, quiet lagoon at the mouth of the Paria River on their way back to the parking lot. "There was a great difference between the way I crossed with a few gliding strokes and the way he inched across exceedingly slowly."

Despite the obvious signs that something was amiss, Harvey was still not convinced that his young friend had no business being on the river. Harvey simply thought Boyd would catch on with a little more practice. He tried to encourage him not to quit. But this time Boyd was firm. He wasn't going. Harvey finally chose not to challenge him any further. With their air mattresses tucked under their arms, the two walked back to the parking lot in silence. Their trip had ended after only half a mile.

The somber three-hour drive back to Flagstaff seemed even longer than usual. Boyd felt relieved, perhaps even embarrassed. Harvey was woefully disappointed. Not only had his Canyon-length float trip been a total bust, now even the condensed version was sunk.

Yet as the drive went on, he and Boyd began discussing alternatives. They did have the next week to fool around with, after all. Soon they came up with an attractive plan that lifted both their soggy spirits. They would hike down the next day from Point Imperial into Nankoweap Canyon, visit the remote Kolb Natural Bridge, then merely *cross* the Colorado on their air mattresses before hiking out the Tanner Trail to the South Rim. Boyd may have had his reservations but he agreed to the plan. If they could get someone to drop them off at Point Imperial, they would be in business.

Harvey remembered that Dale Slocum had once mentioned that he wanted pictures of Kolb Bridge. Once back home, Harvey phoned Slocum and asked if he was still interested. Slocum immediately agreed to drive the three of them to the Canyon.

Slocum, a wizened, loquacious man now living in Phoenix, recalled not only their trip to Point Imperial, but also that *he* had gone to Lee's Ferry with Harvey and Boyd the day before. Although Harvey never mentioned Slocum being at Lee's Ferry, Slocum insisted that he had originally planned to join the air mattress float, too.

"When it came down to going it was just Harvey, Boyd and myself," said Slocum, who hadn't met Boyd before the trip. "When we got up to Lee's Ferry

I discovered from talking to this Boyd Moore that he didn't even know how to swim, so I said heck, I'm not going on a trip with some man, floating on a mattress in the Colorado River that doesn't even know how to swim! That's when I told Harvey I didn't want to go on a trip like that. As far as Harvey was concerned, he [said], 'if you don't want to go, I'll go without you'. That was his attitude so to speak."

When asked if Boyd left any impressions on him, Slocum replied, "I don't remember him ever saying much one way or the other. He was kind of quiet." Slocum insisted that other students had also been slated to go—including one Marvin Ratcliff, whom Harvey had listed in his permit request—but all except Boyd had dropped out.

AROUND NOON ON May 24, Harvey, Boyd, and Dale Slocum pulled up to the North Rim at the Grand Canyon's highest viewpoint, 8,803-foot Point Imperial. They emerged from Slocum's Austin Healy a bit stiff-legged after the four-hour drive from Flagstaff. Ponderosa pines and aspens towered overhead and a few patches of snow still lingered in the shade. While the Canyon roasted a mile below, it felt cool here under the midday sun.

Harvey was eager to get moving. He began rummaging in the trunk for his backpack. He would have preferred to arrive earlier but since Slocum had done him a favor by driving, Harvey had not been in a position to keep his own schedule.

Not far from Point Imperial, the Nankoweap Trail led down from the rim some 5,000 feet in 10 miles to the bed of Nankoweap Creek, which was Boyd and Harvey's goal for the day. Even though Harvey had never been down this trail, he felt confident enough to assume that they could make it to the creek in the few hours they had before sundown. As usual, they would go light, carrying only enough water for the afternoon, meaning they had little time to waste.

Slocum on the other hand was packing plenty of water plus his bulky medium format camera. He seemed in no hurry. He planned on photographing the recently discovered Kolb Natural Bridge, which lay only a couple thousand feet below Point Imperial. Although Boyd and Harvey were headed to this bridge too, Slocum would try to bushwhack his way to it from above via a much shorter and less certain route than coming at it from below like Boyd and Harvey.

Before getting started, Slocum could not resist the view from Point Imperial. He insisted that they pause so he could photograph Boyd gazing at the landscape. As soon as Slocum packed his camera, Harvey led them through the thick alpine forest and down off the rim.

The rarely used Nankoweap Trail proved hard to follow in the maze of thick vegetation. Harvey thought they would likely pick up the trail farther down and became impatient when Slocum repeatedly stopped to inspect his map. "After protesting Dale's needless delays a few times," Harvey wrote, "I suggested that we part company and that Boyd and I could then perhaps reach water before time to camp. That suited Dale too, so we hurried ahead while he went on studying the map. Later I learned that he spent the night in the woods at a high elevation with his water, heavy photo equipment, and no blanket." Indeed, Slocum didn't make it near the bridge that day, though he photographed it a year later while on assignment for *Life* magazine.

Meanwhile, Boyd and Harvey headed down and eventually picked up the trail. They made a wrong turn, however, and darkness found them sidetracked on Saddle Mountain, the large butte that rises adjacent to Nankoweap Canyon. Now, they were stuck for the night, too, also without water. "Well," Boyd declared as he shared the last drink in his canteen with Harvey, "we're in this thing together."

That evening, bivouacked on their desolate patch of shale, Boyd and Harvey discussed the day's hike and their plans for the rest of the trip. At some point, the subject of Lee's Ferry came up. Boyd finally allowed that there had been more to his quick exit from the river than Harvey knew. Referring to an earlier trip when the two had camped on Lake Mead in Harvey's boat, Boyd said, "Remember, when we were on Lake Mead, you went swimming in the evening and I didn't? I didn't like it." Boyd admitted that he had a tendency to panic in water, though he still did not go so far as to tell Harvey precisely why. Boyd's courageous declaration, however, did not change their plans to get on the river the following day. Perhaps Harvey felt he could help Boyd face his fears.

The next morning, instead of backtracking to locate the lost trail, they found a crack in the Supai Formation that allowed them to down-climb to a ridge sep-arating Nankoweap from Little Nankoweap Canyons. Once there, they picked up the trail, then scrambled the rest of the way to Nankoweap Creek. Water gurgled into their canteens as they shoved them into a pool, and only after empty-ing them twice did they rest. Both men gorged on the previous evening's dinner and that morning's breakfast, as they had been too thirsty to eat until now.

Refreshed and restored, they headed upstream in Nankoweap. After scram-bling for miles over boulders and circumventing a tricky 120-foot dry fall, they reached the isolated, muscular-looking Kolb Bridge. Future presidential candidate Barry Goldwater had discovered it while flying his helicopter over Grand Canyon in 1952. Both Boyd and Harvey snapped photos, only the second time the bridge had been photographed. Harvey measured the width of the opening using a piece of string and reckoned it to be 147 feet across, making it the largest natural bridge in Grand Canyon. They retreated downstream toward the river to make camp.

Kolb Natural Bridge. *Elias Butler*

Harvey arose before dawn, as was his habit. Within 20 minutes they were hiking in the cool morning air of May 26, going three miles downstream until they met the rumbling Colorado. The river had grown since they'd seen it last, now surging at over 30,000 cfs. Harvey wanted to get on his air mattress and ride, a much more appealing prospect than bushwhacking through thickets along the riverbank, but he kept the thought to himself. Boyd's admission two nights earlier made it clear that Harvey needed to minimize their time in the water.

Even so, as they hiked downstream through groves of scratchy willow and mesquite toward Kwagunt Canyon, the next major tributary on the right side of the river, Harvey's reserve broke down. He finally suggested that they try their air mattresses. To make it less scary, he said, they could hug the riverbank and thus avoid the hazard of being swept into the main current. Boyd seemed willing to give it another try. They inflated the mattresses and waded into the torrent.

Boyd and Harvey floated for nearly a mile by sticking close to the bank, weaving in and out of small coves and bouncing off limestone boulders. Boyd tried to practice his technique, but again, as at Lee's Ferry, he began to grow rigid. Harvey decided to try towing him by a short rope, which proved workable, if awkward. Yet Boyd's confidence began to improve—at least, as far as

144

Harvey saw it. "Boyd got along quite well and seemed quite pleased with that method of travel," Harvey wrote. "But we didn't get far from the west bank and were careful to land safely above Kwagunt Rapid."

If Boyd was indeed "pleased," or at least not stricken with fear, perhaps it was because he had a safety net close at hand. Like a new swimmer who stays at arm's length from the side of a pool, Boyd had that nearby bank to provide a quick physical and psychological bailout. Yet any time they needed to fight against the current, such as when crossing the numerous eddies that plague the Colorado's banks, it became obvious that Boyd's weight made it nearly impossible for Harvey to keep control of them both. "I can see," Boyd remarked, "that we're strictly on our own when out on the river."

Boyd told Harvey he would just as soon walk rather than float any farther to their crossing point. Harvey had not yet decided on the best place to cross, so they simply hiked downstream while he judged the possibilities. Harvey passed up the relatively calm four miles immediately downstream from Kwagunt Rapid, where there were no rapids of note, in favor of a spot just upstream from 60-Mile Rapid, at mile 59 1/2. This was two miles above the confluence with the Little Colorado River, where Marble Canyon comes to an end.

It was getting late, about 5 P.M., and they had planned to make camp on the other side before dark. Harvey quickly chose a huge eddy that extended halfway across the Colorado, surmising that this mass of cycling river could help ferry them to the opposite bank. For safety's sake, Harvey lightened Boyd's backpack by taking his camera and all his food into his own pack. To make the float look as easy as possible for his nervous young friend, Harvey would go first.

They stripped naked. Each stuffed their clothes into their packs. Harvey stepped into the river. He instructed Boyd to wait until he crossed to the other side before trying it himself; Harvey wanted to make certain that this would work before setting Boyd loose.

Harvey shoved off. Immediately, the flood-swollen river proved less cooperative than he had anticipated. After riding the eddy as far as he could, the main current grabbed him and sent him out of control downstream. He went around a bend and disappeared.

Harvey and his micro-raft had spun willy-nilly through 60-Mile Rapid before being forced back toward the right bank below. It was obvious that crossing the river was not going to work after all. The river was simply too high and too swift for air mattresses. He gave up and walked ashore only several minutes after he had started. Harvey realized that he and Boyd would likely need to retrace their steps to Point Imperial.

Harvey had left Boyd with clear instructions to wait for his signal. But he had not mentioned what to do in case he happened to get swept out of sight downstream. Boyd stood on the riverbank anxiously waiting, wondering what to do, his air mattress tucked under one arm, straining for some sign of Harvey. Soon his waiting became unbearable. He looked at the river rushing past and fear struck his heart. As terrifying as it was to think about getting in the water, however, neither did he want to become stranded here alone. For all Boyd knew, Harvey might have been carried miles downstream. If so, Harvey would probably be expecting him to follow. Deep in Grand Canyon, alone and naked, Boyd felt the overwhelming uncertainty break down his resistance to the river. He climbed onto his air mattress and made the fateful decision to follow.

Harvey was just getting ready to walk back upstream toward Boyd when he stopped short. "I was deflating my air mattress," Harvey said, "and was going to carry it back, and we'd do something else besides cross the river. But just as I was about ready to walk, here I saw him in the middle of the river, coming downstream lickety-split."

To Harvey's horror, Boyd raced past wearing a look of panic as he dropped into the three and four-foot waves of 60-Mile Rapid. Harvey frantically re-inflated his air mattress, which took several minutes, then jumped back into the brown froth.

He paddled furiously to catch up. But Boyd had a sizable lead on him. Harvey fought to gain ground for nearly an hour as Boyd hurtled downstream, paralyzed and helpless with fright. This stretch of the Colorado is notorious for large eddies that materialize in high water, making downstream progress—even with a boat and a good pair of oars—tremendously difficult.

Despite these numerous obstacles, Boyd somehow managed to travel two and a half miles before Harvey finally closed the gap. "I might not have ever seen him again," Harvey wrote, "but he got caught in a big eddy and was swirling around slowly when I caught up with him, below the mouth of the Little Colorado."

Harvey's relief evaporated when he saw how rattled Boyd was. His former student hung upside down with both arms and legs locked in a death grip around his rolled-up, log-shaped mattress. Boyd's nose poked only a few inches above the water. His face had turned ashen. When Harvey yelled at him, Boyd's garbled reply made it all too clear that he was "not thinking clearly."

Worse, the current was working against them. Try as he might, Harvey could not get within reach of Boyd in the giant whirlpool. Logs and other accumulated flotsam swirled in a dangerous, tangled mass, which made navigation all the more difficult. Desperate to rescue Boyd, Harvey changed tactics by propelling himself in the opposite direction to wait for Boyd to cycle around. However, while Harvey was holding steady, the eddy flung Boyd back into the main current, sending him downstream again.

Almost immediately, Boyd got sucked into another, larger eddy on the right side of the river at mile 62 1/2. Harvey wrote that this revolving morass "seemed as big as three tennis courts."[1] Boatmen who have been caught in it at high water know it as one of the worst on the river. Harvey needed to paddle with everything he had just to penetrate its outer line. Even after making it inside, the pair made two lazy orbits before Harvey could finally grab Boyd's arm.

Between labored breaths, Harvey tried to calm his petrified friend. He spoke clearly and directly, telling Boyd not to panic. Harvey now realized why Boyd was hanging so low—he was still wearing his waterlogged backpack. After multiple commands, and with Harvey's help, Boyd jerkily freed himself of the anchor-like pack and even managed to climb atop his mattress.

For the moment, Boyd was safe.

But Harvey needed to get him to shore, somehow. He decided to try towing him as before. Harvey instructed Boyd to hold onto his feet while he paddled with all his might toward land. The two floated with the eddy's current to gain momentum. Although they passed within a few feet of a projecting rock several times in a row during repeated circuits, the eddy's current always proved too strong. The boils and whirlpools simply pushed them away. Harvey desperately struggled for another 45 minutes in this manner but with no success. Boyd's 165 pounds were just too much for him.

By now the two hikers had been in the chilly water for nearly two hours. They had also hiked at least 20 miles that day. Boyd stammered to Harvey, "I don't have much strength left." Harvey knew that time was fast running out on his own ability to function as well.

Harvey thought quickly, groping for a solution. If Boyd could just stay afloat on his own for a bit—and stay in the eddy's grasp—perhaps Harvey could get to shore and throw him a line. It seemed the only option left. It would mean letting Boyd go of course, which was risky. Boyd might easily slip under his mattress again and drown, or the river might yank him back into the main current and send him downstream. But this eddy was like a liquid black hole. It seemed unlikely that Boyd could escape it without a huge effort.

Harvey decided to take the gamble. He told Boyd to let go. Boyd had always trusted his older friend. His death grip on Harvey's feet relaxed.

The cycling current quickly separated them. Harvey pleaded with Boyd to try to paddle as he made his own desperate dash for shore. But before Harvey could reach the bank, the unthinkable happened: The fickle river pulled Boyd into the main current once again. At that moment, Harvey was at the opposite

---

[1] Later, Harvey identified this eddy as being just upstream from the wash that comes in from the west, north of the place where debris fell from the mid-air collision that occurred in 1956, aka "Crash Canyon."

end of the eddy, unable to do anything but watch as Boyd departed downstream. The gamble had failed.

In a moment of hope, Harvey saw Boyd turn sideways and prop himself up on his elbows in an attempt to keep his head above water. Just as quickly, however, Harvey's heart sank as Boyd rolled upside down again, slipping from view under his air mattress. Only his face poked above the water. Boyd's arms and legs clamped down for dear life as rigidly as before. He silently melted downstream into the growing dark, completely at the mercy of the implacable river.

"That was the last," Harvey wrote, "I would see of the best hiking friend I ever had."

Harvey made a frenzied effort to escape the eddy, freeing himself and hurrying downstream. He strained for some glimpse of Boyd. But he had disappeared.

Seven miles and three hours downstream from where he had entered the Colorado, Harvey was now not only exhausted, but also nearly in the throes of panic himself. He willed himself to keep paddling after Boyd until a small rapid knocked him underneath his mattress. His backpack immediately filled with water, as had happened to Boyd. Harvey was unwilling to jettison his belongings and struggled to get back atop his mattress. But like a punch-drunk boxer, Harvey was now barely hanging on.

The sun had set by now. Harvey's waning strength and the vague light convinced him to give up and save himself while he could. Already he could hear the ominous roar of Lava Canyon Rapid (at mile 65 1/2). He knew Boyd would have gone through this cataract, but there was nothing he could do for his friend now.

Harvey worked his way over to the south bank. His soggy backpack felt heavy as a boulder. But with a few strokes and one mighty heave he was soon climbing out of the river. He dumped the pack and ran blindly downstream. Thick brush and the dark made it impossible to search any further. Harvey stumbled about in shock, trying to fathom what had just happened. He returned to his pack and collapsed onto the sand.

After many minutes, he sat up and lit a small fire. He was too distraught to feel hunger but mechanically pushed a few bites down. He knew he needed to keep up his strength for the appalling job of hiking out the next morning to report Boyd missing. The remainder of the night passed in a surreal concoction of tortured thoughts and utter fatigue. Sleep proved impossible.

At first light the next morning, May 27, Harvey began searching for a sign of Boyd. "Walking along the bank the next day," Harvey wrote, "I prayed, hoping that somewhere I would see a miracle and that Boyd would be waiting for me on the bank; it was all a waking nightmare."

Harvey was now facing not only Boyd's death, but also the fact that it was *he* who had talked Boyd into going on this trip in the first place—*after* Boyd said

Lava Canyon Rapid. *Steve Miller*

he did not want to go, *after* Dock Marston had suggested they bring life jackets, and, *after* the park superintendent had warned in writing of the very dangers that had doomed Boyd.

At the foot of the Tanner Trail, Harvey dropped off Boyd's food. Maybe that miracle would still happen, perhaps Boyd might yet show up, famished and ready to hike out. As Harvey began the long trudge to the rim, guilt and grief hammered down in equal blows. He vomited in anguish, the dry heaves wracking his numb body. Nevertheless, he made it to ranger Joe Lynch's home at Desert View by 5 P.M. and weakly reported the calamity. "He [Harvey] was pretty upset," Lynch said, "and I felt bad for him. But I couldn't understand why anyone would do such a darn-fool stunt to begin with." The ranger began making arrangements for a search.

Harvey then called Roma and broke the news in a faltering voice. She nearly fainted. But the worst came when Harvey called Boyd's parents. Few griefs are as heartbreaking as the loss of a child, and as a father himself, Harvey knew full well the depths of suffering the Moores faced. He spoke with Boyd's father, Carl D. Moore, and explained the circumstances of Boyd's death.

Harvey's brand new son-in-law Sam Madariaga was fresh off his Las Vegas

Boyd Moore circa 1953.
Courtesy Anne Madariaga

honeymoon with Anne. He arrived at the South Rim to find Harvey incoherent with grief. Tears welled in both their eyes as Sam gave Harvey a pat on the shoulder. It would be the only time in over 50 years that Sam saw his stoic father-in-law cry. They drove home in silence.

Fifteen year-old Jim Butchart never forgot the look on his father's face when Harvey walked into their Flagstaff home. Jim had never before seen such raw despair and grief. A somber mood hung in the house for weeks. It was a sharp contrast to the joy and elation of Anne's wedding only days earlier. Roma, Jim, Anne, and Sam all felt Boyd's loss. The friendly young man had been a frequent visitor to the Butchart home.

"I was sick for a week in bed over that, emotionally," Harvey admitted, "and depressed for six months about that experience...I was no help for the search party."

On May 28, the NPS sent a search plane into the Canyon just above river level. They found nothing. On May 31, rangers Ken Patrick and Donald Black hiked down the Tanner Trail and then along the river but they too returned empty-handed. "The Park Service started a search along the banks for about a week," Harvey said, "but they didn't find anything. So he was gone."

A memorial service was held at the Federated Church in Flagstaff that was well attended by ASC students and faculty, and, of course, Harvey and his family. At the end of the month, Boyd's father arrived in Flagstaff to speak in person with Harvey, then drove to Grand Canyon to meet with Superintendent Patraw. Patraw had already begun contacting river runners to ask them to keep a lookout for a drowning victim.

One of those boatmen was Plez Talmadge "P.T." Reilly of Studio City, California. A former Norman Nevills boatman now running his own non-commercial trips, Reilly received a humble, hand-written letter from the Moores politely pleading for help with finding Boyd's remains and/or evidence of his fate:

Dear Mr. Reilly:

Mr. P.P. Patraw supentendt [sic] of Grand Canyon National Park Informed me that you were taking a trip down the Colorado river about June 20th.

As Mr. Patraw will inform you our son Carlton Boyd Moore was lost at the

Grand Canyon on May 26-55 trying to cross the river on an air mattress.

We would appreaceat [sic] any reports from you on what you might see on your trip.

We realize you are on a vacation and do not want to bothered with other Pepels [sic] Troubles but this is Very real to us, and we are not opposed to re-emburs [sic], for Information received.

Sincerly [sic],
Mr. + Mrs. Carl D. Moore
By: Carl D. Moore

Reilly's reply was inspired and heart-felt:

June 16, 1955
Dear Mr. and Mrs. Moore:

Please accept my sincere sympathy on the loss of your son Carlton Boyd. A life span cannot always be measured in chronological time, as some people live to be a hundred, yet experience little that life has to offer while others, more intense in their living, may condense several life times in a few short years.

You are to be commended for raising your son whose daring nature contended with aspects of his environment not ordinarily challenged by the average individual.

You may rest assured that I will utilize all my powers and experience to assist you in your tragic hour. Much depends on whether the river rises above its level succeeding the day your son was lost. Any news will be reported to you from Phantom Ranch if we are successful by then. Otherwise I will write you a full report at the end of my trip, which will be after July 8.

Sincerely,
P.T. Reilly

As fate would have it, when Reilly passed by Unkar Rapid at about river mile 72, six miles downstream from Lava Canyon Rapid, he spotted something on shore. He rowed over. It was Boyd's backpack, split open and empty.

Reilly found no other evidence of the lost man. Thinking it would not be of interest to the family, he left the pack on the beach. A short time later river runner Georgie White Clark picked it up and eventually brought it to the South Rim where it was discarded.

In the days and weeks following the incident, Harvey gave multiple interviews, all of them difficult. One of the toughest renditions was the one he gave to Dock Marston. Had he been wearing a life jacket, Boyd, in all likelihood, would have survived.

Somewhat uncharacteristically—for Dock had a reputation as a severe critic—Marston held off sending Harvey a scathing "I-told-you-so" letter, instead offering only a gentle reminder about the necessity of life jackets.

June 24, 1955
Canyoneer Harvey,

I am glad to get the details from you as you clear a number of points. I had not known that you had been with Moore but guessed it due to the relatively novel method of flotation.

I have recently been compiling the list of tragedies in the River in the Grand Canyon. There is no case of loss of life where there was a good boat, a life-preserver and the person was in good health. In line with your report, it is pertinent to note that most tragedy has been attended by panic, this started with the loss of the three men who left the first Powell party. They would not have left had it not been for panic in the leader.

The tragedy cannot be helped now but it can serve to provide means for prevention of other losses. I put down the life preserver as the most preventative measure.

I think we will have to judge navigation without a boat to be extra hazardous and only justified when done by expert swimmers. Even with them, I believe that a life preserver is essential. I swam Dubendorff Rapid without a preserver but was exhausted at the end.

In our cruises with motors, the top rule is the use of life preservers whenever anyone is afloat on the River.

Again my thanks. You know I regret the tragedy.

Truly,
Dock Marston

In all likelihood, Boyd drowned not long after drifting into Lava Canyon Rapid. No one will ever know. Though Harvey was never officially blamed for Boyd's death, it lingered on his conscience for the rest of his life. Forty years later, Harvey spoke frankly about his role in the drowning.

"He [Boyd] said something that really kind of burns into my consciousness every now and then," Harvey said. "That when we were short of water in getting down to Nankoweap Creek...he said, 'Well, we're in this thing together,' and he shared his last drink with me. I think of that remark, 'We're in this together,' and it turned out that I didn't stay with him, and take whatever was coming to him. I didn't share. That is something on my conscience."

Harvey also realized he failed to heed the warning signs. He later wrote it was "mostly bad judgment that I thought Boyd could handle it when he was so scared of water. Maybe if we'd stayed tied together..."

Hiker Lost While Attempting Air Mattress River Crossing

By BILL DEAVER

Search has been abandoned for Boyd Moore, 23-year-old graduate of ASC at Flagstaff who is presumed to have perished in the cold and muddy waters of the Colorado River Thursday afternoon.

Moore, who with Dr. JJ. Harvey Butchart of the ASC faculty, had hiked down from the north rim to see a newly-discovered natural

Moore became panicky ir water as they were crossing a three miles above the juncti the tributary Little Colorad was swept downstream.

The two had packs on backs and had reached mi current of the river gra Moore and took him downst his air mattress on top of Soon they were both caught

From the *Arizona Daily Sun*, 1955. *Courtesy Anne Madariaga*

When Harvey met with Boyd's father, he made a disturbing discovery. It was only then that Harvey learned of Boyd's near-drowning experience at age three in a Michigan river. Boyd, the elder Moore said, had never completely recovered from the incident.

Neither would Harvey.

Last known photograph of Boyd Moore, Point Imperial, May 24, 1955. *Dale Slocum*

Chapter Thirteen
LEGWORK FOR THE HISTORIAN
1955–1959

You certainly have been covering ground. It keeps me busy just following you on paper.
If you would let me know where you have ideas you may be going, I might be able to give you some leads of things to look for...

Dock Marston,
Letter to Harvey Butchart (1956)

WHEN THE CALLS FINALLY STOPPED and the reports were all made, Harvey divorced himself from Grand Canyon. His role in the incident remained unequivocal, and therefore tormenting. There could be no going back.

He tried to move on by being a good father, husband, and college professor. Harvey attended church regularly and relied on his faith to see him through, as his mother had when she experienced similar trauma. As the days and weeks turned to months, life slowly returned to a semblance of normalcy. But Harvey continued to question his own judgment and replay Boyd's final hours.

He led a few trips as sponsor of the college hiking club in the fall of 1955, taking his students to other destinations besides Grand Canyon. His attitude toward the hiking club changed. He now watched over his students more carefully, making sure not to lead them beyond their limits. Harvey vowed never to repeat the mistakes he made with Boyd.

Amidst his efforts to put the past behind, Harvey gradually began to feel a yearning to return to the Canyon. He missed hiking there, though that was only part of it; he was aching for closure to Boyd's death.

In November, he took a solo backpack trip to Clear Creek. This side canyon below the North Rim where he and Boyd camped on one of their last backpacking trips together meant a round-trip trek of 35 miles from the South Rim.

What passed through his mind as the trail passed beneath his feet is unknown, but clearly Harvey was in the midst of a psychological tug-of-war: The lure of Grand Canyon pulling in one direction, the specter of death pulling in the other.

Harvey snapped a few photos of the Canyon's tallest waterfall, Cheyava Falls, located in upper Clear Creek. Taking its name from a Hopi word meaning "ephemeral" (the falls run only rarely), Cheyava gave Harvey the chance to enjoy a fine spectacle. But the effect was fleeting. After spending the night, he decided that hiking in the Canyon again was tolerable but not wholly pleasant. Not yet. In the end, it failed to bring the reconciliation he yearned for.

Harvey waited another five months before returning. By April 1956, nearly a year had passed since Boyd died. It was time to revisit the scene of the tragedy. He backpacked alone down the Tanner Trail to the Colorado then upstream toward Palisades Creek. As he neared this tributary, Harvey saw Lava Canyon Rapid where Boyd disappeared and likely drowned. Harvey stepped to the bank, quietly observing and photographing the cataract. Then he walked to the spot where he had crawled ashore in his physically and emotionally drained state. The indifferent river hissed at him from beyond the willows.

After a few minutes, he continued toward the Little Colorado River, about four miles upstream, sticking close to the bank in order to scrutinize the stretch of eddies and riffles where he struggled to save his young friend. The spring flood was just beginning. Flotsam sailed past. Thoughts of that black day lingered in Harvey's mind.

As he clambered over small dunes, he eventually came to an abrupt cliff formed by the Tapeats Sandstone. This chocolate-colored, 200-foot escarpment demanded that he either walk atop its flat lid, or below, along a rough slope that angled steeply down to the river. Harvey chose the latter.

He soon began to have misgivings, for the cliff edged closer and closer to the river the farther upstream he went. Finally the bank pinched away to nothing. He was left facing a 30-foot wall rising straight out of the deep, swirling water. Looking north, he saw a colossal wedge of sedimentary rock named Chuar Butte towering directly opposite the mouth of the Little Colorado. Harvey reckoned he was within two miles of the confluence of the two rivers. He needed to retrace his steps and find another route.

Then something unexpected caught his eye. He stopped short and stared, trying to make sense of it. With the same surprise and curiosity anyone feels when finding a man-made relic in a place of profound desolation, Harvey drew closer for a better look. A makeshift ladder of driftwood poles leaned against a cliff covered in salt deposits. Only one rung remained, the others missing where rusted nails showed. Perhaps it was a miner's ladder, but leading to what?

Harvey wanted to find out, but even if
the crude artifact had been sound, he
decided he did not want to scale the
10 feet of vertical rock that waited
beyond its reach. Whatever the
unusual salt-draped wall and the mysterious ladder meant, it would have to
remain a mystery.

He retraced his steps to Palisades
Creek and made camp. Perhaps it was
a conscious act of atonement, choosing to sleep where he had spent the
worst night of his life a year earlier.
Thoughts of Boyd's death would never
completely leave him. But today, the
grief he had associated with the
Canyon for the past 11 months finally
began to fade, while his long-dormant
curiosity was reawakened. By the flick-
ering light of a driftwood fire, Harvey
mulled over the intriguing relic and
the salt cliff.

The crude ladder Harvey found in April
1956. *J. Harvey Butchart, courtesy NAU
Special Collections*

Once home from this soul-searching reconnaissance, Harvey sat down at his
typewriter and composed a letter to Dock Marston, the first time in a year that he
had written his Canyon pen pal. Harvey figured if anyone knew something about
the old ladder, it was Marston.

Glad to receive news that Harvey was back in the Canyon again, the river
historian quickly replied that there had long been a rumor of gold at the mouth
of the Little Colorado River. This indeed attracted prospectors to the area in
the late 1800s, but Marston surmised that the ladder pointed toward another
possibility. What lured the first miners to the Little Colorado, wrote Marston,
was not gold but *salt.*

Harvey, it turned out, may have stumbled upon a clue to one of Marston's
latest fixations: The hunt for two sacred Hopi Indian connections to Grand
Canyon—a long lost salt quarry, and a mythic doorway to the spirit world
known as the *Sipapuni.*

Marston had been searching for both for several years. He was excited by what
Harvey found, and immediately suggested that Harvey take over the hunt.
Marston had long recognized Harvey's potential as a backcountry explorer and
fellow Grand Canyon historian, and was now reentering Harvey's life at a crucial

time. It is no exaggeration to suggest that Harvey may have given up on Grand Canyon were it not for Marston's encouragement in April 1956. Of course, Marston did have some personal motivations. With a backlog of stories such as the Hopi sites to investigate in the backcountry, and with no illusions as to his own abilities as a hiker, Marston knew Harvey could do the legwork for him. "I am openly in admiration of your vim on getting over the trails," wrote Marston. "It's a good job but a strenuous one."

More than anything, Marston simply wanted his friend to get back into Grand Canyon. Dock had exercised restraint to allow Harvey time to get over Boyd, but he jumped when Harvey reported the strange ladder at the salt cliff.

Dock began by telling Harvey what he had learned of the Hopi salt expedi-

Otis "Dock" Marston. *The Huntington Library, San Marino, California*

tion, the story that formed the basis of his search. For centuries, the Hopis had performed an annual ritual of trekking 80 miles from their home at the southern tip of Black Mesa to the bottom of Grand Canyon to gather salt. The Hopis prized this sacred salt for ceremonial use and believed it brought good fortune to the entire tribe. The trek also served as a rite of passage for young men. The way was rough, the rituals exacting, and depending on the pilgrims's behavior and thoughts while trekking, the spiritual implications could be either beneficial or disastrous.

Marston told Harvey where to find a record of the last known Hopi salt trek, which had taken place in 1912. Yale scientist Mischa Titiev had interviewed a Hopi man who took part in that final pilgrimage. Titiev then published his account in the 1937 book *Sun Chief: The Autobiography of a Hopi Indian*. Sun Chief was Don C. Talayesva, a member of the Sun Clan from the village of Oraibi on Third Mesa, the oldest continuously inhabited settlement in North America. Talayesva gave Titiev a general description of the long route his party used to reach the salt source, which was located somewhere along the Colorado River.

After Talayesva's 1912 journey, Hopi interest in the Canyon's salt withered, for white traders began to provide salt much more readily. By 1956, the tribe including Talayesva himself had forgotten the details of the journey. *Sun Chief* thus became the only available "map" for locating the old route, the salt source, and, hopefully somewhere along the way, the sacred spring known as the *Sipapuni.*

Harvey was at first intrigued, and then inspired by what Dock told him, and agreed to continue the hunt on his own. He quickly found two items of interest in *Sun Chief* that seemed to offer important clues. Talayesva explained that the War Twins, a pair of brother-deities, had pioneered the route down the Little Colorado River gorge to the salt source. These mythical beings turned themselves to stone at critical points in the journey to help future travelers find their way. The first War Twin did so at the rim of a defile named Salt Trail Canyon to mark the correct spot to descend toward the Little Colorado. The other chose to become a rock that served as a necessary rappel anchor, just above the final cliff near the river.

Talayesva's vague description of the route and the salt source indeed proved difficult to decipher. But Harvey was able to locate where the Hopis had started down from the rim of the Little Colorado. He noticed on his map that a Salt Trail Canyon met the Little Colorado River six-and-a-half miles upstream from the river's mouth. Beyond this detail, however, he knew little else of the route. From a 1965 article Harvey wrote for *Arizona Highways* titled "The Lower Gorge of the Little Colorado":

> Sun Chief related that when they came to the junction of the two rivers, they followed the Colorado, but he failed to specify whether they went up or downstream. Since he was a boy of seventeen when he went on the famed pilgrimage and it was twenty-five years later when he gave his verbal account, it is hardly to be wondered at if he was sometimes a bit unclear about minor landmarks along the trail. He did, however, recall that at the end of the trail it was necessary to use a rope to get down to the river. He was also definite in remembering a peculiar rock where they fastened the rope. This rock, shaped like a man's chest, was where a demigod had changed himself into stone…

Using these clues, Marston suspected an obvious deposit of salt he had seen five miles upstream from the mouth of the Little Colorado, near Kwagunt Rapid. He told Harvey that he doubted the salt mine could be located in the area of the old ladder. "I cannot recall any special deposit of salt in the Canyon about three or four miles below the mouth of the Little Colorado," Marston wrote. "There is plenty at the Kwagunt site." And, Marston added, Kwagunt was located around a bend in the river, which agreed with Talayesva's account.

Harvey decided to start his search by covering the stretch from Salt Trail Canyon to Kwagunt Rapid. A month after his hike to the mysterious ladder, he started off. He wasn't familiar with the confusing maze of reservation roads that led to the head of Salt Trail Canyon, so he chose to go at it in reverse. He descended the Tanner Trail, headed upstream to the Little Colorado, and then continued six-and-a-half miles up the Little Colorado toward Salt Trail Canyon.

An impressive, deeply sculpted drainage, the gorge of the Little Colorado River runs for nearly 60 sinuous miles from the Navajo Reservation town of Cameron before ending at Grand Canyon. By virtue of its steeply graded bed, which drops an average of 28 feet per mile (more than three times that of the Colorado in Grand Canyon), the river has cut a dramatic, narrow slit in the surface of the Colorado Plateau. The extensive upstream drainage basin runs dry much of the year, leaving the bed a largely dehydrated mud flat snaking between locomotive-sized boulders. But closer to the Colorado, a perennial flow equal to three times that of the next largest Grand Canyon tributary, Havasu Creek, bubbles up from Blue Springs at a rate of 300 cfs. The high concentration of calcium carbonate in the water creates a powder-blue river (when it's not pumped full of flash flood silt from upstream tributaries), hence the name for the spring.

Flanked by 3,400-foot reddish-brown walls, the turquoise water produces an improbable scene of great contrast. Small travertine dams form numerous lagoons, lending an almost Caribbean appearance. Were it not located adjacent to Grand Canyon, this stretch of the Little Colorado would likely have been made a national park, but back in the 1950s it remained nearly unknown. As far as Harvey knew, no one had ever made a full descent of the "Little C" on foot. He described his first impression of the gorge after peering down from its rim in 1945:

> This gorge is different from anything we had seen. At first you may wonder whether there is a bottom below those walls and towers. Of course there is, but down there it seems like a different world. Could a walker follow that sandy riverbed? Would he meet some impossible waterfall or go crazy hemmed in by prison walls for so many miles?

Although Harvey's reason for venturing there in May 1956 had more to do with sleuthing, he became enamored of this wilderness on his initial visit. Indeed, he soon embarked on a personal project to rediscover all of the routes that penetrate the canyon. He also wanted to be the first to walk its complete length. During that first hike into the gorge's depths, it must have been alluring indeed, an unexplored, wild canyon where Indians previously traveled on a sacred journey. An impressed Harvey wrote:

Each bend in the canyon presents another terrific vista of upsurging walls cut by ravines into towers and ramparts. My senses could only appreciate a limited amount of this overpowering grandeur, and I began to notice the little things—a deer track or a water ouzel doing its dipping curtsy between dives. A few men have come and gone here, but the wilderness remains as it has been for a million years.

The Hopis believe that the Little Colorado gorge marks the birthplace of all mankind. As he made his way upstream, fording the river here and there by walking across travertine bridges, Harvey easily understood their conviction. The unlikely river and the utter isolation lent a mythic atmosphere to the awesomely deep chasm.

Harvey was struck with wonder when he came upon a unique spectacle a few miles upstream. This was the place where legend became reality: The origin of all life to the Hopi, the *Sipapuni*. Harvey had never seen anything like it. An elevated mineral spring made of travertine, about 40 feet high and 75 feet wide at the base, the *Sipapuni* formed a doorway between two worlds, according to Hopi belief. Talayesva explained that the first people and deities to inhabit this world, the Fourth World, had ascended from the Third World and the pool inside the dome by using a reed as a ladder.

Harvey walked atop the *Sipapuni*, as Talayesva had done. He gazed into the five-foot-wide hole where spring water arose mysteriously from inside the great mound, noticing that a Hopi prayer stick, or pahoe, had been placed beside it. Talayesva had indeed mentioned that his group deposited pahoes at the *Sipapuni* in 1912. Harvey also inspected the spot beside the spring where Talayesva had collected yellow clay that would later be used for ceremonial purposes.

After taking a few photos, Harvey continued to follow the Hopi route upstream. Picking his way through brush, over rocks, and along gravel bars, he went two miles until meeting the first major side canyon coming in from the north: Salt Trail Canyon. He detoured up this drainage toward the rim, noticing that Hopis had piled bright red pieces of chert upon boulders here and there, while petroglyphs and clan symbols appeared on other boulders. Once at the rim, Harvey encountered the younger War Twin shrine, where the deity had turned himself to stone. "I realized how much more this trip would mean to a Hopi believer," he wrote, "than to a vacationing mathematics professor."

Having found two of three objectives, the *Sipapuni* and the first War Twin, his focus swung back to the Hopi salt mine. He considered what Marston had told him about the site, but something failed to add up. Although Talayesva had stated that it "was around a bend in the river," and the Kwagunt site indeed fit this description, Talayesva had also said a rappel was necessary. During his hike past Kwagunt with Boyd the previous year, Harvey had noted that one could merely walk the bank to the site Marston had suggested. Could Talayesva be wrong in remembering "the need for a rope" to scale a cliff at the site? Perhaps Dock's hunch was wrong. Harvey decided to head home and gather more information before making his next move.

Unfortunately, his next move would have to wait. A few weeks after Harvey's trek, the worst airline catastrophe up to that time took place when two full passenger planes collided 18,000 feet above the mouth of the Little Colorado, killing 128 people. The collision scattered grisly debris over the terrain west of the confluence with the Colorado, and park authorities closed the area to all except investigators of the disaster. Almost 14 months would pass before Harvey could continue hunting for the salt mine.

But the interruption did little to slow him down. Harvey's passion for exploring had returned. It was now stronger than ever, thanks to Marston and his infectious zeal for Grand Canyon history. Theirs was a powerful bond, this shared passion for the gorge, and Dock was going to show Harvey just how deep you could get into it.

That summer, the two canyoneers met for the first time when Harvey drove to Lee's Ferry, where Dock was rigging for a river trip. They gabbed as long as time would allow before Marston finally had to launch his boat. Harvey may have watched after him wistfully. The river stories Marston told, and the sight of his boat floating downriver, once again fired Harvey's urge to get on an air mattress.

Memories of Boyd Moore still haunted him. But Harvey decided that although he would never again be responsible for another person on the river, he had never lost confidence in his own abilities, or his method. As long as he went solo, he reasoned, he could float the river again.

This time he decided to venture elsewhere, for not all of Marston's river tales had centered on Grand Canyon. Dock told Harvey that one place he must see was Glen Canyon, and two months later, in August, Harvey decided to take Dock's advice. He began planning a solo mattress float through Grand Canyon's sister gorge, which wound for 170 miles upstream into southern Utah.

There had been a recent surge of public fascination with Glen Canyon. In October 1956, the Bureau of Reclamation announced plans to begin construction on a dam 16 miles upstream from Lee's Ferry. Scheduled for full operation by 1963, Glen Canyon Dam would not only flood Glen Canyon, it also would make swimming and air mattress activities in Grand Canyon a practical impossibility due to the resulting great drop in the river's year-round temperature.

Harvey figured he better see Glen Canyon while he had the chance. From a

1960 feature-length article in *Appalachia* magazine called "Backpacking on the Colorado":

> By the summer of 1956 I had heard enough about the scenic boat trip down the San Juan to want to try it for myself. The lowest professional rate for the ride was $100; I also wanted the thrill of being my own skipper and I wanted to demonstrate the feasibility of my system. No one seemed to care to share the experience, so I did it solo.

Harvey made arrangements to be dropped off at Mexican Hat, Utah, one of the put-in points for Glen Canyon river trips. From Mexican Hat, he would float the San Juan River to its confluence with the Colorado in Glen Canyon, then ride the Colorado all the way to Lee's Ferry. Few rapids stirred the Colorado in Glen Canyon, thus making for a far less hazardous outing than running Grand Canyon. Those who floated Glen Canyon did so not for the excitement of whitewater, but rather for the Glen's mesmerizing beauty and for the diversity of its numerous, various side canyons.

Harvey carried rations for 10 days and a rough list of tributaries he wished to explore. Floating in the warm, silty San Juan was easy, especially in the low water of August; there were few whirlpools, no fast currents, no significant holes or falls. This was a run that invited contemplation. For two days Harvey drifted lazily below red sedimentary rock walls, attended to by only the occasional squawking raven or singing canyon wren.

He soon lost track of where he was. He could only guess at the identification of the side canyons that he passed such as Grand Gulch and Slickhorn Gulch. By the time he reached Paiute Farms, a tributary on the Navajo Reservation (south) side of the river, he finally encountered a "touch of civilization" and exchanged waves with an Indian couple. They stared at the improbable visage of the floating *bilagana* (a Navajo term for "white man"). Harvey imagined them wondering about the "strange way of

Harvey floats Glen Canyon solo, 1956.
Courtesy Anne Madariaga

some whites." He had become a bit lonely, and felt like talking to someone, but knew the Indians might not speak English. He kept going.

Harvey camped alone that night on a beach at the mouth of Copper Canyon. The following day the San Juan deposited him onto the smooth, bronze-hued Colorado. Navajo Sandstone cliffs painted in black desert varnish rose hundreds of feet from the water's edge. At 10,388 feet, Navajo Mountain stood guard over the confluence of the two rivers. Many agreed that this arresting and wild section of the Glen marked one of the finest stretches of the entire Colorado. On the other hand, the oven-like walls made it all tremendously hot. Harvey stayed cool by dipping himself in the quiet river and seeking shade in side canyons.

Scores of inviting tributaries passed his slowly moving craft, each an elegant portrayal of sculpted rock, each a work in progress that changed with every flash flood. Many had never been named. Harvey spent his first night on the Colorado at Hidden Passage, a narrow slit that merged seamlessly with the main canyon walls so as to be nearly invisible to passers-by. Once inside the subtle fissure it opened into tall, smooth-walled chambers floored by pools of clear water. Reflected sunglow cast this interior world in varying shades of red and orange. Struck by the spectral beauty, Harvey lamented Glen Canyon's forthcoming loss to the soon-to-be-rising waters of Lake Powell:

> As I walked up this famous glen among the ferns and flowers, I enjoyed the luxury of the first clean bath of the trip. The next morning I crossed the river and followed a trail through the willows to the back of Powell's Music Temple. Here one can still see the names of Powell's men. It seems a shame that the resonant acoustics of this beautiful chamber will be stilled forever by the rising waters of the lake named for the man who loved this spot.

From Music Temple, Harvey kept his eyes peeled for Forbidding Canyon, where a route led to Rainbow Bridge, the largest natural bridge in the world. But he missed the correct beach and floated by without stopping. He spent his fifth night upstream of West Canyon. Harvey was nearing Last Chance Creek the next day when the *Rattlesnake*, a motorboat piloted by river runner Rod Sanderson, buzzed by en route to Rainbow Bridge. Sanderson stopped to visit with the unusual air mattress floater. After a 125-mile run, and with much of Glen Canyon behind him, Harvey was ready to call it quits. He took Sanderson up on his offer to give him a lift to Lee's Ferry and saw the rest of the doomed canyon at a much faster clip.

Marston was impressed with Harvey's latest adventure. Dock sent a letter to convey his respect, and to entice Harvey into more Grand Canyon adventures by including a list of various backcountry mysteries that needed clearing up. Most of them meant off-trail bushwhacking, so Harvey could look forward to seeing something new no matter what he chose. Dock's conundrums appealed to Harvey's love of problem solving and offered what Harvey called "a consistent program of exploration."

Harvey's next bit of legwork for the historian proved fateful, for it sent him off the rim of Grand Canyon in search of a new way to reach the river. This sort of challenge ultimately became Harvey's most consuming passion—discovering his own rim-to-river routes. It happened for the first time on the eastern flanks of the North Rim, at a point where a river-man-turned-prospector had clambered down to the Colorado decades earlier.

Dock told Harvey the story of Harry McDonald. McDonald had been a member of the 1890 Robert Stanton river expedition. Tensions arose during the trip that persuaded McDonald to desert his boat mates and strike out on his own into the unexplored backcountry of Crystal Creek. He managed to ascend the North Rim via an unknown route (which Harvey would one day investigate as well) and made it as far as Kanab, Utah before stopping.

McDonald bought supplies in the small Mormon town, loaded everything onto his burros and then returned to the Kaibab Plateau. He intended to prospect near the Colorado River in the vicinity of Lava Creek. After crossing the Kaibab, McDonald led his burros somewhere off the east side of the Walhalla Plateau down through the cliffs to the river.

Marston wanted to know where McDonald managed to achieve this feat. No one knew of a route between the Nankoweap Trail and the North Kaibab Trail, a distance of 35 river miles. Marston suggested that a promontory named Cape Final would have been the most logical place for McDonald to descend. Harvey drove to the North Rim in the summer of 1957 to look into it.

He started by walking east on a compass bearing through the forest from the paved Walhalla Plateau road not far from Cape Royal, making his way to Naji Point. From this vista, he could see the series of cliffs along Dock's suggested route below Cape Final. The route appeared promising. Harvey could read small details in faraway ridges and walls that would indicate whether a person might be able to climb through otherwise impossible-looking terrain. He did this in much the same way a boatman might scout a navigable line through a hazardous rapid. With a general route sketched in his mind, Harvey headed toward Cape Final to begin.

Setting foot off the rim without a trail would be dangerous. Loose rocks presented a constant hazard, steep grades promised to make a return hike extremely taxing, dense thickets of thorny vegetation tangled the way, and, of course, if something went wrong, no one would happen along to offer help. On top of all this, there was no guarantee of success for the hard work.

Harvey reached the edge at Cape Final and allowed gravity to draw his body down the duff-covered slopes. He grabbed trees and boulders to use as brakes, sliding his way through the Kaibab and Toroweap layers. At the top of the Coconino Sandstone, he noticed a lack of deer trails leading down—not a promising sign—but continued anyway until he faced a 40-foot drop off that no burro could manage. Clearly, he had not found McDonald's route.

But this was part of the game, the hunt for the correct variable in a long chain of possibilities. Harvey knew this failure meant at least one step forward in knowledge. After returning to the rim and his car, he decided to have a look at another possibility just up the road. He drove a couple of miles north and spied a clear way to get down from a promontory named Atoko Point. Even though he had scheduled a meeting with a friend later in the day, he rushed over to try it.

Harvey again scrambled all the way to the bottom of the Coconino Sandstone, a vertical distance of about 800 feet, before being stopped by another sheer drop. Still refusing to quit, he panted back up to the rim, checked the next bay to the south and spotted a deer trail leading down.

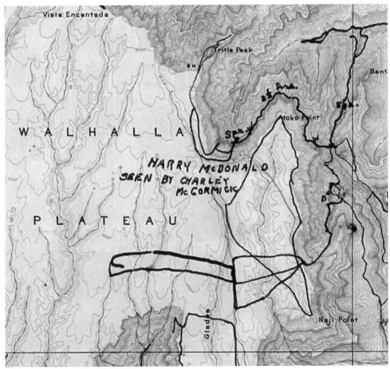

Harvey's notes and route near Atoko Point. *Courtesy NAU Special Collections*

Impulsively, he went for it, descending for the third time that day. This time, he succeeded in walking all the way through the Coconino. He would have kept going too, but time forced him to turn back. Later he returned and discovered that this route indeed allowed one to descend all the way to McDonald's mines along the river.

As he dusted himself off at the rim and shook the pine needles from his sweaty head, Harvey felt a wave of hard-won satisfaction. He had just achieved his first route-finding victory in Grand Canyon.

He felt fascinated by stepping where no one had been in decades. It meant confronting the sort of raw challenges that only a pioneering explorer could know. Genuine discoveries might be made, ranging from hidden beauty spots to untouched Anasazi ruins to never-before-photographed natural bridges. Harvey's experience at Atoko Point had a transforming effect. He would thenceforth gravitate almost exclusively to routes, ignoring the established trails in Grand Canyon as objectives, hiking them only as necessary to reach a particular piece of unexplored backcountry. He was still sponsor of the hiking club and would make his share of humdrum treks with greenhorn students, but seen through the portal opened to him by Dock Marston, Grand Canyon suddenly held unlimited possibilities for exploration.

Marston made sure to encourage Harvey by heaping praise upon him for his success. Dock's respect was genuine. He was astonished by Harvey's singular determination, his uncanny knack for a route or a lead buried in some book. Dock carbon-copied for Harvey the following letter to a friend:

> I have wondered a lot about Harvey. Just what is the drive? And you are correct—who would think it just to meet him?
>
> I rather imagine [miner John] Hance did some of the same thing but not with the zeal of Harvey...
>
> You can do me a real favor if you can slow that Harvey down so he can take a little more time to look—and to take pictures so I can get prints.

With Marston forming such an attentive and eager audience, Harvey became all the more inspired. And Marston's projects kept piling up, 20 or 30 in all. Harvey's passion for Grand Canyon grew in proportion. "As we have said before," he wrote to Marston, "there are enough interesting places to visit along the Grand Canyon to keep one busy for a lifetime."

EVEN THOUGH THE AIR WRECK and subsequent closure of the mouth of Little Colorado had halted Harvey's search for the Hopi salt mine, an illuminating clue came to his attention in the intervening months. He found a second account of the 1912 Hopi salt trek in *Sun Chief,* Don Talayesva's biography (edited by Leo Simmons). Talayesva's description of the salt mine proved essentially the same as that in the previous account Harvey had read, except for one very significant difference: Talayesva stated that about 30 feet from the spot where the Hopis rappelled down the final cliff to the river, they saw a ladder of driftwood poles made by a white man. Harvey, remembering the ladder from his earlier trip, now knew that he had already been within one rappel of the Hopi salt source.

In the fall of 1957 the restricted area near the mouth of the Little Colorado was reopened, and by May of 1958 Harvey was hiking toward the ladder. Walking along the Beamer Trail near the confluence of the two rivers, he watched closely for the ravine where he could go down to the ladder and the salt. He scrambled down and soon found himself facing a 30-foot drop to the riverbank.

Allyn Cureton lays a hand upon the second War Twin rock, just above the Colorado. *J. Harvey Butchart, courtesy NAU Special Collections*

This was the right place—I could now see the ladder. I crawled under an overhang to a pocket directly above the ladder, but I was afraid to test the crumbling wind-eroded ledges below. I even had some bad moments while getting back. I must have been a bit shaken, for I forgot to look for the fabulous rope-support rock that is shaped like a man's chest. Halfway to the Beamer Trail above, I remembered it and went back to look. It is in plain sight, the most peculiar example of erosion of bedrock I have ever seen in the bed of a wash. It stands out like a saddle horn a foot in diameter, and it is located exactly where you need to fasten a rope for the shortest rappel.

Harvey had found the elder War Twin who turned himself to stone. He wanted to be able to "provide a full report" complete with pictures. But he had already used all his film, so would have to return yet again. At home, he quickly wrote letters to Marston and NPS backcountry ranger Dan Davis, telling them how to find the mine. He promised to return and make definitive pictures in cooler weather unless they beat him to it.

As it turned out, someone else did get there first. Davis passed the word about the mine's location to Fred Eiseman Jr., a writer and outdoorsman. Eiseman had been interested in repeating the Hopi expedition for years. His wife, Margaret, had even glimpsed the ladder from the river during a river trip in the summer of 1956. Using Harvey's directions, Eiseman and two friends hiked down Salt Trail Canyon, then along the Little Colorado to the salt cliff. There they rappelled down off the War Twin rock, found the cave, and made the first photographs of the Hopi salt source.

Eiseman had the salt analyzed and published a full account in the October 1959 issue of *Plateau*, the journal of the Museum of Northern Arizona. Eiseman was gracious enough to acknowledge his debt to Harvey by writing, "In May 1958, J. H. Butchart of Flagstaff, Arizona, on a solo hike in the vicinity of the Little Colorado River all but discovered the salt mine." Yet Eiseman mentioned little of Harvey's extensive legwork. Because Harvey failed

Allyn Cureton rappels off the second War Twin rock to reach the Hopi salt source. *J. Harvey Butchart, courtesy NAU Special Collections*

169

to make the last rappel of the 13-mile route to the salt caves, Eiseman felt the discovery of the mine was still up for grabs. Thus it was Eiseman's party that garnered credit for the "discovery." Harvey later told Marston in a letter that he wasn't bitter; he just wished he had been invited.

Not to be completely outdone, Harvey returned in 1959 shortly after the *Plateau* article appeared. This time he brought a young student friend named Allyn Cureton, a skilled climber from the railroad town of Williams. With Cureton's help, Harvey rappelled over the cliff using the War Twin rock as an anchor. After so much detective work and so many months of waiting, reaching the salt cave at last proved exciting and gratifying. Harvey had unearthed that which had supposedly been "lost" for the previous five decades.

He owed this victory to Marston and his all-consuming Canyon fanaticism. In 1970, Harvey acknowledged Marston's impact in his guidebook, *Grand Canyon Treks:*

> For suggesting projects pertaining to the history of the Canyon, Otis "Dock" Marston was outstanding. From his voluminous files he has sent me copies of pictures, letters and articles. More than anyone else, Dock Marston has maintained my enthusiasm for exploring the Grand Canyon.

Not only did Marston supply Harvey with information and ideas, he also connected him with others in the Canyon community. In 1958, Dock introduced Harvey to his on-again, off-again friend, P.T. Reilly, the man who had found Boyd Moore's backpack. Reilly was a proud, sensitive river historian in his own right who predictably locked horns with Marston on numerous occasions. During one of their friendly stretches, Dock wrote the following letter to both Harvey and Reilly, which began a decades-long correspondence between the two:

July 22, 1958
Canyoneer Pat,

> If you get the opportunity, make a point of having an evening with Harvey Butchart in Flagstaff. He lives at 907 West Summit Avenue. I am sending him a carbon of this letter.
>
> Harvey knows the trails of the Canyon far beyond anyone else. He is the one who dug out the trail to the head of Grapevine. He has a fine collection of 35mm color.
>
> His trouble is something like yours. You go like hell flying over the country and he goes like hell walking the trails. If we can get him slowed down a

few seconds, the increase in pix record will mount hundreds of percent—but he gets some telling pix just the same altho [sic] how he does it remains a mystery...

Reilly too, soon suggested projects for Harvey to look into. For example, Reilly had spotted Keyhole Natural Bridge in 140-Mile Canyon from the air, and asked Harvey to hike there in order to make photographs. Harvey willingly obliged, but this poses a question: Was he starting to feel used by the likes of Marston and Reilly?

Apparently not. Such trips served Harvey's needs too, after all. By now Harvey was well aware, however, that Dock harbored a dark side. "The problem with Dock Marston," Harvey wrote, "was that he spent his time thinking of the weakness of people, rather than their strengths and virtues." Harvey tried to stay out of Marston's numerous feuds with other prominent canyoneers, but since these feuds happened so often, Harvey often became an unwilling participant in Marston's drama.

Naturally, Harvey became curious about what Marston said behind *his* back. True, he had given Dock a fine opportunity to lambaste him following Boyd's death, an opportunity Marston had gracefully passed up. Still, Harvey wondered.

In 1963, his doubts came to the surface after Reilly and Marston had a falling out. In the aftermath, Reilly suggested to Harvey that he thought Marston was using Harvey.

Harvey confronted Dock in a letter about Reilly's accusation:

> Pat once said that you had only divulged enough about the Hopi Salt to get me to do the legwork. Then he thought that you would combine what I could tell you with what two or three others could contribute and wind the story up over your name.

Marston pooh-poohed this notion. He replied:

> ...[Reilly] is always suspicious, which of course, reveals his own concern over what he is doing....Basically I feel the Canyon is big enough for a thousand serious students. Unfortunately, there are too many who want to look at the Rim and get someone else to do all the work—then they put it into print and gather the credits.

Marston proveed true to his word. He never exploited Harvey as Reilly suggested. Dock only wanted Harvey to keep up the exploration, and for this,

Harvey remained his friend.

Harvey's appetite for achievement and redemption had not just been revived—it had grown beyond all previous bounds. Yet Marston was not the only one who deserved thanks for this transformation. In 1957, Grand Canyon's reigning climber showed Harvey just how one could ascend to greatness. That path led not down some off-trail route, but rather down and *up*—atop the summits of Grand Canyon's forbidding buttes.

Harvey at the Hopi salt source, 1959. *Courtesy Allyn Cureton*

Chapter Fourteen

THE G. C. TRAMP
1957–1958

No matter how many trips you have made, you always return knowing there is much you haven't yet seen, even some places no one has ever been. Nobody knows all about Grand Canyon and probably no individual ever will. It is fantastically complicated.

Professor Merrel D. Clubb (1953)

HARVEY ENJOYED GETTING up in the wee hours while it was still dark. Sometimes, he lounged in bed a bit while waiting for the sun or a companion to rise. On the morning of May 28, 1957, Harvey was reading a magazine in his sleeping bag in Grand Canyon when a flash brightened the pre-dawn sky: A 12-kiloton nuclear "test" in Nevada, about 65 miles northwest of Las Vegas.

That year the American government was detonating nukes on its own soil on a near-monthly basis. Instead of foreign enemies, the desert bore the brunt of our Cold War arms buildup. The Colorado Plateau, including Grand Canyon, harbors an abundance of uranium in certain of its sedimentary rocks, which worked in America's favor— both mining and weapons testing could be prudently restricted to the Southwest, a sparsely populated area of the country.

The blast served as a grim

"Boltzman," a 12-kiloton nuclear bomb, detonates on May 28, 1957. *U.S. Department of Energy photograph*

reminder of the world's doings. But also provided an interesting diversion for Harvey and hiking pal Allyn Cureton. Cureton, an ASC hiking club member, had observed such explosions from his home in nearby Williams. He smartly predicted from his sleeping bag that they would hear the bomb's report in 21 minutes. As they packed up, they checked their watches at the appointed time. The unearthly rumble shook the ground exactly when Cureton had said it would. They quickly left camp.

The two hikers were on their final day of an off-trail marathon, circumambulating the South Rim peninsula called Great Thumb Mesa. They had set out to follow in the footsteps of Edwin D. McKee, a ranger-naturalist who wrote one of the few published accounts of bushwhacking in the Canyon in the book *The Inverted Mountains: Canyons of the West.* McKee's Boy Scout troop leader in Washington, D.C. had been none other than cartographer Francois Matthes, and his secretary at the Museum of Northern Arizona was none other than Roma Butchart. With characteristic confidence, Harvey chose to mimic McKee's 90-mile trek in only three days, something that Cureton—an avid runner who could easily keep pace with Harvey—readily agreed to.

Part of the reason for such a workout had to do with scheduling, as Harvey did not want to miss his son's high school graduation that evening. As fast as he and Cureton were moving, however, Harvey decided to cut his plan short that afternoon by climbing 1,200 feet to the rim at Hamidrik Point so that they could trot along a dirt road back toward the car. Harvey did make it to Jim's ceremony in time, but the near miss was indicative of Harvey's changing priorities. Just about everything—outside of the more pressing family events and teaching—now took a backseat to his blossoming obsession. Grand Canyon presented a constant, nearby temptation that he was less and less willing to resist. Like that nuclear bomb, Harvey's level of involvement with the gorge was about to explode.

As a measure of how things changed in 1957, Harvey notched 43 days and over 500 miles below the rim that year—equal to what he had done in the previous six years combined. The hikes themselves became more and more intense, sometimes bordering on the outlandish. In April he made an 85-mile solo loop hike in four days, from Hermit's Rest to the Bass Trail and back along the South Rim. It was as if he had been pulled back in a slingshot for the past dozen years, the tension growing until it finally released him with terrific speed into the abyss.

His fervor expressed itself in other ways besides the mega-hikes. One of Harvey's favorite pursuits included talking to the old-timers who had preceded him at the Canyon. He learned a great deal by chatting with Emery Kolb, a permanent South Rim resident since before Harvey was born. Emery's brother, Ellsworth, had arrived in 1901 at Grand Canyon from the Kolbs's native state of Pennsylvania. Emery joined him in 1903, whereupon the pair of photographers established the famous Kolb Studio. Although Ellsworth had parted from his brother in 1924 and moved to California, Emery had kept the business running ever since.

The Kolbs had done their share of exploring over the years. Emery was familiar with much of the territory laying within sight of their studio, including Shiva Temple, a broad, flat-topped 7,618-foot mesa standing at the eastern edge of the Hindu Amphitheater, just south of the Kaibab Plateau. In 1937, Emery had made it a point to beat a well-funded team of scientists to the top of Shiva, which earned Kolb the honor of making the first recorded ascent of this inner Canyon butte.

At the Kolb Studio in May 1957, after watching the Kolbs's film that documented their 1911 epic Colorado River journey, Harvey asked Kolb about Shiva Temple. What Harvey learned from Emery about the route convinced him to give Shiva a try. He figured as long as Cureton—his trustiest sidekick since Boyd Moore—would join as his climbing partner, Shiva should be his next project.

In early June, the two friends made the 200-mile-long drive to Tiyo Point on the Kaibab Plateau, where they began their climb. It took an entire day of route finding through the woods just to descend 1,500 feet to the saddle connecting the North Rim to Shiva. They started their ascent early the next morning and scrambled up Shiva's steep but forgiving walls until a short cliff forced them to negotiate a narrow chimney. Harvey made it above this obstacle with Cureton's help, from which point they were able to continue to the summit.

Like a big game hunter, Harvey had bagged his first butte-climbing trophy.[1] He and Cureton scoured the

Harvey inspects a pre-Columbian agave roasting pit while en route to Shiva Temple, June 1957. *Courtesy Allyn Cureton*

---

[1] This is the first butte Harvey climbed according to his logs, though it is possible he may have climbed another butte earlier without mentioning it.

wild mesa top and found Anasazi potsherds, indicating that the Indians had beaten Kolb for the honor of first ascent hundreds of years earlier. But it was the panoramic view that really grabbed Harvey. The fact that he could now survey the Canyon from *within* it, instead of from the rim, lent a whole new perspective to an otherwise familiar scene. The pair ate their lunch with feet dangling over the edge, enjoying the swath of butte-studded country falling away from Shiva on three sides.

Shiva was similar to those Fourteeners in Colorado, only with this difference: Harvey had never heard of people climbing the Canyon's buttes for the hell of it. In fact, no one seemed to bother with these summits, while elsewhere in the West, such as in Yosemite and in the Grand Tetons, climbing was experiencing its golden age as an American sport.

Harvey returned to the Kaibab Plateau one month later, on July 4, this time for a solo trek to nearby Widforss Point. The view from Widforss would give him a different angle on the same cluster of buttes and canyons he had observed from Shiva. He never made it that day. On the way to the trailhead, he stopped at the NPS office to talk with his friends Ray and Art Lange, a pair of brother rangers. Over the course of their conversation, the Langes mentioned that a man was staying at the nearby campground that Harvey ought to meet. The man's name was Merrel Clubb. The Langes told Harvey that this Clubb character was just like Harvey—he spent lots of time exploring off-trail.

Harvey had heard the name before. Dock Marston picked up Merrel Clubb on his Canyon radar over a year earlier, and in April 1956, Marston encouraged Harvey to contact "the two men who have covered a lot of the Canyon trails, Dr. Allan MacRae and Dr. Merrel D. Clubb." Harvey replied, "I believe I'll get a letter off to Dr. Clubb. It will be interesting to swap notes on the trails." But as of 1957, he still had not written either Clubb or MacRae (unlike Marston, Harvey rarely initiated a correspondence; he typically wrote those who wrote him first. He didn't contact MacRae until the early 1970s).

Not wanting to lose this perfect opportunity, Harvey walked over to the campground, unaware of how his life was about to change. He found a large white wall tent, stepped to the doorway and called out to Clubb. A graying, slightly built man emerged. As they introduced themselves to each other, Harvey realized that his reputation had preceded him.

"Oh yes," Clubb said. "You're the man whose companion drowned in the river."

Fortunately, the conversation quickly steered toward less painful subjects, such as exploring Grand Canyon and that old fossil Emery Kolb. The more they talked, the faster their rapport grew. They not only had similar interests, they discovered, they had *exactly the same* interests.

They also could not have helped but notice how much they resembled one another—it was as if each was looking into a mirror. Clubb was a decade older, but there the differences ended; both stood five feet, seven inches tall, weighed 130 pounds, and wore thick bifocals.

Apparently subject to some ill-understood law of nature, Harvey Butchart and Merrel Clubb comprised a highly specialized archetype, the professorial route finder, the plumb obsessed, intellectual Grand Canyon fanatic.

It was an historic meeting. For 12 hours in the campground that day they swapped stories, carrying on far into the night by the light of Clubb's crackling fire. Harvey discovered that Clubb, who had been exploring the Canyon longer than he, had done things no one else

Merrel Clubb at the North Rim campground. *Courtesy Merrel Clubb, Jr.*

had, not Kolb, not McKee, not MacRae, not even Harvey himself. Clubb, unlike those others, was a climber. He enthralled Harvey with stories of the Canyon's heights, of what it was like to challenge lonely summits such as Cheops Pyramid, Wotan's Throne and Vishnu Temple.

Clubb made it a point to state that he had made more first recorded ascents and climbed more buttes than anyone—at least 10 of the Canyon's 140-odd named summits. Harvey was not accustomed to meeting people who had outdone him in the Canyon. The idea of going after the Canyon's buttes as trophies had never occurred to Harvey. But it made sense—if you got a first ascent, you were in the record books for good. Clubb's enthusiastic stories and proud declarations sharpened Harvey's imprecise Canyon desires to a fine point. Climbing suddenly sounded like something he needed to get into.

Equally intriguing as Clubb's collection of butte climbs, though, was the man himself. Harvey had never met anyone like him. Clubb possessed a scholarly, mild-mannered personality, but he transformed into a fervent romantic when the subject turned to Grand Canyon. Clubb spoke about it with the most consuming *passion*, the most genuine *reverence* that Harvey ever came across—in anyone.

Harvey wrote about Clubb in a 1977 article in the *Journal of Arizona History*:

He weighed no more than 130 pounds and wore thick-lensed glasses to make up for his near-sightedness, but he was rugged. He insisted on carrying a pack weighing over sixty pounds at the start of a trip. He moved slowly and limited his wanderings to a few rather restricted areas, but when he talked about the climbs he had done and the discoveries he had made in Shinumo Amphitheatre, he revealed himself as the most enthusiastic and dedicated Canyon explorer I have ever known.

No hiker or climber ever influenced Harvey to the same degree as Clubb, who provided a role model for what Harvey had been yearning to achieve—a degree of lasting significance in Grand Canyon—and also someone to measure himself against. Had there been no Clubb, it would be hard to imagine Harvey's evolution taking the same streaking arc that it did in the years following 1957.

The English professor told the mathematics professor his story. Merrel Dare Clubb was a southerner born in Chattanooga, Tennessee in 1897. From the beginning, there were striking parallels to Harvey's life. Clubb too, was the son of a Disciples of Christ missionary who had saved souls in China in the late 1800s.[2]

Clubb's father eventually moved the family to Pomona, California. A natural athlete, Clubb Jr. became a high jumper on his high school track team. He also enjoyed hiking the hills and canyons around Pomona, and spent many of his boy-hood days exploring—that is, when not practicing piano. Clubb proved good enough on the ivories that he had to decide between careers after graduating with an English degree from Pomona College, either concert pianist or professor. He chose the latter, eventually earning a Ph.D. in English from Yale after completing his dissertation, *Christ and Satan: An Old English Poem*. Clubb nurtured a rich appreciation for all the arts, including drama, painting, and poetry. One day, poet Robert Frost dropped in at Clubb's home for a conversation that lasted all night.

Clubb met Edith Jordan while at Pomona and married her in 1919. They had three sons, Merrel Junior (actually Merrel Clubb III, but he would be referred to as Merrel Jr.), Will, and Roger. For years Clubb taught a variety of subjects, bouncing from school to school, including Miami of Ohio, Stanford, and the University of Texas. While teaching at Oklahoma Agricultural and Mechanical College in the 1930s, he lived only 200 miles from the Butcharts, who were just beginning to explore the West from their home in Enid. Clubb

---

[2] Whether Harvey and Clubb's fathers actually met or knew of each other is unknown, but given the tight-knit Disciples community that existed in late nineteenth-century China, it remains an intriguing possibility.

taught a variety of subjects but his specialty was Old and Middle English literature. He studied Chaucer, Jonathan Swift and Shakespeare, as well as the classic Anglo-Saxon folk tales, such as *Beowulf*, and Clubb's favorite, *The Junius Manuscript*.

Clubb, like Harvey, also took his family on extended summer vacations out West. There were camping trips to California and New Mexico. Clubb loved to hike and climb mountains, and took his enthusiastic sons up numerous peaks in the Sierra Nevada and Sangre de Cristo Ranges.

Clubb also visited the Canyon for the first time as a middle-aged man. What the 42-year-old saw beyond the guardrail on that initial view in 1939 claimed him completely. He felt an immediate urge to hike into the Canyon. As soon as he set up his family at the South Rim campground, he did just that. During this solo maiden trek he managed to lose sight of his return time and showed up a day late. Edith was so worried that she told him she would not be coming back for any more Grand Canyon trips.

Clubb decided that he and his wife could amicably spend their summers apart. He thereafter began an annual tradition of setting up his wall tent at the North Rim campground during summer vacations, then reuniting with Edith back home when the fall semester began. He thus fed his new Grand Canyon preoccupation at his leisure, without restraint, sometimes disappearing for up to week at a time in the backcountry. His sons joined him during those first few years at the Canyon in the early 1940s, but after 1947, Clubb did most of his exploring solo. "He was totally taken with the Canyon when he got going

Summits below the Kaibab: From left, Siegfried Pyre, Hubbell and Poston Buttes. *Elias Butler*

there," wrote his son Merrel Clubb, Jr.

That Clubb decided to make the North Rim his base camp is telling. Though he enjoyed hiking the South Rim trails, and even explored remote south-side areas such as Great Thumb Mesa, Eremita Mesa, and Cape Solitude, Clubb quickly discovered that his real passion lay in the terrain below the Kaibab Plateau, where the majority of Grand Canyon's buttes and prominences are located.

Benefiting from more aggressive geologic uplift than her neighboring plateaus (there are four distinct plateaus forming the North Rim), the Kaibab has been bestowed a distinctly different character than its more popular sister rim to the south. Its edge rises up to 1,800 feet higher than the South Rim and thus towers higher over the chasm; one looks *far* down upon the Canyon from the Kaibab Plateau.

For hikers and climbers, there are important differences. Because the Colorado has had to adjust to the Kaibab's loftier altitude, the river has over time hugged closer to the South Rim. The few trails north of the river thus challenge hikers with greater relief and greater distance than those to the south. Contrast the 14 miles and 5,850 feet of elevation change that a hiker must negotiate on the North Kaibab Trail with the 6.5-mile, 4,860-foot climb presented by the South Kaibab Trail. In the same way, with a greater amount of upraised land to be eroded, the north side is home to many more buttes, castles, temples, spires, mesas, towers and monadnocks than the south. This profusion of heights makes the Kaibab Plateau the doorway to a climber's landscape.

When Clubb began haunting the North Rim, it had been centuries since anyone had done much climbing in the Canyon. The Anasazi indeed ascended many buttes, as evidenced by their telltale artifacts that mark scores of inner Canyon summits. Since the Indians's departure, however, few during the ensuing years of Anglo occupation had bothered to climb there.

Trapper James Ohio Pattie, one of the first white men to see Grand Canyon after the Spaniards, arrived in 1826. He cursed these summits below the rim with his famous phrase "horrid mountains." Ironically, one of those prominences that had so repulsed the mountain man now bears his name, Pattie Butte. The miners and tourists of the late nineteenth century who followed somehow found reason to climb a few of the more accessible summits. Written documentation of these "prospector" ascents remains scant. Prior to 1900, guides John Hance and William Wallace Bass, each bringing tourists, climbed 7,108-foot Coronado Butte near the New Hance Trail and 6,275-foot Mount Huethawali off the South Bass Tail. By 1912, The Battleship, adjacent to the Bright Angel Trail, had been climbed, as attested to by the earliest date inscribed in the Hermit Shale on its 5,600-foot crest.

Yet what little interest there was during this period waned as quickly as it had started. The buttes remained unvisited for decades, with no first ascents recorded for over 30 years, even as climbing began to take off elsewhere.

Climbing in Grand Canyon has always been a far cry from climbing in other regions. It often means a brutal full day or even two days of trekking to haul gear and supplies to the base of any given butte. "Hiking [in the Canyon] is mountaineering with essential differences," Harvey wrote in *Grand Canyon Treks.* "The main differences include the summer heat, lack of water and the fact that the uphill portion of most trips is usually done on the way out, when one is the most tired."

As Harvey noted, high temperatures and a scarcity of water form thorny barriers to those wishing to stand atop an inviting Grand Canyon summit. Bringing enough water to last for the duration of a climb often translates to a staggering load. When combined with the usual difficulties of hiking off-trail, such a problem conspires to defeat the will of all but the most dedicated.

Aesthetics also play a role. The Canyon's summits do not resemble the shapely granite peaks of Yosemite, nor the mighty glaciated massifs of the Himalaya. Instead, these variously eroded sedimentary knobs and mesas, especially when viewed from above on the rims, do not scrape the sky. Compared to traditional mountains and big walls, the Canyon's summits would likely not earn a second glance from most climbers.

Nevertheless, Clubb referred to the Grand Canyon as "a climber's paradise." He felt charmed by the buttes's isolation, their intriguing names, and became seduced by the views they could offer. Clubb withstood the difficulties and pushed himself into the maze of cliffs and untracked terrain below the Kaibab in search of routes and personal satisfaction with only the Matthes-Evans map as his guide. Clubb's passion allowed him to cheerfully endure the incredible toil and substantial suffering this invited. Time and time again he

Merrel Clubb with torn shirt. *Emery Kolb, courtesy Merrel Clubb, Jr.*

fought his way up and down steep, brushy gullies, or along exposed narrow ledges without any assurances that he might succeed.

He did not look it, but Clubb was a hardened outdoorsman. Pound for pound, he was as strong as a badger and just as tenacious. When he made his annual move to Grand Canyon he transformed from a conservative-looking professor to a desert mountaineer, trading suit and tie for pith helmet, boots, rope, and sturdy clothing. On average, he toted 60-75 pounds (Clubb brought what he called "cold grub", i.e., canned fruits, canned vegetables, canned meats, cheese, and as much as two and a half gallons of water). He even, a time or two, backpacked over 100 *pounds*—a figure that amounted to more than 75 per cent of his body weight. Despite such loads, he managed to lug his homemade, wooden-framed backpack up one rocky Canyon summit after another. To top it off, Clubb always did his exploring in the scalding summer heat.

His climbing philosophy was simple. In 1966, he stated in a *Lawrence Daily Journal* newspaper article:

> The important mountain climbing technique is finding the right route. Now and then I use a spike or a rope, but these moments are few and far between. I take a good topographic map along with me, and sometimes I take the long way around to avoid dangerous areas. My objective is to just keep walking—uphill.
>
> It doesn't make too much difference whether I climb alone or with a companion. Climbing is always fun...I climb for the sheer joy of climbing...and the mountaineer has the feeling he is the first person ever to see this bit of nature's beauty.

Clubb's plan of attack netted him several impressive first ascents.[3] In 1941, he undertook his first Canyon climb with sons Will, 18, and Roger, 14, to the summit of 5,200-foot Cheops Plateau near Phantom Ranch. That same year, Clubb and Will also climbed Shiva Temple. On top they found and then *ate* a can of tomatoes that had been left by a party of scientist climbers four years earlier.

In 1945, Merrel and Will again joined forces, this time tackling a more difficult objective: 7,633-foot Wotan's Throne, an imposing, flat-topped mesa protruding south from Cape Royal. Using ropes to rappel past the cliffs below the

---

3 The term "first ascent" may carry a different meaning in Grand Canyon than elsewhere. Pre-Columbian Indians were the first to scale many buttes, but of course these incidents were not recorded. Therefore, "first ascent" most often means "first recorded ascent," though it may not signify the first actual ascent.

Wotan's Throne from Cape Royal. *Elias Butler*

famous viewpoint, the father-son duo fought their way across waterless miles of steep slopes until reaching the actual climb. There they struggled up rockslides amidst swarms of biting juniper gnats and unrelenting heat. Yet they eventually gained the summit of one of Grand Canyon's most recognizable buttes for what Clubb believed was a first recorded ascent.4

Feeling confident with this success, Clubb quickly set his sights on perhaps *the* most prominent summit in all of Grand Canyon, 7,537-foot Vishnu Temple. Although not technically demanding, Vishnu would require Clubb to cross several miles of rough terrain and then locate a route up 1,500 feet of eroded cliff bands unmercifully exposed to the searing sun. Doing so with a limited supply of water would mean a dangerous race against time and the heat. Even today, climbers using a well-known route often find Vishnu's combination of height, dry terrain and distance from the rim a daunting challenge.

Clubb teamed up with his son Roger this time and followed the same route below Cape Royal that he had used to approach Wotan's Throne. Once below the Coconino Sandstone rappels, they veered to the east toward Vishnu, which meant an up-and-down scramble through numerous ravines and minor canyons. Finally at the base, the pair then slogged up small

Inverted mountains: From left, Krishna Shrine and Vishnu Temple. *Courtesy Richard L. Danley*

---

4 More on this controversy in Chapter 15.

cliffs and loose talus dotted with boulders too hot to touch. The sun burned any uncovered skin. Although they closed to within an hour of the summit, they had to bail out when Clubb suffered an incapacitating bout of hemorrhoids. Vishnu remained unclimbed.

Clubb had a stubborn streak. His way was to thrust himself without compromise toward his ambitious goals, both in climbing and his career. It was a trait that rubbed some people the wrong way. He landed a new job in 1946, taking over as English department chair at the University of Kansas at Lawrence. He remained there for the rest of his career, but his chairmanship would not be permanent.

"He was always a very strong man with a strong (too strong at times) personality," wrote his son Merrel Clubb, Jr., who also became an English professor and even worked under his father at Kansas for a couple years in the late 1940s. "His strong personality and rather strong-mindedness made him enemies among his faculty only too soon, and he was replaced as chairman after some eight or ten years."

Vishnu Temple, first ascent: Merrel and Roger Clubb (photographer), circa 1946. *Courtesy Merrel Clubb, Jr.*

Yet however much Clubb's mulishness irritated his peers, it would become an absolute requirement for what Clubb had in mind the following summer at Grand Canyon. He and Roger gamely returned for another attempt on Vishnu. With a clean bill of health this time, they excitedly rushed past where they had been stopped the previous year. The exposed crux below the summit required a risky move. Clubb drove a piton into a crack and attached himself to the rock. He scrambled up this final pitch, belayed Roger, and finally father and son found themselves poised upon a small cap of Kaibab Limestone: The summit of Vishnu Temple.

In awe, Clubb called this place "one of the two most thrilling spots in the Park visually." Perhaps no butte, other than the technically challenging Zoroaster Temple in the Canyon's main corridor, could be considered a more significant first ascent.

In 1947, Merrel and Roger returned to the summit of Vishnu. During both trips to Grand Canyon's signature butte, they detoured during their return to the rim for an ascent of Wotan's Throne. And each time atop Wotan's, they spent two nights on the summit, a remarkable feat considering that the butte is devoid of water. How they managed to keep themselves watered on these treks far from any known source remains a mystery.

Yet Clubb felt that the difficulties only added to the rewards of standing where so few had stood before him. Wotan's Throne symbolized his deeply personal, even spiritual affinity for Grand Canyon. He regarded Wotan's and the other Canyon buttes, especially those with names that had been culled from his life's other passion— Old English literature—as sacred ground. Writing to Dock Marston in 1955, he explained that the summit of Wotan's Throne was "clear out of this world, of course."

Wotan's Throne (back) and Thor Temple (front) from Francois Matthes Point, 1951. *Merrel Clubb Courtesy Grand Canyon National Park Museum Collection*

Likewise, Clubb's many treks into the remote Shinumo Amphitheater were in part spurred by its surfeit of Old English appellations. For example, Holy Grail Temple, King Arthur Castle and Excalibur summon the Arthurian mystique, as do Lancelot, Galahad and Bedivere Points. The very deep Merlin and Modred Abysses became favorite haunts. Clubb even decided that he wanted a butte in the upper end of Shinumo Amphitheater named for him after his death.[5]

Clubb was particular about names. In response to a controversial movement in the 1950s that proposed replacing the exotic nomenclature attached to the Canyon's summits with Native American and local politicians's names, Clubb wrote:

> The Canyon belongs to the entire human race. What's wrong with having such a wide variety of names? Many people think it's appropriate. Besides, we

---

[5] As of this writing, Clubb's name has yet to be ascribed to any feature in Grand Canyon.

are now used to those eyebrow-lifting names. Once you get accustomed to 'Zoroaster,' no other name for the lump of rock will do.

Clubb himself participated in a bit of naming in the Canyon. Following the death of Francois Matthes in 1948, Clubb applied to the U.S. Board on Geographic Names for a point to be dedicated in the topographer's honor. Clubb chose a location above the Ottoman Amphitheater and Clear Creek, at a southern tip of the Walhalla Plateau near Wotan's Throne. This spot has since become known as Francois Matthes Point.

"Clubb reveled in the Canyon," said archeologist and author Douglas Schwartz. "And he loved to share his tremendous knowledge." Schwartz was a young man when he met Clubb in the mid-1950s. Clubb had approached Schwartz with intriguing questions about the Shinumo Amphitheater, where Clubb claimed that ruins he had found showed evidence that the Indians who once lived there had been sun-worshippers. Although Schwartz could not confirm Clubb's hypothesis, he recalled that Clubb was "extremely immersed and totally dedicated to the Canyon."

Caver and climber Donald Davis, a man who would share many Canyon adventures with Harvey in the 1960s, experienced Clubb's generosity and fascination with Middle Age folklore. After learning of Clubb, Davis passed through Kansas for a visit in the spring of 1964. Davis recalled:

> I found his home, introduced myself and explained my cave quest. I remember him as a courteous academic gentleman of the old school (I surmise that he and J.R.R. Tolkien would have had some things in common). His living room had rather comfortable and in some cases, interesting furnishings; I recall an octagonal stained-glass lampshade in the shape of a medieval castle turret. He took me at once to his kitchen where he had a Matthes-Evans East and West Half of Grand Canyon topographic maps mounted on the wall, and pointed out the exact location of the caves, which I carefully recorded and later found the caves just where he said.

In September 1950, Clubb made a final trek to perhaps his favorite Grand Canyon mountain, Wotan's Throne. His partner this time was Bill Beaty, an amputee walking on a wooden leg. Although few would bring a handicapped man on such a demanding trek, Clubb had met Beaty while hiking to the summit of Mt. Whitney in California a year earlier. That alone impressed Clubb. Beaty neglected to bring camping equipment up Whitney, and Clubb offered to share his sleeping bag that night. Beaty removed his wooden leg and used it as a pillow. Astounded by Beaty's hearty resolve, Clubb invited him to climb

Wotan's Throne the following summer.

Starting at Cape Royal, Clubb led Beaty down a pair of rappels through the Coconino Sandstone, but they lost an entire day retrieving a knapsack that Beaty accidentally dropped onto a hard-to-reach ledge. Once down to the Hermit Shale, they began hiking to the base of Wotan's. It took two days for them to fight their way to the summit. By this time, their supply of water was gone. They also got caught after dark on the summit, having left their bedrolls in their camp below. The pair spent a sleepless, cold night—Clubb's fifth and final on Wotan's—trying to stay warm by sitting back to back.

Their return to Cape Royal took even longer than their approach. At one point Clubb left the game-legged Beaty behind to go for help but later returned and cajoled him to keep going. Finally, two days overdue and weak from dehydration, they reached the final cliffs below Cape Royal. Worried rangers arrived to help lug Beaty's knapsack up the last pitch to the rim, though Clubb proudly declined help with his own backpack. In all, it took the men an eternity—six days—to reach the summit of Wotan's and return.

The audacity of this incident later prompted Harvey to question some of what he had been told by Clubb regarding his climbing methods. In a 1996 letter, Harvey wrote:

> On Clubb's third ascent of Wotan's, he and Bill Beaty used a rope tied to a redbud tree root. Clubb told me that just reached, but he left me with the impression that he and Beaty climbed hand over hand without Jumars or Prussik knots [climber's tools used for ascending a rope]. That seems like an impossible athletic feat, especially since they were so dehydrated that Beaty went goofy.

What Harvey didn't realize was that proof existed to verify Clubb's claim of climbing hand over hand up a rope, a difficult and dangerous technique (indeed, a nearly impossible technique except for instances when a climber can place his feet on a sloping wall for leverage). Clubb was photographed ascending as he had claimed, without traditional aids. From the look of unbridled exuberance on Clubb's face in this photo (see following page), we can surmise that he did not mind the attendant dangers.

Clubb continued his yearly pilgrimages throughout the 1950s. His final tally of climbs included: Vishnu twice, Wotan's three times, Shiva twice, the Battleship, Oza Butte, King Arthur Castle, Cheops Plateau, Cheops Pyramid and Mt. Huethawali. Clubb had tried for more, but several ended in failure. He and his son Roger attempted 7,012-foot Isis Temple in the mid-1940s, but upon reaching the bottom of the 500-foot Supai Formation, they lacked both the

Clubb ascends a knotted rope below Cape Royal. *Courtesy Merrel Clubb, Jr.*

equipment and skills to climb a 75-foot cliff that blocked further progress. Not giving up without a fight, they circled the entire temple hunting for a break, only to eventually turn around and go home.[6] Clubb also attempted Brahma Temple with Little Colorado River boater Kit Wing in the early 1950s, but "failed entirely because of a silly exhaustion of mine." He did, however, reach the summit of the easy Horseshoe Mesa near the Grandview Trail with parachutist rescuer Dr. Allan MacRae in the 1940s.

By the time Harvey and Clubb started yawning that evening at the North Rim campground in July 1957, Clubb had told Harvey enough to keep his mind abuzz for days. Harvey walked away bit hard by the climbing bug. He never considered himself a true technical climber, for he always left the advanced techniques to others, but he was immediately hooked on the thought of scaling Grand Canyon's buttes.

Time would reveal that Clubb had roused not only Harvey's fascination, but also his competitive spirit. Harvey always kept score of his own feats and could not help but gauge himself against others. He felt that he and Clubb now had a friendly, subtle rivalry.

Although Clubb made many more hikes in the coming years, his days of ascending the heights were slowing. In 1955 and 1956, he had traveled to Egypt as a Fulbright fellow and contracted viral hepatitis. This forced Clubb to take his first yearlong hiatus from hiking and climbing in 17 years. Clubb was still getting his legs back in 1957. It is thus tempting to view his encounter with Harvey as a passing of the Grand Canyon climbing torch.

Yet Clubb was not ready to give up just yet. In fact, he ended his Canyon climbing drought only a week after meeting Harvey. On a scorching mid-July day, Clubb topped out on Cheops Pyramid, earning him yet another coveted first ascent.

---

[6] Isis wasn't climbed until a quarter of a century later when an NAU student named Al Doty soloed it on 9/26/70.

Still, following this feat, he perhaps sensed that he would not be able to continue the hardcore climbing trips much longer. A message he scrawled on the
back of a photo, which was taken while hiking out of the Canyon after his
climb, gives some insight into Clubb's spirited personality, and his realization
that he had passed his prime mountaineering days.

Clubb rests beside
the Kaibab Trail
on his way back
from climbing
Cheops Pyramid,
July 1957.
*Courtesy Merrel
Clubb, Jr.*

Inscription on
the back of
photo (at right).

> Merrel
> and Valerie
>
> The G. C. Tramp,
> back from Cheops Pyramid,
> at that cedar ridge on
> the Kaibab Trail.
> The pack is not mine,
> but a young collegian's on
> way to join George White's
> river party at Phantom.
> I had to fix up his pack
> with my old Vishnu rope
> for shoulder straps.
> My gear is back of legs.
>
> Grizzled & wasted but
> still tough in 60th yr.

As much as Clubb loved to tout his achievements, it was the simple act of
experiencing the Canyon on a vigorous, raw level that gave him his greatest
reward. He explained in a July 17 letter to Dock Marston—his first to the historian in over a year of recuperation—that he looked to Grand Canyon not
only for adventure, but also for healing and wholeness:

> I thought of writing you, but haven't, because much of the time I feared
> that my Canyon doings would prove a chapter that was closed. (Sometimes,
> thoughts of G.C. were just too painful.) Only last month, on the doctor's
> promise it would be so, have I begun to feel like myself again—of course, the
> Canyon itself is the reason.

Given that Clubb and Harvey shared such a tremendous fixation with
exploring and climbing, it poses the question: Why didn't they join forces and
climb together? An essay Harvey wrote in the late 1950s titled "Backpacking in

the Grand Canyon" provides one answer: "Whenever I could find a good team-
mate, I would take him along, but no companion is better than one who is accident prone or who can't keep a fair pace."

By Harvey's standards, Clubb could not keep "a fair pace." Douglas Schwartz
hiked with both men, Clubb in the late 1950s and Harvey in 1968. "Merrel
Clubb was very wise but slow, like a barn owl," Schwartz observed. "Harvey
Butchart on the other hand, also extremely knowledgeable, was a contrast in
speed. He was ten years younger than Clubb, and more intense and focused, and
more energetic, like a hummingbird."

In a letter to Dock Marston, Harvey explained his lack of interest in hiking
with Clubb, and his competitive relationship with him:

> Merril [sic] Clubb and I had a good visit and I got a lot of details on his
> routes. He and I wouldn't make very good hiking companions, I am afraid,
> because he likes to start off with a 60-pound pack and move only a few miles
> a day...He is ahead of me on the temples since he has been up Wotan's three
> times and Vishnu twice. Besides Shiva twice, he has climbed the plateau
> behind Cheops and also Cheops Pyramid. He has also covered quite a bit more
> of the rim than I have, but I am ahead of him with respect to the Hopi Salt
> Trail, the Old Trail, the lower parts of Horseshoe Mesa area, the Great Thumb
> Trail, and the Thunder River area.

While Harvey loved to cover ground, Clubb loved to spend extended time
within the Canyon for the feeling of connection it gave him, as well as for the
physical challenge. Despite their hare-versus-tortoise disparities, both men perhaps did share similar motivations. A popular book from the era offers some perspective on their unique bond. In 1939, James Thurber, one of America's best-
known humorists, wrote *The Secret Life of Walter Mitty.* The story's protagonist
is a very unassuming, middle-aged, middle-class man who escapes from the routine drudgery of his suburban life into repeated daydreams of heroic conquest.

Merrel and Harvey could have been Thurber's poster children. Both clearly
had ambitions far beyond the cerebral world of chalkboards, textbooks and
classrooms. Restricted by early academic pursuits and family demands, they
nevertheless nursed testosterone-driven aspirations to become explorers who
accomplished feats of astonishing physical endurance and stamina. And quite
unlike Walter Mitty, Harvey and Clubb acted on their desires and took real
risks in the process.

They continued their correspondence in the coming years and met whenever the opportunity arose to watch each other's slides or to talk routes. They were
friends, and once they got rolling in conversation, there was no stopping them.

Yet while Harvey accelerated his pace in the Canyon following their 1957 meeting, Clubb found himself increasingly standing in Harvey's shadow.

By 1957, Harvey faced little "competition" from the tiny handful of other off-trail hikers covering Grand Canyon. He had simply out-hiked them all. Only Clubb and his collection of summits stood in the way of Harvey's supremacy as the premier backcountry expert. From his essay, "Summits Below the Rim: Mountain Climbing in the Grand Canyon," Harvey made it clear who had given him the inspiration to climb:

> When Clubb passed his experiences on to me, his memory was remarkably detailed and accurate, though he was unsure on a few minor points...He used to introduce himself as the man who had been up more Grand Canyon summits than anyone else. He generously shared his knowledge of routes with me and infected me so thoroughly with his enthusiasm that his title didn't last long...

Harvey's self-diagnosis was accurate. He soon went from "infected" to a full-blown case of summit fever, the likes of which the Canyon had never seen. Harvey set his sights on climbing—and Clubb's record—with a single-minded intensity that likely surprised and humbled Clubb. Scores of unclimbed peaks lay waiting like plums in the Canyon orchard in 1957, and much of that fruit still hung low to the ground. There simply was no one else beyond Clubb and the occasional one-timer trying to collect first ascents. This was Grand Canyon's golden age. One did not need to be a world-class alpinist to put himself into the record books, if one acted quickly.

Tellingly, Harvey's first few climbs after meeting his predecessor took him to the very summits Clubb climbed. For example, the following July, Harvey ascended Mt. Huethawali, a gentle dome of sandstone near the South Bass Trail. Part of it was practical, for Clubb was able to give Harvey—a cautious man when it came to climbing of any sort—the route information he needed to feel confident.

But following in Clubb's hand-and-toe holds also provided a yardstick by which Harvey could judge his nerve, and he quickly found just how tough Clubb was. After climbing Cheops Plateau in July 1958, Harvey wrote a letter to Dock Marston:

> Dear Dock,
>
> On Sunday I came back down the open part of Phantom. I was on my way to follow Merrill [sic] Clubb's example and climb the plateau behind Cheops Pyramid. I made one false start which led nowhere and had to come down to

the creek level before I got started up to the top of the talus below the north-west ridge. If Clubb's other climbs are any more risky than this one, I'm afraid I don't want them.

Cheops Pyramid from Cheops Plateau, July 1958. *J. Harvey Butchart, courtesy NAU Special Collections*

Yet Harvey had proved to himself that he had what it took to repeat Clubb's daring feats, and quickly began chasing after unclaimed summits.

Following his encounter with Clubb at the North Rim, Harvey now perceived the Canyon in all its heart-pounding potential. Not only were there routes to rediscover, but dozens and dozens of untouched buttes to climb. An irresistible path unfolded before him into the future as far as he wanted it to go. He almost did not know where to begin.

Chapter Fifteen

WOTAN'S OR BUST!
2004

HARVEY WOULD HAVE BEEN IMPRESSED.

Our little rafts are light and well made (and expensive), a far cry from the cheap air mattress that Harvey favored. Elias and I waste little time inflating them at the mouth of Cottonwood Creek in the inner gorge. We spend a few moments admiring our handsome fleet of two before happily swapping our hiking boots for river sandals and snapping on lifejackets. We break into big sweaty grins. Months ago, we decided floating the Colorado River was a necessary part of our Harvey homework, and right now, the thought of following in his wake is much more appealing than eating any more of his dust. With aplomb and high-fives, we shout "Wotan's or bust!" and step to the river's edge. Time to shove off.

The Colorado is amazingly quiet in this stretch; Grand Canyon's famous whitewater makes no claim here. Not that we mind. We will enjoy this ride, rapids or not. It is already much more comfortable than hiking. Close to the surface of the water, it feels like I've opened a refrigerator door, a sharp contrast to the hot, dry and dusty conditions we experienced while scrambling down.

Our large packs make awkward cargo. They claim the lion's share of space in the three-by-six-

Inflating a trail raft. *Elias Butler*

foot inflatables. Getting them aboard without tipping the rafts proves a delicate operation. The steep riverbank does not help. Elias holds my raft as I clumsily slither in. The last thing either of us wants to do is overturn and fill a pack with water and add to the load we will be toting as we hike up Vishnu Creek. I manage to climb aboard and squirm into what seems like the best position, draping my legs over the sides of the raft. Seconds later there is no turning back. The current hustles us downstream. Harvey saved himself days of hiking by crossing the Colorado on his air mattress, and now that we are doing the same, all that work it took to lug rafts down here is finally paying off.

Despite the calm water of this stretch, Elias and I remain acutely aware that we need to pull out on the opposite bank only a mile downstream, at a spot just upstream from the mouth of Vishnu Canyon. Should we miss our landing, we will easily be swept into the Class-IV whitewater of Grapevine Rapid. Just thinking of it makes my mouth go dry. There will be no second chance to make the correct landing. Here in the inner gorge, the glassy black walls are too steep to climb, making escape from the river nearly impossible. Every now and then, as if to remind us who is in charge, I feel a feisty boil well up beneath my raft and shove it capriciously off course.

But after a minute or two of floating, my anxiety melts. I'm too caught up in the novelty of floating the river on such a miniscule raft. Soon we are concocting spurious, dramatic accounts of hairball rides in upstream rapids that we can tell to another river party should one happen by. Conversely, we try to imagine our own surprise and laughter if we came across the likes of ourselves, perched in such unlikely watercraft on this mighty river. We hope to meet a large motorized commercial trip, in fact, and the bigger the better. More contrast to amplify the odd sight of our tiny rafts, like an aircraft carrier versus Curly and Moe on pool floaties.

Some of our swagger evaporates as we imagine Harvey Butchart on his air mattress, floating alongside us. Nearly 50 years to the day have passed since Harvey made his first air mattress run through this same section. I can almost see Harvey as he bobs alongside, his hands dog paddling, his feet kicking at the river. He is wearing a canvas backpack and vintage, Chuck Taylor high-top basketball shoes. But what stands out most is what Harvey is *not* wearing.

He has no lifejacket.

Today, anyone who viewed a middle-aged math professor down here on an air mattress without a lifejacket would be inclined to assume it was Larry, making complete our river version of the *Three Stooges.* Truth is, even Elias and I would probably stare, mouths agape in disbelief, "No way!" spilling from our tongues.

Yet there were undeniable advantages to Harvey's floating the Colorado, as

Afloat on the Colorado. *Tom Myers*

risky as it was. To hike to the mouth of Vishnu Creek without crossing would take at least two days between the long drive and longer bushwhack. Another advantage is logistics. Even if one did have all that time, reaching Vishnu Creek on foot would be no easy task. The vast majority of Canyon hikers, including us, would probably never visit Vishnu Creek simply because there is no trail. Arriving by river makes it easy.

The final reason for our float is more subjective: It is fun. In fact, we are enjoying it so much that we try to go as slowly as possible. Elias and I agree that this lazy float is likely to be the highlight of our trip, so there is no sense in rushing. Even though I have crossed the river similarly once before, I feel the need to pinch myself to remind me that this is indeed "backpacking." Harvey felt the same way. He summed up his love for floating the Colorado by air mattress in his 1960 article "Backpacking on the Colorado":

> If there is a better way to see terrific scenery while keeping cool all day, keeping warm at night with very little bedding, portaging a five-pound boat that you can sleep on at night, I would like to hear about it. I suppose the next thing will be to ride a surfboard through the canyons.

I envy Harvey for the era in which he floated. Back then it was the "wild," warm, muddy Colorado River. Once upon a time this river ran blood red loaded with silt and reached nearly 85 degrees in summertime. Nowadays, it is freezing. It runs clear, a deep shade of unnatural green and is nearly 30 degrees colder than before the construction of Glen Canyon Dam upstream. The river has since it comes from deep within Lake Powell where there is no solar warming. As a result, it looks and feels more dead than alive, at least when compared to its former self. The silt is gone, now trapped behind that 10-million-ton concrete stopper, where the Colorado continues to deliver 12,000 dump truck loads of it per day. My butt grows numb from the frigid river water, and as it does, I can't help but think of Frankenstein's monster.

Harvey Butchart floats the Colorado in the post Glen Canyon Dam era, late 1960s. *Courtesy Jorgen Visbak*

When the dam was finished in 1963, the Bureau of Reclamation argued that it provided flood control and steady, small releases, thus making the "new and improved" Colorado less dangerous. Like Dr. Frankenstein in the novel, the Bureau did not seem to consider that its "creation" would turn deadly. Or that it would actually increase the danger. Cold rivers kill more people than warm rivers, simple as that. Rapids are always dangerous, but add shock and hypothermia to the equation and the combination suddenly becomes much more deadly.

Elias and I find it hard to accept that Harvey Butchart actually supported the construction of Glen Canyon Dam. He, like many of his generation, believed dams were symbols of American ingenuity and progress. Yet the dam curtailed Harvey's floats by lowering the river's temperature until it became too cold-blooded to stand. By the mid-1960s, Harvey completely lost his zeal for air mattress travel. His feelings, like the Colorado itself, went from hot to cold.

Indeed, after 1964, when Lake Powell started to rise, all Harvey could muster was a handful of crossings (of about two dozen total). Before the decade ended, he would swap his air mattress for a small inflatable raft somewhat like ours. Just like the warm, silty Colorado and Glen Canyon's enchanting beauty, Harvey's mattress floats marked a bygone era:

> I wouldn't want to cross the river on an air mattress now except in very warm weather, and I wouldn't try to go downriver for any distance at any time of year any more. The water released from Lake Powell comes from far beneath the surface and is cold the year round. However, I now use a 3 1/2 pound Sevylor inflatable that keeps me dry as I lie face down and paddle over the sides. I would use it only for quiet stretches of the river.

Staring back upstream, I lament what is lost while I enjoy what remains. The Colorado is shimmering in the sunlight. It is a gorgeous silver ribbon, strangely beautiful despite its dam-disfigurement. Okay, if this is not Frankenstein's monster, the Colorado just might be Frankenstein's bride.

Our joy ride ends much too quickly. Dead ahead is the only spot on the right bank suitable for landing. A tiny beach, barely big enough to hold our rafts, lays 100 feet upstream from the mouth of Vishnu Creek. The thunderous snarling of Frankenstein's Bride in Grapevine Rapid, a few hundred yards ahead, tells us the beach will not only have to do, but also that we better not miss it. We pull in and step once again onto land.

Ditching the rafting gear under a ledge of Zoroaster Granite is almost as gratifying as using it to float the river. Our packs are a welcome 10 pounds lighter. Feeling satisfied that our stash is well hidden, we halfheartedly talk about hiking again. It is only mid-afternoon, but after the leisurely float and lunch, all I can seem to muster the energy for is a nap. But Elias reminds me we need to make some miles, then he pulls out a few wadded pages copied from *Grand Canyon Treks*. Vishnu Canyon is new territory for us. I yawn but somehow manage to stay awake during what most would find a bedtime cure for insomnia, or just plain-old Canyon mumbo jumbo:

> Various routes are possible in and around Vishnu Canyon...There are springs in Vishnu Creek near the top of the granite, in the Tapeats narrows,

and near some cottonwoods at the Tapeats-Shale contact. Getting down the Archean rock from the west requires care in following of a narrow ledge of travertine. It is impossible to go down the main bed to the river, but these falls can be bypassed by some rugged climbing over spurs east of the bed.

Here again Harvey has painted a stick-figure portrait of what lies ahead. His writing is about as engaging as the selected answer section of a math textbook and almost as baffling. He offers terse, dense answers to difficult questions, and conspicuously absent is any "work" showing how one finds the solution. We read it again, as well as the sections that precede and follow, hoping for better illumination. *None.* Feeling like two of Harvey's dimmer-witted students, we decide to reread the head-scratching segment in reverse, like solving a math problem starting with the answer first. After all, we are going *up* the drainage.

Ahhh…it starts to make a little more sense.

Although vague, Harvey's advice does indeed contain vital answers, especially about the water. And within its opacity lie some important data. We know it is impossible to go up the main bed, but *somewhere* to the east, with some "rugged climbing over spurs," we will be able to reach the Tapeats Sandstone level. And, *somewhere* to the west, we can get down, and therefore presumably up, on a "narrow ledge of travertine" that "requires care in following." At least his obfuscation, we conclude, is consistent.

We amble up and over the small cliff that separates us from the mouth of Vishnu Creek. The creek runs several feet deep along the base of this cliff, so we remove our boots, then step barefoot into the side canyon's rushing waters.

Leaving the security of the river for what will eventually become remote, bone-dry desert is disconcerting. The deep narrows of this side canyon, which quickly twist out of sight, make us wary. A flash flood would be tough to evade down here. And there is something else. From the few fleeting glimpses up the mouth of Vishnu Canyon I've had while floating by during river trips, it has always looked deep, dark and uninviting.

Fortunately, Vishnu Canyon proves much less spooky than I had envisioned and far more beautiful than anyone would guess from Harvey's pokerfaced prose. Sunlight fills the gorge, and with pink Zoroaster Granite more dominant than the darker Vishnu Schist, the canyon warms and brightens into a cheery glow. In fact, this turns out to be a stunning defile. For nearly two miles it continuously coils and bends on itself. The water of Vishnu Creek, a small perennial spring-fed stream, provides a comforting companion throughout this stretch.

The canyon offers an easy walk over sand and cobbles, but twice we have to remove our boots to cross small pools. Twice more we have to scramble up small cliffs—Harvey's "rugged climbing"—to bypass small waterfalls in the polished rock. Fortunately, we are relieved to find "rugged" doesn't mean "you're an idiot to try this without a rope," or translate to the equivalent of "this place startled me." But hiking up Vishnu Creek is time-consuming. The delays mount. Marching on, I listen to the hypnotic tempo of our feet. Like molars, they crunch the creek-bed cobbles over and over again. It reminds me of an old phrase in mountaineering: "Climbing mountains is like eating an elephant. The only way you can do it is one bite at a time." Our elephant is enormous, and for all our ferocious chewing today, we have hardly made a dent. I feel like we are gnawing a bone.

By 6 P.M., daylight begins to fade and we find we have gone about as far as we can. Our bed of smooth walking abruptly ends in a 40-foot cliff of polished Shinumo Quartzite. Backtracking a quarter mile, we find a nice, open, level area in the drainage where we can camp beside a spring. We lay out our beds, fill our water bottles, and fix our freeze-dried dinners. Cracking open a couple of beers, we toast the day, the river, each other's efforts, and Harvey.

Having bowled along at a Harvey-like pace all day, we've covered plenty of ground. Yet we have not gone as far as we had hoped. By inspecting our map, we realize that we are at least a couple miles short of our original goal of climbing to the Tonto bench and camping half way up Vishnu Canyon. Elias continues to study the map. He thinks he sees the route up Wotan's. My eyes drift sleepily. All I see is an elephant.

The last ASC Hiking Club trip Harvey Butchart would lead as sponsor, Sycamore Canyon, 1957. Harvey is at center, and Dave Hewlett, who became lost, is at far right. *Courtesy Allyn Cureton*

Chapter Sixteen

THE LURE OF THE VOID
1957–1964

Why muck and conceal one's true longings and loves, when by speaking of them one might find someone to understand them, and by acting on them one might discover oneself?

A 1934 letter from Everett Ruess to a friend,
written while Ruess was camped at Navajo Mountain.

"Butchart! Him again?" harrumphed Coconino County Sheriff Cecil Richardson. The perturbed lawman knew the name all too well. He had bailed out Harvey four years earlier when the hiking club sponsor lost two of his charges at the San Francisco Peaks. A search party later found the hikers holed up in an abandoned cabin, but Richardson had not liked the way Harvey had sped ahead of the people he was supposed to be watching. When Boyd Moore drowned a year later, the sheriff lost any remaining faith he had in Harvey's judgment.

And now, in the fall of 1957, two students were telling him that a young ASC faculty associate was lost in Sycamore Canyon. Richardson probably groaned. Forty miles southwest of Flagstaff, Sycamore is known as "Arizona's Little Grand Canyon" due to its dramatic red sedimentary rock walls, seven-mile width, and 1,500-foot depth—all of which made it a terrible place to search for a missing person, and, an ideal hiking club destination.

Harvey had led his group of eight down from the rim of Sycamore along a trail to the bottom of the gorge. During their descent, Dave Hewlett said he wanted to bushwhack off trail to go exploring. Harvey advised against it. He knew that Sycamore Canyon, gouged out of Arizona's convoluted Mogollon Rim country, was no place for a tenderfoot getting his first taste of route finding. But Hewlett had made up his mind. Hewlett was a faculty associate, not a student, thus Harvey let him do as he pleased and only asked that he return that afternoon when the group would be on its way out.

Yet when the appointed time came and went, the young teacher failed to show. Harvey waited as long as he could, then led the club to the rim. There they waited, and waited some more, but by then Hewlett had been benighted deep within Sycamore's clutches. Harvey finally resorted to sending the two students to Flagstaff to alert Sheriff Richardson.

Richardson arrived a few hours later with a large search party. Though they quickly found Hewlett waiting beside a campfire, the sheriff made it clear to Harvey during the long drive back to Flagstaff that perhaps he should consider absolving himself of his position as hiking club sponsor. It was more than a suggestion; it was a firm request. After 12 years at the helm, Harvey decided to resign.

The embarrassing episode turned out to be a blessing in disguise. No longer would Harvey spend his weekends guiding students to the same old places. His only lasting regret was not quitting sooner. He later claimed that his stint with the club prevented him from achieving more in the realm of serious exploration.

Combined with meeting Merrel Clubb, climbing his first butte and making his first rim-to-river route find, leaving the NAU Hiking Club proved Harvey's final, pivotal move in 1957. From now on, he would spend his Canyon time doing exactly as he wished.

And what better time to be footloose, for 1957 represented the last of a passing era in the Southwest, when Arizona and her neighboring regions still enjoyed relative anonymity. A tremendous population surge had already begun to change everything. Between 1950 and 1960, Flagstaff more than doubled in size, going from 8,000 to 18,000 residents. Still, in 1957, the Arizona skies remained unsullied by pollution and the stars undimmed by city lights. The Colorado River ran free, no one needed a permit to hike on public land, and much of the Colorado Plateau and Sonoran Desert remained quiet, wild, and unspoiled.

But the trickle of people moving to the region was showing sure signs of becoming a flood. Word was getting out regarding Arizona's charms. Articles kept cropping up in national magazines touting some newly discovered pocket of desert beauty for the adventuresome to visit. As the region's top attraction, Grand Canyon became more popular than ever. Harvey thus found himself in prime position, as an explorer, writer and photographer, to become the acknowledged Grand Canyon specialist for the Southwest's newly arrived. He had unknowingly been preparing for this role over the previous decade.

His notoriety had begun in 1954 with that small radio piece detailing his first air mattress float. He again made it into print in 1955 with a feature in *Arizona Days and Ways Magazine*, a weekly supplement in *The Arizona Republic*. That article's lead paragraph shows that Harvey's reputation had solidified even then:

> John Harvey Butchart is a professor of mathematics. He is also a demon hiker. This son of missionaries to China, slight, bespectacled and quiet-man-nered, looks on the surface like a typical absent-minded professor, but student members of the Hiking Club at Arizona State at Flagstaff will testify that the professor's legs are made of material so durable it can scarcely be called human.

His prominence continued to rise. Though he could be quiet and even shy in crowds, Harvey developed an increasing knack for getting himself into print. In 1958 he managed to reach his largest audience yet with a notable discovery. He was playing sleuth in May by hunting for the once-popular lower Grandview Trail, a forgotten bit of history that had been obliterated by several decades of disuse. In the 1890s, this trail had teemed with tourists who descend-ed from the old Grand View Hotel (the Grand Canyon's main lodge back in those days, located near Grandview Point) to the river near Grapevine Rapids. The trail seemed simple enough to find on paper, for it was clearly marked on the Matthes-Evans map. Harvey had also found a photo in a tourist book made in 1899 that showed the foot of this trail in the inner gorge. But the tortured schist where the trail led would not answer at first. It became a challenging hunt that took several trips to solve.

When Harvey finally triumphed in May, he decided he had made news. Rather than try talking a reporter into covering the story, however, he wrote it up himself. In the October 1958 issue of *Plateau*, Harvey had his first magazine article published, titled simply "The Grandview Trail." He related his discovery with an authoritative but not boastful tone and made use of the considerable knowledge he had soaked up from Dock Marston and other sources. His writing is clear, direct and unusually free of attempts to describe the park's beauty. Instead, he gives a didactic rundown of the trail's human history and the methodology he used to unearth it.

By the beginning of 1959, another bit of detective work brought Harvey still greater recognition. He discovered a map buried away in the Coconino County recorder's office, submitted by miner John Hance in 1893, which revealed sever-al asbestos mines in Asbestos Canyon below the North Rim. Harvey set out to relocate the mines on a five-day solo backpack through the unexplored country that lay between Clear Creek and Asbestos Canyon (a distance of five rugged miles separates these two tributaries). His decision to reach the mines on foot when it would have been much easier and faster to cross the river using his air mattress was rooted in Harvey's newfound sense of self-preservation. He had decided to avoid riding flows over 10,000 cfs following Boyd Moore's death. But more to the point, he wanted to challenge himself with unraveling a stretch of new territory.

The route finding proved difficult as he crossed unnamed side canyons barring the way to Asbestos. Harvey relied on guesswork, and a lucky throw, to get across one of these major obstacles:

> The long canyon whose head is below Wotan's Throne seemed discouraging to walk around, so when I saw a chance to cross it, I took the gamble...After some study, I decided that the only way to continue was to use a crack just wide enough for one foot to go in. The handholds were mostly a matter of bracing with the elbows to get friction. I knew I would feel insecure with my pack on so I tossed it down ahead of me. It bounced and rolled about 100 feet farther but stopped just above another similar drop.

By the time he reached Hance's diggings, Harvey succeeded in hatching his next magazine story. He promptly told an ASC journalism professor named Melvin Hutchinson what he had found, whereupon Hutchinson decided to write an article and submit it to *Desert Magazine*. This Palm Desert, California-based travel publication was aimed at desert rats in the Southwest, but it also boasted a broad national audience. When Hutchinson's "Backpack Adventure in Remote Asbestos Canyon" appeared in the January 1959 issue with a photo of Harvey emblazoned across the top of the page, Harvey's public persona—the one he would forever after be known for—became set.

There were other significant discoveries during this period of exploration, and not all were limited to manmade features. Harvey took a weeklong solo backpack trip in August 1958 along the Butte Fault, a natural avenue for foot travel between the foot of the Tanner Trail below the South Rim and the

Nankoweap Trail below the North Rim. Also known as the Horsethief Trail (according to legend, rustlers once ran stolen stock between Arizona and Utah along the route), this little-known route was spiced with intriguing human history, a combination that Harvey found irresistible. He happily hiked down in the blistering August heat with the intent of writing an article about whatever he found.

As he strode across the furnace-like interior of Lava Canyon, he decided to try connecting to his route from Atoko Point, the one he had found while searching for Harry McDonald's burro route two years earlier. He managed to do so, but no burro could have followed him, he decided. Yet Harvey more than made up for failing to answer the McDonald mystery with a more dramatic discovery.

On his way out of Lava, he looked up and noticed a large natural bridge in the Redwall Limestone. Senator Barry Goldwater made a big splash when he discovered Kolb Bridge in 1952, after which he wrote and photographed a related feature piece for the February 1955 issue of *Arizona Highways*. Excited about discovering his own remote natural bridge, Harvey made photos and measurements with the intent of announcing it to the world when he returned.

Once back at the rim a couple days later, he drove straight to the backcountry office. His smile faded when the ranger replied that a commercial pilot named Hartman had already spotted Harvey's find two years earlier. Harvey may have silently cursed the pilot. Like Goldwater, Hartman had discovered the bridge from his aircraft without exerting any more effort than a turn of the head. But Harvey did take solace in discovering Hartman Natural Bridge from the ground—the hard way. He had also produced the first photos. Harvey's account of the trip, complete with his photographs, would be published in a 1962 issue of *Appalachia*, a Washington D.C.-based periodical, under the title "Old Trails in the Grand Canyon."

Following this trek, Harvey decided to sort out the rest of McDonald's burro route once and for all. This time though, he planned to drop into the Canyon off the North Rim near Atoko Point and then exit via the Nankoweap Trail. As usual, Roma was willing to shuttle him to his adventure. On the Walhalla Plateau, husband and wife bid farewell at the side of the paved road with firm plans to meet the following day at Point Imperial.

Harvey followed the route near Atoko Point that he had discovered in 1957 and dropped through the Coconino. From there, he located a deer trail that led down the Redwall into Kwagunt Canyon, a trail that he felt was "a good bet" for a burro. Once in Kwagunt, he entered unknown country—no one in modern times had been down all the way into Kwagunt by this route. The bed of the canyon, so easy to follow, soon led him to a sheer dry fall.

Instead of backtracking, he impatiently rock-climbed around it, risking his neck in the process.

The rest of the route went much easier. Six hours later he reached the bottom of Kwagunt, victorious. He felt certain he had finally located the route McDonald had used. Harvey lit a large fire to signal his location to Roma.

She never saw the communiqué. By the next day, Harvey was feeling in the mood for adding even more new territory to his Canyon tally. Instead of simply hiking up the Nankoweap Trail, which would have led him to Point Imperial and his wife, he headed up the unknown bed of the adjacent Little Nankoweap Canyon in hopes of discovering another route. This bid eventually ended in a sheer cliff that Harvey backed away from, which cost him nearly three hours by the time he had retraced his steps to the foot of the Nankoweap Trail. Already tired from making this detour, he scrambled up the trail in the intense afternoon heat to try to make up his lost time.

Harvey's stomach began to cramp, delaying him further. When he reached an exposed portion of the Nankoweap Trail in the Supai Formation—reputed to be one of the hairier bits of trail in Grand Canyon—he found that washouts had destroyed the margin of safety. The trail crossed an exposed cliff that offered little purchase save for steep, crumbly dirt. Harvey backed off and decided to try his luck on a crack above the trail that might lead past this obstacle. His log for September 21, 1958 records this risky climb:

> At this point there is a very unusual break in the top cliff of the Supai...I started up. I put the gallon canteen in the pack and used both hands for climbing, but when I was four-fifths to the top, I encountered a mean step. The next toehold was about as far away as I could step without jumping across the face of a 20 foot straight drop, and the space where I wanted to be was occupied by a clump of brush. I almost gave up and went back, but that prospect seemed worse than taking the chance. I hooked one arm around the brush and got a friction handhold on the rock nearby and made the step. Somehow I wiggled until my pack came clear of the brush and I knew that nothing but a long grind would prevent me from reaching Point Imperial.

It was an accurate prediction. Harvey stumbled for eight hours through the dark without food or water, fighting miserable, brushy slopes and countless ravines along the way. He lit two signal fires, hoping Roma would notice. But she was too busy driving back and forth between Point Imperial and the spot where she had dropped him off the day before. Harvey finally staggered into the parking lot after sunrise. Not bulky to begin with, he had lost nine pounds during the hike. Roma arrived shortly afterward. She immediately offered her stricken husband food and drink, and a helping of remonstration.

The problem was not merely that he was late. It was that he was ridiculous-ly late—again. His Canyon pursuits had been escalating past all reasonable lim-its lately and her anger had been simmering in direct proportion. The incident only confirmed to her that Grand Canyon had cast its spell upon her husband. Roma—like any faithful spouse would—had been growing steadily more resent-ful of the new favorite in Harvey's life. Harvey apologized, likely promised to spend more time with Roma, and then returned to the Canyon for another backpack trip a month later.

Roma's discontent can be traced to at least the beginning of that year. In January, Harvey had written to thank his Canyon enabler Dock Marston by crediting him with "90 % of the responsibility" for his current trekking. He also reported that Roma was complaining about the amount of time he was spend-ing at the Canyon. Marston responded, "You have provided me with a new worry with my 90% responsibility for your treks into the Canyon. Probably Roma will take a shot at me for sending her husband away all the time."

Harvey's reply to Marston reveals his ambitions with forceful clarity. Roma's anger had become an afterthought.

> On the subject of your responsibility for my wanderings—I remember now that I had the ambition to cover all the trails which were shown on the map of the Grand Canyon before you began sending me dope on the historic trips. Then when I read the chapter on trails in the *Inverted Mountains*, I resolved to try to cover the area as well as McKee had seen it. I remember that you heard of me through a bit of publicity about air mattress travel, so I guess Roma shouldn't blame you for all my wild ideas!

Looking at the frequency of his treks in 1959, Harvey obviously paid little heed to Roma's wishes that he spend less time in the Canyon. He had been averaging a full month there during each of the past two years, a figure that would continue to increase over the coming decade. Harvey not only felt an overwhelming desire to explore Grand Canyon, but for the first time in his life, he was receiving major recognition, too—a combination that was proving too tempting to resist.

Indeed, Harvey found it hard to consider reigning himself in. The Canyon offered an unambiguous, physical reprieve from his otherwise mainstream exis-tence. He had followed the conventional American blueprint for the first half of his life—earned his education, got married, pursued a career, raised kids. He had been responsible to his family, society, and faith. But he had never really let loose, not the way his restless legs and heart yearned to. Now some of the most exciting times of his life just happened to be arriving in his sixth decade. After years of devoting himself to others, he intended to indulge himself in his pas-sion—selfishly, yes—with or without Roma's approval.

Marston had inferred correctly that Roma frowned on of him and his geeky Canyon mania. One can almost see Roma rolling her eyes whenever she got the mail—the two canyoneers had faithfully been keeping up a correspondence to the tune of several letters per month. In September, following Harvey's all-nighter at Nankoweap, the pen pals discussed Roma's latest tirade. "It seems to me that Roma is unreasonable to worry that you are only twelve hours late," Marston wrote. "After all, she knows you are crazier than I am."

Of course, Marston was wrong about Roma, but he was not about to con-demn his friend. To help stoke Harvey's resolve, Marston defended him by writ-ing, "Your job is important since you not only go to these places, but you also report accurately—which is rare." This got to the meat of Marston's true con-cern. Nothing was more important to him than records and history—not even a marriage.

Lately he was haranguing Harvey good-naturedly to begin recording his treks with camera and pen so that he might have documentation of Harvey's findings. Harvey did not need much convincing. He knew firsthand the scanty information passed down by his hiking predecessors, especially Merrel Clubb. Harvey later explained to an interviewer that he decided not to make the same mistake. "I remember one reason I started keeping the logs," Harvey said. "I talked to Emery Kolb about his hiking in the Canyon, and he seemed to be clear enough, he would tell you very positively what he had done. Exactly. And then maybe he'd tell somebody else a slightly different story [laughs]. So I decided to put mine down in typing, even though I wasn't a very good typist. And so I've been keeping logs that show almost a page for each day I was on any interest-ing hike in the Canyon."

By 1959 he began typing up each of his treks, usually as soon as he returned home, a routine he would stick to for the rest of his hiking days. If Roma thought he had been devoting too much time to the Canyon before, this new develop-ment could not have been welcome. Now, even when he was home, between typing up logs and corresponding with Marston, their time together as a couple continued to dwindle. Harvey pecked away nonetheless. And he typed *slowly,* using one finger from each hand. He also decided to document all the trips he could remember going back to his first hikes in 1946. He had already spent close to 200 days in the Canyon by 1959, but of course most of those days did not equate to off-trail hikes. Still, it would all amount to a great deal of writing.

That he chose not to write by hand is significant. By typing his logs he made them presentable, easily understood, and easy to copy for future distribution.

And thanks to his photographic memory, he could record the minor details of each trek with uncanny clarity, without the need for notes from the field. He was even able to recall particular conversations from 10 years earlier.

Harvey also heeded Marston's advice in 1959 by taking more pictures of whatever he encountered in the Canyon: Breaks in the cliffs that permitted passage, items of historical interest, and so forth. Such photographs would be important, Marston reminded Harvey, now that he was entering places no one with a camera had ever been.

In the summer of 1959, the river historian and Canyon trekker finally had the chance to share a real adventure. On June 9, Harvey backpacked down the Tanner Trail and then upstream to the Little Colorado gorge. He knew from correspondence with Marston that his party would be passing the Little Colorado any day now. When Harvey arrived at the confluence, he was disappointed to find fresh tracks in the sand: Marston's river trip had already come and gone.

He backtracked to Palisades Creek and spent the night. Harvey awoke the next morning to see seven boats lined up on the opposite side of the Colorado at Lava Canyon. A boatman noticed Harvey waving and came over to pick him up. When Harvey stepped on shore, everyone crowded around while Marston introduced the man who knew the Canyon's trails better than anyone. Down here, Harvey was a celebrity.

Marston was guiding a production company from Walt Disney for the filming

Actors working on the film *Ten Who Dared. Otis Marston, courtesy the Huntington Library, San Marino, California*

of the movie *Ten Who Dared*, which dramatized John Wesley Powell's 1869 river trip down the Colorado. In addition to the Disney crew, the group included future river company owners Rod and Larry Sanderson (the same Rod Sanderson who had given Harvey a lift in Glen Canyon in 1956) and Grand Canyon swimming veteran Bill Beer.

Harvey reveled in the attention. Hanging out in the Canyon with Marston was proving to be much more fun than exchanging letters. They spent the day motoring upriver to the Little Colorado to shoot some scenes with the replica boats (Harvey even made it into one scene in the final cut), then had a bonfire that night with the crew. The following day, with the river flowing around 30,000 cfs, Harvey showed everyone what he could do on his air mattress. Ignoring his I-don't-run-the-river-if-it's-over-10,000 cfs rule, Harvey ran Lava Canyon Rapid twice—the same rapid where he had lost Boyd Moore four years earlier—while everyone watched from shore. Harvey wrote:

> The water was fast and the waves, especially at the end of the tongue, had a way of coming to a peak which were about six feet above the trough, but the mattress carried me up the steep side easily, and only the small crest would slap me in the face. I made two runs and thought it was as much fun as skiing.

After this show, it was time for Harvey to head downstream. He had hoped to grab a lift from Marston, but the crew was stuck repairing a replica boat, so he simply hopped on his air mattress and paddled away. Despite all the ground Harvey and Marston had covered on paper and the obsession they would share for another 20 years, this would mark their only meeting below the rim.

As Harvey hiked out the Tanner Trail that afternoon, he was buzzing from the experience. But amidst all the fun, he had forgotten Roma and the date he had made with her. When he opened the door of his home at 9 P.M., he found her "mad as hops." She had canceled two invitations to bridge parties that night. Her estimation of Marston—and Harvey's Grand Canyon obsession—was dropping by the day.

While Roma was disappointed with Harvey, *he* was not disappointed with Grand Canyon. Or the rest of his life for that matter. Somehow he was juggling the Canyon with his responsibilities as math department chairman, professor, and, to a certain extent, father and husband. Things had been going well at work. While not known for his dynamic teaching style, Harvey made it a point to always be available for students who needed extra help. In October, the school recognized his efforts by naming Harvey ASC homecoming dedicatee. He sat with the homecoming king and queen in the convertible Volkswagen beetle that led the parade through downtown Flagstaff.

Yet it was the Canyon that Harvey remained most excited about. At this point in his canyoneering career, he could count on new experiences just about every time he dropped below the rim. Good things kept happening for him down there. In fact, he made one of his most significant discoveries only two months later, in a side canyon named Royal Arch Creek.

This south-side tributary chisels a broad bay into the Coconino Plateau, a recess so large that it warrants its own name, Aztec Amphitheater. In 1959 it constituted *terra incognita* except for a travertine cathedral at the canyon's mouth which topographer Richard Evans had named Elves's Chasm. A favorite attraction for river runners, Elves's Chasm continues to draw thousands of people each year to its crystalline pools and photogenic waterfalls. But most river runners generally venture only as far as one cold beer from the Colorado, and by 1959 no one had ever seen an arch in that short distance. In fact, no one seemed to know which arch Evans had been thinking of when he gave this side canyon its name; no arches appeared on the Matthes-Evans map. Harvey decided to investigate in October by making a solo backpack trip off Apache Point.

He quickly picked up an old Havasupai trail and made his way down to the Redwall in Royal Arch Creek. After spending the night, he continued down the side canyon toward the river, but was soon stopped short by an unusual sight:

> Just a few more minutes and I was thrilled to see a very shapely natural bridge spanning the main creek. It's about 60 feet in span and about the same height from the water up to the ceiling. One can go on beyond the bridge for about 100 yards and then you come to the end. There is a sheer cliff of around 150 feet drop. If there were a real flow in the creek, what a fall would be there! This is the only bridge known in the Grand Canyon which spans a main canyon with a perpetual flow.

Harvey made the front page of the *Arizona Daily Sun* in October 1959 as ASC homecoming dedicatee. *Arizona Daily Sun, courtesy NAU Special Collections*

The first photo of Royal Arch. 1959. *J. Harvey Butchart, courtesy NAU Special Collections*

This discovery more than made up for his disappointment at not being the first to see Hartman Natural Bridge. With the bad taste of that incident still in his mouth, Harvey wasted no time in telling the world about Royal Arch. *The Arizona Republic* published a letter to the editor only a week later in which Harvey detailed his discovery. As was his right by finding, he also named the natural bridge. In this case, accuracy was less important than history (it was technically a natural bridge, not an arch). He called it Royal Arch.

Harvey would have a long time to savor the triumph. The Royal Arch trip would be his last Canyon excursion for nearly half a year. Just before Christmas in 1959, Harvey, Roma, and their son Jim were headed for eastern Arizona to spend the holidays with the Madariagas in Springerville. Roma drove one car, while Harvey followed in another with Jim riding shotgun. They were on Route 66 near Winslow. It was snowing, hard.

Like watching a horror movie at a drive-in theater, Harvey witnessed a shocking scene unfold through his windshield. Roma spun out of control at 60 mph on the wet pavement. Her car rotated 360 degrees, slid to the other side of the highway in a blur of glass and metal, and then smashed into the embankment. The driver-side window shattered. Roma was ejected just ahead of the car, which then landed on her, crushing her pelvis.

She spent the next few miserable weeks at the hospital in Winslow. In addition to her excruciating pain, Roma also suffered bad reactions to sedation. In January 1960, Harvey wrote to Dock Marston of his wife's condition:

> She is still very nervous and upset at having to lie in one position on her back, but by next Wednesday she will wear a girdle and be allowed to roll over in bed and also she can be brought to the Flag hospital. She has been in Winslow all this time and I have been visiting her all I can in my old hiking trip car. This is putting a stop to Grand Canyon trips for several more weeks, but the weather has been so wintry that there is no regret on that score.

By March of 1960, Roma had healed enough to get around by herself in Flagstaff. Satisfied with her recovery, Harvey immediately resumed his feverish pace in Grand Canyon. He was finding that his extensive list of goals would not shrink, no matter how many trips he made. With each new line he traced onto his Matthes-Evans map to show where he had been, he grew ever more eager to fill in the adjoining blank spaces. It was like a game. And because he was the first to reach most of those blank areas, it became all the more enticing to claim more and more territory.

On July 30, after making a first ascent of Diana Temple (a butte located about 10 miles west of Grand Canyon Village), he wrote without dismay of his inability to make headway on his list:

> There were some fascinating things to be seen from the top, especially a couple of caves near the upper end of the Redwall in Slate Canyon. The ones in Slate Canyon looked like something the prehistoric Indians would have liked. Thus, my backlog of projects lengthens as fast as I chalk one off.

One item on that backlog which Harvey felt he needed to finish right away was his dream of running the Grand on his air mattress. Ever since Boyd Moore had drowned, Harvey had wanted to vindicate his unique method. Harvey made a furtive one-mile run below Pipe Creek, taking care to avoid being seen by rangers near Phantom Ranch. He wrote this defensive entry in his logbook about the float:

> Apparently I had been influenced by the people who cry horror at the mention of an air mattress on the Colorado River, because I didn't push off into the water until I was definitely past Pipe Creek Rapids. I really know that I can bounce right through about anything on the mattress when I ride it cross-wise under my chest...

Although he avoided getting caught for his illegal run, when Harvey sloshed ashore with his clothes and air mattress in hand, he passed a pair of astounded hikers. One remarked to the other, "See, I told you that wasn't a log!"

Harvey's indignation flared in July when the NPS refused his offer to help with a search for a lost 16 year-old hiker named John Manson Owens, who had disappeared on a makeshift raft after hiking down the Tanner Trail (Owens was later found alive). Harvey had told the NPS he could search the river from his air mattress, but they had dismissed it—he felt—as a crackpot idea.

So when Harvey decided to float the entire Canyon in August, he did not bother asking the Park Service for permission. Roma felt this a mistake. She never quite believed Harvey about how safe the river was, no matter how confident he sounded. But Roma could not persuade him to change his mind. As usual, Harvey would not be taking a life jacket. This alarmed Roma to the point where she wrote a letter to Marston pleading for his help in talking some sense into Harvey. She also asked Dock to persuade Harvey to quit going solo on his hiking trips.

Marston's response was sensitive, but noncommittal. On August 23, the day before Harvey left on his river trip, Roma received Marston's letter:

Dear Roma,

I assure you that I understand your concern over the trip and trips by Harvey. When it comes to values in relation to risk, I am not so sure we are realistic. You experienced trouble on the highway and the narrowest escape I had during a trip involving the River this year was on the road in Nevada.

I wish that Harvey would not go alone walking in the Canyon and I have pointed out the risks to him. I see no purpose in drifting down the Canyon on a mattress. I have told Harvey that but I recognized that I made little impression.

I feel quite sure that any protest from me would not bring the result you wish as I think I understand enough of his drives.

Once he determines to make a trip, I feel I should help to the extent which I can. This I intend to continue to do unless someone can show me I am in error.

I will be glad to have any suggestions but they must have sound bases for belief in success. I know I am not going to reform Harvey, or anyone else, merely by expressing opinions or by wishing.

Truly,
Otis Marston

One wonders how Harvey felt about such an exchange, or even if he knew about it. In any event, by the next day he was inflating his air mattress after hiking down Jackass Canyon, a tributary eight miles downstream of Lee's Ferry. Roma's plea for safety—by all means a reasonable and sensible one—had gone unheeded.

Harvey meant to float as far downstream as he could with two weeks worth of food. But the usual low water of late summer changed his plans. He put on below Badger Rapids, and, after taking three hours to reach Soap Creek Rapid (only five miles downstream), he knew the going would be much slower than he had anticipated. Harvey decided to leave as soon as he reached the Tanner Trail. As he had promised Roma, Harvey portaged every major rapid he could. He wrote in his logbook:

> I had heard terrible things about the rapids at Miles 24.5 and 25, but at this stage they didn't seem particularly impressive. Of course I walked around them, but I did that for all the riffles. I must have landed 25 times in the course of a day's travel.

The aptly named Sheer Wall Rapid, however, demanded that he run its course. Harvey would write his account of this run in a 1960 *Appalachia* article, "Backpacking on the Colorado":

> Even from a distance I could tell by the sound the places where single rocks cut through to the surface as against a real drop in the bed. Rocks breaking the surface sounded like tearing paper, while a real drop in the whole river made a roar like a fast freight...As I approached Sheerwall Rapid I thought both sides furnished good detours. I approached the right bank, and it was only when I was too close to turn back that I realized that one could not get out. I tried a landing instead of using my chance to stay clear of the rocks, and I was swept over the drop right against the rocks.

Sheer Wall Rapid. *Elias Butler*

He came away with a bruised knee. When Harvey rode the section below the Little Colorado where the tragedy with Boyd had occurred, he had a chance for reflection. "I recognized the place where Boyd and I were swung around and around," he wrote in his logbook. "Now there was no difficulty to keep out of the back eddy. In fact, I was never given an undesired ride upstream in a back eddy on the entire trip." Tellingly, Harvey began his *Appalachia* piece with a large dose of denial. Hailing the merits of air mattress travel, he writes, "My system for seeing the wild canyons of the Colorado in safety and comfort is suggested by the title of this article." In other words, Harvey's air mattress idea was not to blame for Boyd's drowning.

After hiking out the Tanner Trail, Harvey arrived home to find a letter from Grand Canyon Superintendent John McLaughlin. It stated that the NPS had been made aware of Harvey's illegal float, and McLaughlin warned him not to do it again. Harvey wondered how he had been found out. He later learned that Marston had asked Bill Belknap of Boulder City, Nevada to pick Harvey up at Lake Mead. Belknap figured it was a better job for Park Service personnel and had notified them. Still, Harvey felt his trip had been worth the wrist-slap.

He later returned for yet another stab at running the length of the Canyon, again without official permission. In August 1962, with Glen Canyon Dam almost complete, he tried floating the 68 river miles from Pipe Creek to Havasu Creek. Once more riding the low summer water, Harvey battled eddies and suffered numerous delays, averaging a measly mile-and-a-half an hour. By the time he reached Hermit Rapid not far downstream, he realized it would take much longer than anticipated to reach Havasu. He hiked out the Hermit Trail.

Harvey's river exploits, though not entirely successful, leave us with an intriguing clue to a controversial chapter in Grand Canyon history. Like many canyoneers, Harvey had heard the story of James White. In 1867, two years before John Wesley Powell's first run of the Colorado, White had been found in an emaciated and dehydrated state 340 miles downstream of Lee's Ferry at Calville, Arizona. After reportedly starting somewhere over 100 miles upstream in Glen Canyon, he had been riding the Colorado on a log raft for 14 days with no life jacket, no clothes, no food and no clue about where he was or where he'd been. Others quickly theorized for him that he had been the first man to float through Grand Canyon.

But to lay legitimate claim to the all-important first traverse, White would have had to average nearly 40 miles a day over the time he had been on the river. Harvey frequently averaged less than a mile per hour on his air mattress. From this fact alone, Harvey felt White's alleged journey would have been virtually impossible. "Even if James White had come through shooting all the rapids," Harvey wrote in his logbook, "he couldn't have done any better since he couldn't have paddled the raft forward or even enough to take advantage of the best current."[1]

Two years later, in August 1964, Harvey tried to run the Canyon one last time. The penstocks of the new dam had closed a year earlier, and the resulting reservoir called Lake Powell had already submerged much of Glen Canyon. As a consequence, the Colorado in Grand Canyon was growing colder by the day. It was now or never for Harvey and his air mattress.

This time he put in at the tail waves of Hermit Rapid with plans to make it to Havasu Canyon. Harvey had allotted himself extra days to explore multiple side canyons. Unfortunately, his unwieldy and uncharacteristically heavy 35-pound Kelty backpack became a problem on the river. The frame forced his head down in an uncomfortable position and made it tough to paddle. Harvey's river trip bogged down. Due to the delays and difficulties, he had little time to hike into the tributaries he wanted to see, such as Crystal and Dragon Creeks.

Below Tuna Creek Rapid he went over a small pour-over, landed on a rock, spun around in the washing-machine-like whitewater, and bashed his elbow. His air mattress sprang a leak, too. The going got worse while navigating the "Jewels": Agate, Sapphire, Turquoise, Emerald and Ruby Rapids. This string of cataracts proved too furious to float and very difficult to portage. Lugging his tired body and soggy backpack past angular blocks of schist and through slick mud proved exhausting and dangerous. He decided to forego any more side canyon hikes and focused only on getting down the river. Between wet socks chafing his feet all the while and stopping every 15 minutes to re-inflate the mattress, he finally threw in the towel and hiked up the South Bass Trail. In his logbook he would wearily write, "...shorter trips are more to my liking than the lonesomeness of 11 days by myself," and "...so much for the navigation."

After 1964, the temperature of the Colorado River released from Glen Canyon Dam nose-dived. It became too cold for the 57-year-old or anyone else to consider without a heavy wetsuit. His "river backpacking" trips would dwindle down in the coming years to a few quick crossings.

Though Harvey fell short of his goal of running all of Grand Canyon on his mattress, it did not douse his enthusiasm for more adventures. He was on a roll in Grand Canyon. He simply shifted his focus back to his countless backcountry projects. Harvey wanted to set a record in Grand Canyon that would be hard to beat—and he knew just how he was going do it.

For more on the James White story, read *Hell or High Water: James White's Disputed Passage through Grand Canyon,* by Eilean Adams

7,600-foot Wotan's Throne looms over the 2,800-foot inner gorge. *J. Harvey Butchart, courtesy NAU Special Collections*

Chapter Seventeen
SUMMIT FEVER
1961–1965

SOLO CLIMBS ARE NOT PERMITTED
The climbing of any cliff or butte in Grand Canyon National Park shall be
undertaken only with the permission of the National Park Service.
Permission for any such climbing shall not be granted unless all members of
the party are properly clothed, equipped, are qualified physically and
through experience to make the climb, and that the necessary water and
supplies are carried.

NPS hiking and climbing permit (1965)

It was then that the deep feeling of isolation and loneliness overcame us.
We could see the far off specks of light from the El Tovar Hotel on the
south rim. The immense silence, the awareness of being completely cut off
from the civilized world and the close contact of nature made us realize how
insignificant are the petty problems and anxieties of mankind. They meant
nothing here.
Unfolding our cramped bodies at the crack of dawn we wolfed down a
can of applesauce for breakfast, dropped a supply of water for our return,
and started for the temple.

Dave Ganci,
"Zoroaster Temple" (June 1960)

THE SUN HIT HIM like a hammer. In the shade of burrows or trees, other creatures wisely hid themselves during this ruinous phase of the day, all except for
the lone human who tried to walk as fast as possible through their midst. Miles
from civilization, Harvey drained the last tepid drops of water from his canteen.

The parched South Rim west of Grand Canyon Village claims a cow. *Elias Butler*

There was nothing to do now but get down the deserted dirt road. He checked his watch every few minutes, running the numbers through his mind. Could he maintain a fast enough pace to reach the nearest water at Hermit's Rest before his dehydrated body gave out?

Harvey had cracked his four wheeler's oil pan on a rock, leaving him stranded 15 miles west of Grand Canyon Village. It was mid-afternoon on July 16, 1961—high summer in the Arizona desert. The breakdown could not have come at a more dangerous time. He had just returned from hiking all day in the South Bass area and had already downed most of his water supply by the time he was forced to shut down his wounded engine.

Coincidentally, only a couple miles away as the bird flies, Merrel Clubb was below the rim, two days overdue from a solo hike somewhere near the South Bass Trail. Concerned rangers had sent a search plane for Harvey's mentor and friend that same morning. Clubb had only misplaced his pack and would later turn up unharmed.

Meanwhile, Harvey might have wondered if he would need a rescue himself. The road burned underneath the cooked soles of his shoes. His tongue swelled and grew leathery as he walked the arid expanse; dizziness and weakness came in waves. His body fought to heed his demands, but dehydration soon reduced his determined stride to a stumbling gait. Heat waves shimmered in the distance as cicadas sang shrilly from the junipers, adding a weird, single-note drone to the passing landscape.

As he and Clubb unknowingly shared the same blazing afternoon in Grand Canyon country, only Harvey was aware that today he had become the Canyon's new climbing king. If he lived to tell anyone about this accomplishment, then perhaps he might even feel that this death march was worth it.

He'd had an eventful two days of exploring. After camping on the rim near Toltec Point (about 10 miles west of Grand Canyon Village), he trekked to the east past Chemehuevi Point, then descended the Canyon a short ways to climb Fossil Mountain. This modest butte rises just off the South Rim and required little effort to climb, but it had a name on the map and therefore counted as an official butte. Once on top, Harvey claimed his 13th summit in Grand Canyon—one more than Merrel Clubb's summit total. In only four short years since meeting him, Harvey had surpassed Clubb as the Canyon's top "crag rat." The icing on this cake appeared in the form of an Indian ruin, a natural bridge, and bear tracks on the return hike—the latter being a rare sight in this area.

When he finally staggered to Hermit's Rest that night, his clothes reeking of dried sweat, Harvey was on the verge of collapse. The stricken mathematics professor called some friends who lived at the South Rim Village. "The Ken Todds took care of me with a good meal," he wrote in his logbook, "and [it took] about four glasses of lemonade and four of water before I got over my dehydration. After three more cups of soup near midnight, I still weighed only 122 pounds, the lightest I have been for years."

Roma arrived the next day, annoyed at having to make yet another rescue but dutifully toting quarts of oil and a bar of soap. The soap was not for bathing but rather for automotive repair—they drove back to the disabled jeep, where Harvey smeared the soap into his cracked oil pan and then carefully drove to the nearest garage. "The soap finally held the leak to a very slow drip," he wrote. "It was a day to remember—a rope route below the Coconino at Chemehuevi, Fossil Mountain, a fine granary, a route down the Kaibab at Jicarilla, a natural bridge, bear tracks, and finally a broken oil pan."

That Harvey would risk his life for such a bounty did not strike him as strange. But it was difficult for Roma to understand. Few, in fact, could fathom why someone would go through so much trouble in the hottest part of summer to stand atop a nondescript lump of dirt. Only when speaking to another long gone Grand Canyon climbing fanatic could Harvey find a truly appreciative audience for such stories.

A month later, driving with a repaired oil pan, Harvey was able to do just that when he met Clubb at the North Rim. Clubb was camped in his wall tent, making his annual stay. The two spent the morning discussing buttes and comparing recent misadventures like sailors showing off their scars. Clubb laughed when he told Harvey about that day near

Fossil Mountain at left and Mt. Huethawali at right.
Elias Butler

the South Bass Trail—he had hidden from the search plane to avoid embarrassment over losing his pack. Harvey conveyed his own mishap.

There were also victories to discuss. Only days earlier, Clubb had succeeded in making a first ascent of King Arthur Castle, a 7,326-foot butte located within Clubb's favorite Grand Canyon arena, the Shinumo Amphitheater. It had taken Clubb three attempts to summit the remote sandstone mountain. He impressed upon Harvey that the solo undertaking had been nothing short of a battle, which was fitting, for King Arthur would mark Clubb's Grand Canyon climbing finale.

The previous year, at age 63, Clubb had suffered what he called "a good healthy thrombosis"—his oxymoron for a heart attack. Still, he had insisted on returning to the North Rim in 1961 to continue his annual explorations. In light of his close call only 12 months earlier, and the fact that he was no spring chicken, managing to summit King Arthur stands as one of Clubb's more remarkable—or foolhardy—feats.

Harvey may have been caught off guard; he and Clubb were tied. Harvey's recent Fossil Mountain victory had put him on top for less than a month. Yet by now, Clubb could have easily predicted the inevitable, that he was going to lose this race. Perhaps the most difficult pill to swallow was that Clubb himself had inspired Harvey to make a determined assault on his climbing record. Indeed, less than two weeks later, once more fired up over his conversations with Clubb, Harvey would build the first cairns on 4,830-foot The Tabernacle and 6,800-foot Juno Temple, both in the vicinity of Cape Royal.

Still, Clubb would not have to relinquish his crown just yet. He doubtless explained to Harvey that it's not just the number of buttes one climbs, but *which* buttes one chooses to climb. Level of difficulty, aesthetics, and a peak's degree of distinction—in other words, how imposing and prominent a butte might appear—all played a part in its worthiness as an objective.

It would have been hard to argue. Clubb's first ascent of what Harvey called a "Matterhorn in the desert," Vishnu Temple, might be worth 10 climbs of lesser "dirt piles" such as Fossil Mountain. Likewise, Clubb's debatable first ascent of Wotan's Throne—a butte close to Vishnu in terms of significance—was another heavyweight. Harvey realized that he would need to kick it up a notch or two before he started tooting his own horn.

This discrepancy only deepened Harvey's hunger to follow Clubb's footsteps up both Wotan's and Vishnu. Harvey had one more compelling reason to climb Wotan's in particular: Clubb had insisted from day one that he and his son Roger had been the first (after the pre-Columbian Indians) to stand atop its broad summit. But a party of scientists had claimed years earlier that *they* in fact had made the first ascent. Clubb became hot and indignant whenever the subject came up. He believed that the scientists had lied about their climb. Harvey spent the rest of that morning asking Clubb detailed questions about the route and Wotan's history.

Clubb began by explaining the significance of the butte's German appella-tion. In the hierarchy of deities that form the Teutonic pantheon, Wotan stood alone at the top. An omnipotent warrior king who could change shape at will, Wotan employed both violence and trickery to maintain his powers and was said to wander the land as a gray-bearded man with a wizard's hat and walking stick. The deity had hired giants to construct Valhalla (which Francois Matthes had recognized by naming the adjacent Walhalla Plateau), where Wotan's valkyries brought slain warriors to the afterlife. Two ravens, one representing thought, the other, memory, attended to Wotan when he sat upon his great throne, which was named *Hlidskjalf.* From Wotan's throne, it was said that one could behold everything in the world.

The west face of Wotan's Throne and the route to the summit. *Courtesy Douglas W. Schwartz*

Francois Matthes had seen something in the isolated mesa south of Cape Royal to suggest just such a perspective. However, it wasn't the opportunity to observe to the world's doings that had persuaded the first Anglo climbers to attempt Wotan's Throne. Rather, it was the possibility of discovering relict ani-mal species.

In 1937, park rangers suggested to Dr. Harold Anthony, curator of animals for the prestigious Museum of Natural History, that the handful of broad, flat-topped mesas found within Grand Canyon were potential treasure chests of unique life forms. Isolated by sheer cliffs, these "sky islands" might be home to creatures that had evolved in a kind of biological solitary confinement. The 300-acre summit of Shiva Temple and the 134-acre roof of Wotan's Throne were ideal lost worlds where such species might exist.

Anthony was sold on the notion. He made plans to lead the first scientific expedition to 7,618-foot Shiva, which was unclimbed in modern times. The intriguing mission created a wave of unscientific hoopla in both the national and international media, catapulting Grand Canyon climbing to its 15 minutes of fame via movie newsreels and magazine and newspaper articles. Most stories tended to highlight the question of Shiva's faunal residents. What animals might have evolved there? Better yet—what if Shiva was the land that time forgot? Maybe it was home to prehistoric men. Or dinosaurs! The trip had not even begun and already rumors and expectations were flying.

Anthony, however, was a scientist. In a magazine article published later that year, "The Facts About Shiva," he cut through the hype:

> When...the story broke into the press, we discovered that the public had taken the expedition from us, made it their own, and that it was front page news.
>
> Discounting the sensational accounts which had us searching for Dinosaurs and other relics of bygone geological epochs, something that no scientist could ever expect to find outside the covers of a novel, the bulk of the press news covered the facts of the undertaking, and even the daily events, which usually go unrecorded, seemed to be worth paragraphs or columns....Now I get mail addressed to me "Shiva Temple, Grand Canyon, Arizona." Shiva Temple is on the map, it has been featured in political cartoons, or as a catch-phrase in a radio program. What is there about Shiva to thus capture the popular fancy!

Anthony needed someone to lead the expedition, which was when photographer Emery Kolb stepped up to offer his services. The 56-year-old South Rim resident had credentials. In addition to being familiar with the country, he had made an epic river trip down the Green and Colorado Rivers from Wyoming to Mexico with his brother, Ellsworth, in 1912. He was a proven outdoorsman and expeditionary, and, at least in Kolb's own eyes, the perfect choice to lead the trip.

Anthony thought otherwise.

He turned down the local hero in favor of a more qualified climber, Walter

Wood, a young mountaineer with the American Geographical Society. The year before, in 1936, Wood had led the first ascent of 16,644-foot Mount Steele, Canada's fifth-highest peak. Wood's wife Foresta, who would join the Shiva and Wotan's climbing teams, had been part of the Mount Steele party, which was unusual at a time when female climbers were few. Their story had been featured that same year in the second issue of *Life* magazine.[1]

Kolb's pride was stung by this rejection. But rather than fume over the matter, the feisty five-foot, six-inch, 120-pound photographer instead climbed Shiva Temple immediately with Gordon Berger, a summer employee from Kolb's studio, thus claiming the first recorded ascent ahead of Wood. Then, after Kolb heard that Wood was taking a woman up Shiva, Kolb quickly returned to the summit with his daughter, Edith, and Ruth Stephens, another studio employee, making them the first known women to stand atop a butte in Grand Canyon. Just to ensure that Anthony would know who had beaten him, Kolb deposited a few choice items on top before leaving.

Wood's team made its own ascent of Shiva on September 18, 1937. Although they found Indian potsherds and Kolb's film canisters, soup cans, makeshift flagpole complete with agave stalk and burlap bag, and, perhaps most insulting, tissues with lipstick smudges, Anthony would later claim a first ascent. Kolb could not make a public announcement about his own ascent. His relations with the Park Service were already worn thin from years of petty squabbling, and Superintendent Minor Tillotson had given his full support to the Museum's expedition.

Atop Shiva, the scientists collected no new animal specimens. Given the modest nature of the findings, and despite boasting of being the first whites to climb Shiva, the expedition brought Anthony more derision than acclaim. *Time Magazine* thoroughly bashed the entire trip in an October 1937 article, "Treasureless Island": "...it seemed to some skeptical observers that the expedition which started out with the trappings of a scientific undertaking, had by last week assumed the cap and bells of a scientific joke."

Anthony and Wood gamely continued their expedition. Anthony wondered whether a "sidetracked descendant" of the bushy-tailed Kaibab Squirrel—a rodent native to the Kaibab Plateau—might exist on Wotan's Throne. A few days after leaving Shiva, Wood attempted a much less-publicized climb of Wotan's with Foresta, Elliot Humphrey, a local Mormon rancher named

---

[1]Wood would later make several other noteworthy first ascents, including Mount Alverstone in the St. Elias range in Alaska in 1958. Wood's victory on Alverstone would be tainted by tragedy, however; on the descent, he would learn that Foresta and their daughter Valerie had died along with their pilot in a plane crash nearby. Mount Foresta, near Mount Alverstone, was named in her honor.

Preston Swapp, and George Andrews.

Andrews emphasized the perilous nature of pioneering a route up Wotan's Throne in a companion article to Anthony's Shiva piece:

> No rock climber can tell you what it is that makes him risk his life to stand on a pinnacle that has never been scaled. It is one of those subtle things that can only be felt—not told.
>
> I had climbed in Wales and Switzerland. [Walter] Wood was a veteran of the greatest mountains in Alaska and the Himalayas. But never did we have a more dangerous climb than getting down to the base of Wotan's Throne.

Wood published his own version of both the Shiva and Wotan's ascents in *The American Alpine Journal* in 1938:

> The descent [of Shiva] presented no difficulties whatsoever of a mountaineering nature below the rim, through the extraordinary dryness of the air which, combined with the September heat of the sun, dehydrated us in a very short time. Water, being totally absent in this part of the Canyon, was carried in limited quantities due to its weight, and was rationed by the thimbleful.

The 1937 party that claimed a first ascent of Wotan's Throne (which rises in the background): (left to right) Elliot Humphrey, Walter Wood, Foresta Wood, Preston Swapp and George Andrews. *Museum of Natural History*

Both Andrews and Wood detailed their climb of Wotan's without revealing much about their route. They claimed a first recorded ascent and the world went about its business. Yet no evidence was ever produced to substantiate their claim. Eight years later, in 1945, Clubb and his son Roger became the next to attempt Wotan's. After gaining the summit, and finding no evidence of the Museum's ascent, Clubb became skeptical. He noted several inconsistencies in the scientists's reports and thus decided that he and his son had made the first ascent.

For example, when Clubb questioned a park ranger about Wood, the ranger said that no one had seen a signal fire atop the butte. Yet Wood had indeed written that his party had built a midday fire on the summit to signal observers on the rim. Another issue raised doubts—a lack of conclusive photographs. Compared to the extensive photographic coverage given to Shiva Temple, only one photo was ever published of the Wotan's climb—and that photo shows the climbers merely standing at Cape Royal. A respected geologist, historian, and author named C. Gregory Crampton later made an exhaustive search of the Museum of Natural History's files in New York City but failed to turn up any additional photos.

Clubb never published anything about his climbs or claims, which made it difficult to cast doubt on the success of the Museum's expedition. When Harvey met with Clubb in 1961, he wasn't sure what to believe. Harvey resolved to climb Wotan's Throne and then track down the surviving members of the summit team to see if he could sort things out.

Harvey had already tried to climb Wotan's once and failed. In May, he and Allyn Cureton had descended from Cape Royal with ropes and enough food for a two-day assault. Clubb had described a route that required two rappels to descend to the point where approaching Wotan's was possible. Harvey had located the steep chute where Clubb had gone down but when he met an abrupt 80-foot fall, Harvey's courage wavered:

> There is a pinyon pine on the rim of the rock here but I didn't have either the experience nor the guts to take on the climb back up a vertical 100 feet even with the prussic slings we had brought. Allyn's 120 feet of nylon rope went unused. Maybe I'll practice going up a wall like that and come back for another crack, but my respect for Clubb and the Walter Wood party, who climbed Wotan first in 1937, went up 100%.

After speaking with Clubb in August, Harvey decided he would descend from Cape Royal via a less demanding, ropeless route Clubb had heard about from Ed Laws, the ranger who helped rescue the parachutists in 1944. This

Harvey executes a Dulfersitz rappel, 1961. *Courtesy Allyn Cureton*

route began about a mile north of Cape Royal. Clubb warned, however, that he had found this route so slow, so brushy and tedious, that he advised using the faster and more dangerous rappel route that Harvey had shied away from. Harvey knew his limits, however, and a month later, in September, he slept by his car at Cape Royal to get an early start at the "easier" route.

He ambitiously planned to climb Wotan's solo and return the same day. But the Coconino stopped him yet again. Within 50 feet of the underlying Hermit Formation, upon which it would have been possible to walk to the base of Wotan's, he came upon a sheer cliff that he dared not try without a rope. Frustrated once more, he called off the attempt and headed to Flagstaff for a game of bridge with Roma.

The failure burned in his mind for months. He practiced his rappelling technique over the winter, and in June 1962, returned for the third time with the gear and confidence he had previously lacked. He also realized the need for an experienced hand and brought Allyn Cureton.

At the 50-foot cliff at the bottom of the Coconino—where Harvey had been stopped last time—he and Cureton anchored their rope to a small tree and "went down in style." Now on relatively level ground, the pair started the long traverse to the base of Wotan's along the Hermit Shale—what Clubb had called "about the most miserable bushwhacking I had ever done." After four tedious hours, they completed their approach and arrived at a sloping Coconino Sandstone talus that pointed up toward the great butte. In the growing dark they began their ascent.

Nighttime caught them negotiating slabs of pulverized sandstone, yet they found a level spot and settled in for the night. Between the mosquitoes, the heat, and the excitement of perhaps finally making the summit the next day, Harvey tossed and turned in his sleeping bag most of the night.

Harvey had talked in detail with Clubb about the route, but he and Cureton ran into several dead ends. Finally, the route unraveled as a single possibility between boulders, bayonets of agave, and hedgehog cacti. The pair scrambled through this obstacle course up to a notch below Wotan's final cliffs, which gave access to the butte's weakness, its northwestern face. From this vantage,

they enjoyed a spectacular
view of the bay to the north
and the huge Coconino
wall that forms a causeway
connecting to Cape Royal.
A small Indian ruin guards
this portal, which evoked a
bit of envy in Harvey.
"What a place this would
be from which to see the
half-real canyon by moon-
light or the morning sun
bringing out the rough
angles!"

Harvey enjoys the view of Vishnu Temple on the way
to Wotan's Throne, 1962. *Courtesy Allyn Cureton*

Now on the brink of
success, they contoured
below Wotan's north rim,
seeking a break that would allow passage to the summit. They bypassed a ridge
that Harvey believed too dangerous to try, the same one that Wood claimed to
have used. "In fact," Harvey wrote in his logbook of Wood's team, "the description of their going up a projecting ridge more easily than [the one] they had
come down from the Cape Royal rim using ropes is the part of their account
that looks extremely suspect." This critical remark reveals Harvey's limitations
as a climber, however, rather than his superior judgment. The ridge is indeed
easily scaled, as attested to by the scores of scramblers who have since used it.

Harvey and Cureton continued until they reached the steep talus where
Clubb had ascended. A strenuous but straightforward final push brought them
to a last ledge, then the rim of Wotan's Throne, where Harvey immediately
spotted a substantial cairn: Clubb's triumphant summit marker.

"As you explore the summit, you feel that you are in a world apart," Harvey
would later write in a 1965 *Summit Magazine* article titled "Wotan's Throne." "For
the next two hours we felt like Robinson Crusoe." They roamed the sky island, finding remnants of stone walls, proof that Indians had first ascended centuries earlier.
Harvey was fascinated and guessed that the occupants might have climbed the
butte for protection from enemies, or perhaps to complete a rite of passage.

Wotan's Throne would now become a symbol for a new era in Harvey's
explorations. With his successful ascent, it is no stretch to suggest that the sport
of canyoneering was born. Although others had previously explored Grand
Canyon—such as Merrel Clubb, Georgie White Clark and John Wesley Powell,
to name a few—none had combined climbing, white water navigation and

backpacking as Harvey had now done. Back in 1962, Harvey could not have known that what he was doing would one day become so popular.

MERREL CLUBB MAY have felt conflicting emotions after hearing about Harvey's success. It meant that he could no longer make those declarations about being up more buttes than anyone else. But such matters paled compared to the devastating event that took place the following summer.

On August 3, 1963, Merrel Clubb's 36-year-old son Roger brought his own son, eight-year-old Roger Jr., to Grand Canyon for the boy's introductory hike. Father and son would take it easy their first time down the trail together by hiking to Indian Garden and back. Although Merrel was busy in England studying *The Junius Manuscript,* he was pleased that his son and grandson were continuing the Clubb hiking tradition.

Roger Sr. was a chip off the old block. Like Merrel, he had earned a Ph.D. from Yale and became a college professor. Roger taught Renaissance Drama, a subject close to Merrel's heart. And, of course, the father-son team had made history by making the first ascent of Vishnu Temple in 1946, and had also spent four nights together atop Wotan's Throne. Now that the third generation of Clubbs was hiking the Canyon, Roger Sr. and Roger Jr. could begin to share their own adventures in the national park.

From the book, *Over the Edge: Death in Grand Canyon:*

> Leaving his wife, Jean, and four year-old son, Eddie, on the rim in the El Tovar Hotel, Roger Sr. took Roger Jr. down the Bright Angel Trail to Indian Garden. This was more than 3,000 feet below the South Rim and about halfway to the river. It was August 3, 1963. Monsoon season.
>
> The 36 year-old veteran of Wotan's Throne and Vishnu Temple and his impressed young son made it to Indian Garden okay. Then the rain fell. As it typically does during the monsoons, it pounded hard and fast. Nearly an inch-and-a-half fell on the elevations above them.
>
> Upstream of Indian Garden, in the Garden Creek drainage, much of the water funneled and cascaded in a gathering flood toward the normally peaceful oasis. Meanwhile, several hikers, the Clubbs among them, took refuge from the rain under the cottonwoods at Indian Garden. No one, it seems, was adding up two and two to imagine the result: that the canyon above them was directing a new river of mud, boulders, and desert vegetation into a semi-liquid monster soon to explode upon them. If anyone did imagine it, apparently no one voiced his suspicions.
>
> The rain stopped. So, after eating lunch, father and son headed back up

the trail from the Garden. About 400 yards up the Bright Angel Trail, Roger, Sr., heard the roar. This trail is one of the safer looking places in the Canyon. Deceptively so.

The roar presaged the arrival of the debris flow by several seconds. Clubb saw that they would have time to rush to a safe high point on the canyon slope. As he turned to hurry his son, he saw to his horror that the boy was missing. Where was young Roger?

As a 10-foot wall of water and mud exploded into view from the canyon immediately upstream, Clubb saw that his eight year-old son had lagged dozens of yards downstream—in the path of the tumbling flood.

Forsaking the easy route to safety that was so close, Roger Sr. instead made a mad dash downstream to scoop up his son before the flash flood hit. Other hikers who witnessed his desperate race against disaster reported that, although he was running as wildly as any human being could, he never made it.

Searchers later found the faithful father's body about 400 yards downstream, nearly buried by debris. Five days later, after a second, much smaller flood had eroded some of the debris deposited by the first flood, searchers finally found little Roger Jr., only about 100 yards downstream of where his father had been found.

Their deaths were the first in recorded Grand Canyon history of hikers being swept away by a flash flood.

Roger's brother Merrel Clubb, Jr. made the incredibly difficult phone call to relay the ghastly news to Merrel Sr. It was perhaps little consolation that Roger Sr. died a hero trying to save his son. For someone who had enjoyed such a profound connection to Grand Canyon, Merrel Sr. now had to accept that it had become a graveyard for his own family.

Despite this heartbreak, Merrel Sr. would continue to make his annual stay on the North Rim. His love for Grand Canyon would endure. He was, however, never quite the same. Thereafter he began a slow, downward trajectory into erratic moods and unpredictable behavior.

Roger Clubb Jr. and Sr., shortly before they died in a Grand Canyon flash flood. *Courtesy Merrel Clubb, Jr.*

EVEN THOUGH HARVEY was taken aback by the severity of his friend's loss, these were heady times for the mathematics professor. With Wotan's Throne now under his belt, he lost little time going after summits, routes, and the unknown with ever-increasing fervor.

Harvey understood that the more prominent buttes counted as status symbols, but being the second or third person on top meant little in terms of history. Only first ascents guaranteed a permanent place in the record books. Because many of the Canyon's named buttes amounted to scrambles rather than technical climbs, Harvey quickly went about gathering easy first ascents like Easter eggs, stuffing as many as he could into his basket.

But each "egg" would have to be well documented to avoid the kind of murkiness that clouded Wotan's Throne. Harvey took photos on each summit he reached and recorded everything in his logbook. His quest to become the all-time champion in Grand Canyon climbing took shape. Within three weeks of the Clubb tragedy he climbed Barbenceta Butte, Nankoweap Butte, and Nankoweap Mesa, all three qualifying as first recorded ascents. In all, Harvey would make it to the top of nine summits that year, seven of which were first ascents.

His obsession with climbing took him out of Grand Canyon as well. In between the flurry of weekend trips, he wanted to find out once and for all whether Walter Wood or the Clubbs had been the first up Wotan's Throne. While on a family vacation to Fairfax, Virginia, Harvey called Wood, who lived nearby, and interviewed him about his climb.

"I didn't let on that I was suspicious that he had failed," Harvey said. "I was trying to be tactful. There were no photographs taken on Wotan's Throne, or even on the way up. So I asked Walter Wood over the phone about pictures, if they had any, because they mentioned taking a camera to the top of Wotan's in the article. And Wood said 'Oh yeah, I have photographs, but it'll take me a while to find them.'"

Harvey brought up the mysterious signal fire. Wood later wrote Harvey a letter explaining that he would not have built a fire for fear of starting a wildfire, yet a *New York Times* article and Wood's own 1938 article plainly states the opposite. Harvey remained dubious, especially after Wood failed to send the photographs he had promised, but he did not go so far as to accuse Wood of being a charlatan.

More inconsistencies surfaced in 1964 when Harvey traveled to the remote Arizona Strip north of Grand Canyon to speak with another member of Wood's party. "I did go to Kanab, Utah, and found the Mormon that they had along on that trip, Preston Swapp," Harvey said. "And there were several things about his story that made me wonder. One of them was that he had never told his wife that he had climbed Wotan's Throne. And then I asked him what the route

SHIVA TEMPLE PARTY ON 'WOTAN'S THRONE'

Signal Fires Show Climbers Reached Unexplored Plateau of Sky Forest

GRAND CANYON, Ariz., Sept. 24 (UP).—Signal fires burning on Wotan's Throne, the unexplored plateau near the "Sky Forest" of Shiva Temple, heralded tonight the safe arrival of climbers who blazed

New York Times, October 1937. *Courtesy NAU Special Collections*

was, and he didn't know *beans* about the route."

Swapp did mention one item, however, that became perhaps the most intriguing clue of all. He had been searching for pothole water at the southern extremity of Wotan's summit when he found a rusted tin can beside a small basin of water. Swapp had shown the can to Andrews, who neglected to mention it in his article. If Swapp's memory was correct, then neither Walter Wood nor Merrel Clubb was the first in modern times to stand atop Wotan's.

The verdict would remain inconclusive. Harvey decided that, despite his reasonable doubts, Walter Wood's party had likely made the first recorded ascent. Clubb of course disagreed. He would always maintain that he owned the honor of making the coveted first ascent.

Still, such distinctions did not matter to Clubb nearly as much as simply being in the Canyon. "What memories it brings back of the sacred ground!" Clubb wrote to Harvey with characteristic enthusiasm in September 1965. Clubb had just finished reading a gift Harvey had sent: The latest issue of *Summit Magazine,* which contained Harvey's article about Wotan's Throne.

Harvey had been tactful enough to state Clubb's feats upon both Wotan's and Vishnu Temple in his article. Harvey even made a gracious, deferential admission by writing "The closer I come to the base of Vishnu, the more I ever despair of climbing it." Indeed, Harvey had climbed most everything that Clubb had by now, but each time he considered Vishnu, his confidence seemed to falter. It is easy to imagine Clubb—who never minded letting others know what he had done—beaming with pride as he read the piece.

Although what Harvey and Clubb had accomplished on Wotan's and on scores of other buttes in Grand Canyon may not seem audacious by today's extreme standards, it must be remembered that climbing constituted a fringe activity in those years. Techniques that are now common were still in their infancy. Available equipment was primitive at best. Gear might be found in military surplus shops, or ordered from Europe; basic items such as carabiners and pitons were practically unobtainable elsewhere.

Truth be told, Harvey never attempted a fifth or sixth-class "technical" (pro-tection-requiring) climb in the Canyon. Harvey freely admitted that this style of climbing wasn't for him, and at times even referred to himself as a "poor climber." Most of what he accomplished falls in the third or fourth-class range, which means he generally made steep scrambles more than true climbs.

But this sort of labeling can be deceiving. Some light can be cast upon the dicey nature of Harvey and Clubb's feats by looking at the first ascent of Zoroaster Temple. In August 1958, Phoenix climbers Dave Ganci and Rick Tidrick made the first true technical ascent in the Canyon by climbing this shapely peak that stands in prominent view from Grand Canyon Village. To surmount Zoroaster's near-vertical upper walls, which had defeated five previ-ous teams, Ganci and Tidrick overcame debilitating heat, a lack of water, a bru-tal approach, and their own extreme fatigue. Such difficulties and lack of prece-dent make their feat the most significant climb in the Canyon's modern era.

After receiving a copy of Ganci's account of the climb from Dock Marston, Harvey wrote to Marston, "That surely makes my type of climbing seem pretty tame."

"I would refute that," said Ganci, who now runs an outdoors shop in Prescott, Arizona. "I think maybe he was in awe of that simply because he hadn't been exposed to it [technical climbing]. He had the drive, the strength, the daring in some of the stuff he's done—pretty wild stuff. Exposed stuff. Some of his descents into the Canyon are *exposed.* Fourth-class climbing on exposed stuff is scary. Much more scary than when you're fifth-class climbing with a rope—at least in my estimation. I've been more scared on fourth class climbing than I've ever been on fifth class. He did tremendous things, as far as I'm concerned, from a climbing standpoint—without any gear!"

"You could almost call what [Harvey and Merrel Clubb] were doing 'techni-cal,' without gear," Ganci continued. "Harvey did some stuff that scared the shit out of me! A perfect example was when [Flagstaff climber] George Bain and I went down and climbed a Redwall butte off the Hermit Trail, Cope Butte. You get up on the side of it, and then on a little fin that goes out to Cope that's maybe eight inches wide, and it goes out about 30 feet and drops off a thousand feet on either side of it. And I'll tell you what—I got on my hands and knees to go across it. And Harvey didn't really elaborate on that particular spot. I looked at that and said, 'If that's indicative of some of the things they did, I'm very impressed.'"

Harvey kept up his torrid pace by making 10 climbs between 1964 and 1965, adding five more first ascents in the process. He amassed a total of 42 climbs and 19 first ascents by the middle of the decade. By the time he quit climbing in the 1980s, Harvey had stood atop 83 buttes, making the 1960s by far his most productive era.

Zoroaster Temple, first climbed by Dave Ganci and Rick Tidrick in 1959.
Courtesy Richard L. Danley

Of course, he was not only climbing at the time. He was also hiking more than ever. The year 1965 marked Harvey's most active 12 months yet. He set a new personal record of over 620 miles, 52 days, and 30 trips that year.

Yet as resilient and driven as Harvey was, the sheer ruggedness of the terrain took its toll on some days. There were bad trips, and even instances where he felt sure he would give up Grand Canyon for good. "Walking by myself was lonesome, and I was wondering whether I really enjoyed this type of activity," he wrote in his logbook in March 1964 after a solo hike along the Esplanade. "However, when I topped the rise of the Sinyala Fault and looked down into the Matkatamiba basin, the old lure of the unknown came back."

In August, he again tried soloing Wotan's Throne. The 57-year-old later wrote to Dock Marston:

> This time I felt shot by 11:30. First I blamed it on my age and decided that this was a young man's game, but when I got out, I blamed it on my cold...going up the rope was about the slowest and sloppiest piece of Prusikking I have done

yet. I was so sure I would never indulge in that sport again that I left my brand new rope right where it was tied. I had decided that I would retire and write about my past or answer letters of people who wanted to know about the canyon. It was a depressing thought. Changing your attitudes that abruptly is most unsettling...After I get clear over this cold, I may decide that I have a year or two more before I have to call it quits.

Harvey was back five days later for a three-day backpacking and climbing trek during which he made two climbs, one of them a first ascent of a spire called Dragon Head. Apparently, Harvey's climbing obsession would not be cured by a common cold, after all.

On the summit cairn of Siegfried Pyre, 1971. *J. Harvey Butchart, courtesy NAU Special Collections*

236

Chapter Eighteen
THE MAN THAT TIME FORGOT
1962–1963

Now, it is one thing to be the first man somewhere and quite another to know, or to be almost sure, that you are only the second.

Colin Fletcher,
The Man Who Walked Through Time

HARVEY AND ROMA, AT HOME during Christmas break in 1967, opened the package at once when they saw the return address. Inside lay an advance copy of Colin Fletcher's Grand Canyon book *The Man Who Walked Through Time.* Five years had passed since the well-spoken Welshman had stayed with the Butcharts while conducting his research. They hadn't seen much of him since then. But Harvey remembered well the day in early 1963 when he had made a symbolic wager with Fletcher.

"Bet you a nickel I make it," Fletcher had said. "A brand new nickel that I can mount as a souvenir." Harvey had had his reservations about what Fletcher proposed to do. Nevertheless, after teaching Fletcher all he could about how to travel in the Canyon, Harvey knew the man was ready to try. Harvey shook his hand and grinned as he told Fletcher that this was one bet he hoped to lose.

With that bit of encouragement, Fletcher set out on a solo two-month back-pack trip in Grand Canyon. He began at Havasu Canyon and planned to walk some 100 river miles upstream to Nankoweap Canyon. These two tributaries marked the boundaries of Grand Canyon National Park in 1963 (today, the park boundaries extend much farther and include all of Grand Canyon, from Lee's Ferry to the Grand Wash Cliffs). As far as Harvey knew, *nobody* had ever attempted such a hike. Fletcher planned to write a book about his feat and was banking on the fame of becoming the first man to walk the length of the park below the rim.

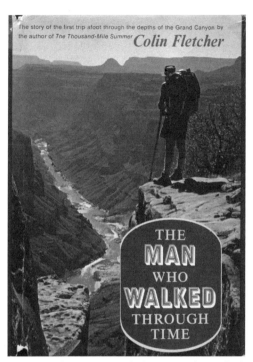

Harvey's advance copy of *The Man Who Walked Through Time. Reprinted wtih permission of Random House*

Harvey leafed through Fletcher's book, curious to see how Fletcher had captured him in print. Harvey had played a vital role in the story. Without his hard-won route information, Fletcher could not have hoped to find his way through so much country in a single trek. Perhaps Harvey could already sense that *The Man* would change his own life. Indeed, the book would sell briskly upon its release in 1968, introducing him to thousands of readers.

Though the two were friendly when they had met in 1963, Harvey and Fletcher had since had a falling out. Any number of factors could have played a part. Perhaps it came down to the usual explanations, simple differences in personality. Or maybe it was just a case of two men falling in love with the same object of desire—in this case, the same canyon.

Whatever the explanation, we do know this much: Back in 1963, Harvey had decided in the last hour that the coveted prize that he had long been chasing was too valuable, too rare, and had been labored toward for too long to allow the Welshman to claim it.

Looking at the new book, Harvey realized that it no longer mattered what he had done back then. Fletcher had gone ahead and walked away with the prize anyhow.

PLOWING HEAD-ON through thickets of two-foot high sagebrush in his Jeep wagon, Harvey decided that if he couldn't find the road, he would make one. Shocked birds fled his path as his bumper swallowed the furry-barked scrub, which cracked loudly beneath the frame. He steered for openings between the trees, following the land's slight northward tilt into a thickening pygmy forest of juniper, pinyon and cliff rose.

Harvey tended to be hard on his vehicles but nowhere did they take more of a beating than at Great Thumb Mesa. Cornered at one point by a wall of junipers, he put the jeep in reverse and impatiently backed up. The rear window shattered on a protruding branch. He came forward and a side window fractured on another sturdy limb. Roma had been right to insist he get his own jalopy for hiking trips.

"If we don't get invited to a bridge party this coming Saturday," Harvey had written to Dock Marston a few days earlier in December 1962, "and if our fine weather holds, I believe I'll jeep out on the Great Thumb and fill in that last leg below Tahuta and G.T. [Great Thumb] Points." No invitations for bridge had materialized, which had freed Harvey to carry out his plans. Now, if he could just negotiate his rig in one piece to the far-flung Tahuta Point.

Harvey was trying to reach the most remote, northern-most spot in the park along the South Rim. Barren, waterless, and nearly trackless, Great Thumb Mesa extends some 25 miles farther north than Grand Canyon Village, jutting so far into the gorge that the Colorado has been obliged to make a wide detour around its distant tip, where Tahuta Point stands over the river's bend. Only the occasional Havasupai hunter, cowboy, or Anglo hiker such as Harvey ever cared to wander this way.

A remnant of an old Supai trail drops off Great Thumb Mesa near Tahuta Point. After descending 1,500 feet, the trail deposits the hiker upon the Esplanade, the broad, level platform of Supai sandstone that stretches throughout Grand Canyon west of the Bass Trail. This friendly, spacious bench tends to form natural potholes that fill with each rain, making it, in the right weather, the preferred avenue for inner-Canyon travelers.

Just to the east of this trail, however, below Great Thumb and Tahuta Points, the Esplanade uncharacteristically pinches to a steep, narrow talus. Still, this stretch of demolished rubble is the only practical route for those wishing to contour around Great Thumb Mesa below the rim.

Given its remote and rugged character, it was thus no mistake that this short stretch of Esplanade became the last piece Harvey needed to sew up a major goal in Grand Canyon: To become the first person to walk all the way from one end of the national park to the other.

He had been whittling away at it for the past 17 years. Side canyon by side canyon, trip by trip, Harvey had methodically unraveled a spidery line on his Matthes-Evans map between Havasu and Nankoweap Canyons that now lacked only three steep bays along the Esplanade, which today he hoped to finally complete.

In November 1961 he first wrote about this ambition in his logbook, right after covering the next-to-last leg downstream near Havasu Canyon:

The attraction of this project for me, in addition to fine views of Havasu, Mooney, and Beaver Falls from the Redwall rim, was that it would be closing the next to the last link in a project I have been working on for quite a few years—going from the northeast boundary of Grand Canyon National Park to the southwest boundary altogether below the rims of the canyon. My other goal is a three mile stretch below Great Thumb and Tahuta Points...

Aside from nabbing first ascents, there existed very few "firsts" for Harvey to claim in the Grand Canyon. This had less to do with previous explorers's accomplishments than an inherent lack of such trophies in canyoneering. Compared to, say, mountaineering's abundance of noteworthy prizes—first ascents, first ascents using new routes, collections of the world's highest mountains, etc.—canyoneering offered few exploits worth proclaiming on the world's stage. There was one exception, however: Being the first to go through the most famous canyon in the world. Pioneering from end to end in Grand Canyon by boat proved to bring lasting fame. Note John Wesley Powell and his crew's alleged first descent of the Colorado in Grand Canyon in 1869. Harvey did not fail to recognize the distinction that awaited him if he could repeat part of Powell's accomplishment on foot.

Harvey's long-term approach to this quest stemmed from his professional and family responsibilities as well as the nature of the undertaking. Even with the help of the 70-odd-mile Tonto Trail running lengthwise in the park, Harvey could only chip away at the whole in small chunks. Much of his trans-park route required toilsome, often frustrating route finding to solve. He returned several times to certain short stretches before succeeding. Three weekends might produce only a couple miles of new route.

The Tahuta-Great Thumb Point leg proved to be one such stretch. He had already failed to cover it once. Two months earlier, he had willed his jeep to within eight miles of Tahuta Point, a significant gain from his previous best on the Great Thumb Mesa road. But with all the walking just to reach the rim, there was no time to descend to the Esplanade. Instead, he and a friend just walked along the rim, overlooking the stretch in question.

Now, in December, after terrorizing the local bird population, breaking windows and getting out time and again to check for any semblance of road, he finally managed to park within reasonable walking distance of Tahuta Point. He started down the rough trail by moonlight early the next morning, December 16, eager to make good on his longtime goal.

Once down at the Esplanade, he headed east and entered the first large recess west of Tahuta Point, where he immediately noticed an abrupt end to wild horse and deer tracks. Only bighorn sheep hooves led farther. Harvey knew this meant no water, and at least some tricky scrambling ahead.

He picked his way through the first few steep boulder fields. They proved difficult, time consuming. He saw by mid-morning he would never make it, as he needed to be back in Flagstaff that night. Notching up the trip as another reconnaissance mission, Harvey told himself that now at least he knew how to get his jeep near the trailhead. He would have to return yet again.

During the hike back to the rim, Harvey stopped to check a spring marked on the map. Instead of a reassuring flow, he found the grisly remains of a previous traveler that had been cheated by fate.

> I'm rather certain I found the right place, below a grove of cottonwoods, but it was now bone dry. What was rather sinister was a dismembered skeleton of a horse as if it had died of thirst and been taken apart by vultures or coyotes. I wouldn't count on this as a source of water in the future…

DR. BUTCHART SENDS THIS CORDIAL INVITATION: "If any…hikers…want to do some exploring with me in the Grand Canyon, they should drop me a line. If our schedules permit, I would love to have some company for some of my 'unfinished business.' About half of my hiking has been solo, simply because no comrade seemed available at the time."

This footnote accompanied Harvey's 1962 *Appalachia* article "Old Trails in Grand Canyon." Harvey's invitation had caught the eye of at least two fascinated readers. One was a man named Dr. Francis Worrell, who had contacted Harvey and joined him in October for that initial hike along the rim near Tahuta Point. The other was a man named Colin Fletcher.

Fletcher, a 40-year-old veteran of World War II, had recently taken a keen interest in anything having to do with Grand Canyon. Earlier that year, he had been mesmerized upon seeing the gorge for the first time. Only a short time later a friend happened to show Fletcher the magazine containing Harvey's article, which Fletcher took as an omen. He had already resolved, after just one look down from the rim, to hike all the way through Grand Canyon and then write a book about his experience. It was just the kind of confident, spontaneous, and adventurous decision that had characterized Fletcher throughout his life.

Born in 1922 as the only child of a single-parent mother, Fletcher enjoyed taking long walks as a youth in the castle-studded countryside near his hometown of Cardiff, Wales. When he was 19, Fletcher joined the British Royal Marines and went on to fight on the shores of Normandy during bloody D-Day as a 22-year-old. By 1947, suffering the effects of battle, Fletcher sought refuge in Kenya and became a farmer for four years. He also surveyed and helped build a road over a mountain in Southern Rhodesia (now Zimbabwe).

Fletcher continued his peripatetic lifestyle. He migrated across the Atlantic to Canada in the early 1950s to work as a prospector, then wandered south, arriving in Berkeley, California in 1956. The open-minded atmosphere and attractive setting suited him and he stayed. It was in Berkeley that Fletcher finally discovered his real talent lay in toiling the earth—not with plow or shovel, but with boots and pen.

He decided to become a writer and serious hiker. He had a gift for lyrical prose and described himself as a "compulsive walker" who preferred extended, solitary rambles through the American wilderness. Fletcher later wrote in *The Man Who Walked Through Time*, "Any free weekend I am liable to pick a road map, choose a large, blank area that intrigues me, drive to the edge of it, park my car, walk in with a pack on my back and find what's out there."

In 1958 Fletcher spent half a year walking alone from Mexico to Oregon, taking copious notes all the while. He reveled in the beauty and solitude of the Sierra Nevada and Mojave Desert, spending long, serene days submerged in the dramatic landscape and his own thoughts. When he returned, Fletcher had the raw material for his first book. With that manuscript in the works, and now one more planned to document his Grand Canyon adventure, Fletcher had jump-started his new career.

Colin Fletcher, self-portrait in June 1966 below Havasu Canyon. *The Huntington Library, San Marino, California*

However, because he had never set foot in Grand Canyon, he first needed to do some research. After reading Harvey's *Appalachia* article, Fletcher wasted no time looking up the author. Rather than contacting him through the magazine, Fletcher figured the best way to get in touch with Harvey Butchart was to walk three blocks to Dock Marston's place in Berkeley. The two were acquaintances and Colin knew Dock had Grand Canyon connections. Marston passed along Harvey's address and encouraged Fletcher to write the mathematics professor.

Just like that, Fletcher had found the one man who could give him what he most needed: Route information in Grand Canyon. Fletcher was savvy enough to realize that his plan's success hinged largely upon being the first man to walk through the gorge. He had no idea if this had been done before. Without revealing his goal, lest Harvey be tempted to appropriate it for himself, he cautiously introduced himself to Harvey:

```
                                    1216 Spruce,    Apt A
                                    Berkeley 9,   California

                                    7 Dec 62

Dr. J. Harvey Butchart
907 West Summit Avenue
Flagstaff,       Arizona

Dear Dr. Butchart:

       Dr. Otis Marston has recommended that I get in touch
with you.

       I am planning an extended foot trip in Grand Canyon,
probably this spring, and am most anxious to get 100% reliable
information - particularly on waterholes.  Dr. Marston says
that no only do you have more firsthand experience of the
Canyon than anyone alive, but also are willing to impart your
hard-won information.  If this is so, could you spare the
time, at your convenience, to discuss my project at some
length over a map?  Failing all else, I'd come to Flagstaff;
but I understand you visit the Bay Area occasionally.  Is
there any chance of your doing so before, say, the end of
January?  Dr. Marston mentioned that you are in LA more
often than San Francisco.  Perhaps we could arrange a
meeting down there.

       I may say that I've read your very valuable 'Appalachia'
article on trails and remote areas, and have marked my map
accordingly.

       For various reasons, I'm anxious to keep my project
quiet at the moment, so I hope you'll forgive me for not
going into details.

       Perhaps I should mention that although I've seen
Grand Canyon only once and done no exploration, I'm not
totally unused to desert foot travel, or even to the
Colorado.  In the course of a long summer's walk a few
years back, I followed the river from the Mexican border
up to Needles.

                         Very sincerely,

                         Colin Fletcher
```

The Huntington Library, San Marino, California

Fletcher's secrecy confounded and intrigued Harvey. He invited Fletcher to Flagstaff to look at maps and talk things over. Harvey then wrote Marston to tell him of the exchange. In the same December 1962 letter in which Harvey mentioned plans to "fill in that last leg" below Tahuta Point, he also wrote:

> A letter from Colin Fletcher came in the same mail with yours...He seemed quite impressed with the necessity of getting more information before he does what he wants to do. He seems a bit secretive about the project...I wonder whether he has visions of lost mines or is just trying to get some exclusive pictures. He says he has walked from the Mexico line along the bank of the Colorado to Needles. The only sort of person I could imagine doing that would be a prospector. I told him I would be glad to tell him anything I know about the canyon and that I would be glad to mark a piece of a map with all the waterholes I know and also indicate where one can get through certain cliffs.

His guess at Fletcher's vocation was not far off the mark. And how ironic that, just when Fletcher happened to write Harvey in hopes of making the first hike through Grand Canyon National Park, Harvey was making final plans to claim this very goal for himself. It is fortunate that Harvey did in fact fail to complete his route during that second attempt in December 1962. His eventual reaction to Fletcher's plan would speak volumes about how badly he wanted to be the first to cross the finish line.

By MARCH 1963, Fletcher had firmed up preparations to make his Canyon mega-hike. He wrote Harvey to request a rendezvous in Flagstaff in April, just prior to making his trek. Harvey agreed on the date and welcomed Fletcher to stay as long as he needed.

Fletcher charmed Harvey and Roma. The stocky, blue-eyed Welshman had an irresistible accent and a worldly demeanor not often seen in Flagstaff. He was well-versed in literature. Also, there was something gallant about him. Fletcher brought to mind the storied English explorers who marched across India in pith helmets or boldly challenged remote Himalayan peaks. Harvey could tell that even though Fletcher had never hiked in the Canyon, he was no greenhorn to desert travel, or to adversity.

Over the course of their conversation, Fletcher finally revealed his plans to Harvey. It may have been a tense moment for both men. Fletcher must have wondered if Harvey had already walked across the park himself. And Harvey would have suddenly regarded Fletcher as competition for the honor. Nevertheless, they continued to have a pleasant meeting. Fletcher went on to explain his plan in detail and noted that the coveted prize of the first end-to-end hike remained unclaimed.

He told Harvey that he had decided against hiking the entire length of Grand Canyon, as had been his original plan. Instead, he would focus on the national park boundaries. These boundaries had been loosely drawn up years before at the deep side canyons of Little Nankoweap to the east and Havasu to the west—the same area that Matthes and Evans had mapped. Even though this represented less than half of the 277-mile physiographic length of the gorge, it still represented an impressive stretch of 104 river miles, and perhaps 250 miles by foot.[1]

Fletcher's decision to shorten his journey was practical. To attempt to hike the entirety of Grand Canyon would have meant a much more daunting challenge, indeed, about 415 additional miles of walking and route finding. This fact had posed something of a dilemma for Fletcher. Prior to 1975's Grand Canyon National Park Enlargement Act, which lengthened the park's borders to their present day locations, the 1962 boundaries were nothing more than arbitrary endpoints found only on paper. Fletcher would explain his confusion and eventual solution in *The Man*:

> Quite early…it became obvious that 'from one end of Grand Canyon to the other' had been a fuzzy target; no two people seemed to agree about where the Canyon began and ended. So I refocused. I would walk 'from one end of Grand Canyon National Park to the other'—the Canyon's major and most magnificent part.

Fletcher was not alone in his confusion. Even John Wesley Powell had declared that the Grand Canyon begins at the Little Colorado River, instead of at the Paria River. Yet it would have been impossible to find a geologist who would argue that the Grand Canyon existed only between the old park boundaries. Still, hiking the length of the park was a goal that Harvey could understand, as evidenced by his own quest.

The two men spent the next day getting down to particulars. When Harvey pulled out his Matthes-Evans map, Fletcher was impressed, even astounded at the visual version of his host's Grand Canyon resume. By 1963, it was a composition nearly two decades in the making. Fletcher quickly noticed that it offered a nearly definitive answer to his most burning question: *Was it indeed possible to hike the length of Grand Canyon National Park on foot?* From *The Man*:

---

1 Accomplished hiker, guidebook author and statistician George Steck once calculated that every river mile in Grand Canyon equates to an average of 2.4 miles by foot.

Over the years, the ink lines he had drawn on the map to represent his short trips from the Rim had consolidated into a tortuous blue snake that ran almost from one end of the Park to the other. Only one gap remained: a four- or five-mile traverse along a narrow hanging terrace below Great Thumb Point, at the far end of the Esplanade.

Harvey explained that he had already taken a good look at that last gap, and that it had appeared rough, but passable. As Fletcher carefully traced Harvey's lines onto his own map, Harvey told him where each vital break lay in the cliffs, and most important, where to find reliable water. Indeed, Harvey impressed upon Fletcher that his greatest challenge would be avoiding dehydration, not the route.

Harvey had grave concerns about the stretch of Esplanade that Fletcher would hike first. Between Havasu and the South Bass Trail lay some 100 foot-miles of chalk-dry country. What was most alarming was that no one in 1963 knew of a route to the Colorado in those 100 miles, making it the longest such section in the entire Canyon. A hiker crossing this territory would therefore need to rely upon the vagaries of weather to provide temporary pothole water. Harvey told Fletcher he would be risking his life in crossing that country.

Fletcher later confirmed this with the Havasupai Indians. They also believed that hiking the Esplanade around Great Thumb Mesa was dangerous, even impossible. The oldest man in the village of Supai "had nothing to offer," except when he heard where Fletcher intended to go. Much to the amusement of a few Supai youths in black cowboy hats sitting nearby, the old man cackled, "All alone? But you'll die! No water up in that country, you know. No food, either. You'll die up there, I tell you."

Harvey gave Fletcher this advice: "Before you take off from Sinyala Canyon, make dead sure there's been enough rain. You could easily get just enough to make you feel safe out on the Esplanade and then run into a spell of hot weather that would dry everything up fast—including you. I can't imagine a neater trap."

Then there was the unknown leg below Tahuta Point. Fletcher would need to find out on his own if it was indeed passable. This uncertainty set a considerable weight upon Fletcher's shoulders. The success of his whole plan seemed to pivot on whether a man could get across this stretch. Ultimately, Harvey could only say that, with luck, he ought to make it.

By now, though, Harvey was raising his eyebrows at Fletcher's scheme. He wrote Marston about his concerns:

> Colin Fletcher called us from Needles and accepted our invitation to have dinner with us and stay overnight. He impressed us as a most interesting person...

Apparently, an important part of his first consists in staying below the rim for the whole trip. I convinced him that it would be better to place his food stores himself...On Sunday, Roma and I are going to take him to the rim of 140 Mile Canyon and he and I are going to leave food and water a few yards below the rim where he can get it without actually leaving the canyon. That distinction seems rather childish to me, but perhaps it will make a difference in the saleability of his story. If there is no water at the grove where I found the horse skeleton last fall, he will already have been in real trouble. What I am principally worried about is his overweight...

I feel some responsibility but I am glad he is going to talk at length to the rangers before he heads to Supai. The last thing I said before he left for the Canyon today was that I didn't think his weight and condition would allow him to finish the grand traverse in one long interval. He and I certainly don't see eye to eye about foot travel. He is planning to stop halfway down to Supai on the short trail and camp the first day. I believe he spends a lot of time writing notes. Maybe he will carry through without incident, but I am half expecting to be called upon as a consultant for an aerial search for a missing man...

For his part, Fletcher simply said he would hone his body down by spending a week in the Canyon near the village of Supai before beginning his trek. He was, however, duly concerned about water and that unknown Esplanade stretch. When Harvey and Roma drove Fletcher to Apache Point and the Bass Trail to help place Fletcher's food caches, Harvey pointed out this daunting country from the rim.

Despite his trepidations, Fletcher knew that his chances for success had improved immeasurably by finding Harvey Butchart. Fletcher would later write, in gracious and graceful fashion, perhaps the single greatest compliment ever bestowed upon the math professor. From *The Man:*

> At the start of my year of waiting I had begun trying to gather information about foot travel through those parts of the Canyon away from the river and the Rim-to-Rim tourist trail. I inquired of park rangers, packers, geologists, and men who had "run" the river several times. But before long it dawned on me that when it came to extensive hiking in remote parts of the Canyon, none of them really knew what he was talking about. So I set about tracking down the experts on foot travel. In the end I discovered that they totaled one: a math professor at Arizona State College in Flagstaff. But Dr. Harvey Butchart, I was relieved to find, knew exactly what he was talking about. He had been learning for seventeen years.

By April, Fletcher had made all the necessary preparations. Leaving at this time of year meant the best chances for comfortable weather conditions, but more importantly, possible water from late winter and early spring storms along the Esplanade. Finally, he was ready to begin.

What Fletcher had in mind was not simply a physical test or a hiking challenge. He would use his journey as a metaphor for a journey into time itself. He hoped to uncover insights about both the formation of Grand Canyon and the origins of life. Fletcher would look deeply into his own soul, and try to comprehend the eons represented by Grand Canyon's geology. It would be a vision quest of sorts, a return to simple living, and a refutation of the growing chaos of civilization.

To execute his Thoreauvian endeavor, Fletcher's mind would need to be as free as possible for making extended internal flights. Hence, although Harvey never thought of himself this way, Fletcher had thrust him into an unusual role—a key master to the spiritual realm. Clutching the treasure map Harvey had bestowed, Fletcher the prospector would search for a unique ore in the vastness of his solitude.

They shook hands for a nickel, then parted ways.

Meanwhile, Harvey felt that his back was suddenly against the wall. Fletcher's journey held far-reaching implications for him. Although Harvey doubted Fletcher's conditioning, he had seen the look of determination in the Welshman's eyes. He knew Fletcher could accomplish what he set his mind to, that he had a good chance of making it across both the unknown Tahuta section and the rest of the Esplanade. The rains had been unusually plentiful that spring and Harvey realized the potholes would be full for Fletcher.

Harvey also knew Fletcher intended to proclaim to the world that he had made the coveted first hike through Grand Canyon National Park. Though Fletcher's success was far from assured, the thought of another man claiming the honor—a newcomer, no less—roused Harvey's finely honed sense of competition.

On April 15, 1963, two days before Fletcher started hiking, Harvey set out alone in his jeep for Great Thumb Mesa. This would be his third attempt to finally knock off the last leg of his trans-park route, and this time, he brought his backpack and plenty of water. Harvey wanted every chance to succeed at getting across the Esplanade below Tahuta Point. He reached the tip of Great Thumb Mesa and descended to the Esplanade, then stopped to check the spring where he had found the horse skeleton the previous fall. To his surprise, he now saw a small flow of water there.

When he entered the first big bay below Tahuta Point, Harvey found it rough as expected, but not a significant barrier. He kept hiking. A few uneventful hours later, Harvey became the first man to walk across Grand Canyon

National Park. If he celebrated his historic accomplishment, however, he left no record of it in his logbook. In fact, he made very little mention of it at all: "...I had filled in the gap below Great Thumb Point...The water situation seemed better than I had pictured it to Colin Fletcher."

Fletcher's timing would be perfect. The Welshman had chosen a most opportune wet spell to hike and would have no trouble finding water—nor in crossing the bays below Tahuta. Harvey returned to the rim near Stanton Point and went home satisfied.

This time, there was no letter to the editor or magazine article to trumpet his deed. Perhaps Harvey thought it would be poor form to publicly one-up Fletcher just when Fletcher would be getting ready to make the claim himself. Whatever the reason, Harvey told only a couple close friends what he had accomplished.

He did, however, make sure to let Fletcher know. A few days later, while Fletcher was making his weeklong stay at the village of Supai, he received the news from an ASC student who had hiked to Havasu Falls. The message left Fletcher with ambivalent feelings: Happy in one sense, let down in another. His

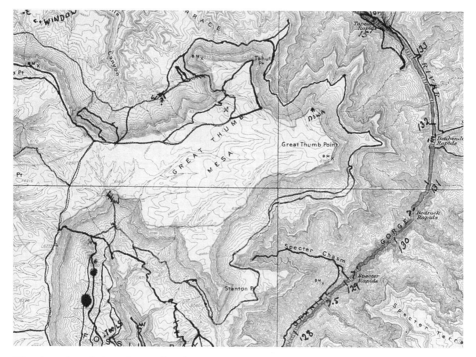

The three bays below Great Thumb Mesa that Harvey crossed ahead of Colin Fletcher. *J. Harvey Butchart collection, courtesy NAU Special Collections*

fears about the three bays below Tahuta and the water availability on the Esplanade had suddenly vanished. But now those fears were replaced by the knowledge that Harvey had run out and claimed the first end-to-end hike ahead of him. From *The Man:*

> Although I felt a sense of loss—a certain slackening in the challenge—it was a relief to know that if the message had not been garbled, as verbal messages routinely are, my way was clear. I felt pleased, too, for a different reason. Without Harvey's help I could have never planned a route. Not with any confidence, anyway. And it was only right that he should be the first man through.
> Much later, I learned from a mutual friend why Harvey had tackled the mystery amphitheaters just before I did. He apparently felt far from sure that I was either competent or in good enough physical condition to attempt a stretch of precipitous country that might well turn out to be impassable. So, in his quietly concerned way, he did something about it.

The day after filling in the gap, Harvey wrote a letter to Dock Marston to give him the news, and to let surface his increasingly critical feelings about Fletcher:

> Speaking about Colin's chances, we are now having a general storm which has put down six inches of snow around here. It must be filling all the potholes on the Esplanade and the going will be fine for the next two weeks with the weather cooling as it is now. Nothing could hold back Colin except his own physical condition. One thing that I predict is…he will lose some of the rapture of the trip after a few days of heading ravines and going down and up and around to make any headway. I'll bet he will wish he were still getting the "impact" like a dude from the balcony before he gets through.
> Your remark about watching Colin with respect to handouts is apropos, I am afraid. He got a $50 pack gratis from a supply store in Berkeley, and he talked Tex Wright, the charter flyer here, into one of the three air drops for free. That, along with the fact that the Oakland telephone company was unable to bill the right number for a long call he made to me from Berkeley, should give us some warning how he operates. Tex thinks that he may wind up getting a helicopter ride out of the canyon. I would guess that whoever does it had better be doing it for the publicity rather than for pay.

Colin had begun to rub Harvey the wrong way. It seems Harvey did not actually like Fletcher all that much. And, one could not blame Fletcher for feeling a bit slighted by Harvey's act of stealing his thunder. Though both men may have said otherwise in public, they were indeed competing with one another. Still, Fletcher was grateful for Harvey's help and acknowledged his decision to complete the route ahead of him. And as fate saw to it, Fletcher—like many other pilgrims in the coming decades—later found himself walking in Harvey's reassuring footsteps.

It happened while Fletcher was crossing the Esplanade below Tahuta Point in the midst of a late winter storm. As he picked his way across the talus slopes, the scene grew vague in the falling snow. Fletcher encountered the shadowy form of a bighorn sheep, which stood silent for a few minutes before melting into the half-light. From *The Man*:

> The other big moment of the day had something eerie about it too…as I padded on half an inch of snow across one of the earth-filled basins, beginning to feel tired at last, I stopped dead. Ahead of me across the snow, dark and definite and impossible, stretched a line of human footprints. Each print turned out to be sharp and clear. And the line cut straight and purposeful, like a pre-echo of my own trail, out and away into the gloom…
>
> I knelt down and examined one of the footprints. It was genuine enough. But almost at once I understood…
>
> I stood up, smiling. When I walked on through the snowstorm, following the dark imprints into the gloom, I found my tiredness had gone. It was good to know, beyond any real shadow of doubt, that I was following, with a most artistic symbolism, the footsteps of the man who had blazed my trail and who had, a week before, fulfilled a seventeen-year ambition. But there was more to it, I think, than feeling glad for Harvey's sake. I found something obscurely yet warmly companionable about these footsteps. And their meaning was so delayed that they did not even begin to blur the solitude.

If he had felt any doubt, here now was proof of the message Fletcher had received in Supai. Yet this did nothing to change Fletcher's plans; he still intended to write his book. He knew that the novelty of his long-distance trek would remain intact. No one—Harvey included—could take that away from him. Besides, he had not come to the Canyon to compete. He had come to escape humanity, to immerse himself within the perfection of nature.

Now assured that his route would go, Fletcher perhaps felt the need to prove himself. After successfully receiving his first airdrop near Fossil Canyon, Fletcher deviated from his goal of peaceful oneness with the Canyon in order to tackle something that Harvey had previously failed to accomplish: Penetrating to the Colorado somewhere in this 100-mile stretch of Esplanade.

For three straight days, Fletcher repeatedly tried to descend to the river via

Fossil Canyon. Fletcher started referring to such bushwhacking as "Butcharting." Harvey may have laughed when he later read this passage from *The Man:*

> Now, Harvey had a local reputation for prodigious feats of sustained speed (he had been called The Flagstaff Flyer even in print), and I was by no means fit enough for real Butcharting...

Given his military background and his overriding confidence, Fletcher was not one to quit. But finally he was forced to admit defeat in Fossil Canyon. He resolved to leave the route-finding problems to Harvey.

Thereafter he moved slowly, taking ample time to absorb the stillness of the Canyon. He became contemplative. Fletcher bathed in rain pools, slept under rock overhangs. He spent hours watching cloud shadows race across the convoluted terrain, or listening to a rill of water on bedrock. His wilderness journey led him to the startling perceptions he had hoped for, both within himself and within the physical realm. This, finally, was the experience he had envisioned.

THREE WEEKS LATER, Harvey hiked down to Phantom Ranch carrying supplies for Fletcher, who had arrived on schedule. Harvey took one look at the new, svelte-looking Welshman and said, "Why, you've lost a good 20 pounds already." He also briefed Fletcher on the remainder of his trip.

After parting ways, Fletcher continued on the second half of his journey. He slowly made his way upstream and crossed the very low Colorado River (Glen Canyon Dam had just been completed and most of the river's flow was being diverted into what would become Lake Powell) on his way north into Marble Canyon. When Fletcher finally reached Nankoweap Canyon a month later, he decided that his odyssey in Grand Canyon had been a complete success. From *The Man:*

> I found myself beginning to list—haphazardly and not at first very seriously— the things I had gained from the journey. I had won a nickel from Harvey Butchart. I had shed twenty surplus pounds and refined my body to such a peak of fitness that when I went to bed the smoothness of my skin sometimes gave me a woman-thrill. I gained a sense of old fears overcome. I had learned that life begins at forty-one: after four sad years in which everything around me had been flat and gray, the world was once again round and shining—rounder and more splendid than it had ever been. And I was beginning to understand too that

the journey had conferred on me a rare but simple gift: an almost perfect confluence of what I thought and what I felt. Had offered me, that is, the key to
contentment.

Two days later, the seven-week pilgrimage was over. Fletcher's lengthy
immersion in Grand Canyon left him deeply inspired to tell the world what he
had experienced. From his onionskin paper journal would arise the book that
would make him famous.

Harvey learned that he had lost his bet. In his next letter to Marston,
Harvey sounds both curious about Fletcher's experiences, and doubtful that he
could stand such a long stretch of solitude himself:

> We got a card from Colin Fletcher written at the north rim after he came
> out. He said he was going to drop in to see us in about six days, which would be
> tomorrow. I will be interested in hearing more details. My only fear is that I
> won't think of all the questions. However, he will have quite a detailed journal,
> and I will try to get all the answers by reading it through. Roma wrote a verse
> to go with the nickel that I owe him for completing the project. Here it is:
>
>> For you the Colorado held
>> Compelling fascination
>> I scoffed for I did not believe
>> You'd reach your destination.
>>
>> But you have conquered heat and dust
>> And drought and rocks and blisters.
>> Among the hikers you are NOT
>> One of the "weaker sisters."
>> So here's your nickel (sixty three).
>> I'm happy to concede it.
>> And when your article comes out
>> I'll be the first to read it.

The only part of this I would not quite agree with is that I scoffed. It was
more that I had serious doubts about his success and especially his desire to continue with it to the end. One of the questions I want to have him answer is
whether it was all fun or whether it became a matter of will power. I am afraid
I would have seen plenty of the canyon long before the two months were over.

When Fletcher visited Harvey in Flagstaff the next day, he collected his nickel, which he later framed and hung on his wall. He also announced his plans to begin work on the book. Though the meeting was initially friendly, Fletcher mentioned something that did not sit well with Harvey. Harvey complained about it to Marston:

> Colin left here on a slightly discordant note. He stayed with us two nights as our guest when his trip was still ahead of him and he had been here a night after it was over. I had given him all the information I knew that might help and we had sat up late talking enthusiastically about the canyon. Shortly after we parted, we mentioned our vacation plans might take us through Berkeley and that if we were close we might look him up for a short visit. He said the following to Roma when I wasn't there, and he evidently meant it very seriously, for he repeated it to me after the plane ride. He told us that he wants no interruptions from his work except for possibly between 1 and 4 in the afternoon. He asked us to call him a couple of days ahead if we were going to drop in. We both felt that if he reacts that way to the suggestion of a short visit, we'll sure as heck not bother to go a block out of our way to say hi!…I suppose you wouldn't say that if we come between certain hours of the forenoon, we are likely to be met at the door with a shotgun, the phrase that Colin used. That struck me as most peculiar since he had been so friendly before parting. I had made a special trip to the south rim to show him how to reach the trail off Apache Point, and I had run down to Phantom Ranch to visit him and give him some special supplies, after which he pulls this crack about wanting to be left alone except between one and four!

Harvey had a willing audience in Marston for his complaints. By September, Marston pronounced that he and Fletcher were no longer friends. Disputes over money matters led Marston to write:

> The beautiful friendship which had developed between Fletcher and me has come to a close at Fletcher's choosing. Apparently he does not approve of my insistence that it not always remain a one-way street. I offered to stake him for some pix cost if he would let me have some pix and take some particular points for me. Now he finds that he never lets anyone have any original transparencies of his and he feels I should weep for him that he ruined his camera…

A few months later, in early 1964, Harvey's estimation of Fletcher dropped even farther. Harvey seemed convinced that every time he heard from him it was only because Fletcher wanted something. Harvey expressed his frustration to Marston:

Colin sent us Christmas greetings, along with a note enlisting my help in getting him a speaking engagement here. I tried a bit half-heartedly, but they don't favor his fee of $150. I thought it was characteristic of him to combine friendship with business. Pat [Reilly] about split when I told him about Colin billing you for the privilege of copying some pix and especially for the time spent in looking at the pictures. Of course Pat shares our view that Colin is interested in nature principally for what he can get out of it in cash.

Harvey seldom wrote anything so critical. Clearly he felt put off by what he perceived as Fletcher's selfishness. Meanwhile, Fletcher's impressive accomplishment in Grand Canyon was garnering attention. He immediately wrote a series of articles that made it into syndicated newspaper circulation. Titles varied from "A View of Trackless Time" and "Out of One World Into Another," to "Cliff Dweller's Thoughts" and "Alone with Time." A unique and interesting subtitle appeared in one article: "The Man Who Walked Through Time." The bold declaration seemed to come from the very depths of the Canyon itself. It suggested an intriguing transparency between this world and another. Fletcher had conceived the ultimate title for his forthcoming book.

His fame only continued to grow in January 1964 when he released his first book, *The Thousand-Mile Summer: In Desert and High Sierra.* It earned good reviews for its flowing style and celebration of the natural world. Although the book did not sell well, it did put Fletcher on the map and paved the way for his next book.

Fletcher wasted no time getting to work on *The Man.* At some point, he may have felt he needed more intimate contact with Grand Canyon before finishing, or perhaps he wished to be avoid being viewed as a one-hike wonder. He made another lengthy solo trip in 1966 by traveling from Havasu Canyon downstream to Diamond Creek. This time he requested no help from Harvey. Fletcher made his way by alternately hiking and floating using an air mattress. This faster-paced trek lasted only 25 days but covered the equivalent of 130 river miles, far more than he had made in 1963.

By 1967, Fletcher had yet another book in the works, *The Complete Walker.* He had paid his dues with two unprecedented mega-hikes in order to qualify as an expert on walking and backpacking. *The Complete Walker* would be the ultimate how-to manual for backpackers, flavored with anecdotes culled from Fletcher's unique experiences.

The Man Who Walked Through Time came to fruition first. Released in January 1968, *The Man* struck a chord with many late-Sixties, soul-searching youths who felt disenchanted with their increasingly industrialized society. Fletcher's eloquent narrative of withdrawal from civilization became a hit (as did a similar book released the same month, Edward Abbey's *Desert Solitaire*; both were reviewed side by side in the *New York Times*). It would go on to be a top seller in the emerging field of nature writing and the best-selling Grand Canyon book ever.

Fletcher's writing beautifully captured the essence of the Canyon—and Harvey's essence. Fletcher devoted extensive page time to Harvey, who is the only character besides the author to appear throughout the book. In many ways, the book pays homage to Harvey, for Fletcher graciously reciprocated Harvey's generosity by giving him full credit for helping him realize his goal. Fletcher also gave Harvey credit for being the first to hike the length of Grand Canyon National Park. No hint of animosity appeared, only appreciation.

One would think Harvey reacted happily to Fletcher's magnanimous gesture. But after receiving the advance copy from Fletcher in late 1967, Harvey wrote a rather sour critique to Marston:

> Colin sent us an autographed copy of *The Man Who Walked Through Time*. Naturally, both Roma and I found it interesting reading. It is surely more extensive in book form than the ms [manuscript] we read earlier. I am afraid that some of his "enlightenments" leave me a little cold. Maybe he is naturally more of a philosopher than the rest of us. Still, I have to hand it to him for getting a lot out of his seven weeks.

Harvey's Christianity and left-brain mindset formed the fundamental opposite of Fletcher's immanent beliefs and artistic bent. To illustrate the wide gap that separated them, we can compare their writing. For example, Fletcher experienced an epiphany at a place he named Beaver Sand Bar. From *The Man*:

> Now on Beaver Sand Bar, the sense of union had become explicit, intimate, totally involving. It embraced everything. Not only man and beaver and mouse, lizard and rattlesnake and toad, sandfly and slug. Not only thicket and willow tree. Not only the sand bar. But the rock as well. The rock from which the sand bar's sand had been fashioned.

On the other hand, a short time spent glancing through Harvey's logbooks reveals the recurring phrase "principal objective." These were two vastly different men.

Harvey's disparaging remarks could easily be chalked up to envy. Fletcher had written a great book about Grand Canyon and was famous as the Canyon's star hiker. True, Fletcher clearly spelled out Harvey's achievements in the book. But Harvey could not have liked all the attention Fletcher was receiving in the press.

Yet there was more to Harvey's reaction than just envy. A blurb emblazoned on the book's cover read: *The story of the first trip afoot through the depths of the Grand Canyon...*

And then, within a running commentary that accompanied a set of photographs showing the conclusion of Fletcher's journey, there was this: *At the last camp, a satisfied look back—for success had meant far more than becoming the first man to walk the length of Grand Canyon National Park.*

When one imagines Harvey reading these dramatic declarations, it is easy to understand the source of his frustration. Although Harvey and Colin knew neither claim was true, those who glanced at the book would accept them as fact. Harvey's competitive nature being what it was, he could not have helped but feel that he'd been unfairly one-upped.

It would have been infinitely more accurate to state on the cover, *Story of the first continuous trip afoot through Grand Canyon National Park.* To his credit, Fletcher fully disclosed this fact within the narrative. But it is no wonder that before Harvey ever read *The Man*, he felt stung, despite the flowering praise and credit he received inside.

Of course, there is nothing unusual about inflated claims when it comes to selling. The blurb makes a dazzling hook, something guaranteed to make people want to invest in the product. Perhaps Fletcher's publisher felt that bending the truth was part of the game when it came to sales. Perhaps Fletcher himself thought the recognition Harvey received in the book more than made up for the erroneous claims. Whether it was the author's idea or the publisher's is perhaps beside the point. As the author, Fletcher allowed it to be printed. *And printed. And reprinted...*

Fletcher continued taking credit for the first end-to-end hike as recently as the 1990s. In 1989, at the age of 67 and after suffering a heart attack, he returned to Grand Canyon, this time in a boat during a 1,750-mile solo river journey from the Wind River Range in Wyoming to the Gulf of California. Afterward, he wrote *River: One Man's Journey*

Colin Fletcher, self-portrait in June 1966 below Havasu Canyon. *The Huntington Library, San Marino, California*

Down the Colorado, Source to Sea, which was published in 1997. In the author profile, Fletcher is described as "the first man known to have walked the length of Grand Canyon National Park within the Canyon's rim." This was closer to the truth, but still not quite the real McCoy.

In 1968, Harvey could only watch as the spoils went to Fletcher, who had walked away with the Grand Canyon equivalent of a first ascent of Mount Everest. Harvey perhaps took solace in the credit that Fletcher gave him in the book, but as far as the world knew, the honor belonged to Fletcher. And simply put, Fletcher's accomplishment was sexier than Harvey's. Few found it noteworthy that Harvey had hiked across the park first, piecemeal, over a number of years; Fletcher's story on the other hand could easily be grasped and appreciated.

Little did either man predict how *The Man Who Walked Through Time* would change their lives. Both became celebrities. Fletcher saw his career launched to a new level. Many regarded the book as a classic and the resulting sales lifted its author out of the starving writer class. Harvey would soon be deluged with young admirers seeking his counsel. As for the Canyon, *The Man* drummed up significant interest in backpacking and hiking, and visitation to the backcountry would rise sharply in the coming decade.

The book also signaled an end to Harvey's relationship with Fletcher. There would be no more visits, no more enthusiastic conversations—not surprising, considering their differences. Both chased recognition in Grand Canyon in their own ways: Harvey hiked to make discoveries in the landscape. Fletcher hiked to make discoveries within himself. Harvey did indeed scoff at Fletcher and his slow hiking times. Yet Fletcher probably dismissed Harvey's hit-and-run approach for the same reason. Each thought the other was missing the point.

In a rare interview in 1997, Fletcher made clear the reason for his books and adventures. When asked about the potentially detrimental effects of calling attention to seldom-visited wilderness areas, Fletcher said, "I'm never really writing about places. I'm writing about my feelings. I loathe guidebooks, particularly for backpacking." Given that Harvey would write three guidebooks, the nature of the difference between the two men becomes clear.

Simply put, despite their close connection to Grand Canyon, they simply could not relate to each other. In a 1995 letter, Fletcher explained his feelings about Harvey:

> Harvey and I looked at the Canyon very differently: to him it was essentially an obstacle course, to be covered, defeated…At one camp, perhaps beside one of the rainpockets on the Esplanade—I'd found a fragment of an article from *Reader's Digest.* "Oh yes," Harvey said. "Probably mine. I always took something like *Digest* with me…I found when I had to stop, time lay heavy on my

hands." Now look, I'm speaking from memory, of a conversation thirty years old…perhaps you should confirm the fact that this reflected his view of things.

I find myself in an oddly dichotomous frame of mind [about Harvey]. I like him, remain extremely grateful for his generosity in sharing the unique knowledge he'd gained of the Canyon, and down the years have kept vaguely in touch…but I…find him something of an enigma.

Harvey was well aware of how Fletcher viewed him. From a 1969 letter Harvey wrote to Dock Marston:

> I read Colin's journal well enough to see the place where he says that I regard the canyon as an obstacle course whereas he regards it as a museum. I would claim that I am more interested in it than just as a place for a good physical workout. I think he really knows that I am interested in a few more things than just seeing whether I can get around fast. If that were all, I would give up right now.

Differences aside, the question remains about the stretch below Tahuta Point. Did Harvey do it solely for himself, or did he have Fletcher's best interests in mind? And how did Fletcher really feel about being beaten to the punch? Fletcher considered the question in 1995:

> Do I resent him in any way for finishing the last segment of the route just ahead of me? Oh, no, certainly not—though there may have been a momentary twinge of something like it at the moment I got the news. But I understood, perfectly at the time, that I would in his boots probably have done the same—partly because, given his 17 years of Canyon travel, it was right that he should be the first one to complete the traverse, under his one-segment-at-a-time rules; and partly because crossing the amphitheaters would assure him that he wasn't sending me into something that might be too dangerous, or even impossible.

Harvey never publicly commented on his reasons for completing that last leg just ahead of Fletcher. Certainly he had been planning to do it anyway, but he also wanted to clear up any uncertainty for Fletcher's sake.

Or did he? According to Jim Ohlman, a hiking prodigy who spent considerable time with Harvey in the 1970s, the answer came one day when he and Harvey were driving to the Canyon. As Ohlman explained, "We talked about Colin Fletcher and Fletcher was not, you know, right at the top of the list of Harvey's favorite people. And I asked Harvey, 'Now I have a bet with some friends of mine as to what the real reason was, and we think you're a little bit more competitive than that. And we also knew that that was the last section that you needed to do to complete the south rim, and we think you just wanted to get ahead of Fletcher.'"

"He looked at me, and said, 'Of course, you don't think I'd want that idiot to do it first before me!' It was like there was no doubt."

ALL THIS BEGS the question: Who *was* the first man to walk the entire length of Grand Canyon?

Kenton Grua, a Colorado River boatman, started on foot at Lee's Ferry on February 29, 1976 and spent 36 days contouring along the south side of the river all the way to the Grand Wash Cliffs, a walking distance of perhaps 650-700 miles. Grua's remarkable feat stands as one of the greatest hiking accomplishments in Grand Canyon history, though he has received little publicity for it. Grua died in Flagstaff while mountain biking in 2002.

Sadly, in 2001, 79-year-old Colin Fletcher was out for a walk near his Berkeley home when he tried to cross a busy street. An SUV traveling 40 mph accidentally barreled into him, sending him flying headfirst into the pavement. He was whisked to the emergency room where he eventually emerged from a coma only to find his body a mess. He had suffered a fractured spine and a severely bruised cerebral cortex, among other injuries. He has since been making a slow recovery and now walks with a cane. Fletcher hopes to one day write and hike again. He unfortunately was unable to answer questions regarding this book.

In the end, both Harvey and Fletcher could say they had accomplished significant "firsts" in Grand Canyon. And though they never were great friends, the two would be inexorably linked through time by their brief bond.

As for the bet? The nickel that Fletcher won from Harvey still hangs in Fletcher's home. It symbolizes Fletcher's determination to overcome the odds and prove himself both to a doubtful Harvey Butchart and to the world. It also represents Harvey's own determination to become the first person to walk across Grand Canyon National Park. It was only a nickel wager, but in terms of Grand Canyon history, it was priceless.

Colin Fletcher, self-portrait in June 1966 below Havasu Canyon. *The Huntington Library, San Marino, California*

Conquistador Aisle from the rim of Great Thumb Mesa, 1951. *Merrel Clubb, courtesy Grand Canyon National Park Museum Collection*

Chapter Nineteen
Unanswered Questions
1965–1971

Breaks in the Redwall formation are rare enough to be a collector's item.

Harvey Butchart,
"Backpacking Grand Canyon Trails" (1964)

Run a finger along the edge of Great Thumb Mesa on a topographic map of Grand Canyon and the side canyons peel back one after another like ragged furrows. From the Colorado, they become something else. When boats run Stephen and Conquistador Aisles, then the Middle Granite and "Muav" Gorges, bouncing over cataracts Fossil, then Duebendorff, then Upset, their boatmen encounter a succession of sculpted, elegant lower worlds: Royal Arch, Blacktail, Galloway, Stone, Tapeats, Deer, Kanab, Olo, Matkatamiba, 150-Mile, Sinyala, Havasu.

For a place lousy with routine drama, most agree that this stretch is quite the country, as the saying goes. This is also quite the bighorn sheep country, for nowhere does the South Rim fall so steeply to the river's edge, especially on the upstream side of Great Thumb Mesa where Forster and Fossil Canyons cut brief gashes into the abrupt rise of the Thumb. No trails lead down to this land of the deep, and back in the 1960s, no one knew of any way out of there at all.

Harvey was troubled by such an enticing expanse of off-limits canyons. With Glen Canyon Dam putting an end to his air mattress floats in the early 1960s, he was looking at close to 50 river miles along the South Rim of Grand Canyon that could be practically reached only via long, off-trail slogs. One hundred and twenty-five miles on foot separated the Bass Trail from well-trod Havasu Canyon, which marked the borders of this impenetrable section. Not a single rim-to-river route in all that country. It was by far the longest such stretch in Grand Canyon.

No sooner did Harvey recognize this glaring blank spot than *the* hunt of his Grand Canyon career was on. Nothing would inspire him more, nothing would keep calling him back like his belief that he could pierce this wild land. No matter how many times he failed, he kept trying, all because of a single clue he had gained while playing canyon gumshoe in the town of Supai in 1961.

Following up on a tip from park archaeologist R. C. Euler, Harvey had come looking for an old man named Walin Burro. Locals pointed Harvey to a small earthen structure beside Havasu Creek. Harvey stepped to the covered doorway and politely called out to Burro.

"It was kind of picturesque because he was in a sweat bath when I got down there," Harvey said of Burro. "And he had on a g-string and that was all he had. But he came out of his sweat bath and he was willing to answer my questions—if he could."

Walin Burro was the son of Captain Burro, who had belonged to the last generation of Supai Indians that roamed freely in Grand Canyon before the arrival of whites. Harvey had learned that Captain Burro once tended a farm on the east side of Great Thumb Mesa, down on the Fossil Canyon delta. On a hunch that Walin might know of a route from the rim of the peninsula down to his father's old cornfields, Harvey had the half-naked Supai man check his memory banks.

"He got his glasses," Harvey said, "which had only one lens intact, the other had been broken and was gone. And he looked at my map awhile, and I said 'Did you go down the Bass Trail and to the river and get to the mouth of Fossil Bay that way?' [He] said no, he didn't think it was that indirect. He thought they had a better way than that. I don't know, maybe he didn't understand maps anyway, but he said, no he couldn't remember, he was too small a boy. But his father had taken him down there."

Harvey walked away from Supai with no more information than this: *Somewhere* in that huge piece of country below Great Thumb Mesa, a route existed that was hardly wider than a pair of feet. A needle in a canyon of hay. It was just the kind of challenge he thrived upon. Thorny route-finding problems required Harvey to fully engage his well-oiled mind and body; the more difficult the problem, the greater he yearned for an answer. By 1961, Harvey wanted to discover as many rim-to-river routes in Grand Canyon as he could, but this one would top them all—if he could unearth it.

When Colin Fletcher interrupted his long walk in 1963 to try blazing a route down Fossil Canyon, he too sensed the importance of such a discovery. But Fletcher was new to route finding in the Canyon. Fletcher described his lone taste of Butcharting in *The Man Who Walked Through Time:*

The idea of pioneering a route down Fossil Canyon had attracted me, and for three days…I walked and scrambled and climbed and inched my way down and along and then back and along and then across and up and along an endless succession of terraces and ledges and cliffs. Twice I followed tapering cliff face cracks until I was out in places I never should have been. And there was one talus slope I hope one day to forget. On the third evening I came back to camp exhausted. My left hand was a throbbing pincushion: in a sudden moment of fear, on a sloping rock ledge strewn with rubble, I had grabbed blindly for a handhold and found a prickly pear. And for the third straight day I had failed to find a break in the Redwall cliff that is Fossil Canyon's major barrier.

The Redwall Limestone would likewise prove to be Harvey's nemesis in this hunt, which only served to heighten his desire. His sphere of mastery in Grand Canyon could not be tied to any particular area, but rather to this formidable remnant of ancient seas. With 500 to 600 feet of relief, the Redwall simply presented too much cliff to defeat without major luck or sharp-eyed, long-term investigation. No wonder then that the Redwall's sheer difficulty attracted Harvey and his love of problems again and again.

When it came to Harvey's Canyon obsessions, routes—especially routes through the Redwall—ranked at the top of his list. His dedication to finding them meant that he sometimes lacked for companions, for the physical demands could be staggering. Susan Billingsley, a former river guide who first came to Grand Canyon in the 1960s, explained, "I didn't do that much hiking with Harvey but I never particularly wanted to. Because he didn't hike, I don't think, for the beauty or anything else, he hiked to get to a certain point. You'd go look at his slides and they would be of the route, you know, there was never a beautiful slide of the Canyon, or

The Redwall Limestone cliff near Fossil Canyon. *Elias Butler*

who was with him, just—the route. He was so focused on that. He'd just get up in the morning and eat in his sleeping bag, and then get up and hike all day, and get in his sleeping bag and eat and go to sleep."

One reason for Harvey's attachment to route finding was the high number of variables involved in the equation—the hardness, texture, load-bearing capability, and shape of its stratigraphic components. Any or all of these characteristics might make a particular route attractive or objectionable. Going from rim-to-river would certainly mean navigating at least four or five and sometimes as many as a dozen different types of rock. With so many possible combinations, there was always the opportunity to be creative with a route.

Harvey became a geologist of sorts, developing a familiarity with each of the Canyon's substratums, including how they "behaved" and where passage might be gained by paying close attention to certain irregularities. As his delving progressed, he slowly built a set of procedures that allowed him to quickly estimate the probability of a route's success or failure. But it was nothing quantifiable. Instead, the answers depended upon hunches and an experienced eye. Was it sandstone he was dealing with, smooth and sticky on the soles of his boots? Or sharpened limestone, which offered more reliable holds? What would the presence of large versus small boulders in a canyon bottom indicate about the terrain upstream?

No matter the rock type, Harvey realized that the common denominator for his success was the geologic fault that can rend the hardest canyon walls. He searched endlessly for faults. He learned to recognize the telltale signs, the steep rockslides or broken stairways of cliff. Harvey twice went with a pilot who flew him into the Canyon, armed with a camera and binoculars, scanning for these breaks like a bird hunting its prey. The faults were there if you knew what to look for. Later, he would check on foot what possibilities he had identified, using his photos as a guide.

"In a lot of places there's no way to get around—you simply can't get through," said George Billingsley, a geologist and former river guide who spent 23 years putting together the geologic map of Grand Canyon. "And I relied on Butchart's maps to help get me through. But I also began to understand the geology enough to where I could do the aerial photography work and find out where the faults are. And I knew those were the most likely routes to get through. A lot of those I'd give to Butchart after I made them and he'd go follow them, too."

The problem at Great Thumb Mesa inspired Harvey to make his first flyover in 1965. These were the days prior to Federal Aviation Administration regulations in the Canyon. If you had a chopper or plane, you could go wherever you wanted, even below the rim—something that today is strictly forbidden.

Harvey teamed with fellow ASC professor and pilot Bill Martin, instructing him to soar past the most unforgiving stretch of Redwall Limestone in the park. From Harvey's March 1966 *Summit Magazine* article "Scouting Grand Canyon By Plane":

> Familiarity may breed contempt most of the time, but not where Grand Canyon is concerned. I have spent more days than there are in one year finding routes through the remote areas, but I am still keen to see and know more. When Bill Martin...suggested a canyon flight, I accepted enthusiastically...the primary purpose of the flight was to help gage possible hiking and climbing routes, but I had to force myself out of a daze, a blurring sense of wonder at the whole great gorge.

Harvey swallowed an airsickness pill, tried to quit gawking, and settled in. At Great Thumb Mesa, he photographed any suspicious creases in the Redwall. One place in particular caught Harvey's eye, a broken, irregular cliff that he had noticed during a prior foot-reconnaissance. "When I had [previously] walked from the Bass Trail to the mouth of Fossil," wrote Harvey, "I had seen an interesting break in the Redwall about a mile upriver from Fossil. As Bill cruised by the place I became convinced that I could get down here but I will keep my fingers crossed until I do it." (See photograph opposite page 1.)

Harvey realized that even when something looked good from the air, it did not always mean things would go well on foot. He waited until the following July before making the drive to Great Thumb Mesa to try his proposed route. He had not yet found a way through the upper rock layers off Great Thumb Mesa's eastern face except in Fossil Canyon, which was at least two miles north of the Redwall break he had in mind. He decided to descend Fossil to the Esplanade and then head south to his break.

Yet bad luck struck before he got very far. From his logbook:

> Perhaps I was trying to hurry, or it may be that I'm getting careless. Anyway, while I was looking for the route two steps ahead, I stumbled. I fell headlong and my canteen flopped up and caught my full weight on its shallow cylindrical surface. The 25-pound pack added to the impact. The blow came right over the heart. I got my canteen and pack off and rolled back into the shade of a large rock to get over the shock and assess the damage if any. I had cracked a rib in Kanab Creek with a lighter blow, and I had done the same with a heavier impact while skiing...The pain in my chest was increasing, and by now a sort of secondary shock was making my knees tremble. I took a couple of pictures and decided that I had had enough for one trip.

Harvey limped back to his truck with a freshly broken rib, wincing with each breath. For all his pain, he had covered no new ground. Thus, when the opportunity came to take another reconnaissance flight in October, Harvey resolved to give himself every advantage before making his next attempt on foot. He made notes on his map while in the air, took more photos of the Redwall break south of Fossil Canyon, and scanned for possible routes through the overlying rock layers.

He put off his next attempt at the route in favor of more immediately attainable goals in other parts of the Canyon. It was April 1968 before he turned his attention back to Great Thumb Mesa by trying to come at its eastern wall from below. He planned to descend via Royal Arch Creek to the Colorado, then make a long downstream hike along the river. Yet no one knew if it was indeed possible to use Royal Arch as a route to the river. He led three friends, Clarence 'Doc' Ellis, Chuck Johnson, and Jorgen Visbak off the South Rim at Apache Point to find out.

From the start of this trek, Harvey did not feel his usual self. After descending to the Esplanade, he failed to remember how to reach the bed of Royal Arch. Harvey prided himself on his bulletproof

Harvey on the Esplanade near Royal Arch Creek, April 1968. *Courtesy Jorgen Visbak*

memory but it had been four years since his last visit to this side canyon. A wild goose chase ensued. By nighttime, the four hikers found themselves still stranded on the Esplanade. They chanced upon a good-sized pothole and made camp.

"In the morning," Harvey wrote in his log, "after I had been a poor guide by leading the group down from the trail, and then admitting that I couldn't remember the better route, we went back up to the trail and proceeded south." Finally they located a route, but part of their descent involved a narrow, exposed ledge requiring careful hand-and-toe work. Harvey never considered himself much of a daredevil and his courage wavered.

"I had the unpleasant feeling through most of this rough going that I have lost self confidence badly during the last few years," he wrote. "The three younger men were taking to it better than I."

However, Harvey managed to get past the obstacle. He joined the others in the canyon bottom where they continued toward the river. The men soon reached a small flow of water in the steadily narrowing corridor then pools appeared, some spanning the width of the creek bed. The pools forced them to either wade or inch along small ledges to get past. Harvey chose to wade, as did Visbak; Ellis and Johnson, however, were climbers. They took to the ledges. In this manner they proceeded, pool to pool toward the bridge Harvey had discovered in 1959.

It was a fine time to visit. Springtime transforms Royal Arch Creek into a colorful oasis of columbines and Indian paintbrush. At one point Harvey abruptly told everyone to look up, and there stood Royal Arch.

After spending the rest of the day in a fruitless search for a route to the river in the vicinity of Royal Arch Creek, they returned to the bridge that night to camp. The next morning, they decided to resume their efforts to reach the river. They loaded their packs and began hiking upstream to a point where they could climb out of the bed. At the first of the wall-to-wall pools, where Harvey and Visbak had previously waded across, Harvey now impatiently looked at Ellis and Johnson. They were exhibiting their fearlessness, already traversing the tiny ledges. Rather than taking the time to remove his shoes and socks to wade the pool, which would have meant making the others wait for him to catch up, Harvey made a hasty decision to try hurdling the water from atop a boulder.

Unfortunately, he forgot that he was now wearing a fully loaded backpack. When he landed, the added weight split his right heel bone with an audible, unmistakable *snap*. His left heel fared only slightly better with a severe bruise. As he writhed in pain on the cool stone floor of the canyon, clutching his feet, Harvey knew there would be no getting himself out of this jam. The others quickly decided to send Johnson to the rim for help.

Visbak and Ellis each took Harvey's arm over their shoulders and helped him back to their campsite beneath the bridge. They made him as comfortable as possible on his air mattress but could do little else. Fortunately, Ellis had experience as a search and rescue man and knew what a helicopter would need to land. In the bottom of a precipitous canyon, with barely a patch of level ground to be seen, he suddenly noticed the top of Royal Arch: It did not look like much, but the helicopter would likely need to land atop the bridge itself.

Johnson made the grueling hike to the rim quicker than anyone had guessed possible. He reached the parking area that night. In the morning, Easter Sunday, he expedited Harvey's 1955 Ford truck 40 dirt road miles to Grand Canyon Village. Johnson reported the accident to one of the few rangers on duty, who immediately arranged for a helicopter.

Meanwhile, Harvey was feeling better but both heels had swollen badly. He could not walk. While sitting in camp near noon, he and his two companions heard a distant staccato beat and quickly got ready. Ellis had cleared the landing site of brush and now clambered up to signal the pilot. Exercising the utmost care, the pilot placed the skids atop Royal Arch without shutting off the engine, ready to lift at any moment should a gust of wind push the helicopter off its slim perch. Harvey gamely willed himself up the steep slope to the chopper with the help of his rescuers.

"On the steepest and loosest part," Harvey wrote, "I crawled on hands and sore knees, but [Malcom] Nicholson piggybacked me up some very tiring parts. His help must have saved a good many dollars in chopper time."

Harvey thrilled at the sights afforded him during the flight to Grand Canyon Village. He even snapped photos of a few faults and vowed to remember them for later. At the South Rim hospital, he was given a cursory examination and ordered to report to Flagstaff Hospital.

Harvey crawls toward the top of Royal Arch with the help of a well-placed boost. *Courtesy Jorgen Visbak*

Roma arrived to retrieve him. One can only guess what admonitions she had for her wounded husband during the 90-minute drive, but it would have been a good opportunity to remind him of the risks he was taking. X-rays would later reveal a wide crack in his right heel bone, which forced Harvey into a wheel-chair for two weeks and then crutches for two weeks more. He walked with a cane for months afterwards. And then there was the bill: The rescue had cost him $145.

NPS Ranger Malcolm Nicholson loads Harvey into the helicopter. *Courtesy Jorgen Visbak*

If anything, this setback only strengthened Harvey's resolve to locate Walin Burro's route below Great Thumb Mesa. In June, he returned to the Thumb with a party from *National Geographic* that was working on a Grand Canyon feature. With his bum heels, Harvey did no exploring on this trip, but photographer Walter Maeyers Edwards did take his photo at Enfilade Point (see cover).

By Thanksgiving, his broken bone had mended and Harvey felt ready for more route finding. He returned to Royal Arch Creek with several companions to make good on his prior mistake. This time they succeeded in reaching the river with the help of a 20-foot rappel, thus completing a new rim-to-river route.

The party then walked downstream along the Colorado for eight miles until making it to the foot of Harvey's proposed route up Great Thumb Mesa. They looked nearly straight up and identified the Redwall break in Harvey's aerial photo. But the walls appeared much steeper from down here than they had from the air. Their collective enthusiasm to climb suddenly waned. "Doc [Ellis] had said that my aerials made the climb seem 75% possible," Harvey wrote. "But now we all thought that the probability was far less. I still want to try it someday, but when I was on the spot, I was about ready to write it off as a bad guess."

This unanswered question stuck in the back of his mind for a year. Harvey decided he had to at least try the route before giving up. Over Thanksgiving break in 1969, Harvey descended the Bass Trail to the river and began the 15-mile downstream bushwhack. It meant a long approach, but by the third morning of this solo trek he was ascending the foot of Great Thumb Mesa.

He scrambled up steep talus slopes to the bottom of the Redwall. It was not an encouraging place. The footing proved crumbly. Although he did notice bighorn sheep droppings leading upward, indicating a route, the unnerving exposure he encountered made for a tough decision. He gathered his courage and went forward along a narrow ledge, the handholds calving off in chunks of rotten rock. After scratching his way across an unstable-looking chute, where he had to trust his life to protruding rocks that looked as if they might give under his weight, he hesitated at the bottom of a precipitous ravine. From here he would need to make an unprotected climb if he wanted to continue.

Suddenly the risk he was about to take seemed absurd. "The way over there seemed especially precarious," he wrote, "and all the chances I had already taken had eroded my morale."

During his cautious descent, however, he happened upon an intriguing clue: Two large rocks that had been piled to make a crucial step below a short cliff. "Now I knew," wrote Harvey, "that Indians had used this route." Even with this encouraging find, he feared that he had finally met his match in the Redwall. "I may never get back here myself, but I would recommend it to strong and careful climbers as the most spectacular route from the rim to the river."

BY THE LATE 1960s, things were changing rapidly for Harvey and the Grand Canyon hiking community. Colin Fletcher's *The Man Who Walked Through Time* was bringing more attention than ever to the backcountry. A crowd of serious young hikers and climbers began arriving in Fletcher's wake, hungry for their own experiences in the wilderness. Harvey no longer had the place to himself.

Amidst this surge of new canyoneers, one pioneer was hanging up his climbing rope for good. Merrel Clubb had been suffering a slow, downward spiral into alcoholism for several years now. Following his heart attack in 1961, he had been drinking a spoonful of vodka each night on his doctor's advice to help him relax. After the 1963 flash flood at Indian Garden that killed his son and grandson, however, Clubb began hitting the bottle hard.

In August 1964, Harvey discussed Clubb's personal and legal problems in a letter to Dock Marston:

Merrel Clubb often wore a hanky on his head, which inspired Harvey to do the same. *Courtesy Merrel Clubb, Jr.*

The news about Clubb is really disturbing. He spent almost two months at the north rim in a very distraught state of mind. He drank a lot and seemed worried about whether his wife had a malignant growth in her throat. Some of the time he didn't seem to know where she was, California or Montana. Then he hiked over to Indian Gardens and back to see where his son and grandson had died. That really cut him up and he drank all the harder.

He drove to the south rim by way of Flagstaff, possibly to visit the package stores. On the way to the South Rim, at Red Lake north of Williams, he was thrown out for disorderly conduct. In the park, he forced two cars off the road. When the rangers tried to stop him, he drove east and parked near Shoshone Point. They found him on a ledge below the point threatening to jump if anyone came closer. I think they used a bottle of Vodka to talk him into letting them help him back to the rim. He was put into a hospital, but I suppose he will face charges of drunk driving later.

Following this emotional breakdown at Shoshone Point, Clubb's drinking habits continued. He repeated his mistake of driving under the influence near Grand Canyon and was later caught weaving in traffic west of Cameron. The NPS levied a $250 fine, which apparently convinced him to cut down to one beer a day. But Clubb's behavior remained erratic. In 1994, Harvey wrote about Clubb:

> He did some odd things. He shared [General George] Patton's belief that one can get used to lack of water in the desert by practice. He came to the South Rim one time and the next day went down to the Tonto and sat in the sun without any water.

On a positive note, in 1965 Clubb had led Emery Kolb on an epic Grand Canyon hiking finale below Point Imperial. For the 85 year-old Kolb, it was a chance to see Kolb Bridge, named for him and his brother Ellsworth. Clubb and Kolb reached the bridge, but the two spent an unexpected, freezing night trying to sleep back-to-back when they failed to reach the rim on the hike out.

In the late 1960s, Clubb's relationship with the Park Service soured once more when he showed up at the South Rim one day to obtain a permit for a backpack trip. Ranger Lynn Coffin hesitated. He felt Clubb would be taking a risk by attempting a solo off-trail trek at his age. Clubb retorted that the Park Service owed him a debt for promoting Grand Canyon with slide shows in Kansas, and that he deserved preferential treatment for dedicating so much of his life to backcountry exploration. Clubb began yelling, "You can't order me around after all I've done for the Canyon!"

Coffin finally relented. But he had been correct to doubt Clubb. The hike turned out to be nearly fatal. Clubb developed heat exhaustion and had to be

assisted out of the Canyon by NPS
maintenance man Marshall Scholing.
When he retired in May 1968 from
the University of Kansas at the age of
70, Clubb headed for the North Rim
to make his annual stay. That summer
he made another pilgrimage to Indian
Garden. In a last letter to Harvey, he
wrote, "Just went down the [Bright
Angel Trail] to the scene of the double
tragedy, as I wish I could always do."

Clubb made his final trip to Grand
Canyon the following year in October
1969. The outing gave him a chance
to reflect on his relationship with the
gorge. "I was (unexpectedly) having
my anniversary, for this was the 30th
year since I started hiking in the
Canyon with Will and Roger. I must

Merrel Clubb in Shinumo Amphitheatre,
1957. *Courtesy Douglas W. Schwartz*

have lived in it 3 yrs altogether in some 20 summers—not a bad record for an
alien unemployed civilian."

Harvey noted that Clubb's "determination lasted longer than his strength."
In February 1970, Clubb suffered severe chest pains and was hospitalized in the
Lawrence Memorial Hospital intensive care unit in Kansas. There he suffered a
second heart attack and this time, there would be no hiking away from it. After
several days in the hospital he died.

IN APRIL 1971, 11 years after interrupting Walin Burro's sweat bath at Supai,
Harvey renewed his efforts to solve the mystery below Great Thumb Mesa. This
time he brought his friend Donald Davis. Davis was a professional caver and
skilled climber with an unusual knack for finding Anasazi pots in Grand
Canyon, including one cache while hiking with Harvey in Lava Canyon in
1968 that produced eight pots and several baskets.[1]

Harvey planned to descend Fossil Canyon to the Esplanade, then hike
upstream to the Redwall break that he had previously shied away from. Before
reaching Fossil Canyon, however, Harvey high-centered his four-wheeler on

---

[1] One of the pots Davis discovered can be seen at the Tusayan Ruins Museum at the South
Rim.

Harvey starting down from Enfilade Point. *Courtesy Jorgen Visbak*

one of the rock ledges that roughen the Great Thumb Mesa road. When he and Davis finally extracted the vehicle, they were still five miles from Fossil Canyon.

Harvey's bad driving would, for once, prove fortuitous. Not wishing to further damage his vehicle, Harvey parked and decided they could walk to nearby Enfilade Point instead. It was a long shot, but he had seen a possible break in the rim there during his last air reconnaissance. And, Enfilade Point loomed almost directly above the Redwall fault that he had previously tried.

Once at the viewpoint, the two men combed the rim for a place to descend. They found a talus slope that permitted them to get down a few hundred feet, as far as the Toroweap Formation, but no farther. Davis tried to chimney down a chute that would have led to the underlying Coconino Sandstone but he nearly panicked while negotiating the powdery rock and retreated. Further searches yielded only more danger, as Harvey noted:

> The rock is relatively soft and one's admiration is aroused for the sheep who nimbly cross these four inch crumbly bits of trail with never a thought for the 300 foot fall that might occur at any time. Donald and I backed away several times and painstakingly pawed our way up the 45 degree or steeper slope to get around a few of the worst parts of the sheep trail.

Harvey's foot had begun to ache, so he retreated to the rim to rest while Davis checked one last possibility through the Toroweap. This time Davis found an exciting sign: Charcoal pictographs scrawled underneath an overhang beside a rock pile step. The Indians had come down here! This made sense, for an Anasazi ruin indeed guarded the rim at Enfilade Point. When he returned to the rim, Davis told Harvey the good news. Harvey wrote:

> We had found a way through the Kaibab and Toroweap with signs of Indian use and this is the much more direct approach to the Supai and Redwall breaks

I have been interested in. Donald plans to go back there immediately while I stay at home and nurse my sore foot and badly blistered lower lip. We really seem to be closing in on the rim-to-river route...

Harvey returned to Flagstaff for work. Meanwhile, the next day, Davis succeeded in following the route off Enfilade Point through both the Toroweap and the 600-foot thick Coconino Sandstone, which put him on the Esplanade only about a mile north of the Redwall break Harvey had in mind. Davis later called an excited Harvey to explain the details.

Harvey returned two weeks later, certain he could finally put it all together.

Harvey on the Esplanade in 1974, gazing at the cliffs below Enfilade Point, where he struggled to locate an Anasazi rim-to-river route. *Courtesy Jorgen Visbak*

His four-wheeler raised a plume of dust as he barreled across the sun-baked road leading to Great Thumb Mesa, bucking and bouncing over ruts and washes, the big V-8 engine snorting like a bull at each obstacle.

From an article of Harvey's entitled "Grand Canyon's Enfilade Point Route," which would be published in the June 1973 issue of *Summit Magazine*:

> I had tried to get a companion, but I felt it was appropriate to tackle this route alone. I wanted to upset the jinx. The project had cost me a broken rib and injured heels and I understood how Captain Ahab felt toward Moby Dick.

He parked a few miles from Enfilade Point and walked hurriedly along the road. He passed through the dwarf forest of sagebrush and junipers that quivered in the day's growing breeze. Harvey kept up his steady gait until the road skirted the edge of the mesa where no obstructions hid the view.

Beyond his perch the land had swallowed itself whole. He gazed down, momentarily awed by the spectacle, as happened no matter how many times he returned to Grand Canyon. Nearly a mile almost directly below, the river appeared as a silvery snake in the morning glare, its rapids visible but moving in silent slow motion from this great a height. A near-vertical succession of broken, leaning, decaying cliffs dropped between the rim and the riverbank. Harvey now realized why he hadn't tried descending from Enfilade Point in the first place: To do so looked impossible.

Harvey quickly made his way down past the pictographs that Davis had discovered, through the Coconino and onto the Esplanade. Instead of resting, he continued to march as fast as possible across this tableland toward the final inner rim. Dried-up potholes marked the clean-swept, smoothed landscape. Everything expressed aridity here, but a few mariposa lilies and Indian paintbrushes bloomed in the sparse pockets of red soil. Harvey always enjoyed the spring flowers but now he barely noticed, such was his focus on what awaited below.

Once at that inner rim, he descended again, this time down 500 feet of shattered red Supai sandstones into a much more gothic-looking chasm enclosed by older substratums. The river sent up a muted rumble, as it was not so far below. Harvey carefully followed its course upstream by picking his way along a slender, exposed causeway formed by the very top of the Redwall Limestone. Harvey knew his success now depended on how forgiving the Redwall would be here. In his previous attempts, the Redwall had meant the end of the road. But he was farther down this route than he had ever been before, and all he needed was a small break. Everything hinged on what he would find next.

The natural walkway continued until suddenly depositing him upon a buttress looming 1,500 feet over the Colorado. His momentum carried him to the buttresses's edge, but there the route tumbled off into space, stopping him cold. Harvey peered over the brink hundreds of feet straight down into a chaotic array of boulders and talus. The man with a penchant for understatement would simply write, "This place startled me..."

Harvey hesitated, thinking of how many times he had faced this particular Redwall cliff, and how many times he had turned back. Although the drop was exposed, he decided he would rather face the dangers of falling than tasting defeat all the way back to Flagstaff one more time. He took off his pack, camera, and even his canteen to give him as much mobility as possible, then stepped off the edge.

The Enfilade Point route from the Colorado. Note the steep ravine at center right in the Redwall Limestone: Butchart Fault. *Elias Butler*

With practiced movements, Harvey felt his way down the vertical limestone wall. Convenient holds appeared exactly where he needed them. He soon reached relatively solid ground, then continued descending the Redwall until he noticed a familiar sight:

> Around the corner I could see where I had turned back 18 months before...I had connected with my former route...over the years I have rediscovered a number of climber's routes from the rim to the river, but for scenery and brevity, this one is foremost.

Harvey never took greater satisfaction in any of his Canyon accomplishments. Not only had this route required his best efforts and a bit of luck, it also allowed him to symbolically link with canyoneers of bygone eras. It dated as far back as AD 950, as evidenced by the potsherds and Anasazi ruin Harvey located near the foot of the route, and the pictographs and ruin near its head. "I felt," he wrote, "like I was part of a chain that dated back to prehistoric Indians and Spanish explorers."

Geologist George Billingsley later commemorated Harvey's success by naming the geologic fault that breaks the Redwall Limestone below Enfilade Point "Butchart Fault." Of all the features that one might suggest to canonize a person in Grand Canyon, perhaps no greater homage could be paid to a route finder than a fault.

Although Harvey enjoyed spreading the word about such accomplishments, when given the chance to brag in person, he was likely to let someone else take the spotlight. While returning from a hike later that year, as he neared the top of the Tanner Trail near Lipan Point, he observed the usual crowd of awed Canyon visitors milling about. He passed through their midst on his way to the parking lot when he heard something that made him stop and turn.

"No one's walked more down there than Colin Fletcher," a woman was saying to her husband. "Yep. I read his book and he walked all the way through the Grand Canyon!"

By this time Harvey had spent at least 950 hiking days in the Canyon; he knew *exactly* who had walked the most down there. And even a few others who had out-walked Fletcher. The urge to correct the mistaken woman's remark was too much for the man driven to "keep ahead of the competition." Sweaty and trail-worn, Harvey approached the couple. He cleared his throat and interrupted.

"Excuse me," he announced. "Actually, there is somebody who's walked more in Grand Canyon than Colin Fletcher."

"Oh yeah, who?" the woman retorted.

"His name is Allan MacRae," said Harvey, referring to the man who rescued the parachutists in 1944. Harvey had never met or talked to MacRae.

"I know Allan!" the woman said. Her response caught Harvey by surprise.

Turns out she was MacRae's neighbor in Maryland. She gave Harvey his phone number, leading to a long-overdue conversation between the two pioneering explorers. Harvey could indeed be modest, if not always to a fault.

Wotan's Throne from Vishnu Creek. *Elias Butler*

Chapter Twenty

THE LAUGHING GERMAN GOD
2004

"GOOD IDEA," ELIAS REMARKS as I stack a pile of rocks atop a prominent boulder. It's early morning on the second day of our trek, and we've just climbed 300 feet out of the bed of Vishnu Creek to the Tonto bench. We used a very steep drainage to make it up here. Looking back, it's clear that identifying this particular trough in the cliff is going to be difficult upon our return. The last thing we'll want at the end of this marathon day is to stumble around trying to find the finish line, hence my cairn.

We quickly traverse to the north, following the canyon's upstream course on the sloping flanks of the Bright Angel shale. The shadowy form of Newberry Butte blots the rising sun to the east. Our eyes remain fixed upon Wotan's Throne, looming over the head of this canyon and looking bigger by the step. We've got at least seven miles of hard hiking and 5,000 feet of elevation separating us from its summit, though it's only a couple miles as the condor flies.

From either the North or South Rim, Wotan's Throne deceives the eyes. Manhole-cover flat, the butte's summit more closely resembles a giant anvil than a mountain. From deep inside the Canyon today, however, it appears very much a mountain, even a fortress. Our siege must be fast and unrelenting if we are to succeed in one day.

As we scurry toward the base of the butte, we enjoy a good look at the opposite side of Vishnu Canyon. Not only does it appear more level on that side, it is a much straighter shot down an obvious and easier-looking ramp leading toward our camp. The drainage we climbed this morning was tricky, and our current side-hilling to circumvent steep drainages below Newberry is tough, especially on the downhill leg. I feel especially wary of shortcuts from Canyon horror stories I know, but that ramp across the way seems certain. We solemnly vow to our aching joints to consider it for the return trip.

It takes a good hour of scrambling before we can drop back into the bed of

Scaling the cliffs in upper Vishnu Creek. *Elias Butler*

Vishnu Creek. The walking becomes easier in the modest grade of the dry creek bottom. Our spirits lift when we reach a true Grand Canyon oasis—a beautiful Muav Limestone "patio" complete with spring, cottonwood trees, and tiny waterfalls purring over small ledges. No doubt, this would have been a better camp than the one we chose. We enjoy it for a few minutes and eat granola bars before trekking on.

As we approach the upper end of Vishnu Canyon, the bed becomes gradually more boulder-choked and difficult to negotiate. The canyon splits into two main arms, then narrows and grows dark, yet the way is obvious and we continue our sprint.

But Vishnu proves to be a tease. It abruptly halts our progress when we come upon an evil-looking pillar of loose rock and debris that guards the canyon's upper end. The pillar resembles a demolished stone building, a haphazard stack of unconsolidated stone perched precariously on pedestal rocks, and the whole thing is eroding from all angles. There is no way around it. We will have to climb this stack of cards.

We dump our larger packs for lighter fanny packs. Elias goes first. Delicately, he climbs only the sections that look cemented in. He knows accidentally kicking or placing too much weight on a keystone could detonate an avalanche. Despite his cautious approach, clods of dirt break free. Small rocks come loose and ricochet like bullets off nearby slabs. I duck for cover. When Elias is done, I follow commando-like, sneaking through the potential danger, convinced that stealth is the best way to avoid rousing this sleeping adversary.

On top we breathe huge sighs of relief, then continue up through 600 feet of successive cliffs in the Supai Formation. At the very last of these, we finally leave the head of Vishnu Creek and step onto the level Hermit Shale just below Cape Royal and the North Rim. Here we allow ourselves a short break, gawking at the arch above us known as Angel's Window. It's a strange sensation to stand just below a tourist hot spot that becomes crowded each summer. But this time of year, the North Rim road is still closed beneath winter snow, and Cape Royal is eerily devoid of people.

We turn south upon the Hermit Shale toward Wotan's Throne. When he first passed this way 42 years earlier, Harvey expressed our thoughts about the Hermit's annoying qualities:

> Travel along the Hermit Shale is necessarily slow. You have to push through brush, watch for skids, and go up or down to avoid steep-walled gullies and huge rocks. Deer tracks may help you find the best route, but you can be sure that the best is not good. To make a mile an hour you have to keep going whether you think you are on the best route or not.

At the quickest pace we can muster, we finally reach the base of our mountain after an hour of slogging. We rest a few moments before starting up the first obstacle, the 500-foot Coconino Sandstone cliff that rings the summit. At only one spot is ascent through this wall possible—right where we stand, at the bottom of a break in this mighty formation. This immense talus slope is a chaotic mess of broken slabs resting at an angle of 40 to 50 degrees.

The temperature is soaring this warm Spring day and the route is exposed to direct sunlight. I continually swipe away streams of sweat from my eyes, trying to stay focused so as to avoid stepping on an errant rock, spiny agave, or off a small cliff edge. Racing against time, we are over halfway through the Coconino when we are forced to stop. The summit is close, probably 500 vertical feet above, but the route is nowhere in sight. Fifteen minutes more into a fruitless search for possibilities, we remain stymied and grow more frustrated. Meanwhile, precious water, time and energy continue to evaporate. I find my anxiety reaching a boiling point...until Elias finally speaks.

Stopped cold in the Coconino below Wotan's Throne. *Elias Butler*

"I think I'm spent."

I am surprised and relieved to hear Elias confess what I too am feeling. Elias is a photographer, and has been talking about wanting to get shots from atop Wotan's Throne. But, he says, he's just too worn out to keep fighting. Besides, through the stinging sweat, my watch shows that it's nearly 2 P.M. Too late. It seems we have underestimated the Canyon, and overestimated our own abilities.

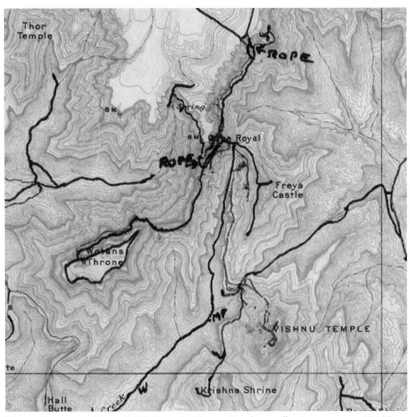

Harvey's route to Wotan's Throne. *J. Harvey Butchart collection, courtesy NAU Special Collections*

Parking under a small overhang that offers the only shade in sight, we sit and say nothing. For all of our work, our only reward is a spectacular view of Vishnu Temple's west flank.

Then, in my mind, the silence breaks: *Don't give up! What if we find a way through these cliffs right now?*

But the summit is at least two to three hours away. Even if we pushed ourselves up there, it would still mean a brutal 10-hour jaunt in the dark to return to camp tonight. We will also be out of water soon. The thought of being stuck high and dry at night on the cliffs of Wotan's Throne turns out to be the perfect antidote for our summit fever. I think of Harvey Butchart and feel a bit sheepish, as if we've let him down. Harvey probably would have made it.

Then, looking back over my shoulder at the butte, I see Wotan. He is sitting in his throne, laughing. Humbled, exhausted, and busted at the foot of Grand Canyon's German god, we turn around.

Elias and I hurriedly lumber along the Hermit Shale back toward Cape Royal, where we can down-climb through the Supai cliffs into Vishnu Creek. As the sun begins submerging itself into the ocean of rock in the distance, we do our best to cover ground. We know if we can get down that awful debris pillar in the Redwall at the upper end of Vishnu Creek before dark, we will be home free. Coming up it had been bad enough, and I dread the thought of doing it again, especially by flashlight. I have been trying to block the climb out my mind all afternoon, in fact, but in no time it appears below.

Peering down Vishnu Creek, spooky shadows are quickly filling the voids and crevasses, making the scene look even more ominous. But our packs are patiently waiting for us at the bottom of this climb, which is comforting. Poised at the edge, I ask Elias if I can go first, not out of bravery, but because I want to get it over with before what little nerve I have left shrivels to nothing. He obliges and sets a hand line. New beads of sweat break out on my forehead. I hold my breath as I slink down the teetering rubble. Elias follows. In less than a few minutes it is over for both of us.

In the waning light, we quickly survey our packs's contents. Our water and food have dwindled drastically. Elias has a bottle of water left, and I am out. I take a few swallows of his, then we hustle down canyon, trying to cover as much ground as the daylight will allow.

An hour of boulder hopping and easy scrambling brings us to the flats of the lower Redwall in the drainage. The sun has dipped below the horizon, so we begin to trot, and within minutes we reach the oasis where we had stopped this morning on

Descending the Supai in Vishnu Creek. *Elias Butler*

the way up. I kneel and drink my fill of unfiltered water. We figure we are probably three miles from camp. Elias drinks from his bottle of filtered water, and feels he won't need to collect any more to get himself back to camp. We can't afford to waste the time anyway. I fill one bottle straight from the spring, and then, decide to fill another. Just in case.

We continue into the deepening dark and before long find ourselves at the lip of a large Tapeats cliff, a dry fall too high to negotiate. To the east lies our route from this morning, long, slow and steep, but guaranteed to take us back to camp. To the west is our untested but easier-looking shortcut that we saw this morning. It is 7 P.M. We are nearly out of food and feeling weary.

We veer west.

Using the dim twilight, we slowly walk in and out of a saw-toothed ridgeline cut by small bays and side canyons. While the terrain is probably more level than what we hiked this morning on the west side, after another hour passes, it becomes obvious that this shortcut isn't any shorter. When we finally arrive at the cliffs above our camp, it's after 8 P.M. and we're more than ready to call it a day. In the moonlight, we can make out something of the dim terrain below. A slope drops about 400 feet to the bed of Vishnu Creek. From there, our tiny camp is an easy stone's throw away, just downstream in the bed of the canyon.

We start bushwhacking down, more cautiously now, as the shadows obliterate our depth perception. The night air is dead calm and muggy. We continue to sweat profusely. I have less than half a liter of water left. Elias has none. I know he's been dry for some time and is probably dehydrated, because he hasn't urinated since lunchtime. But he doesn't want to drink unfiltered water, for fear it might reactivate his giardiasis, contracted long ago. He said he will wait for safe water back at camp.

We pick our way down, down, down this rocky talus. I'm famished, and all I can talk about is dinner. All Elias can think of is water. Soon the top of a cottonwood tree in Vishnu Creek comes into view. I scoot ahead. Only 30 or 40 more feet and we'll be back in the bed of the canyon, which by now I'm fully prepared to kiss.

"It goes!" I holler.

But suddenly things begin to look a little queer. I swallow hard and hold my breath as I descend a few more feet. "Wait a minute," I stammer as a faint rock edge materializes from the shadows.

I glance over the edge: A dry fall. I shine my flashlight over the lip. The cliff is slick and polished, overhanging. The drop is at least 30 feet. With only a short, thin hand line, there is no possibility of rappelling or climbing down.

I brace against the wave of panic surging through me, my heart now jackhammering in my chest. Elias has caught up, and after his initial survey, I can sense him instantly doing the same.

"*Oh no! This can't be right!*" I blurt.

This 30-foot drop is all that separates us from camp. We are closing in on 15 hours of non-stop hiking. We desperately hunt for a way off the cliff, looking at every possibility. There is none.

Our shortcut is fool's gold.

Harvey on the summit of Vesta Temple, 1972. *Courtesy Lee Dexter*

Chapter Twenty-One
THE PAPER TRAIL
1969–1975

No assumption should be made as to how long it might take to traverse any of these routes. When Butchart traveled with a hiking companion, it commonly was a person of considerable capability; one of his frequent companions is reported to have crossed the canyon from rim to rim on the maintained trails in 3 hours. My own experience has been that a route which might be described by Butchart as "interesting" may significantly exceed in difficulty and danger what a normal outdoors person might consider prudent or enjoyable.

United States Geological Survey letter to Don Ziegler, a
hiker who requested a copy of Harvey Butchart's
Matthes-Evans maps (1989)

DEAR MR. PROFESSOR HARVEY BUTCHART:

Through the years I've discovered that if you let nature take its course a sequence of events unfolds in a very natural and logical order. Therefore, since I see your name mentioned over and over again in books and articles, it seems the natural and logical thing to write to you.

I have a dream—germinated when I spent a week on the Colorado River last Sept. My dream is to hike down into the Canyon. Aside from having a dream, I'm a wild bird. And I'm sure, since you're a wild bird yourself, (why else would the Grand Canyon be your habitat?) that you will understand what I'm driving at.

I'm 48, 120 lbs, 5'5", peppy and enthusiastic —
Would you take me under your wing and show me how to soar?

T. Geary
February 1975

Harvey politely declined such propositions. But for a 67-year-old "wild bird" who had hardly seen a date in college it must have been flattering. And ironic. He never expected his feats to make him a sex symbol. It was amazing what a little publicity could do. Roma thought it bad enough that Harvey spent so much time in the Canyon and writing his pen pals. Now adoring women were sending letters too.

Ever since the 1970 publication of Harvey's first guidebook, *Grand Canyon Treks*, and its 1975 sequel *Grand Canyon Treks II*, hardly a day went by that somebody wasn't writing to ask for route information, or for advice on what kind of sleeping bag to bring on their backpack trip. Or to ask if he was available.

Treks had carved a unique position for its author. Harvey the Canyon expert suddenly had more friends than ever. Even complete strangers were paying attention to him. It was sweet redemption for this once-bullied "weakling" to now attract people by his physical prowess and tough-as-nails reputation. He welcomed the flood of letters that poured into his mailbox.

Harvey knew things had really changed when he started running into fans below the rim. "While I was still on the Redwall I had a shouting conversation with a lone hiker down on the trail below," wrote Harvey in May 1973 after a day on the Bass Trail. "I learned that he wanted to get to Elves Chasm and I contributed some advice. He finally asked whether I could be Harvey Butchart, and he said he was going by my book." This scene would be repeated numerous times in the most out-of-the-way places, and it never failed to thrill him. Harvey had become a fixture in the national park, as natural and recognizable a part of Grand Canyon as a bighorn sheep, Lava Falls, and the heat.

It had all come about as a result of a casual meeting years before. Walt Wheelock was the owner of the independent La Siesta Press, a tiny publishing business he had formed in 1960 with the printing and distributing of a mini-text called *Ropes, Knots and Slings for Climbers*. At the time, Harvey was soaking up all he could about basic climbing techniques and bought a copy. When Harvey noticed Wheelock's name on a list of guest speakers scheduled for a 1961 writing conference at ASC, he decided to meet the author and publisher. Wheelock later described the encounter:

> Shortly after arriving there a slight well-dressed gentleman introduced himself to me, Dr. Harvey Butchart, professor of mathematics. Since I had majored in math at UCLA, I started to make small talk in this field, but was quietly turned off.
>
> The year before I had written and La Siesta Press had published *Ropes, Knots and Slings for Climbers*. Harvey was finding that more extensive exploration in

Grand Canyon was requiring skills in this field and this was to be the subject of our conversation.

It was the start of a friendship, and eventually, a successful business relationship that would last more than two decades. By the late 1960s, Wheelock had developed a niche for La Siesta by printing quirky guidebooks to the West, including works by such authors as pioneer climber Royal Robbins. Wheelock kept his eyes peeled for new opportunities and decided he had one in Harvey Butchart after reading the huge plug Harvey received in Colin Fletcher's *The Man Who Walked Through Time.* Wheelock called the mathematics professor in 1969 to propose a Grand Canyon backcountry guidebook. It just might sell, Wheelock encouraged, and besides, no such guidebook had ever been written.

What existed in the way of an off-trail Grand Canyon hiking guide was limited to *Escape Routes*, a small NPS handout the government provided to river runners. This was the brainchild of ranger Dan Davis who in 1956 assembled the guide to provide means of escape to the rim in the event of trouble on the river ("It is hoped you will not find yourself and party in a situation requiring the use of this booklet..."). In 1958, Davis sent it to Harvey for what additional information he might be able to include. When Davis received his edited booklet back, the number of river-to-rim routes had jumped from 40 to 88.

Yet *Escape Routes* offered little to a hiker or climber starting from the rim of Grand Canyon. Harvey realized that here indeed was a literary void as Wheelock had suggested. Although initially dubious, citing a lack of public interest as a concern, Harvey eventually concluded that a guidebook fit his natural talents and passions—teaching, writing, and of course, exploring Grand Canyon. Several months later, after many nights huddled over the typewriter, Harvey delivered his manuscript to Wheelock with a note saying, "Do what you want with it."

The first in a trilogy of books spanning 14 years, *Grand Canyon Treks* would become as prominent in the Grand Canyon pantheon of written works as John Wesley Powell's *The Exploration of the Colorado River and Its Canyons* or Fletcher's immensely popular *The Man Who Walked Through Time. Treks* would not achieve such status for its literary qualities, but for the secrets it divulged.

Essentially a compact version of Harvey's dense logbooks, *Treks* offers not only nuts and bolts guidance on the maintained trails, but also a number of backcountry routes the author uncovered. Although a casual hiker could use *Treks* to negotiate the beaten paths, Harvey presents the trails as mere frames upon which to drape the more exciting information, his routes that lead into the wild. *Treks* thus introduced the sport of canyoneering to a generation of eager practitioners. There had never been anything like it. "It was an instant success!" wrote Wheelock, 40,000 copies later.

The unpretentious, 70-page paperback marked both the end and beginning of an era. No longer would the Canyon be a no-man's land where the wilderness was an unknown quality. *Treks* opened Grand Canyon's backcountry.

Wheelock had a good sense of timing. Interest in outdoor recreation boomed in the early 1970s, with the number of backpackers in the U.S. growing from 9 million in 1965 to 28 million in 1977. But the change went beyond statistics. A wilderness ethic had arisen in the public consciousness. The environmental movement was still in its childhood yet had already left its mark in Grand Canyon when the Sierra Club inspired the public to oppose a 1965 Bureau of Reclamation plan to construct two dams in the national park. Suddenly, it seemed, America was realizing the need for preserving—and experiencing—the remaining Southwestern wildernesses.

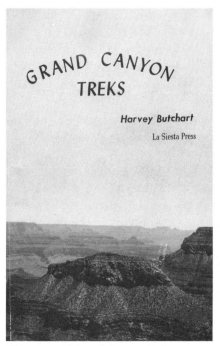

The result in 1970 was an unprecedented wave of people heading for the canyons. And waiting for them was the college professor who had what they would need. Harvey's years of exploration, which in the past had been of interest to a small contingent of friends, now made him something of a legend. *The Man Who Walked Through Time* had started it; *Treks* made it official. Harvey was Grand Canyon's

The cover of *Grand Canyon Treks.*

equivalent of a martial arts master—all knowing, deserving of respect, and someone necessary to confer with, should one wish to enter the backcountry.

"When I started, you had to have Harvey's book," said Pam Foti, an NAU Parks and Recreation Management professor who made her first Canyon hike in 1972. "The trails were bad. It was very different back then. You needed to know little things—like how to get through the Redwall in certain places. That's all disappeared now. The trail guides are not all that critical now."

Treks embodied the do-it-yourself philosophy. Both author and publisher strove for frugality in words and design. Presentation became an afterthought. This approach allowed the stark essence of the Canyon—and Harvey's all-business attitude—to permeate the modest yellow-and-red booklet. Subtitles appear slightly askew, as if hurriedly pasted just before going to press. Illustrations exhibit a crude, hand drawn look. The radioactive-landscape cover suggests not a fun walk in the park—as do *Treks's* modern day counterparts wrapped in their quaint covers—but rather an introduction to a harsh, otherworldly reality.

Inside, Harvey likewise makes no attempt to describe the Canyon's beauty. His minimalist sentences hold facts. In 72 pages, he presents much of what a serious hiker and climber might need to negotiate the national park—the reliability of particular water sources, the location of breaks in the cliffs, good shelter overhangs, even particular boulders on which rainwater gathers after a storm.[1] Harvey showed not just where to hike but how to move and stay alive in this desert. *Treks* thus amounted to a continuation of a very old practice—just like the Indians before him who had discovered and passed route information among themselves, Harvey now gave his own tribe the knowledge they needed to navigate this labyrinth.

Beyond the guidance lay a wealth of stories. Harvey integrated what he had learned from people such as Dock Marston and what he had gleaned from his years of reading everything on Grand Canyon he could find. In the course of his research, Harvey had made himself the locus for all the Canyon's varied clans: Cavers, climbers, Indians, boatmen, park officials, writers, guides, photographers, historians, archeologists, cowboys, backpackers, botanists and geologists. He took these people's collective wisdom, placed it into *Treks,* and made it his own.

Yet Harvey did not include *everything.* His Matthes-Evans maps, which would have made for a much more accessible guidebook, are missing. It is his maps, after all, which make unraveling the routes much easier. Perhaps Harvey felt he would be giving away too much if he included them. Hence, compared to many modern guidebooks, in which GPS coordinates, detailed maps, and driving directions to trailheads are near requirements, *Treks* was by no means a golden key to the backcountry.

"My book," he admitted, "is intentionally sketchy so the reader might have to do a little guessing about the details." Harvey wanted people to experience the Canyon by earning their way through it, as he had. It was a natural decision for someone who had made a career of providing students with the means to solve difficult problems. Harvey wanted to inform without going so far as to rob the reader of experiencing discovery, or the possibility of a misadventure. It was

---

[1] *Grand Canyon Treks* covered what was the national park in 1970, marked by the borders of Nankoweap and Havasu Canyons. *Treks II* expanded the coverage to include Marble Canyon and parts of the Western Grand Canyon, areas that had been made part of the national park in 1975 with the Grand Canyon Enlargement Act.

Typical illustration from *Grand Canyon Treks.*

his way of being generous.

A proclamation on the back cover reads, "We must warn the reader that this guidebook is not to be taken lightly, often a short paragraph or a few words, opens up a trek that may take two or three days to check out."

Harvey's philosophy wasn't wholly premeditated. He simply believed that it was more fun when you figured things out for yourself. Years before he decided to write a guidebook, after descending a new route into Marble Canyon in 1961, Harvey wrote, "I arrived at Soap Creek in time to drive out to the rim and take a picture from above the rapid. I purposely didn't inquire for directions as I thought it was more interesting to do my own exploring."

The fundamental paradox about the first Grand Canyon backcountry guidebook, then, is that it was written by someone not all that interested in guiding.

In 1995, a gifted Grand Canyon explorer named John "J.D." Green wrote his own guidebook called *Hiking in the Grand Canyon Backcountry* (edited by Jim Ohlman). Aided by the inclusion of Harvey's Matthes-Evans maps, *Hiking* covers the same areas as *Treks* but with more reader friendliness. Green composed his book after finding Harvey's pithy style to be of limited efficacy. "This guide [*Treks*], along with its two companion volumes is a high speed romp through the wilds of the Grand Canyon 'outback,'" Green wrote. "Harvey's books are classics, but they should be used to provide incentive and motivation rather than actual guidance."

Indeed, many have complained that Harvey's guides lack practical information for the average hiker, or even for the experienced hiker. *Treks* is too hard to understand, too difficult to follow, say the critics. Difficulty ratings are absent. Often Harvey tells that something *can* be done but not *how*, such as this sentence describing the route into Royal Arch Creek: "There are several ways to get down to the Redwall rim [through the Supai Formation] but only the bed of the wash will take one through this formation."

George Steck was an experienced bushwhacker and Grand Canyon backcountry guidebook author in his own right who struggled with Harvey's oblique words. Steck said, "We spent a lot of time the evening before we went out, wondering, what does that mean exactly? There are many ways through the Supai! Are they easy to find? Are we going to find them? That was not a helpful description!"

Indeed, Harvey's writing style could be generously described as *the art of conciseness*. Perhaps no book has ever crammed so much into so few pages. Transitions tend to be absent. The matter-of-fact delivery can make for cryptic reading. A familiarity with obscure landmarks, the geology, and even Harvey's friends is necessary to understand *Treks*. The casual tourist who leafed through it perhaps found it not so different from a television repair manual. The route descriptions, though not quite as opaque as those found in Harvey's logbooks, frequently leave room for guesswork. Even among proficient route finders such as Steck, the missing details are at best a challenge, at worst, demoralizing and confusing.

Yet for those who need answers regarding out-of-the-way places in the Canyon, Harvey's guides have always been considered *the* source—as long as one doesn't mind filling in some blanks.

Michael Kelsey, a Utah guidebook author who exchanged letters with Harvey while researching his popular *Canyon Hiking Guide to the Colorado Plateau*, explained, "Harvey's books weren't meant to be like most guidebooks. He wanted it to be a mystery for others, as it was for him when he explored it. Most people enjoy the drama of exploring. Some guidebook writers leave out maps—I suppose for the same reason. On the other hand, it helps those who are a day late and a dollar short if they have a little more info. I guess that's where I come in."

Artist and former river guide Ellen Tibbets was a member of the NAU Hiking Club in the late 1960s. She feels that *Treks* makes perfect sense—at least to experienced canyoneers. "Well, we [NAU Hiking Club members] understood it," Tibbets said. "It's the kind of language that people who have hiked in the Canyon understand. And they all speak it. It's like 'I got through the Redwall in 20 minutes.' Well, that means something to me and other people who've done it. But to other people, it wouldn't help them. That's not very descriptive."

Still, anyone who has relied on *Treks* to cross unfamiliar country can attest to the sparsity of Harvey's descriptions. Robert Eschka, a man considered to have been one of the most accomplished hikers to ever set foot in Grand Canyon, decided to use *Treks* when descending into Marble Canyon in 1983. While negotiating what Harvey called the 21.7-Mile Route, Eschka froze at a spot where the route traverses a sheer Coconino Sandstone cliff. In a single, innocuous line, Harvey describes this dreadfully exposed, inches-wide ledge traverse with the sentence, "One can go along a narrow ledge to a place where the sandstone is broken."

Eschka was so spooked that he emptied the contents of his pack and crawled them piece by piece across the bad spot. Eschka's journals are typically terse, but

The 21.7-Mile route and narrow sandstone ledge. *Courtesy Gary Ladd*

he took three long paragraphs to describe his less reserved reaction: "H.B. [Harvey Butchart] mentions the bypass of this barrier rather casually as 'a narrow ledge to the left.' It looked narrow all right. As a matter of fact, I find the term 'ledge' a great exaggeration unless you are a rabbit or a squirrel..."

Following Harvey's words into the wilderness proved fatal in at least one case. In October 1975, a 22-year-old hiker named Brad Riner began an ambitious, multi-day trek in Grand Canyon. Riner had taken Harvey's advice by first hiking the maintained trails before moving to off-trail routes suggested by *Treks.* Riner died after suffering a fractured skull and broken ribs in Phantom Creek, a tributary to Bright Angel Creek. He had jumped for unknown reasons off a 30-foot fall while making his way through the Redwall near a route Harvey recommended. Pages torn from *Treks* were later found with Riner's possessions. Whatever the cause of his fall, he had been inspired to leave the trail because of Harvey, and, after getting lost in the wrong tributary, never made it back alive.

Riner doubtless read the phrase "very sporty" in Harvey's description of the route in Phantom Creek. Perhaps this should have given Riner pause. Harvey included a few such phrases in *Grand Canyon Treks* that experienced hikers have come to respect: "Sporty," "interesting," and of course, "very sporty." These sparingly employed adjectives are the closest Harvey gets to difficulty ratings in *Treks.* Prevailing wisdom suggests that when Harvey describes a place as "sporty," one should expect to face a terrifying drop-off and dangerous climbing.

Yet this is not necessarily true. Harvey used a word such as "sporty" only as an interpretation of his own experience, which of course varied from trek to trek. Still, it is illuminating to know what he meant.

Harvey depicts a route to the summit of a butte he nicknamed the Wedding Cake, which rises just west of the Tanner Trail on top of the Redwall, as "a sporty rock climb." By applying the Yosemite Decimal system, the standard ruler by which many climbers rate their climbs, Harvey's Wedding Cake route falls somewhere between 5.2 and 5.4. In other words, there are two handholds and two footholds to negotiate each move through the crux, which involves about 15 feet of actual climbing. While challenging for the inexperienced, such a route would not prove to be an obstacle for those familiar with basic climbing techniques or accustomed to modest exposure.

"Routes to the three southern summits of the Sinking Ship are hard enough to be interesting," Harvey noted in his assessment of the butte that stands east of Grandview Point. "Interesting" in this case equates to a short climb that rates at least 5.4, making it a bit more difficult than the "sporty" route up the Wedding Cake. Lest one become confused, the decimal rating system is notoriously inconsistent, as any particular climb will vary according to one's size and ability, not to mention the conditions that can easily change along any route.

Although places that Harvey describes as "sporty" or "interesting" will present more of a challenge than any maintained trail in the park, some places which Harvey gave no such adjective to prove far worse, such as the narrow ledge that Eschka grappled with. One possible explanation for this inconsistency is that Harvey's rather limited daring when it came to climbing caused him

The "sporty rock climb" to the summit of the Wedding Cake. *Elias Butler*

Climbing the "interesting" route up the Sinking Ship. *Elias Butler*

to view vertical ascents—even those that are relatively easy to negotiate—with a large dose of trepidation. Along more level places that feature a great deal of exposure, however, such as the ledge at Mile 21.7, he rarely noted the danger. Harvey would walk the edge without blinking, but he did not want to climb above it.

Guidebooks have always been something of a blessing and a nuisance. Many hikers rely on them, yet the same people often condemn the advertising that the books necessarily give to obscure areas. Especially in the digital age, information that once needed to be discovered on one's own, or through word of mouth, can now be accessed by anyone. This kind of free-for-all rankles those who jealously guard their secret places against the regulation, fees, and destruction that often accompany the crowds.

It was one reason why a few Canyon aficionados criticized Harvey for publishing *Treks.* Ellen Tibbets explained, "One thing we [the NAU student hikers] liked so much about the Canyon was that we were the only ones that knew these cool places to go, where we thought 'No one can get here but us.' And when the books were published we thought 'Oh God, it's going to be this influx of people following these routes.' But then we found out that, because of the way Dr. Butchart wrote them, most people who were from New Jersey or something, and read the book and wanted to come out, were probably lost or dead if they tried to follow his directions." Indeed, Brad Riner became one such fatality.

Harvey of course felt no qualms about sharing his information with the public, even after visitation to the backcountry jumped sharply in the 1970s. "Some hikers have deplored this development," Harvey wrote of the increasing crowds. "Personally, I enjoy meeting other hikers [in the Canyon] and visiting with them."

This attitude highlights a paradox in Harvey's personality. While eager to one-up the competition, he felt inspired to help anyone get around in the Canyon. It was fortunate he felt that way, because after the publication of

Treks, it did not take long for the letters to start pouring in. Perhaps it was the professorial face staring from the back cover. Or the fact that more people than ever wanted to get off trail. Whatever the explanation, Harvey had suddenly become the Dear Abby of Grand Canyon.

No question was too uninformed or complex for his tastes, he answered them all in great detail. "If you were a new hiker and the only thing you'd done was maybe hike down to Phantom Ranch and back or something, and you were excited about your trip and you wanted to tell Harvey about your trip, he'd be glad to listen to you," said Al Doty, a Sedona art gallery owner and accomplished Grand Canyon climber who met Harvey as a student at Northern Arizona University in 1968. "He would never say anything like 'Well, you know, I've hiked 12,000 miles in the Canyon.' He would always be excited about your trip. No matter how insignificant your trip was, he would never talk down to you."

In between hikers and climbers's questions, Harvey also received fan mail, business offers and professional inquiries. The years of hard work had finally brought him an audience that appreciated and needed him.

"He was a clearing house of information," observed Scott Thybony, a Flagstaff author who wrote a guidebook called *Official Guide to Hiking the Grand Canyon*. "Even today there's no central spot where you can go to get information about these more remote areas. There've been guidebooks written now, and more magazine articles, but at that time the Park Service just wasn't getting into the backcountry at all, or very little. They're doing it much more extensively nowadays. But most of the rangers, you'd go to the backcountry office and they didn't know a thing about the backcountry. So if you wanted to know about the backcountry, you asked around and everybody you asked said 'talk to Butchart.'"

At the Special Collections Department of the NAU Cline Library, there are 481 folders containing thousands of letters that Harvey received from over 300 people. If this sounds voluminous, it is, but it only represents the letters Harvey received until 1985. Hundreds more exist within Harvey's personal files still kept by his family. It is no surprise to anyone who corresponded with him that he had written the equal of his massive logbooks in letters.

One wonders where he found the time. He held down a full-time job, had a wife and a family, hiked as much as ever, and maintained extensive logbooks. Yet Harvey still made it a priority to answer his Grand Canyon mail. He rarely waited more than a day or two before responding to a question and always asked for trip reports or at least encouraged a response. The correspondences became yet another extension of his obsession. Whereas exploration offered its own satisfaction, the letter writing affirmed his significance to the world at large, as evidenced by the 40-plus years he spent at it.

December 15, 1959
Dear Harvey:

Your last two letters really made a red-letter day for me. What a fine wind-fall! Your logs were so interesting that I couldn't tear myself away. You are certainly the Grand Canyon Flier.

How much do you generally pack on a two-day trip? Do you use a pack-frame? What kind of food do you take?

Plez Talmadge Reilly

November 12, 1969
Dear Harvey:

It seems I have known you for some years now. Your fame in Grand Canyon follows your every trail. Think back if you will—about a year and a half ago—at Phantom Ranch. At that time I visited with you briefly at the pool. My party was impressed—as was I.

There is a cabin (in ruins that is) at the spring at the Muav Saddle. Could you tell me its history?

Ken Sleight

January 26, 1979
Dear Harvey,

For purposes of identification, I am the gal who has been at the canyon longer than <u>you</u>; oh yes, you say; that old gal!

Never thought I'd be writing you, but I need a bit of help that I think you can do for me...

Gale Burak

June 6, 1989
Dear Harvey,

I was quite happy to receive your most recent letter. Your review of my inner granite gorge routes made me feel more confident in my documentation. In a way, you are regarded as a canyon teacher, and as your student I was compelled to be inspired and make my own mark...

George Mancuso

July 2, 1999
Dear Harvey,

I have some good news! The Park Service has finally found a place for your hiking gear exhibit. It's in the new Museum Collection building in a display case.

By the way, I have a few questions about the Redwall caves in the east arm of Cremation...

Tom Myers

All manner of people crossed written paths with Harvey, some seeking his honest advice, others simply interested in the person who had spent so much time in Grand Canyon. His reputation occasionally brought him into contact with other writers. In 1969, novelist Edward Abbey manned a fire lookout tower for the Park Service on the Kaibab Plateau. In June on his way to a hike, Harvey stopped by to say hello and spent a couple hours in the lookout with Abbey, whose book *Desert Solitaire* had recently been published. In one chapter, Abbey recounts a brush with death while exploring near Havasu Canyon; the two Grand Canyon buffs would have had much to compare notes on. Harvey wrote about the encounter:

> I didn't hear anything about Ed Abbey's hiking this summer. I feel that he would have mentioned it if he had done any, but he is a rather quiet person. When you know how funny he can build up a conversation when he is writing, one wonders what he is fixing in his mind as you talk to him.

Abbey gave his version of their conversation in his journal:

> North Rim—Harvey Buchart [sic], prof. of math at NAU, man who has walked over more of the Grand Canyon than any other alive or dead, visited me in the [lookout] for a couple of hours. A gracious, charming man—invited me to join him on a hike sometime. We agreed it possible that mediocre writers like

Ambrose Bierce (or Everett Ruess) might have deliberately disappeared in a desperate reach for the only fame possible to them.

Although *Treks* became his best-known work, Harvey's logbooks remain the far more significant documents. These weighty tomes represent the most comprehensive record of the Canyon's backcountry ever written, 1,079 pages detailing Harvey's discoveries and explorations from 1945 to 1987. Indeed, it is the logbooks more than anything else that separate Harvey from both his forebears and those explorers who would follow.[2]

Not that they make terribly lively reading. Largely devoid of anything but route information, hard data and emotionless notes to self, Harvey's logbooks were never meant to be entertainment. The resulting thick descriptive consistency means that the reader must frequently come up for air. The following passage is typical Harvey prose as he describes a bit of the route he used to ascend Apollo and Venus Temples in 1965:

> For the second time I used the cutoff near the bottom of the Redwall where I had found that I could climb up a steep ramp in the Bright Angel Shale. This meets the present trail about 100 yards south of the saddle where it leaves the bare green shale and heads north down to the Tapeats exposure. It took me so long to pick my way safely down these crumbly ledges that I decided that it is no real saving. Actually the trace of the old trail that leaves the present trail about three-fourths of the way down the Redwall and heads north with a couple of switchbacks doesn't reach the shale rim at the place where I can climb down. It deteriorates just above this place and continues as a deer trail north around the angle to the west...

Most readers would say *"huh?"* For the hiker looking for a straightforward guide to Grand Canyon, the logbooks are obviously not the place to start. But for someone wondering if it might be possible to drop into some obscure canyon from the rim, or if there is water to be found in a location that hardly anyone has heard of, Harvey's logs will probably give an answer.

Their usefulness stems from a mathematician's touch. A self-described perfectionist, Harvey constantly assessed his hikes in terms of time and distance. Companions remember him as a man absolutely preoccupied with his watch—how long it took to hike from point a to point b, how this compared to the last time he had been across the same piece of ground, how long he could go before

---

[2] A friend of Harvey's, Wayne Tomasi, transferred the entire content of Harvey's logbooks to electronic files, and they are now available online.

having to turn around, etc. "It could be argued," wrote climber Scott Baxter in a biographical essay, "that, next to boots and backpack, the wristwatch has been Harvey Butchart's most important piece of hiking equipment."

Although helpful to future logbook readers who wanted to know what to expect from a canyon or route, sometimes Harvey's fixation with time bordered on the ridiculous. During a hike with Scott Thybony near Aztec Amphitheater, Harvey was determined to locate a prehistoric Indian route, a goal that had eluded him on previous trips to the area. He had promised Roma to be back in time for dinner. When Thybony spotted an interesting archaeological site across a drainage during their descent, he suggested that they check it out. As interested as Harvey was in archeology, he did not hide his impatience for deviating from the day's goal. "He looked at his watch and said 'You've got 10 minutes,'" Thybony said. "I jogged over and it was an untouched site with arrowheads laying on the ground and some interesting rock art. Eventually he came over too, but he was impatiently looking at his wristwatch the whole time."

Butchart's *idée fixe* becomes apparent from the lead paragraph of his logbook entry for June 25–26, 1970:

> I have pretty well covered this route in my logs for 10/12/63, 10/27/63, and 9/20/64. On rereading them I see that I was not moving as fast this time as I had before. Six years of age and the heat would explain this discrepancy. My time from the road to the river was 145 minutes and to go back up I took 220 minutes.

Known to draw geometry problems in the sand or in a pocket notebook during his treks, Harvey could not help but make calculations in the Canyon, even when on a rare leisure trip. During a weeklong river journey with guide Ken Sleight in 1970, Harvey and the rest of the river runners made the customary stop at the large cave in Marble Canyon that John Wesley Powell had named Redwall Cavern. Powell, often accused by historians of being an inaccurate chronicler, estimated in his book *The Exploration of the Colorado River and Its Canyons* that, "if utilized for a theater, [Redwall Cavern] would give sitting for 50,000 people." Harvey decided to test Powell's estimation:

> I paced the depth and breadth of Redwall Cavern and the engineer present did a mental calculation that 10,000 people could stand on the inner terrace. If one should include all the sandbar that would lie behind a plumb-bob tracing the entire overhang, Powell's figure of 50,000 would not be a far miss.

For someone with such a penchant for math and figuring, Harvey fortunately owned a memory that allowed him to write it all down on the fly—in his brain.

"One thing that impressed me about Harvey," Al Doty said, "was that he had an incredible memory for detail on hikes. You could ask him about a trip he'd done, you know, 10 years ago, 15 years ago, 20 years ago, and he could tell you every detail about that trip. Things that most people would have forgotten about, all

Redwall Cavern partially submerged in a flood of 125,000 cfs in 1957. J. Harvey Butchart, courtesy NAU Special Collections

the insignificant details about a route, he could just recall them no problem. He was an amazing person."

Although little pattern exists to the order of Harvey's many hikes, the index of his logbooks does demonstrate the mind-boggling scale of his obsession.[3] The following excerpt showcases the busy month of June 1970. Here we have a full-blown assault on display, in this case facilitated by a 63-year-old college professor on summer "vacation":

"June 2-4: Vishnu Canyon, Sheba, Solomon" (a backpack trip that resulted in two first ascents of these buttes located north of Hance Rapids)

---

[3] A friend of Harvey's, Tony Williams, painstakingly prepared the comprehensive index to Harvey's logs.

"June 8-16: Lee's Ferry to Diamond Creek, Impressions" (a river trip with long-time river guide Ken Sleight, who served as the inspiration for the character Seldom Seen Smith in Edward Abbey's *The Monkey Wrench Gang;* Sleight offered the trip to Harvey for free)

"June 23-24: Kirby Trail to Black Tank Wash" (a backpack trip in upper Havasu Canyon)

"June 25-26: Recovery of the pots at mile 43.3" (During the Sleight river trip, near President Harding Rapid, Harvey had led a small group to an Indian ruin where one of the clients found five unbroken Anasazi pots. After the trip, Harvey urged authorities to collect the pots but to no avail. Later, on one of the hottest days ever recorded in Flagstaff, he returned on foot to do it himself, but was only able to carry two pots, which he brought to the Museum of Northern Arizona. Four months later, he returned for the remaining three pots but they had disappeared)

"June 30-July 2: Up Wotan like an Indian (Almost)" (Harvey's second ascent of Wotan's Throne)

Harvey typed 6,500 words to record these adventures; that is twice the length of a typical feature-length magazine article, and about the length of this chapter in the book you are reading. Harvey did not have much idle time, it seems.

Yet he had what every writer needs, an audience. Even the government wanted his information. He donated copies of his logbooks and Matthes-Evans maps to the Park Service, and for years, these documents would form the basis of park rangers's knowledge of the backcountry.[4]

Between all the lines of hard data contained in Harvey's writing are occasional hints of an appreciation for beauty. Contrary to what some believe, the Canyon did affect Harvey on an emotional level. After traveling alone through a dark chamber called Jumpup Canyon in 1974, Harvey expressed his wonder by quoting an eighteenth century English poet:

> The Redwall aisle both above and below the junction with Indian Hollow Gorge is really something spooky. There were places where the stream cut into the bend and formed a Redwall Cavern effect with the ceiling far over in the middle of the channel. At other places both walls overhung, forming a corridor like a dimly lit cave. The contact between the bright sun and these shaded portions was striking. Often the walls bulged out and cut off a view of the

---

4 William Mooz, a friend of Harvey's, spearheaded the effort to have Harvey donate his logs to the public record.

sky. It is easy and safe walking but to quote Coleridge, 'A savage place, holy and enchanted.'

Harvey had finally made his mark in the world. Yet for all he had written, there remained a plethora of other stories he had not told, and not because these tales lacked in drama or entertainment value. We shall now take the liberty of explaining.

Harvey relaxes with a chess match at Phantom Ranch, 1981. *Courtesy Scott Baxter*

Chapter Twenty-Two
SPRAY PAINT AND GINGERSNAPS

*After a lecture by the arctic explorer Vilhjalmar Steffanson, he was
approached by a little old lady who remarked, "Your talk was very instruc-
tive, but didn't you have any adventures?" The explorer is supposed to have
stiffened and replied "Adventures, Madam! Adventures are a sign of
incompetence."*

*My rambles in the Grand Canyon have been seasoned very slightly by
adventures.*

Harvey Butchart,
Logbook entry (1956)

HARVEY BUTCHART COMES OFF in Grand Canyon Treks as the consummate professional hiker, a cool, levelheaded guide. He is in control, prepared for whatever the Grand Canyon might hurl his way, seldom letting a trace of emotion show.
Any mentions of pain, deprivation, mistakes in judgment, or other unavoidable
consequences of exploration are quite absent in Treks, despite all the time
Harvey gave to his risky pursuits.

But if this was the Harvey Butchart he presented to his readers, there existed yet another Harvey—the one who used cheapskate gear, spray painted boulders, lit runaway fires, and nearly did himself in on several occasions. Like any
writer, he chose to overlook certain humbling aspects of his own personality
and behavior, at least in his published writing. The letters, logbook entries, his
friends, and Harvey himself often told otherwise.

For example, the condensed version of Treks advises readers to take precautions and make wise decisions. One also gets the impression, though Harvey
never states as much, that he placed considerable importance upon preserving
the fragile environment in Grand Canyon. Several appendices remind readers
of Leave No Trace ethics and warn against such activities as hiking during the

heat of the day, hiking alone, hiking in summer, or letting one's goals or desires outweigh good judgment.

Sensible advice. Not that Harvey much bothered with any of it, as he admitted in a 1995 letter:

> I felt rather peculiar about the safety precautions that [editor] Wynne Benti brought up [in *Treks*]. I had, over the years, violated about all the rules. I had been guilty of hiking in the sunny part of the day in the summer. I had gone out alone and had not always given anyone a plan where I was going. I had had wood fires and had not always observed the rules for bowel movements. I was guilty of not carrying out all my trash. And I didn't always take as much water as she advised.

In Harvey's defense, he began exploring long before any notion of environmental responsibility or hiker's guidelines existed in either the public consciousness or the law books. Even so, Harvey was not exactly the embodiment of a land steward. He regularly committed infractions that today would result in punishment.

To wit, from Appendix E of *Grand Canyon Treks* (condensed version), Leave No Trace Rule #8: *Don't burn toilet paper! Bury it or pack it out in a zip-lock bag. Devastating fires have been caused by burning toilet paper.*

Harvey may have helped inspire such a rule. One night in June 1976 near the North Bass Trail, he nearly charred himself and his friend Bob Packard in their sleeping bags. "We camped just below the Tapeats by a flowing stream," Packard said. "And we were in this place where it was quiet, and you know, trickle-trickle, and we're in our sleeping bags. And since we're below the Tapeats, the canyon walls were pretty precipitous on both sides. And I forget what time of night it was, maybe midnight and I was asleep. And I looked up, and the canyon walls are all lit up!"

"And Harvey's up and running around and actually he yells at me that I better get up and move the sleeping bags. He'd taken a shit and he lit his toilet paper and went back into his sleeping bag apparently, and then the little spark on the paper probably got a leaf going—a lot of dried leaves and brush in there—and sometime later he noticed it. We beat out the fire. But, to wake up in the middle of the night and see the canyon lit up! [laughs] You didn't need a flashlight or anything. Of course he was embarrassed. He didn't want the people on the rim to know about it."

Harvey's next accidental blaze came less than a year later. While on a solo hike in 94-Mile Canyon, where he was investigating evidence of a once-proposed cross-canyon aerial tram, he made the mistake of walking away from his tiny gelatin fuel can. Harvey wrote:

The fire under my soup was Sterno and I put the fireplace close to a large rock to cut the wind. There was some very short, sparse grass nearby...When I was going down to the river to wash up, I glanced back and saw that the fire had ignited the grass and had gone like a streak up into quite a thicket of mesquite...There were so many dead limbs on the ground that the whole thing went up like a blast furnace. All I could think about doing was to pull my own gear out of danger...

Harvey was loath to destroy Canyon flora. But he admitted to a soft spot for pyrotechnics when conditions were right, such as in 1962 when he came across a small mountain of logs deposited by the free-flowing Colorado:

I had heard that the Park Service approves of burning piles of driftwood to try to diminish the nuisance of logs in Lake Mead. There was a beautiful pile about a quarter of a mile below Tanner Creek, about three feet thick by eight wide and fully 60 feet long. There was a lot of small stuff caught in with the large, so I set fire to it. I got the thrills of an arsonist without causing the damage.

Harvey had few qualms about behavior that would rub environmentalists the wrong way if it meant a little fun. He cared even less if it meant a new route. In June 1962, he and Allyn Cureton decided to climb Freya Temple, a butte near Cape Royal that Francois Matthes had named for the Norse goddess of love. The route below Cape Royal (the same route that provided access to Wotan's Throne) had always been hard to remember. "This time," wrote Harvey, "I carried a can of green spray paint and sprayed arrows on the rocks to indicate the more elusive turns."

According to rule #13 listed on the back of the modern backcountry permit, *Writing on, scratching, or otherwise defacing natural features, signs, or other property is prohibited.* Most backpackers would be incensed if they saw someone "tagging" a national park. But to Harvey, a route was a route, and rocks were rocks.

Likewise, trees were trees. Later in 1962, after trying to negotiate a faint dirt road that led to the rim of Great Thumb Mesa, he wrote, "If the Park Service would cut a few trees and mark the route with plastic ribbons, it would be a big help."

As for garbage, Harvey ascribed to the adage, "pack it in, leave it in." He surprised several companions by littering whenever and wherever convenient. Geologist George Billingsley, a member of the NAU Hiking Club in the late 1960s, said, "Butchart typically carried a can of food. And then he buried the can when he was done. We'd end up digging it up and clearing it out, and he caught us doing that and said, 'Why don't you just leave it there? It's just going to rot and rust.' And we said 'Well…maybe.'"

"One thing we always laughed about was that he'd been on a trip with another student," Billingsley said. "And when they finished lunch he just threw the can over the cliff and said 'No white man'll ever be down there.'"

Harvey also left full cans of food in odd places throughout the chasm. "We would hike along and he would say, 'I have an old stash over there,'" wrote Jim Kirschvink, a former river guide. "He would find some old Sterno, and maybe a can of Campbell's soup, which he would often eat cold and out of the can."

Although Harvey's photographic memory helped him locate his buried food, he did suffer from occasional spells of absent-mindedness. In May 1957, while hiking near Great Thumb Mesa with Allyn Cureton, Harvey stripped off his pants to stay cool. When the two stopped for lunch, Harvey unpacked his ruck-sack to get his food and laid his pants on the ground. After eating, Harvey began walking away without his pants. "Aren't you going to take your trousers?" asked Cureton. Harvey stopped abruptly, turned around and looked down at his bare legs. His pants held his car keys and cash, and he would have had a devil of a time explaining to Roma why he'd been stranded half naked.

In 1946, while stopped for lunch during a hike in Oak Creek Canyon, Harvey opened up his lunch bag, reached in and pulled out a tennis shoe. He had grabbed the wrong bag.

Yet he could be quick on his feet, too. Harvey rarely bothered with overnight hiking permits, which became required starting in 1971. He felt that he was entitled to hike wherever and whenever he wanted. If confronted by the Park Service in the backcountry, he simply name-dropped—his own name. Kirschvink wrote about one such encounter that occurred while in western Grand Canyon:

> We snuck into the cave at Cave Canyon [a cave that is officially closed to the public]. We poked around a little, and found it to not be very interesting. Out of nowhere, two park rangers appeared. Harvey said we went in until we saw the signs that said not to go in, then turned around. Then he said 'I'm Harvey Butchart', in a casual way of course. One of them said, 'Oh really! I've read your books…'

Harvey enjoyed a largely cordial relationship with rangers throughout the years. But this didn't mean he wanted to see Grand Canyon in the hands of their protectionist agency. In 1966, the Sierra Club was pressuring the government to expand the national park boundaries to include the entire Canyon, from Marble Canyon to the Grand Wash Cliffs, which Congress voted to approve in 1975 with the Grand Canyon Enlargement Act. Most hikers were thrilled with the news. But Harvey knew it would mean more red tape to hike on land formerly controlled by the less restrictive Forest Service. A 1968 logbook entry records his dismay at the prospect:

> I planned two interesting trips, down through the Coconino and possibly the Supai to the Freya-Vishnu Saddle and the next day a trip to the Supai off Bright Angel Point. As it turned out I didn't do either of these things. I ran into a hard and fast rule laid down by the new Chief Ranger that no one should be allowed to go off the rim without a companion.
>
> As an interesting substitute, about 9:30 A.M., I decided to try going out on Saddle Mountain and look for ruins...This would be out of the park so no permit would be needed. (Note that I am not campaigning for Marble and the lower canyon to be given to the park service.)

No, Harvey was not an environmentalist. Noisy helicopter tours, for example, which continue to be a thorny issue for wilderness advocates, bothered him not. Nor did he complain about Glen Canyon Dam, which most Canyon aficionados hate with special vehemence. When the Bureau of Reclamation proposed two dams for Grand Canyon in the 1960s, one in Marble Canyon and the other near Bridge Canyon, Harvey had no objections. Truth be told, he looked forward to reservoirs in Grand Canyon.

In 1966, *Reader's Digest* invited Harvey to participate in a discussion with the media to help form an opinion on the issue. As part of the deal, Harvey took a plane ride over the dam sites with one of the most vocal anti-dam environmentalists, Martin Litton of the Sierra Club. Harvey recalled the flight:

> I went to the bash that the *Reader's Digest* put on to brainwash the news media against any more dams in the canyon and I had a fine plane ride over Toroweap, but no one asked my opinion at that time. I remember how Martin Litton let us enjoy the view for three minutes and then launched into 15 minutes of oratory against building a dam that would make a lake 120 feet deep. As a boat owner, I rather enjoyed the prospect of launching at a ramp in Diamond Creek and checking side canyons by water. I figured there would still be lots of good hiking at the Tonto level and above.

But he could be contradictory. Harvey shuddered at the thought of a dam in the Little Colorado River gorge:

> You wonder whether this Eden is still safe or whether dam builders will harness the spring and summer floods. You hope that a careful calculation will

convince them that hydroelectric development here would be a financial loss. Improvements should be made on the trails so that more people could enjoy these glistening cataracts and turquoise pools, but there the "improvements" should stop.[1]

Although not a consistent preservationist, Harvey was a recycler of sorts. The plastic bread bags that housed his sandwiches came in handy, for example. Instead of leaving them in the Canyon, he wrapped the bags around his ankles to prevent chafing.

Such a low-cost solution fit Harvey's bare bones approach to canyoneering. He favored Spartan gear and a rudimentary diet, even after manufacturers began producing modern, much-improved backpacking products in the early 1970s. "I

Harvey's ankles in plastic bread wrappers, while eating sardines in 1985 with Al Doty. *Courtesy Jorgen Visbak*

have always been careful in spending my money," Harvey wrote, "and my hiking equipment shows the result." Harvey would have had little use for today's gear-crazed outdoors industry, which emphasizes safe, clean, and comfortable experiences and thrives on consumers's urge to have the latest and most advanced knick-knacks. He proved that stoves, fancy boots, chic outdoor clothing, water filters, compression stuff sacks, titanium pots, poop shovels, dehydrated food, GPS units, tents, technical backpacks, headlamps, and trekking poles may make someone rich, but aren't necessary for hardcore desert hiking and canyoneering.

In the 1970s, renowned Northern Arizona climber Scott Baxter was part owner (along with Lee Dexter) of the Alpineer, a climbing shop in Flagstaff. Baxter remembered that he had no luck selling the math professor expensive gear. "He was already a legend at that time," Baxter said. "And he used to get off work there at the university and he'd walk up Beaver Street every afternoon. And we'd look out the window of our little shop and see him striding up

---

[1] The Bureau of Reclamation planned to construct a dam in the LCR for sediment control in the 1960s, but it was never built.

Harvey at the Alpineer climbing shop in Flagstaff, 1972. *Courtesy Lee Dexter*

the street with just that real forceful, determined stride of his. Sure enough one day he strode into our shop and of course we were all in awe of him. And he was shopping for a daypack. So we started showing him our top of the line items. And he ended up buying the cheapest thing we had! Which was his style all the way."

For years, Harvey used the same orange Boy Scout-style external frame pack. There was no hip belt, so he simply used clothesline as a substitute, which also came in handy when he needed to line it over a cliff. As for footwear, he bought ordinary K-Mart or J. C. Penney work shoes. No pair lasted more than two years, even with numerous repairs. His sleeping bag was made of Dacron, the same material used in high-pressure fire hoses. For shelter, he laid a plastic sheet over himself at night. Harvey never owned a stove, instead preferring fires (as long as they didn't threaten his life) or Sterno.

This no-frills system had benefits. Harvey kept his pack at a trim 18-25 pounds, even in winter, which allowed him to move fast all day. Setting or breaking camp was always quick and easy.

Harvey likewise tailored his diet for speed and ease of preparation, sticking to a dreary culinary routine that delivered bare sustenance and nothing more. He admitted that one reason he avoided long backpack trips was that his food was so unappetizing. He would typically pack margarine sandwiches, prunes, sardines and instant soup, although Scott Thybony recalled another item in the menu: "He'd have his meals planned out: White bread and baloney sandwiches wrapped up in a bread bag, two for breakfast, two for lunch and two for dinner. His secret energy food was some ginger snaps that he kept in the front pocket of his pants."

Sometimes the urge to stock up on the super-cookies got out of hand. A June 1961 log entry complains, "My pack wasn't very well planned. I had too many gingersnaps..."

Water is of utmost importance to any desert explorer. Harvey sometimes toted as much as two gallons of water on a trek, but he most often drank what he could find, which occasionally tested his stomach. While hiking Paria Canyon in 1977, Harvey brewed his customary cup of soup with a few extra and unwanted ingredients. The Paria River runs thick with greenish sediment, making it tough to swallow even when one is very thirsty.

> The two quarts of water I had carried from the car didn't suffice for my soup or my breakfast. I doped the creek-diluted mud with iodine and drank it as sparingly as possible as well as using it for my Lipton's soup. When I ate the latter it looked like mud pie, but it tasted like soup. I didn't seem to feel the worse for the mud in my diet, but it had a definite effect on my excrement.

Sometimes, perfectly clean water presented problems. Before the age of portable water filters, shallow potholes posed a challenge for those needing to fill their canteens. Near Sinyala Canyon in 1964, Harvey employed an unusual method:

> ...I found plenty of shallow pools on the flat rocks northwest of Manakacha Point. They were too shallow for dipping the canteen, but I tried a trick I have thought of before, sucking the water into the mouth and squirting it into the canteen. It works all right, but after you have gotten the water by that method, you can be sure your friends won't borrow your canteen.

Harvey didn't mind trekking solo, but he enjoyed company, provided his company could keep up with him. As he became better known, students from NAU often asked to join him in the Canyon. Following a few treks when he ran younger hikers into the ground, grumbling to himself all the while about how they were holding him back, Harvey eventually devised a test to weed out the weak. In June 1967 he brought a group of prospective student hikers to Sunset Crater National Monument near Flagstaff for a qualifying run.

Harvey held up his stopwatch and yelled, "Go!" They had 25 minutes to make it 1,000 feet up the loose volcanic cinders that formed the steep sides of Sunset Crater. Harvey had done it in 18 minutes himself, so he figured an extra seven minutes would be adequate for the students. Those who failed were out of luck. The lucky ones, however, moved on to the second heat of the Harvey Butchart Challenge: Hiking 2,400 feet up nearby Mount Elden in 75 minutes or less. The trail to the summit features an elevation gain similar to that of the

Grandview Trail in Grand Canyon, but with the added strain of loftier altitude (Mount Elden tops out at over 9,300 feet). Those who made it were rewarded with a hot July day hike down to Phantom Ranch and back.

Harvey averaged one student throwing up for each hiking club trip he led in the Canyon, perhaps more during summer afternoons. He set a demanding uphill pace and simply expected others to follow. Invariably, a student who was 40 years younger would erupt from the exertion. And if it didn't happen on the trail, it could happen in the car on the way home. Harvey recalled:

> One boy I walked with was a bit different. He told me that when he hit the rim, he would head for the snack bar and order the biggest milkshake that they had. Then he said that about 20 minutes later he would throw it all up. Sure enough, when we had been driving along for a while, he had us stop abruptly and he threw up the whole thing.

Perhaps Harvey's driving played a part in this incident. If so, it wouldn't come as a surprise to those who experienced Harvey's cavalier attitude at the wheel. Harvey often drove with abandon, sometimes frightening his passengers to the point where his hairball hiking routes paled by comparison. "Has anybody ever mentioned what he was like driving?" asked Susan Billingsley, an NAU Hiking Club member in the late 1960s. "*Oh my God!* He was the scariest thing I have *ever*."

"You'd ride with him and he'd talk the whole way and he would never pay attention to what he was doing. He was really scary! And going over dirt roads you'd just crash! Bang! Boom! You know, and you're just hitting your head [laughs]."

"We went up in a snowstorm to the South Rim one time," Susan said. "And going up around Kendrick Park, I mean, they should have closed the road—it was drifting over the road. And he was going *so* fast, talking 90 miles an hour, you couldn't see a thing and he's just plowing through the drifts!"

Harvey steps on the gas in his V-8 Jimmy near Toroweap, 1984. *Courtesy Jorgen Visbak*

"Or he'd go off the road," said Susan's husband

George Billingsley. "And say 'Let's see, I better watch what I'm doing' then he'd go on about what he was talking about [laughs]. And we were all just petrified. Just wide-eyed. He was just talking about the Canyon, going like hell!"

As dangerous as Harvey was, he never had a serious accident. The same could not be said of his time in the Canyon. Over the years, he accrued the wisdom and confidence to help minimize errors, but anyone who spends over 1,000 days exploring such a landscape is bound to screw up, or be at the wrong place at the wrong time. The odds increase dramatically when going solo.

"I go out alone about half the time, and I like the spice of danger," he boasted in a 1976 issue of the *Journal of Arizona History*. There is no lack of "spice" in Grand Canyon—flash floods, rattlesnakes, rock fall, heat, and lack of water all present possible avenues to death. With the exception of the Boyd Moore drowning, Harvey managed to avoid the worst consequences thanks to his cautiousness and blind luck, but he suffered his share of mishaps nonetheless.

Sometimes he only needed to show up. On August 24, 1970, Harvey and pal Jorgen Visbak joined forces to attempt Siegfried Pyre, a butte east of the Walhalla Plateau (Siegfried is another Grand Canyon summit Francois Matthes named). After descending into the Canyon below Atoko Point, the two climbers scraped out beds at the foot of a Coconino Sandstone wall near a spring. Oftentimes in the Canyon, the only available flat spots for sleeping occur at the bases of cliffs, but there is a risk involved: Cliffs are not permanent. Rock fall in the canyon country has flattened unsuspecting backpackers in their sleeping bags. As Harvey and Visbak snored contentedly on their air mattresses, the ticking of geologic time finally caught up to them.

> About 10:40 P.M., after both of us had been asleep, I woke up to a startling sound. At the top of the Coconino, 350 feet above me, I heard a lot of rock coming down. Without stopping to think, I found myself, still in the bag, hopping seven feet and crouching against the wall with just a second to wonder whether the big stuff would pile down on me. I thought I heard some grapefruit sized rocks land in the brush about 15 feet away...I shouted to Jorgen that I was all right. He had awakened only when the chips and dust landed on him, but our only casualty was that my new air mattress was cut and the metal reel for my adhesive tape was crimped. This experience made me wonder about sleeping here.

Though he came away clean that time, Harvey was not so lucky on other occasions. In 1964, he brought two college students to the Little Colorado River gorge in search of the so-called Damsite Trail. This faint footpath led from the rim of the gorge down to a Coconino Sandstone narrows, a location which surveyors had determined an ideal site for a dam. After leaving the bed of a tributary canyon at a dry fall, Harvey guided the students along a ridge, hoping for a break in the cream-colored Coconino cliff below. As Harvey paced amongst the slabs and weeds, craning his neck over the cliff to see the terrain, he forgot to mind the dimensions of his frame pack:

> I made a foolishly long step up to a shelf beneath a rock ceiling. My Kelty [backpack] caught on the edge of the roof and threw me off balance. I fell backwards on the slope that went to the big precipice about 15 or 20 feet downhill. My reflex action was to throw out my arms to keep from rolling downhill. Unfortunately, my left hand caught between two rocks. When my body weight came down, it broke my wrist into a double right angle. I knew it hurt, but when I looked at my left hand in that very unnatural shape, I felt quite a bit of shock. It took me about 15 minutes before I felt like getting up and making a sling out of my shirt for the bad arm.

With the swelling came waves of throbbing pain that ricocheted up and down his arm. It was a bad place to suffer such an injury, on a ridge laden with small cliffs. With no level ground to accommodate a helicopter, Harvey realized he needed to rescue himself. He used his good arm to make the short climbs, trying in vain not to let anything glance his grossly deformed wrist. Forty minutes later he flopped into the car and ordered one of the students to step on it to Flagstaff. At the hospital, the doctor set his arm and warned Harvey to stay away from hiking until it healed.

It was like telling an alcoholic not to drink. With his arm in a cast the following month, he led a photographer and writer from *Arizona Highways* who were working on a story about the Little Colorado gorge down the rough Salt Trail. Despite his handicap, Harvey set his usual tempo and quickly left his companions behind. When he and the photographer's 20 year-old assistant neared the Little Colorado River, they waited for an hour before deciding to head back up. "We found," Harvey wrote, "that the other three had just come to a decision not to go any further toward the bottom." After the hike, *Arizona Highways* editor Raymond Carlson asked Harvey to write and photograph the story himself, which he did. "The Lower Gorge Of The Little Colorado," which detailed Harvey's long-term exploration of this side canyon, eventually appeared in the September 1965 issue.

In June 1970, Harvey found more danger while soloing a virgin summit. Under the glare of an early summer sun, he dropped off Cape Royal, hiked past Vishnu Temple and Krishna Shrine, then in and out of Asbestos Canyon to put himself within striking distance of two unclimbed buttes, Sheba and Solomon

Temples. His reward for the long approach came when he easily climbed Sheba, a first ascent. Solomon, however, held a surprise for him as he approached its upper cliffs:

> There was a problem in route finding and the only way through a high ledge seemed to be up a chute. It ended in two vertical cracks both having chockstone caps. I picked the one that seemed a bit easier and was soon even with the top by bracing my feet against one wall while leaning my back against the other. More from habit than necessity I reached my right arm out and put a little weight on the chockstone as I often do. This was a mistake which might have been fatal. With no scraping, this 150 pound rock tipped toward me and came down on my leg.
>
> At first I just held it thinking that I might push it back into balance, but in my position this was impossible. Then the weight of the load fell on my right side and I wouldn't have been surprised if I had felt some ribs cracking. If I had tried to move out I was afraid it would roll farther and take me down the cliff. When I couldn't stand the pressure any longer and did give way...the rock jammed lower in the crack... I was ready to proceed to the top with nothing worse than some very sore ribs and welts.

With his heart racing and legs still trembling, Harvey stumbled off to the summit. By sheer luck he had won again, adding another prized first ascent to his list. As dangerous as Grand Canyon could be, Harvey often found that he was his own greatest threat. In 1968, he nearly hung himself while conducting a climbing workshop for several NAU students.

"He decided he would teach us how to jumar," said Susan Billingsley, referring to the cam-like devices that allow a climber to ascend a fixed rope. "So we met behind the forestry building one day, there was five or six of us, and he was going to come down off the fire escape and jumar back up. And some of us were on top and some of us were on bottom. And he was on the outside of the railing, and he was fixing his ropes and everything. And [student] Jimmy Sears came out, and he was late, so he came out and threw the door open and Dr. Butchart was leaning over and it hit him in the head, and he goes 'Whoaaaaaa' like that [mimics Harvey falling]! He was just dangling over the edge, ready to come crashing down, and we're just grabbing for him and we pulled him up and he said, 'Wow, that was really close' and just never stopped talking."

"Then he starts down, and he was in his teaching clothes, and the rope got caught around the collar of his white shirt. And the white shirt started getting twisted up into the rope and it got tighter and tighter and he wasn't breathing, you know [laughs]? And we're all like 'He's gonna die!' But he never lost his cool. So we finally got him over to some steps and he kinda snapped out of it, and his shirt was all burned there and everything. And all he said was, 'Roma's gonna be really upset when she sees this.'"

Indeed, Harvey possessed limited mechanical aptitude. One of his hiking buddies said that Harvey had no idea whether the engine in his Jimmy was a V-8 or a six-cylinder. Yet he considered himself proficient with jumars. Sometimes they became necessary for a route that would not yield to unprotected climbing. Such was the case in 1969 in Saddle Canyon, a deep trench north of Saddle Mountain (now an official wilderness area adjacent to the national park) that feeds Marble Canyon.

In the 1960s, no known rim-to-river routes penetrated Marble Canyon between South and Nankoweap Canyons, a distance of 20 river miles. Harvey surmised that Saddle Canyon formed a likely place for such a route when archeologist R.C. Euler reported an Indian granary deep in Saddle Canyon's Supai Formation.

In September 1963, Harvey decided to check it out. He descended the bed of Saddle, following deer paths and bypassing several falls until an 80-foot overhanging drop in the Coconino halted further progress. It was unlikely that the Indians would have been able to bypass this obstacle yet Harvey spied a recent-looking landslide below that might have previously formed a talus ramp leading up to the fall. He hadn't brought his rope, so he turned back pledging to one day rappel the 80-foot cliff, thinking he might find evidence of an Indian route below.

He put this project aside for two years, then came back with NAU student Norvel Johnson in June 1965. But Johnson became frightened at the sight of the overhanging drop. Harvey's bitter log entry reads, "I had carried the rope here, but Norvel insisted that I shouldn't try anything that risky. I should have left him the car key in case he had to go for help, and I should have gone down."

Four years would pass before Harvey returned. In November 1969 an experienced climber and geology student, Jim Sears, agreed to try rappelling the cliff with Harvey. It was an ambitious day. Before tackling the Saddle Canyon rappel, they forged a difficult route down to the river at River Mile 30.4, upstream from Saddle Canyon. This route had also stopped Harvey before, but Sears was able to down-climb the crux, a 30-foot cliff, while Harvey chose to rappel. Once again, Harvey displayed an appalling lack of expertise when it came to rope work.

> I tied the rope to a large block 25 feet back from the edge of the drop, but I didn't succeed in getting the rope to stay the way I fastened it. After Jim was

up and I began to put my weight on the Jumar slings, the loop around the big rock slipped and one side came up as if the whole thing might slip off. Jim should have told me to descend and let him fix it right, but instead, he held the rope freehand supporting my weight most of the way to the top. I didn't realize what was going on until I got out on top...

Following the close call, the two headed back to the rim, then drove to the second route-finding operation of the day at Saddle Canyon. Intent on making the rappel that he had been denied four years earlier, Harvey confidently led Sears to the cliff. Once there, however, they both lost heart. "We didn't go down to the very last edge for a close look," Harvey wrote, "but the drop seemed so great that neither of us seemed to feel much courage. For the second time I agreed to retreat without ever uncoiling the rope."

On a cold, cloudless Saturday morning one month later, Harvey returned for his fourth try at Saddle Canyon. Several lapses in judgment, any one of which could easily have proved fatal, would make this trek *the* epic in Harvey's hiking career.

"I came alone," Harvey wrote in his log for December 20, 1969, "determined not to let anything dissuade me from the adventure. I left the car by 7:15 A.M. on the short day in late December and got to the rappel site without delay." He set his anchor on a sturdy pinyon tree and tossed his 120-foot coiled Goldline rope over the edge, now ready to make the descent that had foiled him so many times. Employing the standard precaution when rappelling over a cliff edge, he removed his jacket and attached it to the rope where it rubbed the sandstone to protect the line from abrasion.

An early climbing rope, the Goldline was strong and flexible but not the best for rappelling concave walls where one would hang free in space. The ropes were notorious for twisting when given the opportunity, such as when a climber would be unable to brace his feet against rock to prevent rotation. As Harvey descended, the wall curved inward and the rope began to spin.

When I was 20 feet down, I found a big overhang and soon the rope was spinning me slowly and then faster. Before long I was feeling dizzy and almost sick. The best that I could do was to shut my eyes and proceed to feed slack to the friction carabineer. In a shorter time than I thought it would take to be down, I felt a big change. I had the sensation of swinging many feet sideways, but when I opened my eyes, I saw that I had stopped spinning with my feet touching a bush. I was feeling rather elated that I had finally had the nerve to reverse several frustrating experiences in which I had chickened out of a project.

He regained his balance and continued down Saddle for another hour and 45 minutes to where he could get a good view of the Colorado from atop the Redwall. Here he ate a leisurely lunch, savoring the awesome sight of the gorge as well as his victory in finally descending the troublesome cliff. He did not mention seeing any signs of an Indian route, but this did nothing to quell his sense of satisfaction.

It was time to turn back, as he had promised Roma to return for dinner that night. The afternoon was warm. He had only a flannel shirt. Frozen pools that dotted the bed of Saddle attested to a dramatic drop in the nightly temperature.

By 3 P.M. Harvey was back at the base of the high cliff in the Coconino, attaching his jumars to the rope; the jumars were fastened to his climbing harness by short lengths of webbing. His harness consisted of a diaper-like device that wound around his legs and middle, through which the climbing rope was fed. This system acted as insurance against a fall: Should his hands slip out of the jumar handles, he would remain attached to the rope, no matter what. Harvey began his ascent.

> When I had gone up a few yards, the rope began to twist me around and around. I remembered how ill I had felt in the relatively short trip down and I thought it might be really serious if I became weak on the slow trip up the rope...When I had come to Earth again, in order not to have to use a hand to pull the main rope through the waist band, I decided to leave the waist band off, a nearly fatal mistake.

By removing his harness, Harvey hoped to quicken his ascent by not having to pull the rope through the harness as he went up. But this also meant that he was abandoning his safety net, as there was now nothing that held him fixed to the rope—he would be relying solely on his hands and feet to hold his weight for the entire 80 feet.

There was another dangerous side effect to disengaging himself from his harness. Lengths of looped webbing that act as stirrups, called aiders, hang down from the jumars to accommodate the feet. By alternately stepping up in the aiders and then sliding the opposing jumar up the rope, a climber is able to work his way up. But for the system to work safely, the jumars must be attached to the climbing harness. Otherwise there is nothing to keep one's feet from swinging away from the body at odd sideways angles.

Harvey loosely tied the bottom of the rope to a bush in the hopes of canceling its tendency to spin. He collected himself, then tried to ascend once more.

> When I was about nine feet up...my feet slipped forward away from my

body...I began to descend but my feet came up even with my shoulders. I was supporting my full weight with my hands and was unable to maneuver the clamps to descend. After a few desperate moments I had to let go and hang from my feet which were well fastened and held by the snug slings.

Harvey had hung himself upside down by his feet. Possessions rained out of his pockets onto the ground. The blood rushed to his head. Harvey had made it a point to shun company for this adventure, thinking that alone he could do exactly as he wished. Now his act of stubbornness seemed likely to cost him his life:

I had seen ice in the shade and I knew that dressed as I was I couldn't survive the cold in that helpless position. I knew that no help would reach me for at least several days since...I hadn't given her [Roma] a good location of where on the north side of the Colorado I would be. I had to do something or else it was my life. I said a prayer for calmness in the face of the inevitable, and I didn't struggle aimlessly or give up either. I felt no sense of panic, so I might say my prayer was answered.

Despite his predicament, Harvey had been incredibly lucky in that he had flipped upside down just above the level of the ground. Had he been one foot higher, he would have hung helplessly in the aiders, doomed to death by exposure. Had he been one foot lower, he would have struck a big rock directly beneath him headfirst.

The ground was steeply sloped, however, and by stretching his arms to the utmost he could just touch it. But with the aiders wrenching his feet, all he could do at first

Harvey using jumar ascenders and aiders in Black Tank Canyon, 1968. *Courtesy George Billingsley* was hang and suffer. He steadied his mind, thinking, trying to come up with a solution. He tried pawing at the dirt with his fingers. Several times he made a little progress uphill only to lose his hold and swing back downhill. Finally, after repeatedly trying this for 40 minutes, he was able to grab a small tree in one hand. This freed his other hand to try to unstrap his feet.

He stretched toward his shoelaces but they were too high to reach. He lunged at them, scraping at the bowknots in desperate swipes. Harvey managed to undo his laces after numerous swipes, then willed his bloodless feet to squirm inside the shoes. He worked his left foot free of its shoe, then his right foot. Finally, he flopped onto the ground, yelping in pain when he tried to stand.

Harvey took stock of his situation. He was short on food, low on water, and his feet were a mess. He had neglected to bring matches. Night was only an hour away. He had not told Roma where he was going. In an interview 25 years later, Harvey explained why he had violated this basic rule of outdoor safety. "I guess I was just always cocky about playing it safe enough. I always thought I could manage myself and didn't need any rescues."

The frustrating Goldline rope had eroded his confidence, and though he could have tried ascending again, he felt in no mood to try. He decided he would rather walk out some other way than go back up that twisting rope. Eventually he found he could endure the pain of standing long enough to retrieve his shoes. As he laced them up, he faced some tough questions: Where was the nearest route out? How would he fare in the cold of night with little clothing and no matches to build a fire? Did he have enough food and water to fuel a self-rescue?

Years later, Harvey would learn of a usable route, the 49.9-Mile Route (also called the Boundary Ridge Route) only two or three miles to the south. But in 1969, the shortest route that he knew of meant a long loop to the south around Saddle Mountain to the Nankoweap Trail—maybe 20 miles, 15 of which would be off-trail bushwhacking in the dark. He would also have to somehow find a way across the deep, forbidding obstacle of Little Nankoweap Canyon along the way, and he needed to do it all above the Redwall, because he knew of no way down through this rock layer. He had never been over any of this stretch before. With evening closing in, he made his decision and went back down Saddle Canyon to the top of the Redwall. Here he began traversing to the south.

A chill settled into the Canyon. Only one more revolution of the Earth separated Harvey from the winter solstice, the longest night of the year. He had 14 cold hours of darkness to look forward to. But the moon had risen and was within three days of being full, providing light to work with—for a few hours.

As night descended, the landscape became indistinct. It traded its familiar look and offered instead a gauzy reality filled with ambiguous forms. Harvey fell now and then over rocks, stumbled into cacti, and repeatedly stabbed himself in the face with unseen juniper branches.

Meanwhile, at home in Flagstaff, Roma became concerned when Harvey failed to show. She decided to ask around to see if someone knew his whereabouts. "The night he was missing she called me up," Bob Packard said, "and wondered if Harvey had told me where he was going and what he was up to, and of course Harvey hadn't told me where he was going. And she was worried about him."

Harvey kept up his marching through the quiet hours of the night. He could not see far enough ahead to anticipate ledges and was repeatedly forced to backtrack. Three deep, recessed amphitheaters meant lengthy bypasses around their heads. He was dog-tired by now, but knew he could not stop moving for the cold. Near 11 P.M., six hours after beginning his self-rescue, he turned into the first ravine that marked the major obstacle standing between him and the Nankoweap Trail, Little Nankoweap Canyon.

Steep and circuitously shaped, this defile forced him onto slim ledges where the Redwall constantly threatened to pinch out. By going this far, he realized he had committed himself. He could not turn back if he met an impasse for his food supply would not allow second-guessing. He had to keep going with the faith that his route would go.

The moon went behind the cliffs of Saddle Mountain soon after I entered this biggest detour. The whole place seems impressively steep, and when I finally reached the north side and looked across I could hardly believe that it was possible to go where I had just been an hour earlier. The moon was still shining on high cliffs, but I couldn't see well enough to dodge tree branches and thorns, and I got through with the richest assortment of scratches on my face and scalp to date.

I had filled my two-quart canteen at a rain pool in Saddle Canyon about 5:00 p.m. and all the food I had was four pieces of bread, six cookies, and more prunes than I would want. When I got back to the bed...this ledge went through, although I had to get down on all fours to get under a ceiling. What won't a man go through just to save his life! I began to think that I should have scratched a message on the bare earth at the rappel rope saying that I was heading for the Nankoweap Trail. It was darkest and coldest from five o'clock on. I hadn't eaten much in an effort to go slow on the water, and I often had to sit down and doze for a few minutes with my head on my knees. After a few minutes, I would get chilly and struggle on.

Finally, as the sun rose upon the first day of winter, he stepped onto an actual trail that would lead him back to his truck. It had been 24 hours since he began hiking down Saddle Canyon and he still had seven hours of hard walking ahead. But at least the sun was up and the weather was good. Soon he was hiking without a shirt, laboring up the steep Nankoweap Trail in the growing heat. He found full water bottles along the trail near Marion Point that had been left by NAU student hikers only a few weeks before, and was able to rehydrate himself for the last few miles to the parking lot.

> By 12:30 P.M. I was starting down off the saddle into the snow to the north. From weariness I was clumsy in the snow and fell repeatedly. Even where the ground was bare, the frozen mud with some wet mud on top was a hazard.

At long last, after 31 hours of continuous hiking, considerable psychological torment, and some time spent "hanging around," Harvey was able to lay his hand upon the smooth metal of his vehicle. He had just completed the worst hike of his life. But the 62-year-old man could manage a small smile of satisfaction. He had refused to surrender and helplessly wait for a rescue. Harvey had also avoided screwing up further by injuring himself or worse.

An ordeal such as this would be too much for most hikers, but then, most would never have taken on the risks of rappelling alone, especially after neglecting to inform someone of his or her whereabouts. Yet Harvey escaped all of these mistakes little worse for the wear and even returned to retrieve his rope and jumars only two days later.

He would always recount this long night march through unfamiliar territory as his most extreme physical test. He may also have set a record: Longest continuous off-trail trek in Grand Canyon, from 7:15 A.M. one day to 2:45 P.M. the next, 31 hours in all. Harvey evidently chose to overlook this small fact, for this was one record he never bragged of.

Harvey and Roma in 1973. *Courtesy Anne Madariaga*

Chapter Twenty-Three

SOLO JOURNEYS

Standing at the back of the auditorium, I watched Joe cast his spell. As he spoke, pictures were projected on the huge screen behind him... By then I knew his faults, the weaknesses behind the image. But like everyone else in the audience I was enthralled. I envied him the certainty of his calling. He was the hero I could never be, the hero I thought I needed—without any real inkling of what that would cost.

Maria Coffey,
Where The Mountain Casts Its Shadow: The Dark Side of Extreme Adventure
On Coffey's husband Joe Tasker, who died in a mountaineering accident.

WAITING...WAITING...WAITING...

Late again. How long had it been, now? Four hours? Five? Too long no matter how she looked at it. Something must have gone wrong. Was he hurt? Maybe. Lost? Not a chance. After all, he was Harvey Butchart, Grand Canyon's foremost hiker and explorer. He knew the national park better than anybody, as they were always saying.

As usual, Roma had no idea where he was. Harvey had told her he was going hiking "across the Colorado." That cocky phrase encompassed more territory than a division of soldiers could cover in a month. Harvey had also promised to be home in time for dinner, a meal Roma had faithfully prepared. But now it lay cold and uneaten. She decided to call their neighbor Bob Packard, yet he could tell her nothing about Harvey's whereabouts. She was on her own with this one.

Roma could not have known that at that moment, her husband was just beginning to hike away from Saddle Canyon after nearly killing himself. That he was doing the best he could to right a series of mistakes. All she could do was wonder what the devil Harvey had done this time, and hope that he would show up alive.

This kind of thing had become all too familiar. How many times had she driven to the Canyon to retrieve him for this or that, or spent anxious nights alone while he got himself out of yet another jam? Roma had a hard night ahead, perhaps as difficult as the one Harvey was just beginning to experience.

When he finally showed the next afternoon, disheveled and weak from his ordeal, she was relieved—and angry. She had spent the entire morning a nervous wreck, helpless to do anything. Harvey tended to leave her in the dark when it came to his Canyon pursuits. He had long since given up discussing the nuts and bolts of what he did down there, and hence had not divulged his intentions to forge a dangerous route down Saddle Canyon. Maybe Harvey figured it was best if Roma did not realize the risks he was taking. After all, most 62-year-olds do not make solo 80-foot rappels into deserted gorges.

As usual, however, Harvey simply brushed himself off, expressed the misadventure to his typewriter, and Roma asked few questions. This was the pattern they had followed for years. In fact, they had long ago worked out an agreement: Harvey could have his Canyon time to do as he wished, as long as he made a punctual return for dinner, the weekly bridge games, or simply to be present in the house. If he showed at a reasonable time, she would not raise much of a fuss. In a sense, Harvey owed his amazing track record to Roma. Without her insisting that he promptly return each Sunday night, he may not have moved quite as fast as he did.

Their explicit pact would last for the remainder of Harvey's protracted relationship with Grand Canyon. And for the most part, it worked. Roma's time with Harvey in the home remained inviolable.

But by the 1970s, the scope of Harvey's obsession gradually followed him out of the Canyon and into Flagstaff. *Grand Canyon Treks* changed everything. Harvey began spending more and more time at his typewriter keeping up with the endless correspondence. He also invited hiking buddies to dinner, to chat, to watch each other's slides. Then there were the fans who showed unannounced at the doorstep. Grand Canyon was invading the home, and Roma grew more and more exasperated.

In 1976, the year after *Grand Canyon Treks II* was published, Harvey and Roma faced off in a decision about their future. Harvey turned 69 in May and retired after 31 years at NAU. He could look back on his life with satisfaction. He had come from poverty in a single-mother family of five, had sweated through a Ph.D. during the Depression and managed to become a success with a family of his own. Now he had adoring grandchildren whom he could dote over.

Harvey was also leaving behind a distinguished professional life. He had published 13 mathematical papers and spent 22 years serving as math department chair. He had been one of two math professors when he arrived in 1945, and raised that number to 12 professors during his tenure as head of the department.[1] And of course, in between family and career, he had made history as the most accomplished Grand Canyon explorer in history.

The future remained just as bright, for Harvey was healthy and fit as ever. And *free* now to explore as much as he wished.

But Roma put her foot down. She wanted to move away from Grand Canyon. Wasn't three decades of hiking enough? Roma loved to walk the beach and collect seashells, to listen to sounds of the surf whooshing over the sand. She and Harvey had made several trips over the years to Rocky Point in Mexico, where the Sea of Cortez meets the Sonoran Desert. Roma told Harvey she wanted to move there, or the Bahamas, somewhere far beyond the blustery, snowy winters of northern Arizona and Grand Canyon.

Despite the decades he had spent exploring, Harvey now had a longer list of Canyon goals than ever. Routes, summits—he had only made a dent in that list, as far as he was concerned. He told Roma he wanted to stay in Flagstaff. They had their friends, their place in the community, Grand Canyon was so close— why on Earth would they want to leave?

They went back and forth. In the end, they compromised. The Butcharts would move 120 miles south, to Sun City.

In the Western tradition of boomtowns, Sun City was unprecedented in size and scope. The self-contained conurbation was the brainchild of Del Webb, a real estate baron who who hit the jackpot erecting Sunbelt suburbias for retirees, and who enjoyed an occasional round of golf with his friends Bing Crosby and Barry Goldwater. Sun City arose in the 1960s out of the cacti-laden *caliche* on the outskirts of Phoenix, attracting 100,000 people on its opening weekend. Senior citizens who wanted to live their final years in the Sonoran Desert amidst golf courses, artificial lakes, and manicured neighborhoods flocked to buy a piece of the good life. Young families with children were welcome to visit, but not stay. This "master-planned community for active adults" may not have been either Harvey or Roma's initial preference, but it would be home for the next 25 years.

Yet, the move did accomplish one thing for Roma—it put more distance between Harvey and the Canyon. As a result, in the years following the move, he began spending less time there, averaging about 25 days per year as opposed to 35 in the early 1970s.

But Harvey still burned as hot as ever for the place. After all, he needed to keep building on his records, lest someone try to dethrone him as Grand

---

[1] In 1983, to the surprise of several math professors at NAU, a new NAU mathematics building was named for Professor of Astronomy Dr. Arthur Adel instead of Harvey.

Canyon's undisputed hiking king. Being a mathematician, he knew with precision the numbers that he had amassed. By the early 1980s, he had hiked over 11,000 miles below the rim and had spent nearly 1,000 days—almost three years—doing so. In a 1995 letter, Harvey described the scope of his Grand Canyon dream:

> Yes, I have to confess that I have done some of my hiking for the record. When I began to get the reputation of being the foremost Grand Canyon hiker of a certain period, I did get the ambition to go farther afield and learn something new about every part of the Canyon. I was trying to build a record that would be hard to beat.

It wasn't enough to merely accomplish these records—everything required documentation, and that meant time at the typewriter. When Harvey wasn't hiking, he was writing. Hours and hours of writing about hiking, or writing someone who was writing him about hiking. Then there was the research. Researching old routes, abandoned routes, forgotten routes, new routes—whatever. Add the visiting hikers, the planning, the discussions, and the debates—there was no end to it.

It seemed that Harvey never left the Canyon. But he could leave Roma. And each time he set foot on his own into the chasm, he was on another solo journey. And so was Roma.

Taking everything into account, Roma knew that Harvey could tack at least another year onto those 1,000 days spent in the gorge. Regardless of how much it all added up to, the resulting figure meant different things to each of them.

For Harvey, it reflected an ever-expanding achievement, one that brought him fame. For Roma, it was a monument to loneliness.

She knew better than anyone the emotional cost of Harvey's greatness. Their first two decades together—until his affair with Grand Canyon began—had been good. But ever since the 1950s, things had changed.

One day in 1984, alone in Sun City while Harvey was on yet another trek, Roma could not help but imagine herself a widow. She sat down in front of Harvey's typewriter. The years of exasperation, of putting up with her obsessed man and all the attendant baggage came boiling to the surface and spilled onto the page in an essay she titled...

Confessions of a "Hiking Widow"

> A few days ago, as I was watching my favorite soap opera, the telephone rang.

"Is Mr. Butchart there?" inquired a voice of the type I've learned, painfully, to recognize.

"You've got to be kidding," I replied. "Why would he be here?"

"Well, I'm calling from Crazy Crag, Vermont. I've read his book on hiking in the Grand Canyon. I'm planning a trip out that way in the spring of 1991 and I need to know if it is all right to wear a sweater on the Bright Angel Trail."

"If you've read his book, you ought to know that he doesn't go down the Bright Angel. Besides, sweaters are in the eyes of the beholder. What's good for one isn't necessarily good for all. Are we talking wool or acrylic, long or short sleeves? Cardigan or pullover?"

"Hmmm, I see your point. Still, I would like to call him back. When will he be there?"

"He may be here between five-thirty and six," I said doubtfully. "And again, he may not be here before next Thursday. And even if he is, I'll be needing him to light the pilot light for the furnace. It's getting chilly these mornings, even in Phoenix. All he has to do is move the Jimmy over so he can climb on top of it to get up on the roof of the house. Don't you agree that a man who can rappel down cliffs and worm his way along a three-inch-wide ledge should be able to do that much, even if he is 77 and has a bad hip?"

"Yeah. Well, it's been nice talking to you. So long."

By the time I had returned to the TV, I had missed the latest in Steve's endless struggles, but not to worry. I felt sure that Steve and Betsy would be reunited sooner or later...

As the wife of Grand Canyon's famous explorer, Roma had been subjected to countless inane calls from complete strangers, readers, and fans seeking Harvey's advice. It was painful enough being left behind whenever Harvey needed a Canyon fix, but having to play secretary in his absence only rubbed salt in the wound. She hated the calls, the unexpected visits, the endless string of interruptions in her life. Roma was a skilled writer, much more versatile than Harvey, a well-read woman who had earned her masters degree in French Literature. She delighted in mocking the many Canyon freaks she crossed paths with and their hero in "Confessions of a Hiking Widow":

"There's this really neat girl in from New Zealand," I reported a couple of days later. "She's in this country and she wants to go hiking with you. She worries because you go alone so much. She's climbed the Washington Monument in two hours, twenty minutes, and seventeen seconds, so you can see what great condition she's in. She would only ask you to meet her plane and drive her to the Canyon. She even has her own sleeping bag, and she's a great cook. She thinks hiking in the Canyon with the man who has spent more time in the Canyon than anyone else would be very educational."

"I already know all I need to know, or at least all she might be able to teach me," said Harvey. "And let's face it, raisins and canned sardines don't require much cooking. And besides, if she couldn't keep up with me, I wouldn't want to feel obligated to carry her sleeping bag. My own pack feels heavier each year. And if I couldn't keep up with her, it might damage my ego, to say nothing of my bad hip."

"I wouldn't worry too much about the ego, but if she calls back I'll tell her the truth, that you are a greatgrandfather, your teeth need to be fixed, and you have to go behind the bushes pretty often. If God had meant for you to go hiking with a girl you don't know, He would have put in more bushes. 'Alone' is better."

Roma had seen it all—the Harvey wannabes, her husband's peculiar addiction to timing himself, the letters from female admirers. She had justification in cutting her larger-than-life mate down to size, for she had paid for his fame with 1,000 lonely days and nights of her own.

Roma also had reason to strike back at his fans. Alas, she realized what they said behind her back. A recurring joke in Grand Canyon circles went something like this:

"Why does Harvey hike so much?"

"Have you met his wife?"

Hikers who befriended Harvey, and there were plenty of them in the 1970s and 1980s, usually knew what they were in for when they entered the Butchart home. It was well known that Roma considered canyoneers the lowest of the low. No amount of charm, politeness, or feigned interest could bring Roma around, and that was that.

Scott Thybony, who visited the Butcharts in both Flagstaff and Sun City, was one hiker who had no success with her. "Roma just...she never seemed to like hikers or Canyon people," Thybony said. "It was almost like we were part of this alien world, that was sort of invading her world. So when you would show up to talk to Harvey, she would coldly usher you into his study, and then would have nothing to do with you. She had no interest in the Canyon and those hiking trips."

Stories flourished. Roma greeted hikers with a snarl at the door. She was rude and aloof. Harvey asked hikers to meet him at a Sun City gas station rather than subject them to her anger. Harvey's friend Tony Williams remembered in particular her feral gaze. "Looking into Roma's eyes," Williams said, "was like looking into the steely blue eyes of hatred. She would go off and sulk. Or sometimes she'd just sit right across the table and glower. But usually, she would retreat with a scowl to the TV room."

"She gained quite a reputation," said Jim Ohlman, an engineer who is among the most accomplished Grand Canyon hikers and climbers. Ohlman remembered the day he met Roma in 1975 after he and Harvey returned from a day at the Canyon.

"So we get back," Ohlman said, "and Harvey, instead of dropping me off at campus, we went to their house and it was about dinner time."

"Let me go in and see if Roma has something fixing for dinner," Harvey said. In a couple minutes he returned to collect Ohlman. "Yeah you can come in, we're having dinner."

"So we sit down," Ohlman said. "Harvey was sitting there, I was sitting across from him, and Roma was sitting right next to Harvey. And she went to the kitchen. We had cups of soup—that was dinner by the way, period. So anyway, we're eating our bowl of soup and I'm looking at Harvey, and Roma's right here."

"Where'd you guys go?" Roma asked.

"And we did this and this and this, it was kind of a neat hike," said Ohlman. "And Harvey and I were kind of batting the day back and forth, but in general terms so as to leave the door open for Roma to get in there." In one of these lulls in conversation, Roma began to speak.

"You know Harvey," she said, "I don't approve of all these hikes that you go on. And one of these days, you're getting older and you're going to hurt yourself, and you've got to be more attentive to your age now."

"And another thing," she continued. "I don't approve of these characters that you go hiking with. They're some of the scruffiest lots. Most of them are bums."

"I looked up at Harvey," Ohlman said. "Roma wasn't looking at anything in particular, and I looked at Harvey, like, 'Am I invisible here? Should I not be here? Give me a cue and I'm leaving.' And Harvey just got this real queer little grin on his face. Roma's over here just going on, and I'm like, 'What the heck is going on here? This gal is doing this all like I'm not there, and it's third person.'"

"I had never seen her before in my life," Ohlman continued. "I had only heard about her. And sitting there, it was like I'm invisible, and every story I've heard about this witch is true. So anyway she waxed as eloquent for a few minutes, and then got quiet, back in her soup again. I finish, 'Oh that was pretty good. You know it's getting kind of late, Harvey can you give me a ride to campus?' And Roma didn't say anything more, like, 'Oh nice of you to stop in.' I was like, 'Did you just have a break in personality? Do you have alter egos, like two faces of Eve, except two faces of Roma?'"

During the short drive to NAU, Ohlman decided to voice his curiosity. "Do you normally have such an elegant dinner?" Ohlman initiated.

"Yeah, that's what we normally have," Harvey said.

"Harvey, was your wife mad at me?"

"Oh no," Harvey said with a laugh, "she's that way with all the people I go hiking with. It's just her way. It's just her way."

After Harvey let Ohlman off, the famished hiker trekked to McDonald's for a hamburger. But Roma's reputation had taken another hit. The incident only solidified the notion among canyoneers that, indeed, Harvey had to escape to the Canyon because Roma was an "unholy terror in the house," as Ohlman put it. Behind every good man is a...strong woman, in other words.

Yet Ohlman himself wondered whether this was true. Did Harvey hike so much because Roma was ornery and difficult to live with? Or did she become a scornful and resentful nag because of his Grand Canyon obsession? Was it possible that Roma owned a pleasant disposition, that she had become aggravated only after Harvey began to devote his life to Grand Canyon? After all, Harvey and Roma had once been young, in love, and had lived far, far away from Arizona. If so, it is not difficult to imagine that as Harvey became more obsessed, his wife became understandably more peeved.

Indeed, not all of Harvey's hiker buddies echoed the common sentiments about Roma. Both Allyn Cureton and Jim David, who hiked with Harvey as students in the late 1950s and early 1960s, found her reserved, but pleasant and polite. Obviously, something had changed between the early days and the 1970s.

Not long after their awkward dinner, while driving to the Canyon for a hike, Ohlman asked Harvey point blank about Roma.

"So Harvey, what's with you and your wife?" Ohlman asked.

Harvey in the late 1970s. Was he happiest in the Canyon instead of at home with Roma? *Courtesy Scott Baxter*

"Oh, don't worry about that old bat," Harvey said.

"He used that phrase," Ohlman said. "I just laughed, I looked over at Harvey and he was laughing too."

"Yeah, she does her thing and I do my thing," Harvey said. "Don't pay her no attention, she's okay, she doesn't get on my case."

Judging from this reply, as far as Harvey was concerned, Roma did not give him a hard time about his treks. One can only speculate on how revealing Harvey was willing to be with Ohlman, but honesty was something the math professor took seriously. Perhaps it was just the accompanying fame, and resulting hangers-on (such as Ohlman) that caused Roma to react with such hostility. From "Confessions":

> It was not always so easy to deflect would-be hiking companions. Many years ago in Flagstaff I returned from work late one afternoon to find a strange young man on the porch. "Hello, I'm Henry. I've heard of your husband. I'm a hiker, too, and would like to meet him. How does it feel to be married to the man who has spent more time in the Canyon than anyone else?"
>
> "If you really want an answer to that question," I said, "you'll have to be more specific. If you mean how does it feel compared to being married to him when he <u>hadn't</u> hiked so much, it's been so long ago that I can hardly remember. If you mean how does it feel compared to being married to somebody else, I really can't say because I've never been married to anyone else. Or maybe you mean how does it feel compared to being single?"
>
> "Forget I asked," said Henry. "But as I really do want to meet him, I'll just wait till he comes home, stay for dinner, monopolize your evening, and stay all night if possible." Of course he didn't say all of that in words, but, as everyone knows, actions speak louder than words. After my husband got home and we had had a couple of hours of scintillating conversation about ropes and pitons and Jumar ascenders and backpacks and Sterno stoves, and other equally engrossing topics, I realized that Henry wasn't going to give up without a fight. I finally invited him to dinner, and he somehow managed to stay overnight.
>
> He didn't visit us again, but he sends five-page, single-spaced accounts of his activities once or twice a year. So much for Henry...

Anyone in a romantic relationship can relate to Roma's lament. For example, how entertaining is it for the wife who has zero interest in baseball to listen to her husband discuss batting averages with a fellow fanatic? The first few times, she may politely attempt to sit in on such a conversation. But each subculture has its own language that must be learned before one can participate. Then there are the inside jokes, the sense of camaraderie that a shared passion produces. Perhaps the wife smiles at the lighthearted moments, frowns over the discords, tries to go along with the tone of things. But ultimately, she becomes a bystander. An outsider. Roma experienced this more times than she cared to remember.

Yet she too had once enjoyed Grand Canyon. She made at least six treks with Harvey into the gorge during the 1940s and 1950s. During an interview in 1995, Roma explained why she lost interest. "Well, of course, when we first went to Flagstaff we all went hiking in the Grand Canyon," Roma said. "The children and I, we all went. It was in later years that Harvey got so intense about it. Of course when we all went, I thought it was great. And later on I got resigned to it."

Harvey's behavior had changed quickly once he became bent on pursuing a legacy. He soon had little desire to spend precious days making casual hikes with the family. Harvey explained this shift in his 1965 *Arizona Highways* article "The Lower Gorge of the Little Colorado":

> Our first vacations in the west were family affairs. We hit all the show places: Bryce, Zion, the Grand Canyon's North Rim, and Oak Creek Canyon. We went on ambitious hikes to Supai, Phantom Ranch, and Rainbow Bridge. But as my wife and two children developed other interests, I began to go exploring in the Grand Canyon by myself or with a few college boys. Anything I heard about the Canyon from other hikers became a lure for me. My first-hand knowledge of Grand Canyon National Park grew.

This innocuous line of reasoning takes for granted that Harvey's family would *want* to make Grand Canyon an obsession, too. In reality, he left Roma and the kids no choice but to "develop other interests." In mid-life, Harvey had stumbled upon *his thing* and saw no reason to resist the tremendous pull Grand Canyon exerted. He consistently chose the Canyon over time at home with the kids and Roma. Meanwhile, his family was left to do as they wished.

But what if Roma wanted to spend time with her husband? She could only watch while he drove away time after time to rejoin the Canyon-apple of his eye, and realize that she now played second fiddle in their marriage. In later years, as more and more fans appeared, they became the natural targets for her pain, as she described in "Confessions":

> Then there was David, a man of reportedly superior intellect who couldn't hold a job but could spot an arrowhead in a pile of rubble a hundred yards away. Like so many of the Canyoneers, David was without visible means of support. On one occasion when he was to take a trip into the Canyon with

Harvey, he arrived in his incredibly dirty vehicle, which at that time served as his dwelling as well as for transportation. He informed me that he would leave this vehicle parked in front of our house while they were gone.

I protested to my husband, "But I don't want that filthy old rattle-trap in front of our house. People will think it's ours and that we're ready for the poorhouse, or else I'll be besieged with dealers wanting to sell us a new car, or they'll think it isn't ours, and the police and junkyard men will keep wanting to haul it away. Couldn't David just take it down the street a little way and park it in front of somebody else's house?"

My husband was really shocked. "But this man is a scientific genius. On his high school SCAT tests he qualified as a National Merit winner. He can climb cliffs nobody can reach and finds unbroken prehistoric pots in caves."

"You don't understand," I cried in frustration. "I don't care about his cliffs and his caves or even his pots. He needs a bath and a haircut, his truck is a mess, and he can't even say good morning to me without stuttering, although I notice he is glib enough when the two of you go on about mescal pits and seep springs and gypsum slopes and twelve-foot cracks and ways through the Redwall and sandstone overhangs and catclaw bushes and burro droppings and Indian ladders and bighorn sheep and confluences, to mention only a few. If I ever need to say anything, I can't even get your attention without assaulting you physically. With these guys around, I might as well not even exist."

The truck stayed in front of our house for a week…

Roma's tyrannical father, Bert Wilson, had demanded that Roma accept his stringent beliefs as law. From what Roma has written in personal essays, we know that she privately criticized her father's disposition, his religious beliefs, and the way he controlled her life as a young woman. But she was helpless while living in the atmosphere of fear Wilson cultivated. To defy him meant dire consequences, the scope of which taught Roma to deal with the cards she was dealt.

Harvey was Bert's opposite. He had a gentle personality, and not even his children remember him ever getting angry. But when Harvey welcomed his hiking friends to stay over, or committed much of his free time to Grand Canyon, Roma could rarely change his mind. Once again, she felt obliged to allow the man in her life to make decisions that went against her wishes. Finally, Roma drew the line at intrusions into her home. From "Confessions":

> Gradually I became more wary. On a day when the nephew of an old friend called joyfully and said he was in town with several fellow college students and they needed showers and a place to spread out their bedrolls, I suggested they go straight to the youth hostel without even stopping to see us.

"But we know your husband has spent more time hiking in the Canyon than anyone else," protested the nephew. "We want to meet him and compare notes."

"Listen, Buster, if he has spent more time hiking in the Canyon than anyone else, who do you suppose has spent more time alone than anyone else? I have a few notes of my own to compare. You'll just have to get his book and make what you can out of it even if quite a few words are spelled wrong and some of the commas are in the wrong places."

Roma had lived much as Harvey had, as a shy, quiet intellectual. Neither could be called socially at ease. Their shared perspective on the world had been one of the few things that brought them together in the first place.

But when Harvey became famous for his feats, when the newspaper articles and magazines featured him, when he published his guidebooks, his perspective suddenly changed. He was *popular* for the first time in his life while Roma remained in the shadows. It could not have been easy for her, especially since Harvey had earned his stature in a large measure at her expense. Worse, it meant that when Harvey's fans arrived, they took away not only her husband, but also stole her cherished privacy.

Roma had her own diversions. She taught for a few years then worked as a secretary for the public schools in Flagstaff, giving her an outlet beyond the home. Roma played piano, read voraciously, and craved those walks on the beach. She loved to travel. She and Harvey enjoyed weekends at Lake Powell on their powerboat, summer excursions to Colorado, and vacations to Hawaii, Tahiti, Alaska, and Mexico. Yet she never developed an obsession on the order of Harvey's. When not traveling, Roma simply looked forward to being at home with him, where she and Harvey could play Scrabble or bridge, sometimes with others, but most often with each other. In fact, this was the lubricant for their marriage: Scrabble.

"People relate to other people on a number of different levels," said Ohlman, who is married with children. "Even married couples, you've got a physical level, you've got an emotional level, you've got an intellectual level, and probably several other levels that I can't think of right now. I don't think Harvey and Roma ever connected on an emotional level, and only very seldom initially on a physical level. They were equals on an intellectual level, and I think that's where they challenged each other and that was the glue that held them together, their intellectual compatibility."

"And having seen them play Scrabble," Ohlman continued, "I know they played a tremendous amount. There was fierce competition there. I mean just absolutely fierce competition between the two on a very high mental level.

think that they operated on that level for years. I don't know where they started initially, there had to be a point of compatibility to bring them together, but I think later on that was about the only glue holding them together. And Harvey needed more. Harvey needed something to stimulate, to challenge him physically. I don't think he and his wife did anything that could challenge each other physically. They had totally different interests altogether."

Harvey's need for physical fulfillment and distinction indeed led him away from the home and into the Canyon. But he did spend far more time providing for them than he did hiking. Perhaps Harvey felt that he deserved to do as he pleased with his free time, as long as he upheld his duties as a husband and father.

Defining those duties, however, is a matter of perspective. "My dad wasn't a great father, but he didn't work at it, either," said Jim Butchart, Harvey's son. "He seemed genetically inadequately equipped for the job, being too intellectual. Unless you were a math, chess, or Grand Canyon junkie, you couldn't talk to him. He was completely focused and overwhelmed by his own pursuits."

As a teen, Jim was a good athlete, but unlike his father, he preferred team sports to hiking. Harvey never did see Jim play a baseball game, nor did he see Jim participate in a downhill ski race, despite Jim being the Arizona State Junior Ski Champion during both his junior and senior years in high school.

Harvey takes it to his opponent, Sun City chess match, 1983. *Courtesy Anne Madariaga*

No surprise then that Jim became a decidedly different person than his father. Now a real estate agent living in North Carolina, Jim took his last hike at age 12 with Harvey at Mount Whitney. Not long afterward, Jim discovered girls and quickly decided they were more fun than hiking. In high school he partied with friends, dated, and took up smoking.

"Jim hiked with me until he was 12," wrote Harvey in a 1995 letter. "Rainbow Bridge and Mt. Whitney for instance. Then in junior high he noted that the 'in' group didn't think much of hiking. He dropped out and became a fine skier instead. However, in high school he took up smoking and by the age of 18, his wind was so bad there was no thought of his hiking with me."

Jim has been married three times, and admits that he never saw his parents express much of an emotional connection toward each other, or toward him or his sister. "Both were intellectually gifted, but socially challenged," Jim said. "Neither had a whit. They both had near genius-level IQs, around 160, but socially they were at the other end. I'd say Dad was a zero, and Mom was a little higher. My mother was the more feeling and nurturing of the two, but neither were overly affectionate. In fact, hugs and I-love-yous were essentially nonexistent. Love was a hard word, for both." But, Jim continued, "She loved him [Harvey] very much, and she agonized when he was gone."

Does Jim harbor any resentment towards Harvey for the lack of attention? "No, not now," he said. "But there were some bitter feelings growing up. On an analytical level he excelled. On an emotional level, my dad often failed. Geniuses are quirky. They often exclude all else for compulsion. My dad was without question a Grand Canyon genius, but there's a price for quirkiness."

Harvey admitted to resenting family and social obligations when they stood in the way of the Canyon. In October of 1961, he typed this frustrated entry in his logbook: "We had a social engagement Saturday evening which kept me from a two day weekend in the canyon at this ideal time of year."

Anne Madariaga takes a different stance than her brother Jim. She never minded seeing her father chase his passion, even if it meant that he was gone much of the time. But for Anne, Harvey's absence meant less parental authority to sidestep. She enjoyed boys and partying as much as Jim relished girls and smoking. Anne and Roma had the usual difficulties when she became a teenager, for Anne had a rebellious streak. She tends to remember her mother as the one who instigated turmoil in her parents's marriage.

"By the time I was 16," Anne said, "I was praying for them to get a divorce because she was picking on him—*picking on him!*"

Yet Anne is quick to clarify that Harvey and Roma would have considered divorce unthinkable. She believes Roma's devotion to the marriage was even stronger than Harvey's. "She was a moral stalwart," Anne said. "They both were, but she probably more so. She was incredibly honest, and she had very strong feelings about the vows of marriage."

Roma did not trace her sense of morality to church doctrine. Roma wrote in Anne's 1935 baby book, under the heading "God," *People make up religions to give them a sense of security, but no one really knows if there is a god.* Roma had left the Disciples of Christ shortly after marriage, adopting instead an agnostic philosophy that she discovered by reading books on the subject. Only on rare occasions thereafter on Harvey's behalf could she be found in the pews. Harvey on the other hand remained a devout Christian his entire life, attending church faithfully every Sunday—that is, *if* he was home. To him, divorce would have been an unthinkable sin.

While attending an out-of-state funeral for Harvey's brother Baird in 1963, Jim spent a few days "bacheloring it" with his father. Jim recalled Harvey's surprising remark, "If I had known your mother was going to leave the church, I never would have married her." Jim never heard him mention it again. And neither Jim nor Anne remembers Roma ever broaching the subject of divorce in their presence.

"They both had intense values and belief systems," Jim said. "And, a very loyal commitment to each other and their marriage. In many ways though, it was a marriage of convenience. Harvey's job provided a roof over their heads and stable finances. They often seemed to just co-exist together, separate but in the same household."

Yet Anne emphasized that she had no complaints. "Mom and Dad were good parents. They did the best they could to provide and be there for us. Dad was always concerned about providing for us, especially my younger brother. I certainly felt loved, and I know it bothered Dad a great deal that he wasn't closer to Jim."

Marital discord is not uncommon when obsession is a third party in the relationship. Most spouses simply will not tolerate prolonged absences taken in pursuit of self-satisfaction. Grand Canyon hiker George Steck referred to the Canyon as "the Great Separator" for its tendency to unravel relationships. Roma discovered just how touchy the subject of relationships could be when she questioned a certain canyoneering buddy of Harvey's on the subject. Again, from "Confessions":

> One day Harvey told me to expect a visit for dinner and overnight from A, a professor from a southern college who spent his summers in Colorado and Arizona. All went well through dinner, but as I was clearing away the dishes I asked A how his wife spent her time when he was away so much. I myself am constantly asked this question, which I consider routine and harmless.
>
> Not so A. He became very agitated. "I'd thank you not to cast aspersions on my wife. She is very devoted to me and supports me in anything I undertake."
>
> I tried to soothe him. "That's fine with me. And to show my heart is in the right place too, I've planned to go downtown to the movies tonight. I've seen Harvey's slides more than once, and I suppose yours are quite similar. So I'll just get out of the way so the two of you can look at the pictures and swap information to your hearts's content."
>
> A became apoplectic. His face got very red and he pounded the table till I

was afraid he'd break it.

"You mean to say I traveled all this distance and you aren't even going to look at my slides? Let me tell you, I really am sorry for Harvey. Everyone in Grand Canyon circles knows he is married to a shrew who won't even let him go hiking!"

"Shrews are in the eye of the beholder. But how can Harvey hold the record if I never let him go? He doesn't wait for me or anyone else to 'let' him go. He just goes. I couldn't stop him even if I wanted to."

"I'm not going to stand here and listen to any more of your insults," screamed A. "I wouldn't dream of staying here overnight. I'm going downtown to the Monte Vista Hotel." And he did.

Which was just fine with me, too. But that night I decided that one thing I could stop was running a motel. So I did. After that things were not quite the same, but as far as I was concerned, not quite the same was better.

Three items from this denouement deserve scrutiny. First, contrary to what others may have thought of her, Roma states that she did not try to keep Harvey from going into the Canyon.

Second, who was the man Roma called "A"? None other than Merrel Clubb, whose fracas with Roma had taken place in the summer of 1961. Already ine-briated, Clubb showed up at Harvey's invitation toting a bottle of booze. Following Roma's charged question, Clubb chided Roma, in Harvey's words, "accusing her of not liking Grand Canyon and being a drag on my [Harvey's] progress as a canyon explorer."

"That got her upset," Harvey wrote, "and she lit into him with a shouting match. She was mad enough to get into tears and he was mad, too. I tried to calm them down, but pretty soon Merrel took his bottle and left. I was in bad with Roma over that mess by not getting mad at Merrel and throwing him out." Later, Clubb sent Harvey a letter apologizing for his outburst, but the damage had been done. This incident likely became one more reason Roma became so dismissive towards many future visitors.

Third, Roma makes her defense with the line, "Shrews are in the eye of the beholder." True, it was a matter of perspective. Although she was undoubtedly cold towards many canyoneers, it was not without reason. Each time Harvey attracted another fan into the home, it meant someone was encouraging him to continue his risky behavior, reinforcing his pleasure at being Grand Canyon's master hiker. The Canyon buffs thus came to represent threats to Roma. She regarded each one as increasing her chances of becoming a real widow. Naturally she feared, even detested them.

This was the real burden Roma faced. She had devoted herself to Harvey in

1929 and intended to stick with him to the end—no matter what. But things had changed after Boyd Moore's drowning. From then on, she took a complete-ly different view on what Harvey was doing in Grand Canyon. In one terrible day, canyoneering had gone from a healthy hobby to a dangerous obsession. Suddenly, Roma realized the very real possibility of losing her husband to the Canyon. The numerous broken bones, hospital visits, and close calls—such as the Saddle Canyon debacle—proved that Harvey, for all his cautiousness and experience, took risks that shrouded each new trek in potential disaster.

It is important to remember that Harvey explored a much less crowded Grand Canyon than exists today. There were no search-and-rescue teams on 24-hour standby, no "sat" phones, no commercial rafting companies flooding the river with a steady stream of visitors, no tourist flights overhead. All of this made backcountry emergencies much more difficult to remedy. It's not hard to imagine Roma reeling in her love for Harvey out of self-protection. And with Harvey abandoning her so often, it is no wonder that the Butcharts drifted apart over the years.

"Roma put up with way more than I ever would have," said Janece Ohlman, Jim's wife and the mother of their four children. Janece too grappled with her husband's Canyon obsession, which grew to rival the scope of Harvey's. Yet Janece had once been a hardcore Canyon hiker too, and understood the reasons behind Jim's absences.

The Ohlmans had met as members of the NAU Hiking Club in the 1970s. Both had an intense passion for the Canyon; their courtship included extreme, off-trail hiking and climbing. "Jan and I met," Jim recalled, "doing the same thing that she knew could one day kill me or her." Things went well—for a while. But by the mid-1980s, even Jan was shaking her head as Jim cranked it up a notch, averaging over 1,000 hiking miles per year and knocking off four to five summits a month. Jim acknowledges the physical and emotional danger that his mania created.

"Many people have lost spouses or partners, either figuratively or literally to such an obsession," Jim said. "They often lament the loss, having no clue why their loved one chose to do what they did, knowing they might be left behind. Jan knew *exactly* why I did what I did."

Jim freely admits that Grand Canyon almost cost him his marriage. Shortly after the birth of their son T.J. in 1986, Jan pointed out that he was an absen-tee husband and father. "It came down to me and the Canyon," Jim said, "or my wife and my son. There's no way I would put the Canyon first. The days of 1,000-mile summers were gone when we started a family. If I hadn't, Janece would've divorced me."

Roma would not consider divorce, however, and Harvey could not fathom quitting what he loved. But Harvey was not oblivious to how Roma felt, nor to the sacrifices that she made for him. In 1984, the same year Roma wrote "Confessions of a Hiking Widow," Harvey's third and final guidebook, *Grand Canyon Treks III*, hit the bookstores. In addition to 70-odd pages of stories, advice, and crediting other hikers' accomplishments, the author included the following acknowledgment:

> A large amount of credit is due to Roma, my companion of over fifty years, who has put up with my many absences while exploring the region. And she has been quite tolerant of my affair with her only rival, La Grand Canyon.

"Tolerant" was a word Harvey and Roma both used when discussing their relationship. In 1995, Anne interviewed her parents together and asked Roma to summarize her marriage. "Well," said Roma flatly, "it's more or less like every other married couple's I suppose. We're still married." And, to what did she attribute the longevity of their 66-year marriage? "Tolerance, patience."

When asked to name Harvey's best and worst traits, Roma's comments were equally telling. She matter-of-factly summed up both in one word. "Perseverance. It's good to a point, but you can over do it. Get carried away with obsessions." Then she added, "I think he's good natured. He doesn't get mad. He's tolerant, and he's intelligent."

Anne asked Roma if she carried any resentment about Harvey's years of exploring. "I don't think I was ever really very bitter about it," Roma said. "I don't remember that I did, maybe I did. But he had to do something with his time."

Harvey responded to a similar line of questioning in a letter that same year:

> Yes, my wife has been in the mood at times of resenting the amount of separation my treks have caused, including my being away from home at Thanksgiving (but not at Christmas). She was loath to let a man write me up in the magazine *Runners World*. She made him promise that he would glorify the Canyon, not me. She now seems to be reconciled to an occasional feature article in a newspaper, although she used to think that being a canyon freak was a disgrace.

Even though Harvey had long realized the toll his obsession took on Roma, and the damage he was causing their marriage, it did not stop him from returning to Grand Canyon again and again. From the outside, it appeared that Harvey had it all—his health, a wife and family, a successful career, *and* a place in history as Grand Canyon's greatest hiker. But in reality, Harvey's addiction had eroded a gorge of its own in his personal life. Every time another canyoneer showed up, or he made Roma worry by not returning on time, that gorge widened another few inches.

Body language speaking volumes: Roma and Harvey at Hoover Dam, late 1960s. *Courtesy Anne Madariaga*

View from Cape Royal of Angel's Window, Vishnu Temple and San Francisco Peaks. *Elias Butler*

Chapter Twenty-Four

THE CANYON'S GRIP

I've cried in the canyon, it's so emotional. My relationship with the canyon comes first, and because of that, my personal life has not always been so good.

Hiker and photographer George Mancuso,
June 1997 *Backpacker Magazine*

"IF YOU'RE GONNA GET STUCK IN A RUT," goes the saying, "you might as well get stuck in the biggest rut in the world." Though one might be inclined to laugh at the thought, a few fervent individuals regard it not as a joke, but rather as a reasonable explanation. These people will take on an 80-day, several-hundred-mile walk in the heat of summer to go from one end of Grand Canyon to the other, or devote a week out of every month to systematically backpacking off-trail routes until conquering every side canyon, or scale temples during 20-plus-hour marathon treks so that camping equipment can be left behind and the necessary gear stripped to the barest essentials.

They've been bit—hard. They are the pilgrims and searchers, the obsessed Grand Canyon fanatics.

They're easily spotted. Look for the sunburned face, the ever-present hiking shoes and easy, purposeful shuffle. A certain build is common—imagine a jackrabbit—though by no means the rule. Conversation with them tends to go dead unless discussing their latest adventure, or the next. Independent, sometimes abrasive, often solitary, they simply cannot go long without immersing themselves within this labyrinth of stone.

Men succumb most often to this peculiar, overwhelming urge. "If I had a mistress, it would be Grand Canyon," said Barry Goldwater, a man generally recognized for his right-wing political career but who also photographed, hiked, and boated the Canyon. Everett Ruess, the young artist who for years explored the Colorado Plateau on foot, wrote to his brother in 1931 following a long trek, "Nothing anywhere can rival the Grand Canyon."

A habitual loner, Ruess was comparing landscapes, but he also included human relationships on his scale. Ruess preferred taking "the lone trail" in life, turning away from family, friends and romantic relationships alike in exchange for ever-longer periods of time alone in the canyons. Eventually it got so he never came back.

Harvey Butchart, who was seven years older than Ruess, bore a resemblance to him in one sense, as evidenced by the enormity of his devotion to canyon country and frequent domestic absences. Harvey too chose to feed his desires over those of the people that loved him, though for perhaps different reasons than Ruess. Of course, Harvey was not completely irresponsible. He provided for his family while nursing his fixations.

But calling Harvey a faithful husband in the classic sense would be a stretch. In *Grand Canyon Treks III*, Harvey echoes Ruess's statement by meekly referring to Grand Canyon as Roma's "only rival" for his attentions. This was a case of infidelity but with a unique variation. Some might wonder how a man could leave his wife and family for another woman, but nearly everyone scratches their head at the man who leaves his wife and family for a canyon.

To better understand how Harvey could make such a decision, it can be illuminating to examine a few others who have also fallen prey to the Canyon's grip. Either through *Grand Canyon Treks* or personal correspondence, Harvey helped spawn during his reign a small but fervent group of serious hikers and climbers, and while not all began their own canyoneering odysseys due to Harvey, each has relied on him for guidance and inspiration. Some have built their own legacies, even surpassing Harvey in pursuits such as butte climbing, long-distance hiking, and number of days spent between rim and river. Using his information as a starting point, they have distanced themselves from the master while never really escaping his influence. At the same time, each is an individual, fiercely devoted to his or her own goals. Harvey may have made obsessive Canyon hiking famous, but such a predilection could never be the province of one man. The Grand Canyon is simply too big, too compelling for that.

Like the mathematics professor, Robert Eschka first needed to leave the country of his birth before finding Arizona. In 1975, 19-year-old Eschka traveled from his hometown of Weidenburg, Germany to the United States, looking to make a break from a repressive past. Relations with his father had been strained in Germany, especially after he had dropped out of high school. Willful, determined to live by his own means, Eschka fixed his eyes on the mythic landscapes of the American West where he hoped to find both refuge and challenge.

His visa allowed him to stay in the
U.S. for six months. Eschka hitched his
way toward California, making stops at
Glacier and Yellowstone National
Parks to backpack into grizzly country
before reaching San Francisco by early
1976. But he quickly lost interest in
city life. Eschka was yearning for a
landscape that matched his itching
mind and compact, restless body. He
continued his meandering course by
thumbing a ride to Arizona, and then,
Grand Canyon.

Eschka was stunned. Here was a
landscape completely alien to his
European senses, a stark and surreal
vastness that suggested much within its
gaunt depths and sunburned plateaus.
He decided to cast his body into this
realm and overcome what obstacles he
might find. This, finally, was the challenge he had come looking for.

Yet before he could so much as hike
the four miles to Indian Garden, reality

Self-portrait: Robert Eschka in Grand
Canyon, 1983. *Courtesy Gary Ladd*

set in: Eschka's visa was expired, offi-
cially making him an outlaw. His passport had been stolen in San Francisco,
which complicated matters, and worse, he was broke. He needed to find work
but a regular job would require identification. Eschka drifted to Albuquerque,
New Mexico to weigh his future.

After seeing the Canyon, Eschka had no intention of ever leaving
America—he had only just found home as far as he was concerned. Nothing
could possibly persuade him to return to the stifling confines of Germany. The
problem was convincing the government to make him a U.S. citizen. Seeing no
legal route through that wilderness of red tape, he chose another, simpler solution: Eschka invented a new name for himself, Robert Benson, lifting the
moniker from a tombstone he had seen while squatting in a graveyard during
his travels.

From then on, Robert Benson the American-born son of German parents
became both his disguise and a symbolic split from his father. Eschka would
thenceforth keep his true identity a secret, masking himself behind the dark

prescription sunglasses that he carefully wore at all times.

He managed to obtain a social security card and settled into a surprisingly normal life. Eschka found work as a carpenter and rented an apartment in Albuquerque. He subsisted on part time work, earning his keep for six months and devoting the other half of the year to serious hiking. Over the next five years, he returned to the Canyon for weeks at a time during long, solitary treks into the backcountry. Eschka ignored trails, preferring to make his own way with topographic maps, Harvey's guidebooks, and his own growing skill.

On the rare occasions when he spent time with others, Eschka became fond of announcing that he would take his life before he turned 30. He suffered from a poorly diagnosed case of depression, the onset of which had coincided with puberty. Eschka also became dyslexic as a teenager, which transformed him from an excellent student into a confused young man barely able to pass the most basic classes. His father had thought it all a charade, and tensions between the two had eventually driven Eschka out of the house.

Despite the serious threat to his mental state, he refused to seek medical attention or even to acknowledge his depression. To do so would be an admission of imperfection, something that he avoided at all costs. According to the strict moral code espoused by Adolf Hitler, such a show of frailty would have been tantamount to an insult to the master race that Eschka believed he was a member of.

Eschka's Aryan values had been planted during his membership in a post-World War II Hitler Youth group, compelling him to embody a very strict set of physical requirements. He didn't use ropes on exposed routes, for example, because that would be cheating. Eschka viewed trails and other aids to hiking as paths for the weak. He would push his body to extraordinary levels to prove his worth and fell into periods of self-recrimination when he failed to achieve his goals.

His few acquaintances remember Eschka as a man obsessed with detail and totally lacking in a sense of humor. But if he expressed the more distasteful aspects of Nazi philosophy, no one seemed to notice. Hiker and guidebook author George Steck, who shared many miles in Grand Canyon with Eschka, explained, "Aryan principles. He subscribed to that. But it would never interfere with our interactions with him. He didn't go 'Hup, two, three, four!' as he was going down the trail, or anything like that. But he firmly believed he was a member of a master race. He never said anything for or against Jews, but he'd been brought up in such a way that his wearing glasses was a major imperfection."

Eschka's obsessive hiking no doubt came from a love for adventure and discovery, but it was also self-medicating. Backpacking produced endorphins that alleviated his depression. When he undertook a long, difficult trek, he worked himself to exhaustion on a daily basis, giving him a temporary reprieve from his inner demons. But the symptoms never disappeared. They may have even worsened over time. He began to find it nearly unbearable to *not* be hiking all the time. This, combined with a supreme confidence in his route finding and survival abilities, a desire to prevent any contact with his father, and an urge to make his mark, led him to envision a mammoth project that would keep him hiking for nearly 14 months straight.

It was ambitious in the extreme, betraying an immense drive: Eschka would start near Moab, Utah and hike downstream to Lake Mead, a distance of 560 river miles and perhaps 1,400 miles by foot. His route would follow the north side of the Green and Colorado Rivers through Labyrinth, Stillwater, Cataract, Narrow, Glen, and Grand Canyons. Once at Lake Mead, his journey would be only half done, for he then planned to cross the reservoir and return to Moab via the *south* side of the river. Eschka's *über*-hike would entail over 2,800 continuous miles through the very heart of the Colorado Plateau. It would make Colin Fletcher's journey look like a stroll by comparison. Even Harvey would have to acknowledge that Eschka, if he succeeded, would rank among the most accomplished hikers.

The mega-trek took years to plan and months for Eschka to methodically place caches of food along his route. He sought and interviewed those who could tell him what to expect and made meticulous annotations on his topographic maps. When his preparations were finally in place, he added a symbolic touch by departing on Independence Day, July 4, 1982.

Eschka picked his way down Horseshoe Canyon, just north of Canyonlands National Park. He turned downstream at the confluence with the Green River, crossing Utah's boiling canyons one after another in the high heat of summer. Though river runners threw cans of beer to him and gave him food, he lived in solitude. Once past the noisy rapids of Cataract Canyon, he continued through Narrow Canyon and then skirted the flooded tributaries of Lake Powell along deserted slickrock benches. While he set up camp on tumbleweed-infested shorelines, water skiers and houseboats buzzed past unaware of the solitary nomad in their midst.

Eschka was a capable photographer. He made scores of self-portraits to document his hike. His slides reveal a skilled eye for composition and a variety of imaginative poses: Eschka at ease in one of his well-ordered camps, drinking a beer; Eschka nude, bathing in a stream; Eschka pretending to be asleep in his bag; Eschka striding along the Colorado in a backpack; even, later, Eschka inside the sacred Hopi *Sipapuni* in the Little Colorado Gorge, measuring the temperature of the water.

Robert Eschka clings to a cliff above the Colorado, 1983. *Courtesy Gary Ladd*

When Eschka reached Lee's Ferry two months after beginning his journey, he found George Steck with a group of hikers waiting for him. Steck was beginning a downstream, 80-day, end-to-end, north-side trek through Grand Canyon, and invited the young man to join him. "Opportunities for solitude were important," Steck wrote, "and he didn't think he'd ever like to hike with a group."

Yet Eschka enjoyed Steck's company and ultimately agreed to join. As they headed downstream, Steck noticed that Eschka was often careless while hiking and showed little fear of exposure on dicey routes. "He could take chances like he was defying death to come get him," Steck said. "He could do things I couldn't do. Or, he would do things that I would not be willing to do. One place, down there near Toroweap [Point] would be a good example. Someplace in the Redwall where the Redwall [makes a whistling noise], it goes down. Well, he has a photograph of his feet standing on the edge of that cliff with just his heels on the solid rock, the toes and rest of his boots are out over space, hanging in the air. And he's taking a picture down thru those feet to the river below. It would seem to me that when you're looking that way, you'd get vertigo. Maybe he was hoping that would happen. But that's the kind of a scary thing that he would do."

Eschka detoured from Steck's course to make a side trip through the Shinumo Amphitheater, but here his daring nearly cost him his life. Eschka climbed Elaine Castle, a butte near Lancelot Point, and during his descent, he fell some 30 feet and cracked his pelvis. He crawled for two days to get past the very deep and rugged Merlin Abyss to the North Bass Trail, which led to a rustic cabin below Swamp Point, and here Eschka recuperated for eight days while Steck's party circumambulated Powell Plateau. Park rangers had been alerted to the stricken man's condition and arrived to evacuate him but Eschka refused to go. Instead, he limped down Saddle Canyon and rejoined Steck at Tapeats Creek.

By Thanksgiving, Steck and Eschka reached the Grand Wash Cliffs and the end of Grand Canyon. Eschka took the winter off to allow his pelvis to properly heal. By March, he and Steck reconvened at Lake Mead so that Steck could

see him off for his south-side return
trek. Eschka recorded the moment in
his journal:

George Steck and Robert Eschka make a
toast in Grand Canyon, 1982. *Courtesy*
family of George Steck

> Right at the mouth of the
> Colorado's spectacular gorge we
> anchored for my goodbye celebration.
> George popped the champagne bottle
> while [Steck's wife] Helen pulled out
> four expensive Styrofoam cups. A
> toast to a new adventure!

On his way upstream near river
mile 200, Eschka ran into a pair of fellow extremists in the midst of a mind-
boggling journey of their own. Verlen
Kruger and Steve Landick were pad-
dling their canoes *upstream* in a spring of higher than normal flows, which was
only a small step in a much longer trip. Eschka wrote:

> I took my first morning break, when suddenly I noticed 2 canoes coming
> up the river...I yelled until they noticed me and asked them to come on shore.
> Verlen Kruger and Steve Landick, two pioneers from Michigan, not just
> attempted to canoe up the Grand Canyon, but included this section as part of
> a 3 year-28,000 mile canoe challenge. And I thought *I* was nuts.

In *The Ultimate Canoe Challenge: 28,000 Miles Through North America* (co-
written with Brand Frentz), Kruger recalls Eschka:

> It was a long walk through tremendously difficult terrain, and we were
> impressed and delighted to hear his story. We talked about the kind of feelings
> that led people to take "impossible" trips, how you feel an urgency, that you
> have to do it, without really being able to give a sensible reason.

For the next five months, Eschka hiked steadily upstream, again enduring a
trial of intense heat and loneliness. By September, 14 months after beginning,
he was back at his starting point in Utah. But instead of enjoying the victory,
Eschka ended his journey on a disheartening note. That summer his father had
died, something Steck had known but had decided to withhold until Eschka
returned. Steck never did tell Eschka, who instead received the news from a

Robert Eschka in Grand Canyon, 1983. *Photo by John Shunny, courtesy Gary Ladd.*

family letter waiting for him in Albuquerque.

The death put the mega-hiker in a bind. He was tormented over his family's exhortations to return to Germany to help fill his father's absence. Eschka realized that if he left America, his false identity scheme meant he would likely never see Grand Canyon again. Despite the enormity of what Eschka had just accomplished, and the recognition that went with it, his personal troubles had never disappeared. He fell immediately into a debilitating depression.

Steck said that Eschka began to withdraw from his personal relationships. "He'd told me right at the beginning that he intended to kill himself before he was 30," Steck said. "I guess he didn't want to give me the option of not investing any time in him if he was not going to be around for very long. I don't know why he told me, or felt he had to tell me at the time, but it just must have been on his mind a lot."

"And one time in particular he took us out to dinner, it was around Christmas. After dinner he wanted to speak to Helen [Steck's wife] alone—he didn't want me there—and what he was telling Helen was, he wanted Helen to treat him the same way she would treat the bag boy at the supermarket. He didn't want to be incorporated into our family, the extended family anymore. He didn't want to be invited to the house for dinners and things. And she didn't pick up on that. Later she realized that was his way of saying goodbye to us."

In March 1984, Eschka was found dead from carbon monoxide poisoning in his car outside of Albuquerque, a rubber hose connected to the tailpipe and the windows rolled up. The 27-year-old left no suicide note. Steck and several friends eventually scattered half of Eschka's ashes in Grand Canyon at Cape Solitude. Eschka's family interred the rest in a Weidenberg cemetery.

"Among his effects after his death were shoe and boot boxes full of receipts," Steck said. "Why he kept them I can only guess. Perhaps even then he thought he might write up his experiences in America and all these purchases could be used as deductions against profits. In the pocket of his coat when he was found was the receipt for the hose and the duct tape that he used to kill himself. That was very single minded, obsessive."

NOT ALL WHO BECOME fixated with Grand Canyon exhibit Robert Eschka's extreme approach. Most manage to keep their passions at a simmer rather than a boil. Of all those who would follow Harvey, none has so closely resembled him—at least on paper—as George Steck. Author of the backcountry guidebooks *Grand Canyon Loop Hikes I & II* and a professional mathematician himself, Steck has perhaps lured as many people into Grand Canyon's outback as Harvey has. The reason is simple. Whereas Harvey's terse guides tend to offer little confidence to the novice, Steck wrote his books with the intent of demystifying the backcountry, and they are easier to follow.

Steck also differed from Harvey in that he was no solitaire when it came to enjoying the wilderness. He included his family whenever possible. He welcomed his wife Helen on many excursions and seemed to enjoy himself most when she was by his side. Steck remains one of the few die-hards who succeeded in finding a middle ground for both his family and his love for Grand Canyon.

Steck rambled some 6,000 miles below the rim, 700 of which came in 1983 during his 80-day, trans-Canyon hike with Robert Eschka. Weaving in and out of side canyons, sometimes forging exposed routes across brittle ledges no wider than the spine of a good-sized book, Steck and his band of family and friends accomplished a feat that rarely has been repeated.

By all accounts, Steck was brilliant. He earned two Ph.D.s, one in statistics from the University of California at Berkeley, and the other in physics from the California Institute of Technology. He worked his way into the Mathematical Research Department at Sandia National Laboratories in Albuquerque, where he spent his career studying probability theory.

Both he and his brother, Allen Steck, a well-known mountaineer, made adventure a priority in their lives. George first came to Grand Canyon in 1957 as a passenger of river runner Georgie White Clark. By the end of the trip Steck had fallen in love with the canyon country. Steck immediately bought a boat and began leading his own river trips each summer through Glen Canyon until 1963 when Glen Canyon Dam was completed. Following this disappointing turn of events, he turned his attention downstream.

His first real hike in Grand Canyon came later that year while Colin Fletcher was busy making history on the Esplanade. Steck and hiking buddy Don Mattox trekked to Thunder River below the North Rim. Steck was 38, the same age Harvey had been when he made his first Canyon hike. Steck and Mattox enjoyed the experience so much that they soon returned with their families for a two-week hike. The pair made it an annual event thereafter, making at least a pair of two-week treks into the Canyon, often along routes below the North Rim in the full summer heat.

Steck bought a copy of *Grand Canyon Treks* in 1970 and consequently sent Harvey a few letters. But a friendship never developed and their association was limited to several conversations. "One meeting we talked about our childhood," Steck said. "We were both kind of wimpish kids, picked on, and that may have influenced the degree of satisfaction we took in physical activity in later life."

Ultimately, despite their shared passions for Grand Canyon and the fact that both had written guidebooks, they were more different than alike. Steck never let the Canyon come between him and his loved ones, and he was far less inter-ested in setting records. Steck also enjoyed having a margarita after a day of route finding. His social approach to trekking won him many fans. His guide-books contain such un-Harvey-like advice as how to encourage raft trips to donate cans of beer.

George Steck in the Canyon for the last time, 2003. *Elias Butler*

Steck, who died in 2004 at the age of 79, explained his differences with Harvey in terms of style. "I think of him as spe-cializing in up-and-down routes, rim-to-river kind of thing. And my style was side-to-side, lengthwise. So you need both, you need his accumulation of knowledge on where you get up and down through the layers, and I can help you get lengthwise along the river."

Despite the amount of time he devoted to Grand Canyon, Steck admitted that he was never in it to make a name for himself. "I think it's too big a place for one person to matter all that much," he said. "As far as the achievements, I'm not concerned about a spot in history. I'd rather be known as a good statis-tician than a good hiker."

For murky reasons, the Canyon has a tendency to attract mathematicians who also hike and climb. As he enters his eighth decade, retired mathematics professor Bob Packard bristles with energy, his shock of gray-white hair seeming to stand up straight from some inner electrical charge. Packard's words are pointed and emphatic, especially when he is talking about high-pointing, that off-shoot of climbing that puts emphasis not on the most difficult peaks but rather on amassing the highest points in a variety of categories: The 100 high-est summits in Arizona, the 10 highest peaks in each western state, the high points in each county within the United States, and so on.

Packard, who earned a Ph.D. in mathematics from Dartmouth College, claims he currently holds first place, at 1,276 high points, among county high pointers. This is something he is glad to talk about at length. It takes some effort to steer the conversation toward Grand Canyon, another small project of his for a spell: Packard hiked 5,500 miles, climbed 138 summits (and 31 unofficial summits) and spent 542 days within the Canyon, the results of a zealous pursuit first lit ablaze by his association with Harvey. Packard explained, "I came to NAU in 1968. And got a job in the math department. And it turns out that the house I bought was only two houses away from Butchart's house. So I could run down to Butchart's office, or over to his house with Robbie [Packard's wife at the time] and talk about the next trip we might be doing."

"I've become familiar, you might say, with the Grand Canyon," Packard continued. "But my first trip into the Grand Canyon was with Butchart. It was in October 1968, and we went down Salt Water Wash, and then went south along the river and came out Tanner Wash. And that was the first loop in my eventual quest to finish the Grand Canyon. I can remember telling Butchart at the time, you know, 'I'm not going to do up the Grand Canyon as you have. I'd like to sample a little thing here, a little thing there maybe.' But the trouble with that, over the years, is—you know, you sample this and you sample this and you sample this and you want more. More! More!"

Packard, an avid runner who still enters competitions, began spending weekends going down one side canyon and out another. The systematic

Summit of Pollux Temple, 1970. From left, Jim Sears, Ellen Tibbetts, Al Doty, Harvey Butchart, and Bob Packard. *Courtesy Al Doty*

Ken Walters in 1974. *Courtesy Ken Walters*

approach fit his desire for continuity. Packard's quest soon became a driving passion. He eventually completed a string of routes on both sides of the river through the entire Canyon, though Packard does not like to discuss the effect this time-consuming obsession may have had on his marriage. "I was compelled," Packard said. "I was addicted or something, you know, I was not particularly relaxed. But, now I get that intimate feeling about the place. I still kind of well up going up to the South Rim sometimes. I can look over and say, 'I've been there and there and there.'"

One of Packard's close friends is Ken Walters, who has hiked more than 11,000 miles below the rim and climbed 140 of the named buttes. In the fall of 1973, Walters moved to Flagstaff from Pennsylvania as a graduate student in geology. Packard soon introduced Walters to Harvey. Walters first hiked the Canyon that year, decided it was a "giant playground," and has ever since relentlessly covered his map with lines showing his routes.

He is now a full time backcountry educator for the Grand Canyon Field Institute, which places him in the Canyon for around 100 days each year. Despite his unusual devotion to the gorge, Walters insists that it is simply a love for hiking that draws him. "We [Walters and Packard] used to do two 10-day trips a year in the Canyon," Walters said. "I wouldn't say we were addicted to the Canyon, because we did other things too. We just liked hiking, and wherever there were blank spaces on the map in the western United States, we'd go hiking, and down in Mexico too. But the Grand Canyon was close, and it was a fixed beast. So you just keep, you know, 'Oh let's do this part, let's do that part.' And then gradually over the years you build up this network of routes and just keep expanding it. There's so much empty space so you don't want to keep repeating yourself. Blank spots on the map—that's all you need."

For some hardcore canyoneers, it is not simply about coverage but velocity. Harvey's pal Allyn Cureton carved a name for himself in Grand Canyon by moving through the gorge with the speed and endurance of a roadrunner. When he made his first Canyon hike with Harvey in 1956 Cureton was surprised by his math professor's abilities. "Goll dang! He set a helluva pace," Cureton said. "It was hard to keep up."

But Cureton did more than keep up. He soon surpassed Harvey—and everyone else—when it came to running the Canyon.

The day after climbing Wotan's Throne with Harvey in June 1962, Cureton made the first in a series of runs that would eventually cause jaws to drop. Cureton ran the 21-mile rim-to-rim, down the North Kaibab then up the South Kaibab Trail, while Harvey drove the 215 miles by car. Cureton made it in 4:14:00, only minutes after Harvey arrived. In 1981, Cureton smashed this impressive feat by running the rim-to-rim in 3:06:47, which is the record as of this writing. Cureton also holds the record for the

Allyn Cureton in the mis-1960s.
Courtesy Allyn Cureton

42-mile rim-to-rim-to-rim with the astounding time of 7:51:23.

Still fit at 70, Cureton acknowledges his records with self-deprecation rather than boasting. "Life starts at 40," he said. "It truly did for me. Trouble is, it ended at 45."

A FIXATION WITH GRAND CANYON occasionally funnels down to a penchant for a specific side canyon. When George Lamont Mancuso hiked for the 50th time into the 2,500-foot-deep gorge of the Little Colorado River in 2001 with his companion Linda Brehmer, he had not yet suffered from contempt bred by familiarity. On the contrary, Mancuso had long regarded the "Little C," and more specifically, its confluence with the Colorado River, as the one place where he felt happiest, most at home, most himself. The 46-year-old photographer and expert route finder spent so much time at the confluence that some boatmen thought he might have lived there.

Few Canyon aficionados would argue with Mancuso's tastes. A startlingly deep and narrow defile, the gorge of the Little Colorado features the beguiling

George Mancuso in 1987. *Courtesy Anne Madariaga*

turquoise river produced by Blue Springs and scores of travertine pools set beneath skyscraper walls. Yet for all its beauty, this stretch of the Little Colorado has not seen much visitation over the years. No maintained trails penetrate its wild inner sanctum. Roads leading to access routes are among the very worst of their kind. Punctured tires are so common that it is often preferable to walk miles to the rim. If one does manage to descend to the canyon floor, further travel is frequently impossible due to the unpredictable runoff from the White Mountains of eastern Arizona, or from local thunderstorms that boil up without warning in late summer. The 315-mile-long Little Colorado drains an impressive chunk of northern Arizona, some 27,000 square miles in all. It's not unheard of to see ephemeral floods roaring through the gorge that far exceed the volume of the Colorado River.

None of these factors prevented Mancuso from falling in love with the Little Colorado. He reveled in its solitude and rugged confines. That it was difficult to reach pleased him. It kept out the casual hikers. Time and again the hiker-photographer descended the Tanner Trail to the Colorado River, then walked the long route upstream to the confluence. There he would bask in the quiet splendor of his Shangri-La, swimming in the light blue waters he had all to himself.

He dreamed of bringing beautiful women there. Mancuso placed an ad on his photography website that read, "Basically I am looking for outdoor, athletic women and models to assist me in backpacking and photography trips inside Grand Canyon. The theme and purpose is to capture on film a unique portfolio of prints displaying the sensual, artistic, natural and spiritual expressions of the female form within a beautiful outdoor setting." Mancuso called his project *La Femme de Grand Canyon.*

When Mancuso began a close relationship with Linda Brehmer, a former science teacher, he wasted little time taking her to the Little Colorado. They had been together for six months on August 1, 2001, the day the two left the stark north rim of the Little Colorado Gorge at a remote point on the Navajo

Reservation. Mancuso had chosen the old Hopi route in Salt Trail Canyon, a rarely used but quicker access route than the Tanner Trail. As Mancuso and Brehmer descended, they passed between two large piles of rock—the shrine of one of the Hopi Twin War Gods. The hikers may have been unaware that a cave believed to be the home of the powerful Hopi deity Masau'u—god of fire and death—also exists in Salt Trail Canyon.

Masau'u, according to the Hopi belief, was the first being to meet the tribe's ancestors when they emerged into this world from the nearby *Sipapuni*. For a Hopi man on the salt journey, Masau'u could either grant passage or imprison one within these walls. Don Talayesva, one of the last Hopis to make the salt pilgrimage in the early 1900s, described a dream he had prior to his journey that demonstrates why the Hopis harbor such fear and respect for the Little Colorado River gorge:

> Soon I came to a great canyon where my journey seemed to end...peering deep into the canyon, I saw something shiny winding its way like a silver thread on the bottom; and I thought it must be the Little Colorado River. On the walls across the canyon were the houses of our ancestors with smoke rising from the chimneys and people sitting out on the roofs...Now the canyon was full of smoke, and when I peered down I saw a gruesome creature in the shape of a man climbing the cliff. He was taking long strides with his shining black legs and big feet; an old tattered rag of a blanket was flying from his shoulder as he approached swiftly with a club in his hand. It was big, black bloody-head-ed Masau'u, the god of Death, coming to catch me. One of the Kwanitakas [a guardian spirit] pushed me and cried, "Flee for your life and don't look back, for if Masau'u catches you, he will make you a prisoner in the House of the Dead!"

Mancuso gallantly carried Brehmer's backpack over the roughest sections of the Salt Trail. He wore his pack on his back and hers on his chest while leading Brehmer over a tricky slide of unconsolidated, bowling ball-sized rocks. Though the two had hiked here once before, Brehmer was not nearly as experienced as Mancuso. Indeed, few people knew the backcountry better than Mancuso, a fact in which he took no small amount of pride. The tautly muscled canyoneer considered himself a professional Grand Canyon hiker. He was even featured on the cover of the June 1997 issue of *Backpacker Magazine* as a premier explorer of the national park.

Mike Frick, an artist and Canyon hiker who shared several treks with Mancuso, remembered Mancuso's grit. "He would carry immense packs," Frick said. "For no reason! I mean, there's so much lighter stuff now and he would go old school, and carry two therm-a-rests, and a zero-degree bag even in the summer because he could not stand to get cold. He wouldn't take much food. We went down for two weeks once on just angel hair pasta and oatmeal and that was it, because you can carry a lot of it and it'll keep you alive, but—ugh."

"He was a monster hiker. He'd find routes down stuff where you'd be like, 'There ain't no way you can get down there' and then he'd find this little scree path, goat path and get down. But you had to follow him [laughs]. He was pretty much like a bighorn."

Mancuso honed his skills for 22 years by spending, on average, a week out of every month below the rim. He made his living as a self-taught photographer by selling postcards of Canyon landscapes. It was his dream job, one that he'd created for himself over the course of his long, torrid relationship with the Canyon.

"I'm obsessed," he told writer Annette McGivney of *Backpacker Magazine*. "My relationship with the Canyon is the single most important love affair of my life."

Mancuso became riveted when he first saw the Canyon in 1972 as a teenager from Bloomfield, New Jersey. A natural history buff with a taste for exploration, Mancuso had been nurturing a hunch for years that his real path in life led west. After that first visit, he returned as often as he could, indulging in occasional backpack trips that left him deeply affected and hungry for more. By contrast, returning to New Jersey was depressing; he had become estranged from his father during his late teens, which further exacerbated his discontent with the claustrophobic East Coast.

Mancuso developed an unusually powerful sense of connection to Grand Canyon after only a few hikes. He soon typed a note to himself that cemented his spiritual pact:

> Never again will I allow myself to remain away from the Grand Canyon for extended periods of time. From here on end [sic] the canyon shall be visited at least once a year. The emphasis on trips out west hereafter will be just that. Hiking the canyon, learning from it, enjoying it, but most of all being a part of it. In my opinion there is no doubt that this is my place, this is where I belong, this is where I shall remain one day. So be it.
>
> October 26th, 1977
> —George M.

By 1979, he could no longer tolerate separation and hauled stakes to Flagstaff. Unsure of what he would do for work, Mancuso was nevertheless tremendously excited to start his new life. The first thing he did was drop his last name to cleanse himself of his father's mark, instead introducing himself as George Lamont (Lamont was his mother's maiden name). He also started up a serious interest in photography.

Mancuso took a series of odd jobs in Flagstaff, becoming a janitor and water station technician for the city. Whatever paid his few bills was fine as long as he could explore and photograph the Canyon in earnest. "He was totally amazed by the Canyon, couldn't get enough of it," Frick said. Mancuso's preference for solitude eventually led him away from the main trails. In the course of his deepening fascination, he discovered Harvey Butchart.

No one who maintained a correspondence with Harvey ever expressed more awe and deference. Mancuso quickly came to regard Harvey as his spiritual mentor. Mancuso dubbed Harvey the "Obi-Wan Kenobi" of Grand Canyon, his wise and venerable teacher. Mancuso had a thing for *Star Wars*. He collected action figures and even paid for a personalized license plate for his truck that read "Kenobi." Mancuso began telling others he was more a knight in training, a Luke Skywalker.

In a 1985 letter to Harvey, Mancuso wrote:

> People all have securities, whether it be a car, job, relationship, house, etc. Well, mine's been the Grand Canyon all things considered. Funny, I never thought of it that way until now.
>
> I know my friend, I can tell you these things, because we both share a common love for this super gorge—perhaps in a way that most do not grasp.
>
> You have started something here at this wonderful canyon, and this young man intends to follow right behind.

"Harvey was his father-figure for sure," Frick said. "Because he didn't have a good father. He didn't get along with him." Mancuso quickly began to emulate Harvey's approach and developed a similar hard-core addiction to route finding. The more he learned of Harvey's accomplishments, the more he began to see himself as the heir apparent to Harvey's legacy. Mike Frick explained, "He knew all of Harvey's routes and what Harvey wanted to do, and the ways Harvey got down. But he was really intent on finishing Harvey's routes that he had planned and never did, and then writing Harvey and saying 'This is how that route went.' So I think Harvey was living vicariously through George's letters."

Harvey indeed enjoyed reading about younger canyoneers' accomplishments, especially when he became too old to hike himself. He encouraged Mancuso to keep up the correspondence. But Harvey was unsure how to react to Mancuso's unbridled veneration in person. "He almost embarrassed me by showing more appreciation than is fitting," Harvey wrote in a letter to a friend.

George Mancuso in Flagstaff, 1991. *Courtesy Anne Madariaga*

"He has given me a big framed photo and a copper plaque with a flattering inscription on it." Like Harvey, Mancuso became a fixture at Grand Canyon. He was often seen descending one of the South Rim trails wearing a backpack and heading for the inner gorge to try out new routes in the Vishnu Schist and Zoroaster Granite. In 1986, he started a fledgling business he dubbed Granite Visions Photography. Mancuso was strongly attracted to the First Granite Gorge, between river miles 77 and 117.[1] He began dividing most of his time between this area and the Little Colorado River.

These two locations, he decided, would be his domain, his areas of expertise. He told Harvey of his intentions to become the authority on the Granite Gorge.

> Dear Harvey,
>
> No doubt you, if anyone, can agree in the seemingly overburdening task of dedicating oneself to Colorado River access via drainages, canyons, chutes, etc., starting from the Tonto down. But I feel this is where I'm best and it is most rewarding. I have the experience, patience, tenacity and determination.

Many who met or hiked with Mancuso commented on his tendency for self-aggrandizement, his supreme confidence in his abilities. More than once he touted himself as a "Grand Canyon Knight," the name he created for those elite few who dedicated themselves to exploring the Grand Canyon. To the people who had predated Mancuso and had done much more hiking in the Canyon, Mancuso's claims could be irksome. "Enough about you, more about me," Frick said. "He was always bragging about how he's done more miles than anybody down there, and how everybody hated him and didn't think he was the big canyoneer that he really thought he was."

Mancuso's sometimes-brusque personality was not welcome among the NPS backcountry rangers whose job it was to see that hikers such as Mancuso obeyed

---

[1] The term "Granite Gorge" is a misnomer. The term refers to the three "granite gorges" along the Colorado in Grand Canyon where the oldest rocks appear. But the primary rock types (despite the name Zoroaster Granite) that make up the granite gorges are schist and gneiss.

the schedules on their back-country permits. He had developed a habit of illegally extending his stays in the backcountry. He even boasted to friends that he was beyond the reach of the law, that he played according to the code of the Canyon, not man's petty bureaucracies. When rangers caught wind of this they pointedly cited him at Cocopah Point on the South Rim for prolonging his stay by one day.

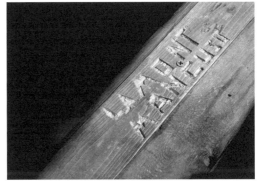

Graffito in the cabin where Robert Eschka once recuperated after breaking his pelvis. *Elias Butler*

On August 1, 2001, when Mancuso and Brehmer made camp on the banks of the Little Colorado about 6 miles upstream from the confluence, he felt no such worries. They were on Navajo land, beyond the reach of helicopters and indignant rangers. They had planned an extended visit—10 days—with plenty of time to make photographs, swim, and hike within the sweltering canyon.

About a week into their stay, the Little Colorado changed on the pair of backcountry revelers. The gentle, clear-blue stream became a heavily silted, trash-laden torrent fed by runoff from recent thunderstorms. August is the height of the monsoon season in the Southwest, when a stream of subtropical moisture from the Gulf of California flows over the superheated desert, creating the likeliest time of year for violent thunderstorms.

Brehmer had been keeping a journal and wrote of her eagerness to wash her hair after the Little Colorado turned too muddy for bathing. Mancuso told her they would find clear, clean pools of water in Big Canyon, a nearby tributary to the Little Colorado. On August 8, they made the short hike to Big Canyon to wash up.

Huge boxcar-sized boulders choke the mouth of this defile, which immediately halts upstream progress. But this was one of Mancuso's secret spots; he knew exactly how to get past the boulder field and into the cool, charmed sanctum he had named Emerald Pool. His appellation perfectly describes the tint of the lovely pool that lies just upstream from the canyon's mouth. With the sounds of the roaring Little Colorado echoing off the narrow walls, the pair delightedly jumped into the clear water, as anyone would when it is nearly 100 degrees in the shade.

Above the swimmers, the walls shot upward for nearly 2,500 feet, eclipsing all but a slice of bright blue sky. Further upstream travel here becomes dangerous, for a slick travertine slide spills over the edge of a 30-foot cliff at the head of the pool. If Brehmer and Mancuso tried to continue upstream, they would have needed to exercise considerable climbing skill to negotiate the small ledges beside the fall. Even so, it would have been an alluring option for a photographer and explorer such as Mancuso. Up above, Big Canyon makes a sharp curve to the east before narrowing into a genuine slot in the Redwall Limestone.

Regardless of where exactly they were, the constricted, winding nature of lower Big Canyon makes it impossible to see what is happening upstream. And that afternoon, the first cold, fat drops from an unusually intense thunderstorm began to spatter onto the sun-broiled rocks of the upper Big Canyon drainage. The ocher sky portending a cloudburst glowered far out of sight of the unsuspecting pair. When the clouds ripped open a few moments later, water crashed down in a blinding deluge that quickly filled Big Canyon's network of drainages, a system designed to efficiently and speedily transport large volumes of water. Rivulets appeared, then streams, and finally, a roaring mass of muddy water and debris. While Mancuso and Brehmer dallied in lower Big Canyon, the flood bore down upon them, gathering speed and depth as the canyon narrowed to almost nothing.

It is likely they heard the approaching bellow. Mancuso had been around flash floods before and would have recognized the impending catastrophe. Terror fueled their flight as they scrambled to extricate themselves from the defile. But there were no quick exits, especially if they happened to be in the Redwall slot above Emerald Pool. Even if he could climb to safety himself, Mancuso may not have been willing to leave the slower Brehmer behind.

Backed by an estimated 9,000 cubic feet of water and debris per second—a rate equal to the Colorado River in Grand Canyon on many days—the initial wave may have been as high as 50 feet, a genuine tsunami in the desert. Brehmer and Mancuso were crushed as if by a giant fist into the unforgiving bedrock of Big Canyon. Boulders gnashed about like grinding molars as the flood exploded over the Emerald Pool and into the Little Colorado River.

More than a week passed before anyone suspected something had gone wrong. Ten days later, on August 18, Brehmer's sons notified the Coconino County Sheriff's Office of the overdue pair. Mancuso had told Brehmer's sons that they would return on August 8, but knowing Mancuso's habit of returning late from his trips, they waited to report them missing. A search and rescue party comprised of NPS and sheriff's office personnel quickly located Mancuso's truck, then the missing hikers's campsite at the mouth of Salt Trail Canyon. Sleeping bags, camera gear, and other items still lay neatly about. Rangers surmised that the pair had not intended to be gone long.

George Mancuso at the confluence of the Little Colorado and Colorado Rivers, May 2000. *Courtesy Lea Parker*

Also at the campsite was Brehmer's journal, which revealed to investigators the couple's plans to visit Emerald Pool on August 8. The trouble was, no one had ever heard of Emerald Pool. When the news broke about the missing couple, Mancuso's friend Scott Thybony teamed with hiker Tony Williams to see if they could offer help. Though neither could provide the location of Emerald Pool, they both knew Mancuso and were familiar with the country.

Before leaving, Thybony enlisted the help of a Hopi seer, a woman with a proven ability to find missing people. She asked Thybony for details about the couple. After a difficult, physically demanding ordeal, the exhausted woman was able to place an "X" on a topographic map Thybony had given her. Thybony saw that the mark was in lower Big Canyon, and this, the Hopi woman told Thybony, was where the two hikers had been.

Thybony and Williams joined NPS rangers to search lower Big Canyon. Thybony soon smelled a faint odor of decomposition near Emerald Pool, but he found nothing. Finally he noticed Brehmer's body, wrapped tightly around a tamarisk trunk.

A shirt identified as Mancuso's—a photo developed from rolls of film left at the campsite showed him wearing it—was also found nearby. But Mancuso himself had vanished.

The Hopi woman who helped Thybony had mentioned that Mancuso and Brehmer had not been getting along. "They were having some kind of trouble," the woman told him. "She wanted to stay in camp but he wanted to go. He got angry and walked off, and she followed him." Startlingly, Brehmer's journal backed up this statement, revealing the details of their argument.

Thybony later learned from the Hopi seer that she had discussed Mancuso and Brehmer with a Hopi priest. When the priest heard that Brehmer had washed her hair in the Emerald Pool, he said that she was preparing herself for the resident deity Masau'u. It is a Hopi tradition to wash the hair of the dead so that Masau'u will accept them in the afterlife.

Three days later, on August 26, at the confluence of the Little Colorado and Colorado Rivers, a flock of ravens drew NPS boatman Greg Woodall to Mancuso's body. The photographer had come to rest in a stack of flood debris. Mancuso still wore his running shorts and boots. His arms were fixed forward as if pushing off a large object. All told, his body had traveled some six miles from Big Canyon before lodging here.

Mike Frick remembered the day he heard the news. "I thought they weren't going to find him. I thought that would be a perfect ending. But it's almost just as perfect that they found him at his favorite spot, and his body somehow went, what, several miles down from Emerald Pool to the confluence. And to be eaten by the ravens, and buzzards, and God-knows-what, humpback chub nibblin' at ya—that seems like a good way to go out."

One of Mancuso's postcards shows the meeting place of these two rivers. It was his best known, best selling image and a rare one at that. Photographers know it is difficult to sell photos made below the rim, as tourists buy the familiar rim views in far greater quantities. But *The Confluence* was different, an excellent expression of Mancuso's love for what became his resting place.

Mancuso never believed his obsession was without risk. He admitted as much in a July 7, 1984 letter to his mentor:

> Harvey ~ even as a young hiker/scrambler I share your thought about the possibility of ending our lives in similar fashion yet ~ if I realized I died attempting or doing something from within my inner self, I'd accept that. It's not a wish, but just a natural accepted thought.

Inevitably, Mancuso's death raised questions. Why did someone with years of experience in Grand Canyon stray into a narrow canyon during an active monsoon? Was it overconfidence? In his *Backpacker* article, Mancuso stressed that he was never out to conquer the Canyon. "Anyone who tries to do that," he said, "will definitely get swallowed."

George Mancuso's tripod beside the Emerald Pool, January 2002 (tripod found underneath a nearby rock and repositioned by photographer). *Elias Butler*

Harvey climbs the Redwall in Spencer Canyon, western Grand
Canyon, 1977. *Courtesy Jorgen Visbak*

Chapter Twenty-Five
UNFINISHED BUSINESS
1976–1988

I'm an old man
I can't do the things I used to do

Lyrics to the blues standard "Done Got Old"

IN SUN CITY, HARVEY QUICKLY became known as the man who took the phrase "active adult" seriously. He cleaned up in tennis, scalping all comers in five tournaments that featured a surprisingly strong field of competition. He was spotted practicing his old air mattress technique in an artificial lake. Harvey's reputation really took off when local publications heralded his feats in Grand Canyon. It made him all the more unusual because he was still at it, while most of his colleagues spent their days piloting golf carts and attending to their TVs.

The problem was that Harvey had officially become an old man. Reminders of his advanced age lay everywhere in Sun City. He realized that time would soon call to a halt what Roma's displeasure could not. This led to an even more sobering perception—his Grand Canyon list contained more unknowns, more projects, side canyons, routes, and summits than he would ever be able to tackle.

Harvey's first reaction was to go on a tear. In October 1976, he hightailed it out of the retirement community for the Canyon where he spent the next eight days rappelling, backpacking, and butte climbing. He knocked off a few projects below the South Rim, then made the long drive past Lee's Ferry and the Vermilion Cliffs toward the North Rim.

Autumn had come to the Kaibab Plateau. Yellow-brown leaves carpeted the dirt roads, a chill spanned the shadows, each breeze wrested fine showers of gold from the trembling aspens that grew in thick stands. Here and there, sunlight broke through the canopy and fell like spotlights upon the Douglas firs and ponderosa pines. The air smelled sugary and sweet. Harvey parked his

Looking north from the summit of Evans Butte, 1976. *J. Harvey Butchart, courtesy NAU Special Collections*

rig at a nondescript spot in a shallow valley near Point Sublime and entered the forest on a compass bearing.

Back in 1964, when he'd first been this way, he was chasing a new route to the river. Today's goal was less ambitious. Climbing a nearby crown of sandstone called Evans Butte (named for topographer Richard T. Evans) promised perhaps less satisfaction than a rim-to-river route, yet the old itch had not left him. It had simply changed direction. Evans would be one for the record, instead of being born from the raw desire to penetrate the unknown.

He headed for a break in the cliffs he remembered, his boots on the pine needles with a soft, thick sound. As he ducked low hanging branches and dodged fallen trees, Harvey may have been thinking of the 75 summits he had already accumulated, just over 50 per cent of Grand Canyon's named buttes. Perhaps his mind fretted over those he had not yet climbed. There was good reason to keep at it. In the past decade, others had already far surpassed Harvey in this aspect of canyoneering.

Gray-white limestone crags appeared where the land tilted toward the void. He paused at the rim to eye his route, then picked up a deer trail leading into the gorge. Stones clattered as he made his way down. It was a precarious place, cleaves of rock and fractured cliffs all leaning inward, but threading such dangers had become second nature.

His feet led him across the steep slopes and down to a saddle between Flint and Tuna Canyons, then up without difficulty to the modest summit of Evans. On top, he took a few snapshots of the deserted Shinumo Amphitheater and its striking array of Arthurian buttes. To the southwest, the Colorado River ran in plain view. But something about climbing his 76th Grand Canyon pinnacle reminded him of his own frailty. In his log he admitted to a sense of foreboding:

I had no problems with my feet or physical condition, but on the way back I began to think that I should try harder to get a companion or two. The story of Pederson's [NAU coach and professor John Pederson] sudden death of a heart attack was on my mind. A companion can't do you any good, but getting the body out is far simpler if there is a witness. Anyway, I seem to be getting less independent.

Harvey, for all his youthful stamina and remarkable health, was feeling his years. During the remainder of his canyoneering career he would often envision himself falling prey to a heart attack or a similar catastrophe. He began to slow down and take fewer risks. His decisions became more cautious. A decade of hiking remained in his future, but Harvey's days of rugged route finding were coming to a gradual close.

Yet during that same eight-day stretch at the Canyon, he also met with reporter Wanda Seglund from the *Arizona Republic* to take her into Mineral Canyon. "At 69, Butchart claims to be walking at a new and slower pace," wrote Seglund, "but he can still maintain a steady speed that left me gasping and grabbing for trees, brush and any rock outcropping to pull myself up to the next level of the trail."

Yet Harvey would never be able to move fast enough. "I have lists of routes and trails that would take at least 70 more years of hiking to accomplish them all," he told Seglund, "more years than I have left."

FOURTEEN MONTHS LATER, after turning back from a challenging stretch of talus above the Redwall in Travertine Canyon, the 70 year-old finally admitted to himself that he had put his best years of physical performance behind:

> I was feeling low because I had had to give up the purpose of the trip, and besides my feet hurt and one knee was feeling bad from breaking the shock of coming downhill. I had fallen in the trail when a rock rolled underfoot and I had put my hand on a cactus. I lay around on my mattress reading *Time* until supper and thought that I would let the younger men have the big time exploring to themselves. It was an unpleasant decision.

Still, it took more than youth to keep up with him. Engineer and hiker Bob Marley was over 30 years younger than Harvey when the pair began a five-day, off-trail backpack in January 1978. Marley believes he hit his physical prime that year and says he fully expected to hang tough with the master Grand Canyon hiker.

Harvey had suggested they take his boat to Lake Mead and motor upstream into lower Grand Canyon. During the drive to the boat launch ramp from Phoenix, Harvey stopped at a gas station to purchase a copy of *Time*, which he had a penchant for schlepping in his backpack to pass the non-hiking hours. Only later, after opening the magazine in the Canyon, did Harvey realize that he should have bought a *Reader's Digest* instead.

"The *Time Magazine* for that week had a big article on heart attacks," Marley said, "and he got really tripped out on this article. And for the whole five days we were hiking he kept thinking he was going to have a heart attack. And I thought he was going to give *me* one [laughs]."

Taking a break, late 1970s. *Courtesy Scott Baxter*

To reduce the strain on his heart, Harvey set a hiking schedule that featured a slower pace but longer days to cover his usual 10 miles. He allowed for a five-minute break every hour. "At that stage of his life he was not a particularly fast hiker but his endurance level was amazing," Marley said. "He would get up at first light and he wouldn't stop until it got dark. He wouldn't move fast but he'd move long. I could see how when he was a stronger man he could rack up some prodigious miles."

The endless toil eventually prompted Marley to invent a handicap for himself so he could rest. "He looked kind of like a walking pack," Marley said. "I just remember walking behind him the whole time trying to keep up and seeing these legs stick out below his pack. After about five days of that, I said 'Harvey I just don't feel good.' I told him that my stomach was bothering me a little bit. He wanted to get another Redwall route up in Spencer [Canyon] and I just wanted to hang out for a while."

"I was 38 or 39, full of piss and vinegar," Marley continued. "And I thought I could do just about anything. If I'd done that for a week following him I guess I would have eventually hardened up. But it would have been like being in the Marines, okay? I thought I was pretty hardened up when we started, but I wasn't so sure after hiking with Harvey." Perhaps this experience inspired Marley to prove himself. Two years later, he would undertake a 55-day, upstream mega-hike (with pal Bob Cree) from Diamond Creek to Lee's Ferry.

Harvey's slender physique allowed him to ramble for hours without working nearly as hard as the stockier Marley. This was nothing new. Harvey had been bestowed with natural gifts for canyoneering and was accustomed to wearing his companions down. But when Harvey hiked with younger men who were similarly gifted, he now found to his dismay that *he* was the one left in the dust.

Twenty-somethings Jim Kirschvink and Jim Ohlman were accomplished climbers and off-trail experts in their own right. They were fit, energetic, and driven. A month after hiking with Marley, Harvey invited the pair to join

The "walking pack," late 1970s. Courtesy *Scott Baxter*

him on a climb of Manu Temple, a butte near Widforss Point. They also intended to investigate a possible route into nearby Haunted Canyon.

Ohlman sweetened the pot further by suggesting they climb Shellbach Butte, a newly named, unclimbed summit. First ascents in 1978 were difficult to come by. All three jumped at the opportunity.

Yet this time, Harvey's zeal would not be enough to overcome his slackening abilities. "I consider that trip to be the turning point of my hiking career with Harvey," Ohlman said. "Because that's when I saw visible signs that Harvey was heading downhill in a real fast way."

Harvey hiked alone down the Kaibab Trail, then his younger companions caught up and passed him. Once in the backcountry, Harvey fell far behind. By the time the two Jims clambered up the Supai Formation in Sturdevant Canyon, Harvey was nowhere to be seen. Ohlman backtracked through the Supai until he spotted him far below, walking away from the route.

"Harvey, where you going?" Ohlman yelled down the Redwall cliff.

"Oh, I'm going to do something else," Harvey yelled back. "I'm going to go over and look at Haunted Canyon."

"Oh, it's easy! We found the way up here," Ohlman said.

"He turned a little bit," Ohlman said, "and started to come back up, and came to a point of indecision. So I hiked all the way back down to where Harvey was—I think I did the Redwall route three times that day. I got down there and it's like, there was no drive—it was gone. He had resigned himself to failure on this one point…and I couldn't understand it. My mindset was, 'We've got a butte. We can do it. It's there. It's a first ascent, Harvey!' I couldn't entice him."

"I think at that point he was starting to resign himself to a lesser physical ability. And physically I don't think that happened right there, but mentally it did. I would say that was a watershed. Prior to that time, I never picked up on his unwillingness to carry through on a project, or having any mental anguish over any aspect of what we'd set out to do. But that trip, it came across loud and clear. And we went on to do several really good trips after that, but they were—different. The trips were different. Slower paced for sure. Everything slowed down."

Harvey wasn't suffering any major physical ailments; it simply may have been too much for his ego to feel that he was now the weak link in the group. He thus returned to the South Rim without accomplishing any of his goals, without covering any new ground. At 70, he had perhaps expected too much of himself. But turning his back on a new Redwall route *and* a first ascent? It was unheard of. His extra slow pace up the Kaibab Trail only deepened his disappointment. "I needed five and a half hours to go from the river to the rim, and I ended feeling pretty discouraged," Harvey wrote. "I will have to plan less ambitious trips with people that are my speed."

A look at the index of Harvey's logbooks following this trek confirms Ohlman's assessment. Harvey made fewer and fewer difficult hikes in the years to come, and although he still enjoyed route finding, nothing would match his efforts from only a few years earlier.

Another pattern emerges from the logbooks. Harvey began spending much of his time in the remote western Grand Canyon. There were several reasons he gravitated to this overlooked area of the national park. It was quieter than the popular central and eastern sections, and Harvey decided he could hike there without hassling with backcountry permits. He also had less experience in the vast wilderness downstream from Lava Falls, and there was plenty new to see in those 100 river miles. And, he'd be giving up nothing in aesthetics, for this lower end of the Canyon equaled the beauty and scale of the more famous upstream stretches.

Perhaps most importantly, Harvey could access western Grand Canyon's many tributaries from below by boating upstream from Lake Mead. Without having to descend first on foot, or make a taxing return hike to the rim, he could save his limited energy for route finding from the side canyons's lower ends.

Harvey steers his boat toward Surprise Canyon, 1980. *Courtesy Jorgen Visbak*

Ohlman explained, "He began taking his putt-putt boat and going up the lower end of the Canyon off Lake Mead, getting into Separation and Surprise, Burnt [Canyons]—he became enamored with Surprise Canyon to a point of obsession, I don't know why. If you want to see anything you better figure on three or four days because it's a huge canyon."

In addition to a number of springs that feed the lush canyon bottom, several arches, a limestone narrows, and assured solitude all made Surprise Canyon an appealing defile. Ohlman believes there was another reason Harvey became fixated with this vast rip in the North Rim. "I think he kept wanting to go back there because he kept failing," Ohlman said. "He'd go up there and *not quite* make it through the Redwall, or he'd *not quite* make it up to a particular point in the Supai. And so it was maybe even a subconscious, maybe self-imposed lessening of one's goals to leave something for the next trip."

River runners who float the length of Grand Canyon encounter excitement and danger in the upper two-thirds of their journey, where rapids frequently tear the river into white foam. At Bridge Canyon, about 236 river miles below Lee's Ferry, a different experience takes over as the Colorado River meets the backed-up water behind Hoover Dam and the upper reaches of Lake Mead. Rapids disappear. In high water years, a motor becomes necessary to whisk over the flat water that marks the remaining one-fifth of Grand Canyon. Excitement gives way to a quieter mood and passengers suddenly realize the journey is coming to an end.

Twin Springs Canyon, a tributary of Surprise Canyon. *Elias Butler*

As Harvey began to spend his waning years in western Grand Canyon, he too encountered a landscape where the ground passed with less recklessness. He returned again and again by boat, sometimes by foot from the rim, always seeking something new and never quite satisfying his urge for discovery. But the scale of his findings shrank and the successes became minor victories.

There were other signs of a passing era. In August 1979, Harvey's old Canyon pen pal Otis "Dock" Marston met his end. While visiting a friend, he fell down a flight of stairs and died several days later from internal cranial bleeding. This came as a shock to Harvey, who had been faithfully keeping up his correspondence with Martson ever since 1954.

IT WAS INEVITABLE THAT Harvey would reach a point where he simply couldn't hack the route finding, where his drive would meet cold reality. In the western Canyon in July 1981, he barely survived his last truly difficult trek, a three-day, 20-mile, off-trail backpack down 209-Mile Canyon and out 214-Mile Canyon. By this point, Harvey preferred having someone along just in case anything went wrong. He did not mind a younger hiker, as long as he would not feel pressured to set a fast tempo befitting the famous author of *Grand Canyon Treks.* Climber and gear shop owner Scott Baxter was eager to hike with Harvey and hear his stories. He accepted Harvey's invitation to tackle the challenging loop.

As the 35-year-old and the 74-year-old set out on July 15th across the deserted pinyon-juniper forest of the Shivwits Plateau, one of the more remote regions in the lower 48 states, they encountered mud from recent thunderstorms. Although it was monsoon season, they were setting foot into a notoriously dry set of canyons during the hottest time of year.

"Well, it was in July," Baxter said, "and we were on the north side of the Canyon, which means you're on south-facing slopes. The sun's beating right down on you, just what you want in July in the west end of the Canyon." Temperatures soared well above the 100-degree mark as the two scrambled into the broiling inner sanctum of 209-Mile Canyon.

Harvey had recently begun to experience trouble with his right hip, which was becoming arthritic. But a more serious problem on this trek would be his choice of footwear.

> I was experimenting with a kind of loafer instead of regular hiking boots. They were fine in that I got no blisters, but the soles of my feet got somewhat sore and by the third day, the shoes were beginning to break up. I tried tape to keep the insoles from coming out, but on the fourth day I gave up and just walked any way that I could in shoes that were coming apart.

Rains had left many potholes full in lower 209-Mile Canyon where they camped the first night. They arose early to avoid the heat and made it to the river around noon the next day. Both men eagerly jumped into the 60-degree water. After cooling off, they started along the riverbank toward the mouth of 214-Mile Canyon, six or seven foot-miles downstream. It was a bleak stretch, rough and exposed to the sun. When some passing river runners offered to give the men a lift, Harvey had no qualms about climbing onboard.

Once the crew and passengers realized who had just joined them (Harvey's photo appeared prominently in the popular Belknap river guidebook), Harvey found himself surrounded by fans. "We ended up spending the night with these people on this river trip," Baxter said, "and they cooked us steaks. We got treated like royalty, and of course Harvey was the center of attention that night around the campfire. Because you know, all the boatmen were all 'Ahhh...'"

Harvey backpacks into 209-Mile Canyon in his penny loafers, July 1981. Courtesy *Scott Baxter*

The last night of a river trip is traditionally the time for a blowout party. The two trekkers happily participated in the evening's camaraderie. Harvey signed at least a dozen copies of the guidebook where his mug shot appeared.

After digesting pineapple upside down cake and corn on the cob, the hikers awoke at first light and hoofed it up 214-Mile Canyon. Harvey had it in mind to camp at the abandoned Snyder Mine, several miles upstream in the side canyon near a reliable spring. The two made good progress until the sun rose, which quickly transformed the canyon into a depressing inferno. Harvey's pace slowed. Several barrier falls necessitated discouraging bypasses among thorny bushes and dreary cliff sides. Following a laborious ascent through the baking Redwall, Harvey's body began to sputter.

They continued a bit farther toward Shanley Springs, which Harvey had visited on a previous trek. A genuine oasis, Shanley Springs is the only reliable source of water in 214-Mile Canyon. Although Harvey had drunk from the spring 11 years earlier, he was now exhausted and dehydrated. He could not remember how to find it.

"He was sure it was there!" Baxter said. "But boy, we couldn't find it and we were out of water. And we still had to get out—a long day out the next day with no water, that's what we were facing. And so we did find this place called Snyder Mine, an old copper mine, just a little shaft, dug back in the bank there, it's about—oh, maybe 30 or 40 feet deep. We crawled back in that shaft where the temperature was a good 30 degrees cooler, so it was just like crawling back into this dark air conditioned room. It was a godsend."

Harvey wrote in his logbook, "Up the last of the Redwall…to the mine, I was feeling the heat. If we had had to go another half hour to get into the cool mine shaft, I might have really been in trouble."

"Harvey got kind of panicky," Baxter said. "And he started coming up with these different schemes how we were going to get water and survive, and one of those included me going back to the river with all our water bottles and hike 5 miles back to the river—a long, long ways back. And I didn't want to do that, that wasn't realistic. So finally what happened was, I told Harvey just to hang out at the mine, chill out, and at the end of the day there, late in the day, I let the temperature cool down a little bit, right before dark, and I went out and just started looking for water. And I found some!"

Harvey takes refuge in the cool air of the Snyder Mine, 1981. *Courtesy Scott Baxter*

"Just the classic, lime-green, skanky, you know, mosquito larvae-filled, wasps-buzzing-around pothole that had been there for months and months probably. But it was water. And I knew that it would get us out of the Canyon. So I went back to the mine, and I played it up. I said 'Oh, don't worry! I've found plenty of water. No problem [laughs].' And I said 'We'll just spend a comfortable night here, I'll get up first thing in the morning and take all our water bottles down there.' I didn't tell him that it was three gallons of this pond scum."

Harvey regained his poise once he learned that his companion had found water. "So I got up early in the morning," Baxter said, "and took our water bottles, strained the water through a t-shirt, and it was just...all that algae, and it's just green, a bright green like Limeade, and stinks really bad, you know, like hundreds of wasps buzzing around and I remember just kind of having to relax and just walk right into this swarm of wasps and sit there when they were landing on me, crawling all over my body while I was filling up these water bottles."

"So when I came back with the water, he took a look at it and he said, 'Oh, pollywog soup. I drank a lot of this before.' You know, it didn't bother him."

The pair then began an agonizingly slow ascent toward the rim, which still lay 2,000 feet above. Harvey could only walk a short distance uphill before tiring, and they straggled from one juniper tree to the next. At each rest, Harvey took 10 minutes to collect his wind. They sipped their putrid water in the hot shade.

As the day wore on, Harvey weakened. His penny loafers barely held together, and the heat intensified. Both men slowly realized the precariousness of Harvey's condition. He had become a liability.

Self-reliance is an unwritten rule in outdoor endeavors such as canyoneering, and Harvey had always taken pride in his ability to fend for himself. Injuries aside, not since making his first hike as a small child to the Three Ancient Trees in China had he relied on another for help. He had in fact complained on numerous occasions about companions who faltered on their way out of the Canyon and slowed *him* down. Yet on this day, he was forced to admit that he was the one who needed help.

"It turned out to be the only time in his entire career where he allowed somebody to carry some of his pack," Baxter said. "I kept saying 'Harvey, let me help you out here.'"

"Okay! Well, I guess I'll do it," Harvey said.

"It was a real point of pride you know?" Baxter continued. "He'd never done that. But then again, he was an old man."

Harvey handed over a few items from his backpack. It was a humbling act that convinced him he had no business taking on such a difficult physical challenge ever again.

Yet even relieved of his gear, Harvey could only manage small bits of progress at a time. "We would look up and say 'Ok, we're going to go up to this tree up here' and walk a couple minutes, get in a little patch of shade, hang out, drink some more water," Baxter said. "I got to where the only way I could keep the water down was to inhale, hold my nose and then take a drink, then exhale through my nose and then swallow. Because of the smell. By shutting off the smell, the taste wasn't so strong. If I was smelling it and tasting it, then I was getting a severe gag reflex."

Harvey admitted in his log that their escape from the clutches of 214-Mile Canyon was as difficult as any hike he'd ever done.

> The final steep part was a miserable talus rather loose and near the angle of repose.... It seemed harder to keep one's footing than anywhere else I have been... When we got to the top, we had a two-hour rest for eating and getting cooled off for the nine-mile hike to the car. Scott had carried water in his pack, and it was a good thing. I had carried a gallon away from the mine up to the rim, but that much needed supplementing soon after I had eaten lunch. It seemed plenty hot even up on the Shivwits Plateau at 6000 feet and I was resting more often, about 10 minutes of progress followed by five minutes of rest.

The ordeal would leave a lasting effect on both men. For Baxter it was an extraordinary experience, a brush with calamity. For Harvey, it meant the end of his glory days. He admitted as much during the hike out. "You could tell that he was on his last legs, that he wasn't going to do anything of that magnitude anymore," Baxter said. "And he kept saying 'There's other areas in the western end of the Canyon that I haven't explored yet and those are easy to get to, I can come up from the lake in my boat.' And that's what he did I think. I think he was just resigned, saying things like 'I'm not going to do anything like this again.'"

By now it wasn't a matter of psychology—Harvey's 74-year-old body was no longer willing to bushwhack down and up 5,000 feet of cliff. His legendary endurance, strength and agility had finally eroded, reducing him to the realm of the average hiker.

THE HIP THAT HAD begun to bother Harvey would soon take him out of the game for good. The problem was a small knurl of bone that had formed on the rim of his hip socket. If he moved his leg back past a certain angle, hot pain shot through his body. He began using a cane on bad days. The handicap did not force him to quit Grand Canyon right away; he would spend almost 100 days— nearly 10 per cent of his lifetime total—in the Canyon following his epic with Baxter. But his treks degenerated into a series of retreats from over-ambitious goals as he surrendered to his body's nose-diving capability.

One of his longtime aspirations had been to complete a route from Lee's Ferry to the Grand Wash Cliffs along the north side of the Colorado. By 1982, he'd done it all save for the stretch between Kanab Creek and Parashant Wash, a shorter stretch near Surprise Canyon, and one final stretch around the Powell Plateau. Once he realized that his time was getting very short, he relentlessly tried to take care of this unfinished business.

In September 1982, Harvey decided to circumambulate the Powell Plateau in one fell swoop, a rough trek for even the hardiest of hikers. Further, he planned not only the circumambulation, but also a climb of two buttes in the area, King's Crest and Masonic Temple. After leaving the North Rim ranger station with his 11-day permit, he made a brief stop to walk the easy, level Widforss Trail for a warm-up. But even this gentle stroll was enough to aggravate his hip. "My physical condition wasn't encouraging while getting back to the car," Harvey wrote. "I felt unusually tired and weak and my left hip joint was a bit painful."

Harvey ended up canceling his plans. As a consolation hike, he did nothing more than walk another rim path the following day, the Uncle Jim Trail near the park visitor center.

He backed off more of his big plans in February 1983, when he wanted to connect a major piece of his trans-Canyon route by hiking solo from Burnt Canyon to Pearce Canyon, a distance equal to the route around the Powell Plateau. On February 10, he started away from his boat at the mouth of Pearce Canyon "…and soon found that I was getting tired rather easily." He shifted his aim and spent three casual days in Pearce Canyon, moving slowly upstream to a place called Snap Point. It was a considerable hike but one that fell far short of his goal.

One month later, he returned for another attempt. He and his friend Jorgen Visbak drove to the rim of remote Burnt Canyon. They planned seven days of hiking in order to reach Pearce Canyon downstream, but Harvey's hip again decided the matter. "I was weaker than ever," Harvey wrote, "and my right hip was bothering me especially on our last day." They changed plans and tried for a spring on the relatively gentle Sanup Plateau, just east of Burnt Canyon. Yet even this was difficult. "The Sanup Plateau is a succession of hills and dales for miles and the walking was rather slow and laborious especially for me. It takes a lot of effort for a man of my age to keep going for hours over this area."

"It was kind of sad," said Visbak. "He was going downhill. But he didn't complain. I never saw him down. He seemed otherwise in good spirits."

In September, Harvey returned to investigate a stock trail leading down from Twin Point into Surprise Canyon. Along with fellow guidebook author John Green, he descended 1,400 feet to the Sanup Plateau, then camped at a place called Neilson Spring. Harvey decided to rest in camp for the remainder of the day, while Green wanted to try making it all the way down to Surprise Canyon via the tributary below Neilson Spring, something Harvey was interested in doing himself. Although Green did not succeed that afternoon, and reported a challenging climb when he returned, Harvey still wanted to try it the following morning. He felt that perhaps Green might have missed the correct route.

Even after a good night's rest, however, the 77-year-old lacked the energy. "I almost elected to try what John had done, but I was feeling my age and didn't have too much confidence in my ability to handle the rough going. We calmly gave up my fine ideas and walked out..."

But the urge to claim one more Redwall route was powerful. He returned to the tributary with Green in June 1986, determined to count coup again on his old Redwall adversary. This trek, however, would represent a great, lasting disappointment.

They took Harvey's boat to the mouth of Surprise Canyon where Green agreed to scout ahead to figure out the Redwall route from below. Harvey would hike alone up the bed of Surprise to the bottom of the proposed route and wait for Green's report.

Green succeeded in climbing through the Redwall to where the two had camped on their previous trip, thus connecting the route. When he returned to

Harvey drinks from a *tinaja* in Pearce Canyon, 1985. *Courtesy Jorgen Visbak*

Harvey, who was relaxing with a copy of *Time*, Green reported that the Redwall had been a tough climb. He doubted Harvey could make it. Yet before Harvey could decide for himself, Green abruptly urged that they end the trip right away, saying he had to return for work. Harvey bitterly turned his back for the last time on his favorite rock formation.

"One of the things that I most regret having missed in Surprise Canyon was a possible route through the Redwall to the west," Harvey said. "I wished I'd gone alone on that trip. But anyway, I didn't get a chance to go through the Redwall, complete that route, but there was one of the most interesting routes of all."

A year later, in May 1987, there was one last hike from the

rim in Surprise Canyon, Harvey's final obsession in the national park. The 80 year-old planned to go from Amos Point down to Amos Spring, a short walk that involved little arduous hiking. He spent two nights at the spring enjoying the scenery. After a short walk on the Sanup Plateau the second day, Harvey had had enough. "When I reached the spring about 2:15...I got so tired that the hiking was no fun, and they didn't have to twist my arm to get me to walk out..."

It was his 1,023rd day in Grand Canyon. As he walked up to the rim that evening, he may have realized it would be his last time. Harvey had left behind plenty that was undone, more routes, more miles to be cover, but he ended with a collection of figures that would be impossible to match: Forty-two years between his first and last hikes, 560 hikes in all; 12,000 miles rambled below the rim; 83 ascents, 28 of which were first ascents; 164 places where he had been through the Redwall Limestone, and, 116 different rim-to-river routes. Harvey had also written 1,079 pages of logbook entries, his three guidebooks, thousands more pages in correspondence, and had taken over 7,000 photographic slides of the gorge.

He could walk away knowing that he had deeply etched his name into Grand Canyon lore. He was respected and loved by many. Despite his declining health, he was still the one person who knew the backcountry the best. He had plenty of slide shows and lectures to deliver. Yet none of this assuaged his sorrow over the projects that would now remain forever beyond his grasp.

In an *Arizona Republic* newspaper article published May 13, 1987, the day after he returned from his final hike, Harvey admitted he was done, but wished for "...probably at least a couple months of hiking if I had the strength to do it."

He got his chance to go below the rim one last time when Arizona Raft Adventures, a river running outfit in Flagstaff, offered Harvey a free trip in 1989. "As a washed up, tired out, Grand Canyon expert," Harvey wrote, "I rated a free $1200 boat ride through the Grand Canyon." This became only the second time he went down the river on a boat. He wrote:

> It was a good trip. The boatmen were able to show me a few things I hadn't seen before, some shafts drilled at the Marble dam site, pictographs near the Whitmore Trail, and a rock cabin about 400 feet above the river opposite Pumpkin Spring.
>
> I am not exploring the western canyon or anywhere else now. I could walk up into Saddle Canyon from the boat going about half as far as the rest and get back about the same time. I staggered up the sand banks and I get winded easily. It is a real struggle to get up when I am sitting on the ground. I can still play a little old-folks-tennis, and I think I am going to spend a couple weeks in August seeing some nice places over again in my little motorhome.

Despite Harvey's sad tone, according to lead boatman Cam Staveley, he seemed content to be in the Canyon one last time. "The thing I remember is that Harvey didn't actually regret that he couldn't do those things anymore," Staveley said. "He felt like he had accomplished something that no one else had. That wasn't spoken in a manner of bravado, it was just very matter of fact."

"And that goes hand-in-hand with the biggest impression I had, that he was familiar with the place—he was content. I think he had some enjoyment out of floating by and looking up at places and certainly didn't feel like 'Well I wish I could do that, or that I could get to places where I didn't go'. That's what he was articulating. But he was a human being! And probably would have liked to have done more."

Staveley said Harvey spent much of his time simply gazing over the passing landscape. Harvey also gave his captive audience anecdotes about many features that they passed. The rafters made the usual stops along this journey—places like Deer Creek and Havasu Creek—where Harvey hobbled about as well as he could to see them one last time. When the trip ended and he disembarked at Diamond Creek, however, he would venture below the rim of the Canyon no more.

Harvey in Pearce Canyon, 1985. *Courtesy Jorgen Visbak*

Chapter Twenty-Six

OUT OF THE MURK
2004

TOM AND I HAVE DECIDED TO HATE OURSELVES.

We not only committed a cardinal sin by placing our faith in an untried shortcut route, but—assuming we'd be in camp by now—we also consumed the last of our food. And left ourselves little water. One thing is certain—we'll be a lot hungrier and thirstier before tonight is over. And two cheeseburgers and a gallon of water sounds perfect right now. As we bitterly hump our loads back up to the Tonto level in the dark, leaving behind that 30-foot cliff that kept us from camp, we say very little.

Once on the Tonto, I dump my pack and stagger a short distance for a look into the neighboring bay, hoping blindly that we simply chose the wrong drainage to descend toward camp. A straight drop of at least 250 feet greets me at the edge.

"I feel dizzy."

"Be careful!" says Tom, sprawled on the ground, shivering in his damp clothes. "Neither of us needs to end up in *Over the Edge*. It would be really embarrasing!"

He's got a point there. It would indeed seem awkward if the next edition of the book he co-wrote, which chronicles fatalities in Grand Canyon, happened to include either of us.

Flattened by the magnitude of our failure, I step back and collapse on the ground beside Tom. No words pass between us. We mutter instead, tumbling into the depths of a most profound regret, wondering what the hell we're going to do *now*. I'm so tired I could sleep right here on the cold ground, and soon I am...

Resting makes sense. But troubling thoughts keep me from drifting off. By morning we'd be thoroughly dehydrated and no closer to water. We might try signaling a plane in hopes of rescue but that seems a little drastic. No, we've got to get ourselves out of this. I take a long look at the stars while my mind first resists, then eventually sniffs at a truly abhorrent thought. We *could* hike back tonight to the last spring we passed in Vishnu Creek, and then spend the night there. Or—*no!*—we could hike *all the way back* to camp tonight. It would mean hours of hard bushwhacking.

Jesus...

Much easier to doze than face such a hellish task. But Tom is more practical. "C'mon, we need to find water," he eventually croaks, "let's get going." Whimpering, we pick ourselves up and stagger into the murk. It's 9 P.M.—right about the time we should be crawling into our sleeping bags. Instead of slumbering, we get to spend tonight retracing our route three or four miles upstream on the west side of Vishnu Creek, crossing to the other side, then hiking an equal distance downstream to camp. To go perhaps a hundred yards from where we stood half an hour ago will require us to trek an agonizing seven or eight circuitous miles in the dark, without food and with a long detour thrown in to reach water.

Too much to think about. I simply concentrate on dodging the cacti and barbed yuccas that lay camouflaged in the dim starlight like land mines. The eroded surface of the Tonto proves incredibly frustrating in our exhausted state. A series of minor tributaries forces us into flanking maneuvers to keep moving upstream. Time and again we drop in and out of these crevasses, or circumvent their heads, taking twice as long to negotiate them as we did in daylight. There is no such thing as a straight line out here.

Deep thirst sets in when we split the last of Tom's unfiltered water. The thought of giardia is the least of my concerns now. We keep quiet to avoid exposing our tongues to the arid desert air but neither of us feels like talking anyway. We have gambled and lost big. Had things gone according to plan today, we'd be celebrating our success at climbing Wotan's Throne right now, digging into sacks of warm re-hydrated chili-mac. Instead, we have condemned ourselves to haunting the desert like a pair of dehydrated ghosts.

The thought of water consumes us. We must sweat to reach more and thus become ever thirstier. But we are closer to what we covet than we realize. Before this trip, while at the NPS Backcountry Office to acquire a permit, I consulted with backcountry ranger Lon Ayers. Ayers has an impressive record of off-trail Canyon hiking. He relished the opportunity to discuss a topic beyond the typical Phantom Ranch inquiries he gets most days. When I told him of our intended route, Ayers made it a point to inform me of a good spring in the Vishnu Creek drainage. I marked the spring on my map, even though it lay on the opposite side of the canyon from Harvey's route, which Tom and I had not planned to deviate from. Still, it seemed good to know such a thing.

As we descend into yet another maddening side drainage, I hesitate. There's a variation in the night's timbre here, but it isn't clear at first what is going on.

"Hey Tom, stop. Listen!"

As soon as our noisy footsteps cease, we shout, in unison, "Frogs!"

Somewhere upstream in this little canyon, a noisy chorus of frog song resonates like a neighbor's backyard party. I suddenly remember my conversation with Ayers and the "X" on my map. The thought of a drink is too much. We lunge instinctively toward the croaking and ribbeting, heedless of the boulders and ledges that block the way. Tom and I push through 50 yards of thorny brush, crazed with thirst, sliding helter-skelter along the steep sides of the canyon. Finally, we stagger upon a crease in the bedrock where a freshet of cool water emerges from reeds and other greenery.

We kneel as if in prayer and cup our hands into the streaming Earth-blood, interrupting the frogs's merrymaking, hogging their fountain, sucking down bottle after bottle of the miraculous water. I can't drink it fast enough to ease the fiery thirst in my gullet. Tom and I agree in between groans of pleasure that surely this is the finest-tasting agua ever to pass our lips, any lips.

Now that we've drunk our fill, there is time for scientific questions. How did creatures of water arrive at this isolated spring, surrounded as it is by such a vast expanse of sun-baked rock? A mystery. Yet the frogs could ask the same of us. At the moment, we only care that we have thwarted calamity. The mental strain of uncertainty has lifted and we laugh and laugh, lying on the cool, smooth rock, dipping our fingers luxuriously into the spring.

We'd walked past this spot earlier without noticing it, and it's easy to understand why, now—the water disappears into the desert almost immediately after surfacing. And the frogs, being nocturnal creatures, had been silent.

Replete, we doze, lulled to sleep by the accumulated struggles of the day and the music of flowing liquid. When it gets too cold for our thin shirts after 30 minutes, we force ourselves back up to face the rest of our mission, feeling slightly refreshed. I glance at my watch: 11 p.m. We thank the frogs for their hospitality and reluctantly trudge from their oasis.

A dull half moon hangs low, giving us some sense of the terrain ahead. But with our attention necessarily focused on our narrow headlamp beams, we get the illusion that we're simply moving in place on a conveyor belt featuring a continuously shifting array of desert obstacles. Even though I can clearly see where my feet land, the perspective is disorienting. I fall hard on a coarse rock at one point, too weary to yelp. I simply pick myself up and get back on the conveyor belt.

Near midnight, we have moved far enough upstream that the Tapeats cliffs have thankfully descended into the bed of Vishnu Creek. We can finally go east, what we should have done in the first place here. Walking the edge of night, and across the divide between east and west in a canyon named for a Hindu preserver of the universe, we have arrived at another beginning in this journey. Ahead lies an 800-foot ascent that will take us back up to the Tonto bench, after which we'll face several more miles of in-and-out scrambling to reach camp.

Hiking the Canyon at night can be a worthwhile experience. Once I made a full-moon solo trek into Havasu Canyon that offered relief from the day's heat and solitude on an otherwise heavily traveled trail. There were other benefits. Without the normal range of eyesight, the other senses became heightened. In the dark, you must feel your way as you go.

But now, with no trail and no food, this tactile experience gradually leads to an unsettling awareness. It becomes apparent that the dark has summoned a more malevolent side of Grand Canyon on this night. Gone are the familiar appearances, the color and sense of order that sunlight brings, all of it replaced by black shapes that blot the shimmering sky. Tom and I quietly agree that we feel a presence imbuing those looming walls. This Canyon in black has the air of a monstrous theater, implacable and vast and demonic. It has expanded its power during the graveyard shift. I can almost feel a throb emanating from deep down in the ground, a hum too ancient and potent to dwell upon.

Yet I can't ignore what it seems to be saying, that we do not belong here, that our presence is not going unnoticed. This is what it must have felt like to those who wandered here in past ages, before science and religion urged that canyons are inanimate things. *This is the belly of the whale,* I think to myself, *move quietly...don't wake it...*

Creeping through this alien nightscape, through the dead grasses and amongst the wreckage of geologic time, our isolation is absolute. I have no doubt that the friendly towns above the rim have vanished. The effects of deprivation and straying at length into this underworld bring a kind of waking dream where thoughts overlap reality. The edges have fuzzed. Once in a while we talk, and the words sound as if they come from far away.

Had Harvey felt this way while making his own marathon self-rescue, during that long night in 1969 near Saddle Canyon? We wonder.

As the hours pass, Tom and I climb past ridges, trying to retrace our steps from yesterday morning, which now seems impossibly removed in time. Our minds are playing tricks on us. What I know to be boulder-strewn slopes appear as gentle wheat fields dotted with harvest bundles. The stars are indifferent to our plight, and we guess at the route. At one point we scream at the Canyon in unison, with all our might. We long for that human sound, I think, just to break the colossal brooding. Yet the answering shriek is disturbingly inhuman and we do not repeat the act.

By 2 A.M., we finally begin our descent toward the bed of Vishnu. The landscape ushers us down to a water-polished chute both of us remember. But it is a tall, steep "half pipe" and we can't find the exact spot where we climbed out of it. In the dim spray of light thrown by our headlamps everything appears too dangerous to climb. We are nearly overcome with the urge to get down and impatiently try a couple of crumbly possibilities, but the fear of falling in the dark scares us back to our senses.

Tom later admitted to building cairns perhaps twice in his life, sounding a little ashamed to admit even this much. I've done so only when absolutely necessary myself. Yesterday morning, however, when we climbed onto the Tonto bench here, Tom had indeed piled a few stones.

"Yes!" Tom shouts when he locates his beacon. It seemed an insignificant act when he built it, but now we can't imagine a lovelier sight.

Descending demands great care. We rain small stone chips as we ease our way down the sharp gully. But it goes quickly. When we finally touch down on the friendly bed of Vishnu Creek, it is 3 A.M., 20 hours after leaving camp, six hours since we turned back from that cliff across the way. A few more steps and we are back in camp. Our utter relief brings us back to reality, like recovering from a prolonged stretch of sedation. We repeatedly tell each other that it's over, it's finally over. We no longer care that we had departed with hopes of heroically ascending a formidable butte; now, merely climbing atop our sleeping pads is victory.

After inhaling dinner, we collapse and drift into fitful sleep.

FOUR HOURS LATER, the heat of the morning rouses us from the sandy wash. Last night might have been a nightmare. I rub my bleary eyes and stand, wincing from sore legs and feet. The Canyon in sunlight is once again friendly and recognizable. We can even look across the way and see Grandview Point, where Tom's Suzuki is parked.

We have told loved ones that we intend to be home tonight, but another difficult hike looms. Neither of us is familiar with Harvey's route across the river, which could mean some delays. Though our bodies scream for rest, we pack our things, determined to make it to the rim before nightfall.

We do have one possible get-out-of-jail-free card, however. A friend named Kevin McClure happens to be on the river and I recall him saying he might pass by Vishnu Creek today. Tom and I decide we'll wait beside the

Bandaging fingers after a night of bushwhacking.
Elias Butler

Colorado for a few hours in hopes of hitching a ride several miles downstream to Phantom Ranch, from which point we could pick up a maintained trail and make a quick exit from the Canyon. This, of course, would be cheating our original plan. We check ourselves for guilt and come up empty. We feel no sense of lost honor, not after suffering defeat at Wotan's Throne and enduring the hell of last night's debacle. We are tired. And getting hungry. We stiffly, dazedly head downstream into the black and gray narrows of lower Vishnu Creek.

When we reach the river, I position a pack where it can be seen by passersby, then attach my red bandana to a long stick and shove it into the backpack. It's too hot to sit in the full roar of the sun and watch, so we'll depend on this distress signal to catch our friend's eye.

A patch of soft and shady sand behind a large boulder lulls us to light slumber. Hours pass, but it's hard to sleep for very long with Grapevine Rapids crashing just downstream. We keep waiting and keep hoping, but no one floats past Vishnu Creek on this day. By 3 P.M. we can afford to wait no longer. Tom will be expected at work tomorrow morning and it'll take at least six or seven hours to hike the 12 miles back to Grandview Point.

Our problem now is not just fatigue but food. I have a couple of energy bars and some raisins; Tom has nothing. It will have to be enough. We inflate the boats, dreading the hard work ahead, then cross just upstream from the boiling rapid. I try to enjoy the feeling of being carried along, of not having to work to move, but it doesn't happen this time. Once on the south side we stash the boats under a boulder. Tom says something about getting a boatman he knows to pick them up. With lightened packs, we are ready to go. When I fetch Harvey's words from my pocket to get a sense of what lies ahead, both of us wilt when we read what we must do:

> Grapevine in the Archean rock is free of barriers until one is near the river. A major fault accounts for the alignment of Grapevine and Vishnu Canyon but the lowest part of Grapevine veers away to the west....Where the bed turns away from the fault, one can climb up and over...

For once, the meaning of Harvey's words is all too clear. We'll have to ascend the 800-foot rise of steep schist directly in front of us, then descend the other side to regain the bed of Grapevine Canyon.

"Aw, god darnit!" Tom yells.

We spit, swear and sweat our way up the loose, brittle rock, finally arriving at the rounded summit of the schist after a sustained effort that leaves my legs quivering. A few minutes of rest

Drinking from a fern-covered spring in Grapevine Canyon. *Elias Butler*

and we spit, swear and sweat our way back down the other side, scratching and sliding along the rough, brushy, boulder-choked route. In the bed of the canyon, we gratefully turn our backs on the mountain of schist we've just scaled and continue marching upstream into the narrowing corridor.

As tired as we are, the beauty of this seldom-visited stretch of Grapevine Canyon offers us some consolation. A perennial stream has cut a deeply incised gash through the gleaming metamorphic rock and many redbud trees have taken root along its course. Their cheerful array of purple flowers provides a pleasing contrast to the black and white striped walls, which wear clumps of greenery below dripping springs. Small pools of water collect in polished basins, and fallen petals swirl in the lazy currents.

For all its charm, and despite being a typically short south-side canyon, Grapevine begins to feel long. It takes two hours to reach the Tonto Trail where it intersects the bed of the canyon. As the last daylight disappears from the sky, we are relieved to abandon the uncertainty of Harvey's routes. "Oh, thank God!" Tom exclaims when we step onto the smooth, foot-pounded trail.

Unbelievable, we tell each other. Another night hike! At least it's all trail from here, even if it is six or seven miles back to the rim. The dark hours pass silently as I measure our progress by the slow turning of the stars against the cliffs. Wotan's Throne stands out in the moonlight across the river, looking mirthful at our retreat. Hard to believe we clung to its upper ramparts only yesterday.

Curving around the headlands that bend the Tonto Trail, I watch Tom's feet ahead of me as they slap the ground, the rhythmic *thump-thump-thump* providing a steady beat to our existence. My own feet are aching like never before.

Small knives stab my heel and arch with each step. I consider telling Tom I have to stop but this won't solve anything. We have to make it out of here while we have the strength; I grit my teeth and plod onward, trying to use other parts of my foot to bear my weight.

By 10 P.M. we reach the arm of Cottonwood Canyon where two days ago we picked up Harvey's route to the river, thus connecting a long loop. We continue on the Tonto Trail to the creek, which flows idly among a handful of empty campsites. Before making the steep climb up the Redwall, we need to rest and gather our wills. I split my last energy bar and raisins with Tom and, like him, I now drink water straight from the creek. The cottonwood trees mumble in the slight breeze.

We sigh, then ascend the long trail up the Redwall to Horseshoe Mesa, a ghostly expanse of moonlight and stunted junipers, where miners once blasted tunnels from the bedrock. In no time we're on the three-mile Grandview Trail that leads 2,600 feet to the rim. Now gaining altitude quickly, the air begins to cool sharply. Though there is no wind, every rest of more than a few seconds sends a chill racing down my sweat-soaked back. We must keep moving to avoid hypothermia but we're too weak to manage more than a slug's pace. Can't stop, can't hardly keep going.

At each tortuous switchback up the Coconino and then Toroweap and Kaibab formations, my will erodes a few more degrees. *Come on!* I think to myself. *It's not that much farther, get going!* This kind of internal dialogue reaches strange proportions until finally I reach the foot of an incredibly steep and long switchback near the rim where I simply cannot will myself to go farther. Tom curses entrepreneurs Ralph Cameron and Pete Berry for building this trail off the highest point on the South Rim. But Tom still has plenty of resolve and mentions that we will be on top in less than 10 minutes. It's a lie, but it works. I lurch forward.

After a few more switchbacks, we finally plod up the last few steps to Grandview Point and hoot weakly in the cold air. It's 1 A.M., meaning we've been marching for 11 hours. Like drunks, we stumble over the alien pavement toward Tom's four-wheeler, flop off our packs with painful gasps, and get the hell away from Grand Canyon.

We never made it up Wotan's Throne, but we made it back. For hours, I've been fantasizing about this moment and to finally reach it induces a supreme and utter feeling of relief. The drive to Flagstaff takes all of our effort. Each of us dozes off in neck-snapping fashion at the wheel, and we must trade off frequently. We try to keep each other awake by keeping up the conversation. Harvey's Saddle Canyon ordeal comes up again as we discuss the painful, disappointing conclusion to our fieldwork. "What kind of a man could go through such misery," I wonder out loud, "and come back for more a few days later?" We both agree. Harvey was simply in another league.

I NEVER WOULD GET GIARDIA, despite drinking untreated water. Neither would Tom. And several days after returning, we learn that a river ranger named Brenton White, the boatman who Tom hoped would retrieve our rafts for us, could not be reached by satellite phone before he passed Grapevine Rapid. By chance, however, White chose to camp where we cached our trail rafts. Despite spending the night and next morning there, White's group failed to notice our gear. Just before leaving, a guide named Clover ducked behind some boulders to urinate and glanced at the rafts at just the right angle. On top of them lay a note we had written, addressed to Brenton White.

"Hey Brenton," Clover said, waving the note at the surprised ranger, "it's for you."

But a more telling revelation finds us at home a few days later. We are flipping through Harvey's logbooks, looking for his experiences in Vishnu Canyon. A startling entry catches our attention.

In 1963, Harvey also planned to climb Wotan's Throne by leaving from Grandview Point, going down Cottonwood Canyon, and crossing the Colorado to Vishnu Creek. Our instincts had been correct.

But, we discover, our instincts had not been quite as flexible as Harvey's. From his logbook:

> "Vishnu Creek, Newberry Butte, and to the Colorado River at Mile 99.8
> November 9, 1963 to November 11, 1963"

> Starting from Grandview Point...I reached the river via the spur trail down from the Tonto...I blew up my mattress and paddled off...The current helped very little and I was shivering some before I made the mouth of Vishnu...now I walked a dry bed for quite a little distance...*I was beginning to see the futility of trying for the top of Wotan's Throne the next day...*

Harvey celebrates his 90th birthday in Flagstaff, 1997. *Courtesy Anne Madariaga*

Chapter Twenty-Seven

THE LAST HAND HOLD
1989–2002

...Kipling wrote one time, 'Ship me somewheres east of Suez, Where the best is like the worst, Where there ain't no Ten Commandments, And a man can raise a thirst.' I didn't go for the last part, but–I guess you might say I got thirsty and drank my canteen water.

Harvey Butchart,

1995 interview

"ONE OF THE PRINCIPAL SATISFACTIONS of an old Grand Canyon hiker whose best days are past," wrote Harvey to his friend Dove Menkes, "is to hear from the current crop."

By the 1990s, Harvey was reconciling himself to reliving past glories, walking the neighborhood in Sun City, and trekking vicariously through his able-bodied friends. Occasionally, a magazine or newspaper ran a feature on him. He still had fans with questions, or stories about following one of his routes. His mental faculties remained as healthy as ever. Harvey could trace over his internal map, seeing in his mind's eye each route, the shape of individual tributaries, and the rough-and-smooth texture of their interiors.

On rare days he might feel up to a real walk in the low desert mountains outside Phoenix, but his arthritic hip made this more and more difficult. Soon he gave up hiking altogether.

"I am finally serious about seeing what they can do by way of a hip replacement," he told a friend in December 1992, "but I have become so weak in the last few years that it is a real effort to stand up from a dining room chair. Day before yesterday I fell on a cement platform with my forearm caught under my chest. I must have broken a rib or two and now I can expect pain when I do certain things for a few weeks. I even have to struggle to get out of bed and stand."

Harvey could have bought himself that new hip, but he never went through with it. Instead, he spent his days traveling with Roma in the motor home, getting clobbered by her in nearly every game of Scrabble, visiting the family, and entering Sun City chess tournaments. Chess gave him a competitive outlet, though it was a bit disconcerting to occasionally lose his foes to a stroke or cancer.

If he worried that his own worsening physical ailments would condemn him to obscurity, however, the world would not allow it. In the summer of 1994, he was invited on the U.S. Geological Survey's "Old Timer's" Grand Canyon river trip, which would reunite a handful of distinguished river rats from the early days. They would travel the Canyon one last time, recounting experiences and giving oral histories along the way. Harvey was excited to go. Like an old prize-fighter, Harvey had his chance to step into the ring one last time.

But shortly before the trip's launch in September, Harvey canceled. Still, he drove to Lee's Ferry to see the trip off. After mingling with old friends and meeting famous river-running canyoneers he had only heard about, he stood in the shade of a tamarisk and quietly watched the rigging. Clearly, he was disappointed. When asked why he had changed his mind, he told me (Myers) that Roma had insisted he was too old and the trip too dangerous. He added, "I don't know if my spirit and psychology could handle seeing all those places I know I can never hike." When asked if he missed hiking, he replied, "Of course, I do."

A 1993 birthday celebration at the South Rim. From left, Harvey, Ken Walters and George Mancuso. Roma stands behind Harvey. *NPS photo by Michael Quinn*

Harvey was indeed listening more closely to Roma's wishes these days. The previous year, in 1993, his Canyon friends had decided to officially recognize Harvey's accomplishments by throwing an 86th birthday party at the national park. There was no special significance to his turning 86, other than that many feared he might not make it to his 87th birthday. Over 100 guests gathered at the old El Tovar Hotel at the South Rim to hear speeches made in Harvey's honor.

Roma was there too. It could not have been easy for her, considering she would see nothing but Canyon buffs. Still, for all her sufferings, she was proud of Harvey. When he shuffled to the microphone, he spoke of his wife, not the Canyon. "He got up to make just a few comments," Scott Thybony said. "The first thing he did was apologize to Roma for having abandoned her...and, he said he was surprised she hadn't divorced him for having basically, you know, followed his bliss and gone off in those canyons for so many years."

Four years later in 1997, at Harvey's 90th birthday celebration held in Flagstaff, he again began by apologizing to Roma. Now that he could no longer leave the house to go hiking, he was spending more time with her than he had in decades. Guilt had caught up with him. It was natural that he should want to make amends at this point. But Roma had endured the kind of loneliness that went beyond public apologies. Their marriage hadn't improved simply because he was around. Indeed, they both knew the truth: Harvey had rejoined Roma not because he wanted to, but because his body left him no choice.

Roma's lingering acrimony was palpable to those who visited Harvey during this period. In 1998, I (Myers) brought my wife Becky and our three children to the Butchart home for a visit. Although I'd already met with Harvey several times and was acquainted with Roma, this was the first time I would see them in Sun City.

Their small, single-story track home occupied a sterile neighborhood typical of the retirement community. A very stooped and frail Harvey greeted us at the door, appearing much older than when I'd last seen him. He welcomed us in. Roma, who looked in better shape, stayed in the background but came forward at the sight of my family. After reintroducing her to Becky and our three children (they had met briefly once before), I was a little nervous about how Roma and Becky might interact, especially with Becky having kids in tow. Becky was leery also, having heard all the stories about Roma's reputation. So far Roma had been polite but stoic. Yet she almost immediately asked Becky, "Are you a hiker?"

"Oh no," Becky replied with a smile. "I've done a few hikes in the Canyon with Tom, but I'm mainly a mom."

Mom was the magic word. Roma broke out in a big smile. She started chatting like I'd never heard. She asked questions about Becky and our kids, talking to all four, relating her own experiences as a mother and grandmother. Enthusiasm punctuated her voice and a sparkle filled her eyes.

I was completely stunned.

Over the years, I had tried my best to win Roma over. All told, between seeing her in person three times and making multiple phone calls to their home, she had spoken less than a hundred words to me. It seemed the only phrases I ever heard were "let me get Harvey" or "you should ask Harvey." Now, however, with the conversation revolving around non-Canyon topics, Roma said more to Becky in a few minutes than she had to me in the previous five years combined. Not only was Roma personable, she was downright charming. I was pleased to see them move outside, where the kids entertained themselves throwing grapefruit around, as Becky and Roma continued to chat.

While Harvey and I made small talk, I began to notice that nothing in their home so far gave any hint that the Canyon had ever played a role in either Harvey or Roma's lives. Instead, the decor veered toward coastline scenes—especially Rocky Point, Mexico. Roma's seashells dotted the tables. Between the entry, the living room, kitchen, and dining room, nothing said "Grand Canyon." *This can't be true*, I thought. The king of Grand Canyon hiking should have a stash comparable to Michael Jordan's trophy collection, or Elvis's gold record wall. Where were his maps, the framed photos and articles, his prized Canyon books—including his copy of *The Man Who Walked Through Time* Colin Fletcher had sent? They had to be here somewhere.

So I asked Harvey. And he showed me.

He wobbled to the far end of the house and led me into a small bedroom about 10 by 12 feet. This was where Harvey slept, alone. Everything was barracks-neat. A couple of Canyon photos and a pair of framed awards hung on the walls. There was also a small desk. On the desk lay Harvey's old typewriter. Other than these few symbols, the room felt very empty.

The message that day was clear: Roma was the main stockholder in the Butchart home, and what mattered most was family, not a lifetime of achievement pursued at a woman's expense. Harvey might as well have tried to hang photographs of a mistress on the walls. I could not help but wonder if it all had been worth it.

THE TWENTY-FIRST CENTURY found both Harvey and Roma sliding into seriously poor health. For Harvey, it was arthritis, failing eyesight, irregular heart rhythm, and an increasing loss of motor control. Friends noticed that Harvey's letters, which had always been models of neatness, now came with the writing literally between the lines.

Hiker Tony Williams explained, "He had, obviously, a lot harder time reading letters. In fact, the last couple letters, I printed in very large type for him. But it was clear that he couldn't see because he'd type these letters, and the margin would be four inches on the left and going off the right margin, you know. So he wasn't able to see. It was kind of painful. And also, his last letter or two were kind of sad ones, just regretting that he couldn't do this [hiking] anymore, and how bad his physical condition had gotten."

Roma was not faring much better. Dementia had begun to unlatch her formidable mind. Anne Madariaga hired caregivers to perform chores around the house for her ailing parents, but Roma routinely fired these people. As it became obvious to the family that Harvey and Roma could no longer care for themselves, Anne's daughter Renee Carrizosa tried to persuade them to move in with her family in Tucson.

"Since I was a little girl," Carrizosa said, "I had always told my grandparents 'when you guys get old, I'm going to take care of you.' I guess I'd been telling them that since I was about four years old. I didn't ever want their last memories to be in a nursing home. When it came time, you know, grandpa got his driver's license taken away, and he was falling."

Indeed, in 2000, Harvey took a wrong turn in a construction zone and ran his Ford Fiesta into a ditch. Shortly after, he crashed into an orange tree in a road median. In both cases, his failing eyesight was likely to blame. Anne and Sam took the 93-year-old man to the doctor and requested, in private, that the doctor recommend that Harvey no longer drive. Harvey surrendered his keys without complaint.

As Renee had noted, it was time for Harvey and Roma to accept full-time care. Renee and her husband Bob arrived in Sun City in May 2001 to bring Harvey and Roma to Tucson. Things did not go as smoothly as planned.

"Grandpa was ready," Renee said. "He had his shaving bag and one pair of clothes. My grandma on the other hand, she was just sitting on the couch with her arms crossed saying 'No, I don't want to go.' And my grandpa was saying 'But Roma, we have to go, we can't stay here anymore. We need help!' It took us an hour to get her in the car because she had dementia."

Even though Harvey was willing to leave, his ankles were swollen to the size of his thighs. He could not walk. "The day we picked them up," Renee said, "we looked at both of them and I said 'Oh my god, Grandpa, we need to take you to the hospital!' He couldn't fit in his shoes. When we left the house, my husband picked him up and put him in the car because he was so swollen because he wasn't taking his medicine. He needed a lot of attention."

Both Harvey and Roma had long feared the idea of a nursing home, and as a result, attempted to care for themselves far longer than they should have. Renee realized how bad things had become when she noticed her grandparents showed signs of malnourishment. "They were in pretty bad shape," she said. "My grandpa was very feeble. He needed help dressing, bathing, he needed help getting up out of a chair. You know he always had that bad hip, but just about six months before they came and stayed with us, he had really gone downhill physically."

Roma, Harvey and grandchild in the late 1990s in Sun City. *Courtesy Renee Carrizosa*

"If they hadn't come to live with us," Renee said, "I really don't think either one of them would have lasted very much longer, because they were in very poor health. Every single week on our days off, the first six months they were here, we had an appointment and we were taking one of them to the doctor."

Following many visits to the physician, and regular meals for the first time in years, Harvey and Roma eventually put on about 15 pounds each. Gradually they improved their health to the point where they were once again able to enjoy the simple act of living.

"From the minute they walked into our house," said Renee, "every single day I think that my grandparents were alive, my grandma would say 'we don't know what we've done to deserve such wonderful treatment. Thank you guys for taking care of us.' And my grandpa used to say, 'we appreciate what you're doing. We know it's not easy.'"

Ironically, it took Harvey and Roma's failing health to renew a physical closeness that neither had experienced in decades. Ever since Roma's pelvis had been crushed in that rollover car accident near Winslow in 1959, she and Harvey had slept in separate bedrooms. She required a specialized bed that tilted at an angle. By that point, Harvey had begun spending more time than ever at Grand Canyon, and their separation went far beyond the bedroom.

In Tucson, however, they again shared the same bed, and slowly began to rekindle the feelings of love that had been there all along.

"It's funny 'cause I never remember my grandparents in my whole entire life ever showing any affection towards each other," Renee said. "You know, like, kissing each other, or holding hands. And they never slept in the same bedroom since I was a baby. We saw that my grandpa wanted a lot more affection from my grandma; it was my grandma who didn't want the affection from my grandpa. I think maybe because she was mad. I don't know why. But she would always keep him at arm's length."

"But here, of course," she continued, "we had them in the same bedroom. And they started sleeping together. And, they became just like two little peas in a pod. I mean, at first, she was kind of like, 'Harvey, you're sitting too close to me!' because he was taking advantage of this. They would sit together on the couch, and my grandpa would always sit real close to her, and he'd put his arm around her. And a lot of times I'd come home from work, and you know, he'd be asleep on her shoulder. So, they emotionally grew very, very close to each other. And it was *really* nice to see that."

Harvey told Renee how grateful he was for the renewed spark in his marriage. "This is *so* nice, I'm having this closeness with your grandma that I haven't had for *years*," Harvey said. "I shouldn't have let this go this far. And now your grandma likes affection."

Renee sensed that Harvey felt guilty. "Well Grandpa, she probably liked it all along, but you know, maybe you just didn't see that, you know?"

Harvey and Roma frolic in a hot spring in Black Canyon, 1970. *Courtesy Jorgen Visbak*

"She lets me sit by her, and she lets me hold her hand now," Harvey said. "You know how long it's been since I slept with your grandmother? All these *years.*"

"I know Grandpa," Renee said. "See—another good reason for you guys to be here with us.'

Harvey and Roma spent hours watching TV. Whenever the family would make a run to the video rental store, Harvey always requested the same movie: *Vertical Limit.* Renee said he watched it dozens of times, despite everyone's plea for something different (the melodramatic flick does veer closer to folly than fact). One look at the film though, and it's easy to understand Harvey's fascination. *Vertical Limit* opens with a climbing scene in Monument Valley, Utah, the iconic landscape not far from Grand Canyon, and ends with a mountain rescue on K2, the world's second highest peak.

The harmony with Roma and the family would not last long. A year after they had moved to Tucson, on Easter Sunday 2002, Roma failed to rise from the bed she shared with Harvey. "I went and got her," Renee said, "because we used to go in and get them out of their bed. It was on my day off, and I got Grandpa up, and my grandma was just lying there. I was like 'Grandma it's time to get up! Grandma, I got you guys breakfast!' She was just lying there on her side. And I went around to the side, and her eyes were kind of glazed over. I said 'Grandma can you hear me?' And her left side was completely paralyzed. But her right side, she could squeeze my hand. And then I realized that she'd had a stroke."

After an ambulance arrived to bring Roma to the hospital, the distraught family received good news. Her stroke had been mild and Roma was expected to recover. Despite the good prognosis, though, Harvey became inconsolable.

"This is it, your grandma is going to die," Harvey told Renee.

"No Grandpa, no she's not going to die," Renee said. "She did not have a major stroke, why are you saying this?"

"Because everybody I know who has had their spouse have a stroke at this age, they never recover," Harvey said. "I will never see your grandma in this house again!"

"So we took him to the hospital every single day," Renee said. "In one week they put her over into a care center. When she got over into that care facility, the second day she was there, we had spent the whole day with her. It was very sweet, we had them both in wheelchairs, and they were holding hands, and my husband was pushing my grandpa and I was pushing my grandma. We'd gone all over the care center and we had lunch and we had a really beautiful day. Grandpa was happy."

"We left there," Renee said, "and we had not been home 30 minutes, and they called and said 'your grandma just had a major stroke.'"

This time, Roma would not recover. At Renee's request, Roma was placed on life support. Renee delivered the bad news to Harvey.

"Grandma had a major stroke and she's in a coma," Renee said. "She's not going to recover."

"I know, I told you guys that," Harvey cried.

"What we did for three days while she hung on is, we went and stayed at the care center and took my grandpa there so he could stay with her," Renee said. "We got him a room there. And let him be there every waking moment, every minute that she had left."

When Roma died on the fourth day, April 3, Harvey was sitting at her bedside, holding her hand. Roma was 96. She had been married to Harvey for 72 years. The next day would have been the 73rd anniversary of their engagement.

Harvey turned to Renee, and in his grief, he delivered an ultimatum. "I'm going to give you a two-week reprieve, and then I'm going to go be with your grandma."

"Grandpa, what are you talking about?"

"I'm going to give you two weeks," Harvey said.

"Grandpa, my gosh, no, no!" Renee said. "We can't do another funeral and go through this again. There's so much to live for! Grandma wouldn't have

Roma and Harvey at Grand Canyon for the last time, at Shoshone Point in 1999.
Courtesy Gary Ladd

wanted that.'"

Harvey reconsidered, and when he had thought it over, he decided to give his family two months.

They attended Roma's memorial service on April 6 at the Evergreen Mortuary Chapel in Tucson. Afterward, Harvey showed signs that he intended to make good on his promise. "He had made up his mind," Renee said. "And everything that he loved to do, he quit doing. He cut his food intake into half, then it went down to like a quarter. And all the stuff after my grandma passed away—the Scrabble that they'd play during the day, the TV programs that they used to watch. You know, his companion was gone! And he'd grown so close to her in the year that they were here. No, he wasn't going to have any part of being around without her. I said to my husband, 'he's going to pass in two months. I know he is.'"

Harvey told Renee and Bob that he would depart with nothing but gratefulness. "Each and every day," Renee said, "he would say, 'I'm so glad you guys gave us the opportunity to be together. And to be close. And to be able to sleep together and hold hands.' And he was very thankful about that, you know?"

"He'd tell us, 'I needed this. This past year has been really good for us. Something that we've needed for a long time.' And you know, knowing that, gosh that made us feel good too."

True to his word until the last, 95-year-old Harvey Butchart died in his sleep on May 29, 2002. It was exactly two months to the day since Roma had passed away. The official report claimed death from complications due to heart failure. But to ask his family, Harvey simply missed Roma too much to be without her.

"I think he really did pass on with peace, and feel good, and feel like maybe he'd made a full circle," Renee said. "Maybe he was able to make up for a lot of the lost time they had, you know? I think in that last year he felt very emotional about things. And emotional about my grandma."

FUNERAL SERVICES WERE HELD in Sun City. Turnout was light. For the people who Harvey had touched in the Grand Canyon hiking community, this quiet observance did not wholly absolve the loss. Harvey might have died in the Sonoran Desert, but his life belonged to Grand Canyon.

In June 2004, a procession of friends and family walked a mile through the ponderosa forest of the South Rim to Shoshone Point, where a mantle of Kaibab Limestone offers a mighty swath of Grand Canyon. The human need for ceremony is elemental, and on this day, the canyoneers bid farewell in tribal fashion to John Harvey and Roma Butchart, as well as to the recently fallen George and Helen Steck.

From left, Renee Carrizosa, Sam and Anne Madariaga place Harvey and Roma's ashes in Grand Canyon, June 2004. *Elias Butler*

Following a round of stories, Anne and Sam Madariaga, along with their daughter Renee and son Kirk and their families, carried an urn holding both Harvey and Roma's ashes to the edge. Below the viewpoint, Cremation Canyon cuts a 4,000-foot gash where Harvey had once explored. According to legend, the Supai Indians who originally inhabited this region cremated their dead and cast the remains into the Canyon here. Anne and Sam now solemnly tipped their urn of ashes into the sky.

There was another reason for choosing Shoshone Point. Harvey had visited Grand Canyon for one of his last times here to attend a Grand Canyon Pioneers Society annual picnic. Harvey was one of the first members of the club and had been its elder statesman. The gathering gave him the chance to swap stories with old friends, while the view could be counted on to inspire memories of bygone feats below the rim.

Harvey had brought three items at my (Myers) behest. I had suggested that Harvey donate his canyoneering gear as historic items to be preserved and displayed at the national park. Although it had been years since he could hike, he had not yet discarded his basic outfit. Perhaps Harvey had been hoping against hope that they might still be of use to him one day.

One by one he pulled each dusty memento from his truck. The items perfectly matched their owner—humble and worn. He handed over his cheap, beat-up, orange, external frame backpack. It had earned its share of Canyon battle scars, but was still holding together. The backpack came complete with a dirty, frayed clothesline—the same line that Harvey used to raise and lower his pack over rocky ridges—wrapped around the base in lieu of a hip strap.

Next, Harvey produced his last pair of Canyon hiking boots, plain workingman's boots, as Harvey called them. He had bought this pair at K-Mart, likely from a blue-light special rack. One boot featured several holes in the sole where the tread had worn through. Earlier, when I had asked over the phone if he still had a pair to donate to the park, he had replied, "I think I have a pair that might be worthy." *They were worthy.*

Finally, Harvey brought out the third and final item from his truck, his canteen. The old metal container wore plenty of dents and scratches, and the striped felt covering was thinned and torn. For a moment he held it in his hands and said nothing.

Like Harvey, his gear was used to its full ability–and beyond. Clearly, the backpack, the boots, and the canteen had given their frugal owner his money's worth. *If any of the articles, in their degenerative state, could speak, what would they say?*

For starters, they would have bragging rights like few others. The backpack could regale the listener with stories of adventure and misadventure. The canteen could enthrall with descriptions of the spectacular and unparalleled views it had been privileged to glimpse. The boots would speak of the thrill of stepping where perhaps only moccasins or sandals had stepped hundreds or thousands of years earlier. Of course, each of the items might grumble a bit too about taking some hard knocks.

But they wouldn't boast.

Instead, they would reminisce about their unique and famous owner, a kind, generous and dedicated teacher, always willing to share his knowledge. Yet there would probably be some regret too, having witnessed pain and heartache caused by his obsession.

Nevertheless, faithful to the end and knowing their master, the hiking relics would likely nod toward the chasm and say, *"Don't we have some unfinished business down there, professor?"*

Harvey reluctantly offered his canteen to me, breaking my reverie. "Wait a minute," he said, suddenly retracting his outstretched arm. He was thirsty. Harvey unscrewed the cap with its little chain attached to the reservoir, and took one long, last slow drink. He sighed contentedly, then screwed the cap back on and gave it to me, knowing he would never need it again. Badly stooped, and nearly crippled from the degenerative arthritis that was ravaging his hip and spine, he smiled, stood as erect as he could, then turned and slowly walked away.

Harvey's well-worn gear, now stored at the South Rim Museum. *NPS photo by Michael Quinn*

Wotan's Throne from near Vishnu Temple. *J. Harvey Butchart, courtesy NAU Special Collections*

Epilogue
IT WAS A SPORTY CLIMB
2004

No farther seek his merits to disclose
Or draw his frailties from their dread abode,
(There they alike in trembling hope repose,)
The bosom of his Father and his God.

Thomas Gray,
Closing lines of "The Elegy"

I wouldn't want to think much about describing myself. I am reminded of
the closing lines of Gray's Elegy.

Harvey Butchart (1995)

TEARS WERE NOTABLY ABSENT during Harvey and Roma's memorial. Mostly, people told stories—hiking stories, climbing stories, anecdotes about what Harvey had said or done below the rim. His Matthes-Evans maps stood tacked to a large easel, which drew a continuous crowd. Any number of his hand-drawn lines, leading down some canyon or atop some butte, was all it took to trigger another story.

Across the Canyon loomed Wotan's Throne, the bold-looking butte that had so captivated Harvey, inspiring him to write in 1965, "Usually I don't care to climb the same summit twice...but Wotan's still fascinates me, and I'll be back for another climb."

Tom and I were still hungry to know what he'd found up there. We started talking about making good on our own failed bid with another attempt, and that was when we knew.

We approached Anne Madariaga about bringing a small container of her mother and father's ashes to one of Harvey's favorite places—*see that butte over yonder?* Anne agreed instantly. Our last bit of research had just become a pilgrimage.

Four months later, on a drizzly October morning, we leave the paved walkway at Cape Royal and take a look over the rim where we're headed. Not an auspicious sight—a coal-black thunderhead glowers like a massive fist over Wotan's Throne. Occasional stabs of lightning tear at the butte's flanks, and thunder reverberates across the Canyon.

The weather makes us nervous but the obesity of our backpacks is more worrisome. We'll need plenty of water, plus climbing and camping gear to get us atop the great butte, all of which adds up to a ponderous load. As the rain runs down our faces, we clumsily descend the first cliffs below the point, trying mightily to keep from collapsing beneath the weight.

We learned a lesson after our first attempt at Wotan's. This time we will follow Harvey's lead to the summit instead of our own foolish notions. Not that it will be any easier, as we soon find out. We spend the day crawling along slim ledges, lowering the cumbersome packs over 20-foot cliffs, rappelling 80 feet where the Coconino Sandstone falls sheer to the Hermit Shale, and then shambling across the shale's steep, corrugated slopes to Wotan's weak eastern flank. In eight hours we manage to move a total of one mile as the bird flies, though our bodies tell us it must be more like fifteen.

Rappelling the 80-foot drop in the Coconino Sandstone below Cape Royal. *Elias Butler*

At sunset we're ascending the same broken, collapsed Coconino Sandstone talus that had been the scene of our failed try the previous April. We heave ourselves up the steeply pitched, slab-ridden route, trying to wring as much ground as we can from the receding day.

We'd planned to spend the night

on the summit, hoping for a rare night up in the Canyon. But again we overestimated what we could cover in a day's time, following routes with all our water on our backs. We'll need to make camp somewhere in this giant rockslide and leave the summit for tomorrow. Halfway up the Coconino break, we unshoulder our dirty, sweaty packs, kick out a couple flat places among the rubble, and flop dead-tired onto our sleeping pads. Not far above hangs the alluring rim of Wotan's, still at least two hours away.

Our outdoor bedroom wears a familiar look. After a moment it comes—we are camped right where we'd been turned back on our last attempt, right where we lost the route. The next move had blended into itself like a page in a closed book here. Tom and I notice the places we had tried, slim cracks in between boulders that led nowhere, possible avenues that ended in overhanging walls— nothing but broken rock heaped upon itself and sloping drop-offs that invited disaster.

Harvey once hunted for the route through this geologic bedlam, too. As we settle into our bags against the night's chill, we read notes from his first ascent of Wotan's 42 years earlier, hoping for clues:

> It was nearing 7:30 P.M. when we [Harvey and Allyn Cureton] arrived at the talus leading to the top of the Coconino on Wotan. It was not altogether clear from below whether we would be able to find the way among the ledges and slabs of the Coconino at the top of the talus...we checked a couple of cracks that might be talus filled ravines to the top. They were no good, but we found an excellent level sandy place below an overhang while we were doing this and decided to make our camp there.

We are surprised and pleased to learn that he too was forced to bivouac within this rockslide. Tom and I peer beyond the glow of our headlamps and make out a few dim shapes in the starlight. We imagine him lying among these rocks, like us, wondering about the rest of the climb. As we read a few more lines, giving voice to his words, Harvey's presence feels close by.

Yet we're unable to make much of his notes. We determine to get going as early as possible and travel light to the summit, leaving everything but the essentials in camp. Until then we are left to worry over the uncertainties and our diminishing water supply.

Morning. We rise in the darkness of 5:30 A.M. as a slice of moon slowly drifts into view from beyond the wall above camp. We ready our daypacks with food, water, and cameras, taking care to stuff in Harvey's notes as well.

Across the Canyon, we can just make out the ghostly sight of low clouds rolling over the Palisades of the Desert in a silent cascade. A few lights pinprick the distant Navajo reservation. The storm that pelted us yesterday is gone. By subtle degrees, the light shifts from nebulous gray to blue until we can see well enough to spring from camp. Once more, we find ourselves in step with the mathematics professor:

> We got a fairly early start, a bit before six...as we had thought, the Coconino gave us some problems. We left our packs... In general the plan for getting through the Coconino is to leave the top of the talus and follow ledges left or right until a way appears where we could climb up...at one place we seemed to be stopped. Careful scouting turned up an easy ramp behind a large rock...

As usual, Harvey's writing offers little detail, only the confidence that there exists a passage amongst the problematical sweep of rock directly overhead. As we scramble around, finding nothing but dead ends, we keep repeating that last phrase. It seems to be our best clue: "Careful scouting turned up an easy ramp behind a large rock..."

Finally the absurdity of such a statement gets the better of us. "Shit, Harvey!" one of us whines. "There's like, a million large rocks here!"

Somehow, we are overlooking the answer that lies right in front of us, an answer Harvey wanted to help us find. With blind hope, we take another look around. After a minute, Tom calls out where a tree emerges from between sandstone blocks. On closer inspection, behind the screen of leaves, we see a ramp leading up that we had missed earlier...*an easy ramp behind a large rock*...could this be it?

We slip through the tangle of branches and pull ourselves through the narrow cleft, emerging on top where a large cairn marks the way. Just like that, we are right where we need to be. We hurry into the predawn light past more cairns, easily picking out the route where Harvey once scrambled.

"Until you get right up to the top of the Coconino," Harvey wrote, "it's not clear how you could proceed, but right there in front of you is a fine gate leading around to the northwest." Indeed, it appears as if we're ascending toward nothing but a sheer wall until a 25-foot wide gap comes slowly into view, a break in the mighty Coconino wall that curves back to Cape Royal. "I came to an Indian rock shelter," Harvey wrote, "a wide ledge under an overhang with wind breaker walls built at both ends." We spot this small ruin that still guards the "gate," which suggests the first summit team used this route to climb Wotan's Throne a millennium ago.

Now on Wotan's western side, the walking suddenly becomes level and easy. We take Harvey's recommendation, hugging the base of the final limestone cliff, quickly crossing a pair of bays to a narrow, 400-foot ridge that connects to Wotan's rim. This was the same ridge that Walter Wood's party used in 1937 to make a first recorded ascent; like a line dropped tantalizingly over a cliff, the rock now beckons to us. Although Harvey refused to consider using this opportunity in favor of a less exposed route to the west, we decide to break from his footsteps to speed our ascent.

We clamber up the giant staircase with growing excitement, squeezing past large blocks of sharp limestone that force us along exposed ledges. Where short cliffs appear, we must stuff our fists and toes into narrow cracks to draw

Ascending the ridge to Wotan's Throne. *Elias Butler*

ourselves up. We climb higher. The sky unfolds around us, exposing fathoms of rock and space on either side. Wisps of cloud race by not far above. We're so caught up in the minutiae of the ascent that we are taken aback to suddenly be facing the final lip of Wotan's Throne. With the help of a convenient juniper root, we pull ourselves up and step upon the flattest ground we have seen since leaving the parking lot 24 hours earlier.

Right away we feel the magical quality, the isolated never-never land atmosphere that Harvey alluded to in his magazine article "Wotan's Throne." The forest here is thick with pinyons, junipers, sagebrush and cliff rose, a primeval desert grove untouched by livestock or wildlife, and hardly by man. We hurry over the downed trees, through the dense brush, stumbling upon weathered stone ruins from past centuries, following the gradual rise toward the summit. This is where Harvey would have come.

Vishnu Temple emerges through the trees, a stone pyramid within a great bowl of plunging space. We are getting close. Bedrock begins to show through

Wotan's thin layer of topsoil. We bypass solitary junipers and small ledges where the cap rock has worn down, exposing deep gaps in the cracked surface. Finally we reach a sculpted white pedestal of Kaibab Limestone, the summit of Wotan's Throne.

Spread open before us are myriad canyons, *the* Canyon, the mute Colorado River, distant volcanic mountains. All of it defies our exclamations, and our thoughts. We stand in silence, not quite believing we've finally made it.

A gust lashes us on the exposed edge. Colder now than when we started this morning, and the sky has clouded again. Raindrops dot the lichen-covered rock. I bring out the film canister that holds Harvey and Roma's ashes.

A photograph of Harvey goes in the container atop Wotan's Throne. *Elias Butler*

Now that this moment has arrived, we hesitate, wondering what to say. I never met Harvey or Roma. Tom remembers Harvey as a grandfatherly figure. For years, Tom's lamented never having hiked with Harvey but now feels this makes up for it. We like to think Harvey would have been pleased knowing someone carried his vestiges—and Roma's—to the summit of his favorite Canyon butte. Yet we are suddenly aware of how little all this matters—us, our gesture, these remnants of human lives. No one, no matter how hard he tries, or how large he looms in the world of man, cannot avoid fading before such time-wrought creation as surrounds us. We have returned to Grand Canyon looking for Harvey's essence, but in the end, we only find what Harvey himself found, what anyone ultimately finds here—a measure of sublimity, the incomprehensible.

We open the cap. Harvey and Roma's ashes float in place for a moment before a gust of wind carries them out over the edge, along the rim, and into the Canyon. A vaporous gray sheet of fast moving stratus clouds looms overhead. Sunlight breaks briefly through the cover to illuminate the rock at our feet.

We leave a final offering, a metal container where people can leave their names if they wish. A small photo of Harvey goes in the can as well as our brief notes. It's getting chilly. We turn away from the summit and start back down toward the ridge that leads to camp.

Much later, past sundown, we are climbing the final limestone cliffs below Cape Royal, feeling our way up by headlamp. Each gust of wind freezes our sopping backs and clouds our light beams with flying dust. After several wrong turns, and much hunting along yucca-studded ledges, and yelling to be heard over the gale, we finally gain the correct route to the rim and step once again onto a paved footpath. We turn our back on the black void that hides Wotan's Throne, no longer able to hear the sound of the wind moaning against its deserted cliffs.

I would plead guilty to the desire to
"leave footprints on the sands of time."

Harvey Butchart, 1975

ACKNOWLEDGEMENTS

Writing this story in many ways was not unlike taking a remote backpacking journey in Grand Canyon. Countless times we found ourselves cliffed out, heading down the wrong trail, or just plain lost. Fortunately, the friends and family of Harvey Butchart and dozens of other nice folks were willing to come to our rescue to help us reach our destination.

First and foremost we are grateful for the assistance that was freely offered by the family of Harvey and Roma Butchart. Daughter Anne Madariaga was especially helpful in trying to sort out the Butchart family history. She was patient with all our pestering, as was her husband Sam. Anne's brother Jim Butchart gave honest answers to difficult questions about his parents. Harvey's granddaughter Renee Carrizosa gave us thoughtful insight about her grandparents's last years.

For information on Harvey's China years, Walter Merwin Haskell of Phoenix, and Kuling Chamber of Commerce spokesperson Moon Dehua were very helpful. The Disciples of Christ History Department obliged our every request for material with efficiency and good cheer. The Kuling American School Association helped in planning travel to China.

Butler University, Eureka College, and Mercersburg Academy breathed life into Harvey's years in Pennsylvania and the Midwest by digging up photos from their holdings, for which we are indebted.

Here in Arizona, the wonderful staff at Northern Arizona University's Cline Library Special Collections went far beyond the call of duty. As curators of Harvey Butchart's sprawling collection, they have painstakingly cataloged each item. Their efforts trimmed months of busy work off our research. We'd like to recognize Peter Runge, Bee Valvo, Todd Welch, Karen Underhill, and especially Jess Vogelsang and Richard Quartaroli ("Q").

When it comes to elusive Grand Canyon history, Dove Menkes is a sleuth without peer. He continually provided us with obscure facts and information for nearly every chapter or personality feature in this book, especially regarding Merrel Clubb, Dock Marston, and Colin Fletcher. He deserves special recognition for going above and beyond the call of friendship.

Merrell Clubb, Jr. provided a wealth of information about his pioneering father, Merrel Clubb, Sr.

Grand Canyon National Park Service Rangers Ken Phillips and Bil Vandergraff provided information on George Mancuso. Mathieu Brown from the Science Center and Backcountry Ranger Todd Seliga assisted in butte climbing data. River Ranger Brenton White rescued our boats (with help from a river guide named Clover). Ranger Bryan Wisher's encouragement never faltered in over a dozen years. Mike Quinn, Kim Besom, and Colleen Hyde of the Grand Canyon National Park Study Collection are a pure joy to work with and in our opinion the dynamic trio. Mike also provided several wonderful photos. From the Backcountry Office, Ranger Lon Ayers saved our bacon with information on that spring in Vishnu Canyon. And from Yosemite NP, Museum Technician Greg Cox provided a Francois Matthes photo at the last hour.

Our understanding of Francois Matthes and Richard Evans would not have been possible without the generosity of Art Christensen, who gave us original maps and rare articles from his impressive personal collection.

Several individuals representing several organizations made contributions including Lee Albertson of the Grand Canyon Historical Society, Todd Berger and publicist extraordinaire Helen Thompson of the Grand Canyon Association (GCA), Mike Buchheit of GCA's Grand Canyon Field Institute, the Grand Canyon Hikers and Backpacker's Association, the University of Arizona Special Collections, Dan and Diane Cassidy of Five Quail Books, and Grand Canyon River Guides historian, writer and spokesman Brad Dimock, who gave priceless words of wisdom.

Curator Bill Frank of the Marston Collection at the Huntington Library in San Marino, California is as valuable as the collection itself. Frank is a selfless, unsung hero who for three decades has assisted students of Canyon history in navigating the colossal maze that is the Marston Collection.

Former Harvey hiking companions who provided insight on Harvey's time "below the rim" include: George Bain, Scott Baxter, George and Sue Billingsley, Kim Crumbo, Allyn Cureton, Donald Davis, Alan Doty, Bob Dye, Jim and Doris Kirschvink, Bob Marley, Bill Mooz, Jim Ohlman, Bob Packard, Chuck Pullen, Douglas Schwartz, Dale Slocum, Scott Thybony, Ellen Tibbetts, Jonathan Upchurch, Ken Walters, and Tony Williams.

Other Canyon aficionados who helped whether they know it or not include: Bruce Aiken, Cathy Alger, John Annerino, Gale Burak, Peter Bremer, Pete Borremans, Dan Davis, Jr., Pam Foti, Rudy J. Gerber, Dr. Michelle Grua, Bill

Hatcher, Shirley Marston, Lea Parker, Glenn Rink, W.L. "Bud" Rusho, Jason Semmelmann, Cam Staveley, Gary Stiles, Aaron and Wayne Tomasi, Sally Underwood, and the late, great George Steck and his family.

Thanks go to Kevin McClure for generously providing a writing sanctuary at the Ranch—and for not rowing past Vishnu Creek that day in 2004 and giving us an easy ride out.

Former NAU math department chairman Everett Walter kindly sent us information regarding Harvey's "other" career as a math professor.

Dr. Mark Crane deserves special recognition. If it not for his unique perspective, we'd probably still be missing "the big picture."

We appreciate writer Scott Thybony's willingness to allow us to add his excellent story regarding George Mancuso and the Hopi seer to our account. Scott also provided precious guidance and advice throughout the evolution of this book, not to mention his two trail rafts for our fieldwork.

We are indebted to Dale Slocum for his unmatched photography of Harvey the river rat, and a poignant shot of Boyd Moore. Al Richmond, a railroad historian, hand-delivered the photo of the railroad workers—thank you.

A big thank you goes to longtime Harvey hiking companion and photographer Jorgen Visbak of Boulder City, Nevada, who spent an afternoon sharing his many fine slides with us. We are obliged for the great photos donated by Douglas Schwartz, Steve Miller, and Gary Ladd. We also owe thanks to National Geographic photographer Michael "Nick" Nichols for helping us find our cover shot. Allyn Cureton's slides were a treasure, and we especially thank him for our back cover photo. A large debt goes to Scott Baxter, whose cover portrait of Harvey and other excellent photographs (and all around insight) helped define this book. Loie Belknap-Evans went out of her way to provide fine photographs made by the late Bill Belknap.

Many thanks go to Richard L. Danley, one of the best and hardest working Grand Canyon photographers, for his stories, advice, taking Elias to Nankoweap in 2002, and of course, those excellent 4x5 transparencies.

Videotaped oral histories of Harvey Butchart by George Bain, Mike Quinn, and Lew Steiger were priceless.

For perhaps the toughest job of reviewing the manuscript, we thank the following: Michael F. Anderson, Chris Avery, John S. Azar, Joe Baker, Scott Baxter, Mike Buchheit, Walker Butler, Hazel Clark, Dr. Mark Crane, Richard L. Danley, Mike Frick, Karen Greig, Tricia Lund, Tom Martin, Annette McGivney, Becky Myers, Jim and Janece Ohlman, Richard "Q" Quartaroli, Scott Thybony, Bil Vandergraff, and former Grand Canyon Superintendent Joe Alston. Their counsel was like gospel.

The talents of Bronze Black, Katherine Spillman, and Mary Williams helped create a handsome book.

Our editor, longtime Grand Canyon river guide and writer Michael P. Ghiglieri, proved invaluable. His critical reviews and brutal honesty helped craft this book. Besides undying gratitude, we still owe him about half a dozen red pencils.

The only thing worse than misspelling someone's name in an acknowledgment is forgetting someone altogether. We apologize if we have done either.

Finally, we thank our families and loved ones for their support and patience throughout our own obsession to write this book, including Brittany, Alexandra, Weston and Becky Myers, Dawn Kish, and Walker, Carolina and the rest of the Butler family.

SELECTED BIBLIOGRAPHY

Books, Articles, and Other Papers

1. ABBEY, EDWARD PAPERS. University of Arizona Library Special Collections, Box 5, Folder 2, Journal, June 18, 1969.
2. ANNERINO, JOHN. *Hiking the Grand Canyon*. Third Edition. San Francisco, CA: Sierra Club Books, 2006.
3. ANDREWS, GEORGE. "Scaling Wotan's Throne." *Natural History*, Vol. 40, December, 1937. pp. 723-724.
4. ANTHONY, HAROLD E. "The Facts About Shiva." *Natural History*, Vol. 40, December, 1937. pp. 709-721.
5. *Arizona Visitors and Greeters Guide*. Phoenix, Arizona: Martin Warren Krause. January 1937, Volume 2, Number 1: p. 2.
6. AUTHOR UNKNOWN. "Canyon hiker bucking for Ripley's." *The Arizona Republic/The Phoenix Gazette*. May 13, 1987: p. 1W-18.
7. AUTHOR UNKNOWN. "Dr. and Mrs. James Butchart." *United Christian Missionary Society, U.S.A.*: 1933.
8. Author unknown. "Hiking Mathematician Sets a Sturdy Stride." *Arizona Days and Ways Magazine, The Arizona Republic*, 1955.
9. BABBITT, BRUCE E. *Color and Light: The Southwest Canvases of Louis Akin*. First edition. Flagstaff, Arizona: Northland Press, 1973.
10. BAKER, RUSSELL. *Growing Up*. First edition. New York, New York: Congdon and Weed, St. Martin's Press, 1982.
11. BEER, BILL. *We Swam the Grand Canyon: The True Story of a Cheap Vacation that Got a Little Out of Hand*. Seattle, WA: The Mountaineers, 1988.
12. BELKNAP, WILLIAM. *Powell Centennial Grand Canyon River Guide*. Ninth printing. Boulder City, NV: Westwater Books, 1969.
13. BUCK, PEARL S. *Fighting Angel*. First edition. NY, NY: John Day, 1936.
14. BUCK, PEARL S. *My Several Worlds*. John Day edition. NY, NY: John Day, 1954.
15. BUTCHART, JOHN HARVEY. *Grand Canyon Treks: A Guide To The Inner Canyon Routes*. Glendale, CA: La Siesta Press, 1970.
16. IBID. *Grand Canyon Treks 11: A Guide To The Extended Canyon Routes*. Glendale, CA: La Siesta Press, 1975.
17. IBID. *Grand Canyon Treks 111: Inner Canyon Journals*. Glendale, CA: La Siesta Press, 1984.
18. IBID. *Grand Canyon Treks: 12,000 Miles Through The Grand Canyon* (edited and designed by Wynne Benti). Bishop, CA: Spotted Dog Press, 1997.
19. IBID. *The Hiking Logs of J. Harvey Butchart, Volume 1, 1954-1964*." Flagstaff, AZ: John Harvey Butchart Collection, Northern AZ University Cline Library Special Collections and Archives Dept.
20. IBID. *The Hiking Logs of J. Harvey Butchart, Volume 11, 1965-1969*. Flagstaff, AZ: John Harvey Butchart Collection, Northern AZ University Cline Library Special

Collections and Archives Dept.

21. IBID. *The Hiking Logs of J. Harvey Butchart, Volume* III, 1970-1975. Flagstaff, AZ: John Harvey Butchart Collection, Northern AZ University Cline Library Special Collections and Archives Dept.

22. IBID. *The Hiking Logs of J. Harvey Butchart, Volume* IV, 1976-1987. Flagstaff, AZ: John Harvey Butchart Collection, Northern AZ University Cline Library Special Collections and Archives Dept.

23. IBID. "Helices in Euclidean N-Space." Ph. D. Thesis. *American Journal of Mathematics* 55 (1) (January 1933): pp. 126-130.

24. IBID. "The Grandview Trail." *Plateau* (October 1958): pp. 37-40.

25. IBID. "Backpacking On The Colorado." *Appalachia* (26) (1960): pp. 176-182.

26. IBID. "Old Trails In The Grand Canyon." *Appalachia* (28) (7) (1962): pp. 45-64.

27. IBID. "Backpacking Grand Canyon Trails." *Summit* (10) (June 1964): pp. 12-19.

28. IBID. "The Canyon Nobody Knows." Unpublished essay (1964): 8 pages.

29. IBID. "The Lower Gorge Of The Little Colorado." *Arizona Highways* (41) (September 1965): pp. 34-42.

30. IBID. "Wotan's Throne." *Summit* (11) (September 1965): pp. 8-11.

31. IBID. "Scouting Grand Canyon By Plane." *Summit* (March 1966): pp. 9-13.

32. IBID. "Routes Into Grand Canyon's Remote Upper Corner." *Summit* (14) (March 1968): pp. 22-28.

33. IBID. "Grand Canyon's Enfilade Point Route." *Summit* 19 (5) (1973): pp.18-21.

34. IBID. "Summits Below The Rim: Mountain Climbing In The Grand Canyon." *Journal of Arizona History*, 17(1) (1976): pp. 21-38.

35. BUTCHART, NELLIE. "A Cheerful Letter from Lu Cheo fu, China." *The Christian Evangelist*. St. Louis, Mo: Christian Publishing Company, June 4, 1908. p. 726

36. BUTCHART, NELLIE. *World Call*. Indianapolis, Indiana: Disciples of Christ. December 1920.

37. COFFEY, MARIA. *Where the Mountain Casts its Shadow: The Dark Side of Extreme Adventure*. New York, New York: St. Martin's Press. 2003.

38. CLARK, GEORGIE WHITE AND NEWCOMB, DUANE. *Georgie Clark: Thirty Years of River Running*. Chronicle Books, San Francisco, CA: 1977.

39. EVANS, RICHARD T., MATTHES, FRANCOIS E., "Map of Grand Canyon National Park." *The Military Engineer*, Vol. XVIII, May-June 1926, No.99, p. 188-201.

40. DIMOCK, BRAD. *Sunk Without a Sound*. Fretwater Press, Flagstaff, AZ: 2001.

41. DRISCOLL, THOMAS. "Reagan at Eureka: Memories of a Student Rebel." *Los Angeles Times WEST magazine*. April 13, 1967: pp. 26-29.

42. DUTTON, CLARENCE E. *Tertiary History of the Grand Canyon District*. Washington, D.C.: Government Printing Office, 1892.

43. FISHER, RICHARD D. *Earth's Mystical Grand Canyons*. Tucson, Arizona: Sunracer Publications, 1995.

44. FLETCHER, COLIN. *The Man Who Walked Through Time*. NY, NY: Vintage Books, 1972.

45. GANCI, DAVE. "Zoroaster Temple." *AZ Days and Ways Magazine, Arizona Republic*. June 26, 1960.

46. GERBER, RUDY J. *Grand Canyon Railroad*. Phoenix, Arizona: Primer Publishers, 1990.

47. GERBER, RUDY J. *The Railroad and the Canyon*. Gretna, LA: Pelican Publishing Company, Inc., 1995.

48. GHIGLIERI, MICHAEL P., AND MYERS, THOMAS. *Over the Edge: Death in Grand Canyon*. Flagstaff, AZ: Puma Press, 2001.

49. GOLDWATER, BARRY. "Natural Bridge Discovery." *Arizona Highways* (2) 1955, p. 8-13.

50. *Grand Canyon of Arizona*. Chicago, IL: Passenger Department of the Santa Fe, 1909

51. GREEN, J. D. (EDITED BY JIM OHLMAN) *Hiking in the Grand Canyon Backcountry*. Kissimmee, FL: Tower of Ra Publishing, 1995.

52. HUTCHINSON, MELVIN. "Backpack Adventure in Remote Asbestos Canyon." *Desert Magazine* 22 (1) January 1959, pp. 19-21.

53. JONES, STAN. *Ramblings By Boat and Boot In Lake Powell Country*. Page, AZ: Sun Country Publications, 1988.

54. KELSEY, MICHAEL. *Canyon Hiking Guide to the Colorado Plateau*. Fourth edition. Provo, UT: Kelsey Publishing, 1999.

55. KELSEY, MICHAEL, AND JENNINGS, RUSSELL AND JENNY. *China On Your Own: The Hiking Guide to China's Nine Sacred Mountains*. Third Edition. Vancouver, British Clumbia, Canada: Open Road Publishers, 1985.

56. KRUGER, VERLEN AND FRENTZ, BRAND. *The Ultimate Canoe Challenge: 28,000 Miles Through North America*. Lincoln, Nebraska: iUniverse, 2004.

57. KRUTCH, JOSEPH WOOD. *GRAND CANYON, Today and All Its Yesterdays*. New York, New York, William Sloane Associates, 1958.

58. LEAMER, LAURENCE. *Ascent: The Spiritual And Physical Quest Of Legendary Mountaineer Willi Unsoeld*. First Quill Edition. NY, NY: William Morrow & Co., 1999.

59. LEYDET, FRANCOIS. *Time and the River Flowing: Grand Canyon*. San Francisco, CA: Sierra Club, 1964.

60. MATTHES, FRANCOIS E. "Mapping the Grand Canyon." *The Technology Review*, Vol. VII, January, 1905, No. 1, p. 1-25.

61. MCCOY, MARION. "Up Grand Canyon Pinnacles With K.U. English Teacher." *The Kansas City Star*. March 20, 1955. p. 6H.

62. MCGIVNEY, ANNETTE. "A Grand Obsession." *Backpacker*. June 1997: pp. 46-56.

63. MCGIVNEY, ANNETTE. "Colin Fletcher is Not Dead." *Backpacker*. August 2002, pp. 49-54.

64. PEATTIE, RODERICK. *The Inverted Mountains: Canyons of the West*. NY, NY: The Vanguard Press, 1948.

65. POWELL, JOHN WESLEY. *The Exploration of the Colorado River and Its Canyons*. New York, New York: Dover Publications, reprint 1961.

66. PRESTON, DIANA. *The Boxer Rebellion: The Dramatic Story of China's War on Foreigners that Shook the World in the Summer of 1900*. NY, NY: Walker and Co., 2000.

67. PRICE, EVA JANE. *China Journal 1889-1900: An American Missionary Family During the Boxer Rebellion With the Letters and Diaries of Eva Jane Price and Her Family.* NY, NY: Collier Books, 1990.

68. RICHMOND, AL. *Cowboys, Miners, Presidents and Kings; the Story of the Grand Canyon Railway.* 6th Edition. Flagstaff, AZ: Grand Canyon Railway, 2005.

69. RUSHO, W.L. *Everett Ruess: A Vagabond For Beauty.* Salt Lake City, UT: Gibbs-Smith Publisher, 1983.

70. SEGLUND, WANDA. "Butchart of the Grand Canyon." *Arizona Magazine* (insert), *Arizona Republic*, December 12, 1976: p. 32.

71. SEVERSON, ED. "Harvey Butchart and His Grand Canyon." *Arizona Highways* (64) (1) 1988, p. 38-45.

72. SIMMONS, LEO W. *Sun Chief: The Autobiography of a Hopi Indian.* Seventh printing. New Haven, CT: Yale University Press, 1967.

73. STECK, GEORGE. *Hiking Grand Canyon Loops.* Guilford, CT: The Globe Pequot Press, 2002.

74. STEGNER, WALLACE. *Beyond the Hundredth Meridian: John Wesley Powell and the Second Opening of the West.* NY, NY: Penguin USA, 1992.

75. STEIGER, LEW. "Dr. Harvey Butchart." *Boatman's Quarterly Review* 16 (1) (Spring 2003): pp. 30-40.

76. STEVENS, LARRY. *The Colorado River in Grand Canyon: A GUIDE.* Flagstaff, Arizona, Red Lake Books, 1983.

77. TESSMAN, NORM. "The Rescue of the Liberator 107 Crew." *Arizona Highways* 73 (7) (July 1997)

78. TOMASI, AARON AND PERNELL. *Grand Canyon Summits Select. An Obscure Compilation of Sixty-Nine Remote Ascent Routes in The Grand Canyon National Park Backcountry.* Flagstaff, AZ: www.Arizonas-Vertical-Web.com, 2001.

79. THYBONY, SCOTT. *Official Guide To Hiking The Grand Canyon.* Grand Canyon, AZ. Grand Canyon Association, revised ed., 2005.

80. VAN VALKENBURG, JIM. "Each Year Finds Local Man Back In Grand Canyon—Afoot, Alone." Lawrence Daily Journal-World. 1953. p. 10.

81. WARDEN, MARIAN. "KU Prof, 68, Is Mountain Expert." *Lawrence Daily Journal-World.* September 22, 1966.

82. WING, KIT AND WOMACK, LES. "Bluewater Voyage Down the Little Colorado!" *Desert Magazine.* August, 1956.

83. WINSHIP, GEORGE PARKER. *Fourteenth Annual Report of the Bureau of Ethnology,* 1892-1893. Washington, D.C.: Government Printing Office, 1896. pp. 574-75.

84. WOOD, WALTER A. "Shiva Temple and Wotan's Throne." *American Alpine Journal,* Vol. 111, No. 2, 1938: pp.137-141.

Audio / visual

1. BAIN, GEORGE, PARSONS, SMITH. "Harvey Butchart: Grand Canyon Pioneer, Parts 1, 11 & 111" Videotaped interview with Harvey Butchart: May 7, 1988. 180 minutes.

2. BAXTER, SCOTT. Cassette taped interview with Butchart, J. Harvey: 1981. 270 minutes.
3. BUTLER, ELIAS. Transcribed interviews with George and Susan Billingsley, Renee Carrizosa, Allyn Cureton, Moon Dehua, Alan Doty, Pam Foti, Dave Ganci, Walter Merwin Haskell, Anne and Sam Madariaga, Jim Ohlman, Bob Packard, Dale Slocum, George Steck, Scott Thybony, Ellen Tibbetts and Ken Walters. 2003-2005.
4. MADARIAGA, ANNE. Cassette taped interview with Butchart, Harvey and Roma: 1995.
5. MYERS, TOM. Videotaped interview with Butchart, J. Harvey. September 1993.
6. QUINN, MIKE interview with Butchart, J. Harvey. May 28, 1994. Grand Canyon National Park Archives. Catalog Number: GRCA #63381
7. SANCHEZ, IRIS interview with Butchart, J. Harvey. May 9, 1975. Flagstaff, Arizona. Northern Arizona University Cline Library, Special Collections, NAU Tape 15-2.
8. U. S. GOVERNMENT. "Harvey at Albright." Grand Canyon, AZ. Videotaped Harvey Butchart slideshow: January 16, 1986. 100 minutes.

Copyrights

Excerpts from Pearl Buck's *Fighting Angel* and *My Several Worlds* are reprinted by permission of Harold Ober Associates. Excerpts from W.L. Rusho's *Everett Ruess: A Vagabond for Beauty* are reprinted by permission of Gibbs Smith.

The following list shows page numbers of images made by Harvey Butchart (excepting the Matthes-Evans maps), available for order from the Northern Arizona University Special Collections Department:

- Inside front cover, Matthes-Evans map (east half): NAU.MAP.550B
- Inside back cover, Matthes-Evans map (west half): NAU.MAP.550A
- Page 1 Enfilade Point route aerial: NAU.PH.70.3.3470
- 107 Inner Gorge: NAU.PH.70.3.147
- 157 Hopi salt ladder: NAU.PH.70.3.548
- 168 Cureton at War Twin rock: NAU.PH.70.3.546
- 169 Cureton rappelling cliff: NAU.PH.70.3.547
- 192 Cheops Pyramid: NAU.PH.70.3.475
- 212 Royal Arch: NAU.PH.70.3.731
- 218 Wotan's Throne: NAU.PH.70.3.3796
- 236 Siegfried Pyre: NAU.PH.70.3.4489
- 304 Redwall Cavern: NAU.PH.70.3.256
- 410 Wotan's Throne: NAU.PH.70.3.6932

NOTES

All letters to/from Otis "Dock" Marston are from the Huntington Library, San Marino, California. Letters to/from Harvey Butchart are from personal collections and the Special Collections Department at Northern Arizona University.

Opening Epigraph:
xi. **"The best explorers are seldom..."** Sam Negri in *Earth's Mystical Grand Canyons*: p. 51

Prologue: Great Thumb Mesa, 2004
1. **"This place startled me..."** Butchart, *Grand Canyon Treks* (La Siesta), p. 41.
3. **"You aren't really living..."** Butchart, "Summits Below The Rim," p. 25.
5. **"It was like he was made..."** Packard speaking to Butler, December 7, 2003.
6. **"There are two reasons..."** Butchart speaking to Myers; also see Myers videotaped interview with Butchart, September 1993.
6. **"a total of four routes..."** Dutton, *The Tertiary History of the Grand Canyon District*, p. 159
6. **"Dutton had much to learn..."** Butchart, "Summits Below The Rim," p. 25.
7. **"I once told him..."** Leydet, *Time and the River Flowing*, p. 87.
9. **"The main thing I think..."** Baxter speaking to authors, 2004.

Chapter 1: To the Titan of Chasms (1901-1906)
11. **"Twenty Yosemites might lie unperceived..."** Higgins, C.A., *Grand Canyon of Arizona*, p 17.
11. **"On September 11, 1901..."** Gerber, *The Railroad and the Canyon*, p. 51.
11. **"mighty miracle."** Gerber, *Grand Canyon* Railroad, p. 1.
12. **"Thirty-eight year-old Louis..."** Babbitt, *Color and Light*, p. 21.

Chapter 2: The Thatch Hut Mountains (1912)
15. **"I want to see the..."** Butchart speaking to Myers; also see Myers videotaped interview with Butchart, September 1993.
17. **"The three hikers strolled past..."** Butler trip to Mount Lushan, January, 2006.
18. **"Although Kuling was new..."** Moon Dehua of the Kuling Chamber of Commerce speaking to Butler. Dehua can be reached at moondehua@hotmail.com.

Chapter 3: From The Wars of God
23. **"If they had not gone..."** Buck, *Fighting Angel*, p. 75.
26. **"Dr. Butchart performed an..."** Author unknown, "Dr. and Mrs. James Butchart."
28. **"The boat has eyes..."** See Butchart's "Recollections of Childhood." Unpublished essay.
31. **"At Kiukiang we changed..."** Ibid.
32. **"Now came, as always..."** Buck, *My Several Worlds*, p. 131.
32. **"I remember the time Father...."** Butchart letter to Myers, 1995.
33. **"A Cheerful Letter..."** Nellie Butchart, "A Cheerful Letter from Lu Cheo fu," p. 726.

Chapter 4: Enter the Mapmakers (1902-1923)

35. **"But the Colorado River?"** Matthes, "Mapping the Grand Canyon," p. 6.
All other quotes and information regarding Richard Evans and Francois Matthes:
Evans, Matthes, "Map of Grand Canyon National Park," pp. 188-201.
and
Matthes, "Mapping the Grand Canyon," pp. 1-25.

Chapter 5: Sea Change (1913-1920)

43. **"After that I never cried..."** Baker, *Growing Up*, p 61.
45. **"It amazes me when I..."** Butchart, J. Harvey. "Childhood Memories," unpublished essay.
46. **"He respected the Chinese workmen..."** Ibid.
47. **"One of my best memories..."** Butchart letter to Myers. January 18, 1995.
47. **"He was an M.D. but..."** Butchart speaking to Myers; also see Myers videotaped interview with Butchart, September 1993.
48. **"James Butchart, doctor, preacher..."** Author unknown, "Dr. and Mrs. James Butchart."
48. **"We were all devastated..."** Butchart speaking to Myers; also see Myers videotaped interview with Butchart, September 1993.
49. **"We did a lot of hiking..."** Ibid.
50. **"We took it for granted..."** Ibid.
51. **"One fearful aspect of those..."** Buck, *My Several Worlds*, pp. 113-114.

Chapter 6: High Grade Points and the President's Daughter (1921-1929)

55. **"I had gone with two..."** Baxter interview with Butchart, 1981.
55. **"I was painfully shy..."** Roma Butchart, unpublished autobiographical essay.
55. **"I decided I wouldn't be..."** Butchart speaking to Myers; also see Myers videotaped interview with Butchart, September 1993.
56. **"Actually, she [Nellie] had a..."** Ibid.
57. **"Mother didn't get a part time..."** Butchart letter to Myers, January 28, 1997.
58. **"I am counting my blessings..."** Nellie Butchart, *World Call*.
58. **"I was sort of a small..."** Butchart speaking to Myers; also see Myers videotaped interview with Butchart, September 1993.
59. **"After I'd been given ..."** Ibid.
60. **"When I was a freshman in..."** Ibid.
60. **"Back in the Middle West..."** Sanchez interview with Butchart, NAU Tape 15-2.
63. **"High school days were a..."** Roma Butchart autobiographical essay.
63. **"I would have given everything..."** Ibid.
64. **"Harvey was at Eureka all..."** Ibid.
65. **"Being the janitor's daughter, Ella..."** Ibid.
65. **"We hardly knew each other..."** Ibid.
67. **"While I didn't play much..."** Driscoll, "Reagan at Eureka," p. 28.

Chapter 7: Southwestern Medicine (1929-1945)

69. **"Arizona, The Year-round State!"** *Arizona Visitors and Greeters Guide*, p. 2.

70. **"My mother went through some..."** Butchart letter to Myers, 1995.
71. **"I got more than the..."** Baxter interview with Butchart, 1981.
71. **"I did a lot of work..."** Ibid.
72. **"That was the time when..."** Butchart speaking to Myers; also see Myers videotaped interview with Butchart, September 1993.
73. **"The reality was..."** Ibid.
73. **"She had been suffering from..."** Ibid.
75. **"Many years ago when we.."** Butchart letter to Bob Packard, Sept. 10, 1981.
75. **"One of the books that..."** Ibid.
76. **"For a pleasant day with..."** Butchart letter to Bob Packard, 1991.
79. **"Since hiking is Dr. Butchart's..."** Arizona State College, 1946, courtesy Anne Madariaga.

Chapter 8: The Canyon Nobody Knows

81. **"Although it was first seen..."** Butchart, "The Canyon Nobody Knows."
81. **"That is quite immaterial..."** All Allan MacRae quotes from letter to Butchart, January 13, 1977.
82. **"three Air Force crewmembers..."** Tessman, "The Rescue of the Liberator 107 Crew," p. 13.
84. **"The canyon is less than..."** Butchart, "The Canyon Nobody Knows."
89. **"the three lightest and most agile..."** Winship, *Fourteenth Annual Report of the Bureau of Ethnology*, pp. 574-75.
89. **"To see something new..."** Butchart, "The Canyon Nobody Knows."
90. **"People have asked me if..."** *Grand Canyon Treks* (Spotted Dog Press), p. 261.
92. **"Each had his mine somewhere..."** Butchart, "Old Trails In The Grand Canyon," p. 45.
93. **"To...nineteenth century Americans..."** Leamer, Ascent, p. 74.

Chapter 9: Getting His Legs (1945-1954)

95. **"At first glance the spectacle..."** Krutch, *GRAND CANYON, Today and All Its Yesterdays*, p. 4.
95. **"Many writers have said that..."** Butchart letter to Jim Ohlman, 1976.
95. **"I'd seen that, day after..."** Butchart speaking to Myers; also see Myers videotaped interview with Butchart, September 1993.
96. **"What hath God wrought!"** Butchart letter to Myers, 1995.
97. **"I knew the Canyon was..."** Ibid.
97. **"Dr. Harvey Butchart, head of..."** *The Coconino Sun*. March 1946.
97. **"We didn't go into very..."** Myers interview with Butchart, September 1993.
97. **"Most of my trips were..."** Ibid.
98. **"There were these old abandoned..."** Ibid.
98. **"I carried a big stick to..."** Butchart, "My First Visit to Supai" *Hiking Logs, Volume 1*, p. iv.
100. **"Mr. Rust knows of a..."** Zane Grey letter to Lina "Dolly" Grey, April 20, 1908. Courtesy of Loren Grey.
101. **"I began to limit most ..."** Butchart letter to Myers, 1995.
101. **"I read everything I could..."** Myers videotaped interview with Butchart, September 1993.

101. **"This contour map..."** Butchart, "The Canyon Nobody Knows."

101. **"Those maps showed a lot..."** Butchart speaking to Myers; also see Myers videotaped interview with Butchart, September 1993.

101. **"There are a number of..."** Butchart, "Old Trails In The Grand Canyon," p. 49.

102. **"It's your turn Doc..."** Butchart, "My first visit to Phantom Canyon (date unknown)" *Hiking Logs, Volume 1*, p.iii

103. **"Too long. You could get..."** Butchart, "Grandview, Tonto, and Hance Trails in one day, January 23, 1954," *Hiking Logs, Volume 1*, p. 6.

103. **"I felt in the mood for..."** Ibid.

104. **"We were kindred spirits..."** Butchart speaking to Myers; also see Myers videotaped interview with Butchart, September 1993.

104. **"You have now found out what..."** Butchart letter to Bob Packard, June 18, 1984.

105. **"We got the first hint..."** Butchart, "Grandview, Tonto, and Hance Trails in one day, January 23, 1954" *Hiking Logs, Volume 1*, p. 6.

105. **"I left them with the..."** Ibid.

105. **"It was a fairly long..."** Ibid., p. 7.

Chapter 10: *The Fieldwork*

111. **"One can get through the..."** Butchart, *Grand Canyon Treks* (Spotted Dog Press), p. 52.

Chapter 11: *Backpacking the Colorado (1954)*

117. **"We carried no life preservers..."** Dimock, *Sunk Without a Sound*, p. 77.

117. **"I have never really lost..."** Butchart letter to Otis Marston, December 24, 1954.

117. **"It seems unfortunate that Grand..."** Butchart "Old Trails In The Grand Canyon," p. 48.

119. **"People often asked me how..."** Clark, *Georgie Clark: Thirty Years of River Running*, p. 6.

120. **"The boat? Obviously it must..."** Wing and Womack, "Bluewater Voyage Down the Little Colorado!" pp. 13-18.

121. **"I could cross to the..."** Butchart, J. Harvey, "Hermit Trail to Granite Rapids (August 1, 1954 to August 2, 1954)" *Hiking Logs of J. Harvey Butchart, Volume 1*, p. vi.

121. **"I don't feel secure in..."** Gibson speaking to Myers, 2005.

121. **"That idea of going downriver..."** Myers videotaped interview with Butchart, September 1993.

122. **"If I could do that..."** Butchart, "From Hance Rapids to the Bridge (September 4, 1954)," *Hiking Logs, Volume 1*, p. 2.

123. **"We got into water after..."** Butchart, "From Hance Rapids to the Bridge (September 4, 1954)," *Hiking Logs, Volume 1*, p. 2.

123. **"I can't make it to..."** Butchart, "From Hance Rapids to the Bridge (September 4, 1954)," *Hiking Logs, Volume 1*, p. 3.

124. **"I began to wish I..."** Ibid., p. 4.

124. **"Roma was quite disgusted..."** Ibid., p.4.

124. **"Hansen talked a pretty good..."** Butchart, "From Tanner to Hance by Water (September 18, 1954)," *Hiking Logs, Volume 1*, p. 4.

126. **"the boy was so sleepy..."** Ibid., p. 5.

128. **"couldn't let me have any..."** Ibid.

128. **"So ended another snafu!"** Ibid.

128. **"If you ever wish to..."** Butchart letter to Marston, October 26, 1954.
130. **"He was a son-of-a-bitch..."** Mooz speaking to Myers. December 2005.
133. **"When do we start?"** Marston letter to Butchart, June 21, 1955.

Chapter 12: Boyd (May 1955)

137. **"I found that a heavy..."** Butchart, "Tragedy between Point Imperial and Desert View (May 24-27, 1955),"*Hiking Logs, Volume* 1, p. 7c.
137. **"I'll tell you right now..."** Dimock, *Sunk Without a Sound*, p. 123.
138. **"May 4, 1955..."** Butchart letter to Patraw, May 4, 1955. Courtesy National Archives and Records Administration, Pacific Region.
140. **"practically a non-swimmer..."** Butchart, "Tragedy between Point Imperial and Desert View (May 24-27, 1955)" *Hiking Logs, Volume* 1, p. 7a.
141. **"In the short distance from..."** Ibid.
141. **"When it came down to..."** Slocum speaking to Butler, December 27, 2003.
143. **"After protesting Dale's..."** Butchart, "Tragedy between Point Imperial and Desert View (May 24-27, 1955)," *Hiking Logs, Volume* 1, p. 7a.
143. **"Well, we're in this thing..."** Steiger, "Dr. Harvey Butchart," p. 36.
143. **"Remember, when we were on..."** Ibid.
145. **"Boyd got along quite well...."** Butchart, "Tragedy between Point Imperial and Desert View (May 24-27, 1955)," *Hiking Logs, Volume* 1, p. 7b.
145. **"I can see that we're..."** Ibid.
146. **"I was deflating my air..."** Steiger, "Dr. Harvey Butchart," p. 37.
146. **"I might not have ever..."** Ibid.
147. **"I don't have much strength..."** Butchart, "Tragedy between Point Imperial and Desert View (May 24-27, 1955)," *Hiking Logs, Volume* 1, p. 7c.
148. **"That was the last..."** Myers videotaped interview with Butchart, September 1993.
148. **"Walking along the bank the..."** Butchart, "Tragedy between Point Imperial and Desert View (May 24-27, 1955)," *Hiking Logs, Volume* 1, p. 7c.
149. **"He was pretty upset..."** Lynch speaking to Myers, 2004.
150. **"I was sick for a..."** Steiger, "Dr. Harvey Butchart," p. 38.
150. **"The Park Service started a..."** Ibid.
152. **"He [Boyd] said something..."** Ibid.
153. **"mostly bad judgment that I..."** Butchart speaking to Myers; also see Myers videotaped interview with Butchart, September 1993.

Chapter 13: Legwork for the Historian (1955-1959)

155. **"You certainly have been covering..."** Marston letter to Butchart, November 23, 1956.
158. **"I am openly in admiration..."** Marston letter to Butchart, January 17, 1955.
159. **"Sun Chief related that when..."** Butchart, "The Lower Gorge Of The Little Colorado," p. 36.
159. **"I cannot recall any special..."** Marston letter to Butchart, April 30, 1956.
160. **"This gorge is different from..."** Butchart, "The Lower Gorge Of The Little Colorado," p. 34.
161. **"Each bend in the canyon..."** Ibid., p. 37.
161. **"I realized how much more..."** Ibid.
163. **"By the summer of 1956..."** Butchart, "Backpacking On The Colorado," p. 178.

164. **"As I walked up this..."** Ibid., p. 179.
167. **"I have wondered a lot..."** Marston letter to Bruce, January 23, 1958.
167. **"As we have said before..."** Butchart letter to Marston, November 15, 1956.
168. **"This was the right place..."** Butchart, "The Lower Gorge Of The Little Colorado," p. 40.
171. **"The problem with Dock Marston..."** Anne Madariaga interview with Butchart, 1995.
171. **"Pat once said that you..."** Butchart letter to Marston, June 6, 1963.
171. **"...[Reilly] is always suspicious, which..."** Marston letter to Butchart, June 1963.

Chapter 14: The G. C. Tramp (1957-1958)

173. **"No matter how many trips..."** Van Valkenburg, "Each Year Finds Local Man Back In Grand Canyon," p. 10.
176. **"the two men who have..."** Marston letter to Butchart, April 14, 1956.
176. **"Oh yes," Clubb said. "You're..."** Anne Madariaga interview with Butchart, 1995.
178. **"He weighed no more than..."** Butchart, "Summits Below The Rim," p. 30.
179. **"He was totally taken with..."** Clubb, Jr. letter to Myers, January 12, 2005.
181. **"Hiking is mountaineering with essential..."** Butchart, Grand Canyon Treks (Spotted Dog Press), p. 31.
182. **"On average, he toted 60-75..."** McCoy, "Up Grand Canyon Pinnacles With K.U. English Teacher," p. 6H.
182. **"The important mountain climbing..."** Warden, "KU Prof, 68, Is Mountain Expert."
184. **"He was always a very..."** Clubb, Jr. letter to Myers, January 12, 2005.
184. **"one of the two most..."** Clubb letter to Marston, March 6, 1955.
185. **"The Canyon belongs to the..."** Van Valkenburg, "Each Year Finds Local Man Back In Grand Canyon," p. 10.
186. **"Clubb reveled in the Canyon..."** Schwartz speaking to Myers, April, 2005.
186. **"I found his home, introduced..."** Davis email to Butler, December, 2003.
187. **"On Clubb's third ascent of..."** Butchart letter to John Azar, September 23, 1996.
189. **"I thought of writing you..."** Clubb letter to Marston, July 17, 1957.
190. **"Whenever I could find a..."** Butchart, "Backpacking in the Grand Canyon," Hiking Logs, Volume 1.
190. **"Merril Clubb and I had..."** Butchart letter to Marston, July 28, 1958.
191. **"When Clubb passed his experiences..."** Butchart, "Summits Below The Rim," p. 31.
191. **"On Sunday I came back..."** Butchart letter to Marston, July 20, 1958.

Chapter 15: Wotan's or Bust!

195. **"If there is a better..."** Butchart, "Backpacking On The Colorado," p.182.
196. **"The silt is gone, trapped..."** Silt inflow estimate is based on data from Stevens, The Colorado River in Grand Canyon, p. 37.
197. **"I wouldn't want to cross..."** Butchart letter to Dove Menkes, September 28, 1976.
197. **"Various routes are possible in..."** Butchart, Grand Canyon Treks (Spotted Dog Press), p. 109.

Chapter 16: The Lure of the Void (1957-1964)

201. **"Why muck and conceal one's..."** Rusho, Everett Ruess: A Vagabond For Beauty, p. 161.

201. **"Butchart! Him again?"** Allyn Cureton speaking to Myers, November, 2005.
203. **"John Harvey Butchart is a..."** Author unknown, "Hiking Mathematician Sets a Sturdy Stride."
204. **"The long canyon whose head..."** Butchart, "Asbestos Canyon via Clear Creek (April 3-6, 1958)" *Hiking Logs, Volume 1*, p. 38.
204. **"When Hutchinson's "Backpack Adventure in..."** See Bibliography.
207. **"You have provided me with..."** Marston letter to Butchart, January 29, 1958.
207. **"On the subject of your..."** Butchart letter to Marston, February 3, 1958.
208. **"It seems to me that..."** Marston letter to Butchart, September 1958.
208. **"Your job is important..."** Marston letter to Butchart, January 29, 1958.
208. **"I remember one reason I..."** Bain, "Harvey Butchart: Grand Canyon Pioneer."
210. **"The water was fast and..."** Butchart, "Sipapu and the Marston Boat Party (June 9-12, 1959)," *Hiking Logs, Volume 1*, p. 79.
211. **"Just a few more minutes..."** Butchart, "Apache Point, Royal Arches Creek (Oct.17-18, 1959)," *Hiking Logs, Volume 1*, p. 90.
212. **"She is still very nervous..."** Butchart letter to Marston, January 15, 1960.
213. **"There were some fascinating things..."** Butchart, "Diana Temple (July 30, 1960)" *Hiking Logs, Volume 1*, p. 104.
213. **"Apparently I had been influenced..."** Butchart, "From Pipe Creek past Horn Creek to the North Rim (August 20-23, 1959)," *Hiking Logs, Volume 1*, p. 83.
214. **"Dear Roma, I assure you..."** Marston letter to Roma Butchart, August 23, 1960.
215. **"I had heard terrible things..."** Butchart, "Through Marble Canyon (August 24-29, 1960)" *Hiking Logs, Volume 1*, p. 83.
215. **"Even from a distance I..."** Butchart, "Backpacking On The Colorado," p. 180.
216. **"I recognized the place where..."** Butchart, "Through Marble Canyon (August 24, 1960 to August 29, 1960)," *Hiking Logs, Volume 1*, p. 109.
216. **"Even if James White..."** Butchart, "From Pipe Creek to Hermit Rapids (August 28-30, 1962)," *Hiking Logs, Volume 11*, p. 189.
217. **"shorter trips are more to..."** Butchart, "Hermit Basin to Bass Canyon, Dragon and Crystal Creeks (August 6-11, 1964)," *Hiking Logs, Volume 1*, p. 260.

Chapter 17: Summit Fever (1961-1965)

219. **"It was then that the..."** Ganci, "Zoroaster Temple."
221. **"The Ken Todds took care..."** Butchart, "Toltec, Chemehuevi, Piute, and Jicarilla Points (July 15-16, 1961)," *Hiking Logs, Volume 1*, p. 140.
224. **"When...the story broke into..."** Anthony, "The Facts About Shiva," p. 709.
225. **"it seemed to some skeptical..."** Author unknown."Treasureless Island." *Time Magazine.* Oct 4, 1937: pp. 46-47.
226. **"No rock climber can tell..."** Andrews, "Scaling Wotan's Throne," p. 723.
226. **"The descent presented no..."** Wood, "Shiva Temple and Wotan's Throne," pp. 137-138.
227. **"There is a pinyon pine..."** Butchart, "Wotan's Throne and Kibbey Butte (May 30-31, 1961)," *Hiking Logs, Volume 1*, p. 135.
229. **"What a place this would..."** Butchart, "Wotan's Throne," p. 8.
229. **"In fact, their description..."** Butchart, "Fifth Ascent of Wotan (June 1-2, 1962)," *Hiking Logs, Volume 1*, pp. 172-173.

230. **"Leaving his wife, Jean, and..."** Ghiglieri and Myers, *Over the Edge: Death in Grand Canyon*, p. 99-100.
232. **"I didn't let on that..."** Bain, "Harvey Butchart: Grand Canyon Pioneer."
232. **"I did go to Kanab..."** Ibid.
233. **"What memories it brings back..."** Butchart, "Summits Below The Rim," p. 30.
234. **"That surely makes my type..."** Butchart letter to Marston, November 1960.
234. **"I would refute that..."** Ganci speaking to Butler, December, 2005.
235. **"Walking by myself was lonesome..."** Butchart, J. Harvey. "Topocoba Trail to Sinyala Fault and Matkatamiba Canyon to Supai along the Redwall rim (March 26-30, 1964)." *Hiking Logs, Volume 1*. p. 135.
235. **"This time I felt shot..."** Butchart letter to Marston, August 26, 1964.

Chapter 18: The Man That Time Forgot (1963)

Unless otherwise noted, all Colin Fletcher quotes come from Fletcher, *The Man Who Walked Through Time*.

239. **"If we don't get invited..."** Butchart letter to Marston, December 10, 1962.
240. **"The attraction of this project..."** Butchart, "Above the mouth of Havasu Creek (November 11-12, 1961)," *Hiking Logs, Volume 1*, p. 159.
241. **"I'm rather certain I found..."** Butchart, "Esplanade above 140 Mile Cyn (December 15-16, 1962)" *Hiking Logs, Volume 1*, p. 201.
241. **"Dr. Butchart sends this cordial..."** Butchart, "Old Trails In The Grand Canyon," p. 64.
246. **"Colin Fletcher called us from..."** Butchart letter to Marston, March 29, 1963.
249. **"I had filled in the..."** Butchart, "Below Tahuta and Great Thumb Points (April 15-16, 1963),"*Hiking Logs, Volume 1*, p. 211.
250. **"Speaking about Colin's chances, we..."** Butchart letter to Marston, April 17, 1963.
253. **"We got a card from..."** Butchart letter to Marston, June 22, 1963.
254. **"Colin left here on a..."** Butchart letter to Marston, June 29, 1963.
254. **"The beautiful friendship which had..."** Marston letter to Butchart, September 20, 1963.
255. **"Colin sent us Christmas greetings..."** Butchart letter to Marston February 1, 1964.
256. **"Colin sent us an autographed..."** Butchart letter to Marston, January 1, 1968.
258. **"I'm never really writing about..."** Hogan, Ron interview with Colin Fletcher. beatrice.com, 1997: http://www.beatrice.com/interviews/fletcher/
258. **"Harvey and I looked at..."** Fletcher letter to Myers, April 11, 1995.
259. **"I read Colin's journal well.."** Butchart letter to Marston, March 7, 1969.
259. **"Do I resent him in..."** Fletcher letter to Myers, April 11, 1995.
259. **"We talked about Colin Fletcher..."** Ohlman speaking to Butler, 2003.

Chapter 19: Unanswered Questions (1965-1971)

263. **"Breaks in the Redwall formation..."** Butchart, "Backpacking Grand Canyon Trails," p. 13.
264. **"It was kind of picturesque..."** Quinn interview with Butchart, May 28, 1994.
265. **"The idea of pioneering a..."** Fletcher, *The Man Who Walked Through Time*, pp. 86-87.
265. **"I didn't do that much..."** Susan Billingsley speaking to Butler, December 22, 2003.
266. **"In a lot of places..."** George Billingsley speaking to Butler, December 22, 2003.
267. **"Familiarity may breed contempt..."** Butchart, "Scouting Grand Canyon By Plane," p. 8.

267. **"When I had walked from…"** Butchart, "Scouting Grand Canyon By Plane," p. 13.

267. **"Perhaps I was trying to…"** Butchart, "Fossil Bay and Redwall rim to Specter (July 25-27, 1966)," Hiking Logs, Volume II, p. 360.

268. **"In the morning…"** Butchart, "Aztec Amphitheater (April 11-14, 1968)," *Hiking Logs, Volume 11*, p. 443.

270. **"On the steepest and loosest…"** Ibid., p.444.

271. **"Doc had said that my…"** Butchart, "From Apache Point to Colorado River and Forester Canyon (November 28-December 1, 1968)," *Hiking Logs, Volume 11*, p. 470b.

272. **"The way over there seemed…"** Butchart, "Bass Trail, Arch Creek, Fossil Creek, Tonto Trail (November 25-29, 1969)," *Hiking Logs, Volume 11*, p. 522.

272. **"The news about Clubb is…"** Butchart letter to Marston, August 28, 1964.

273. **"He did some odd things…"** Butchart letter to John Azar, August 15, 1993.

273. **"You can't order me around…"** Butchart, "Memories of Merrel D. Clubb," unpublished essay.

274. **"Just went down the B.A…"** Clubb letter to Butchart, December 21, 1969.

275. **"The rock is relatively soft…"** Butchart, "Scouting the way to the river at Mile 123.7 (April 12, 1971)," *Hiking Logs, Volume 111*, p. 593.

275. **"We had found a way…"** Ibid., p. 594.

277. **"I had tried to get…"** Butchart, "Grand Canyon's Enfilade Point Route," p. 21.

279. **"I felt like I was…"** Butchart, Grand Canyon Treks (Spotted Dog Press), p. 13.

279. **"No one's walked more down…"** Anne Madariaga interview with Butchart, 1995.

Chapter 20: The Laughing German God

283. **"Travel along the Hermit Shale…"** Butchart, "Wotan's Throne," p. 10.

Chapter 21: The Paper Trail (1969-1975)

289. **"No assumption should be made…"** Kieffer, Hugh letter to Ziegler, Don. *United States Geologic Survey.* HHK/213 "Ziegler." August 17, 1989.

289. **"Dear Mr. Professor Harvey Butchart…"** Geary letter to Butchart, February 1975.

290. **"While I was still on…"** Butchart, "Port Hole and Grand Scenic Divide (May 5, 1973)" *Hiking Logs, Volume 111*, p. 691.

290. **"Shortly after arriving there…"** Wheelock, *Grand Canyon Treks 111: Inner Canyon Journals*, p. 5.

291. **"It is hoped you will…"** Davis, *Escape Routes.*

292. **"The number of backpackers…"** McGivney, "Colin Fletcher is Not Dead," p. 49.

292. **"When I started, you had…"** Foti speaking to Butler, 2004.

293. **"My book is intentionally sketchy…"** Butchart, Grand Canyon Treks (Spotted Dog Press), p. 13.

294. **"I arrived at Soap Creek…"** Butchart, "Soap Creek (March 4, 1961)," *Hiking Logs, Volume 1*, p. 125.

294. **"This guide, along with its…"** Green, Hiking in the Grand Canyon Backcountry, p. 177.

294. **"There are several ways to…"** Butchart, *Grand Canyon Treks: A Guide To The Inner Canyon Routes*, (La Siesta Press), p. 47.

294. **"We spent a lot of…"** Steck speaking to Butler, November 15, 2003.

295. **"Harvey's books weren't meant to…"** Kelsey email to Butler, 2004.

295. **"Well, we understood it..."** Tibbetts speaking to authors, January 8, 2004.
295. **"One can go along a..."** Butchart, Grand Canyon Treks II: A Guide To The Extended Canyon Routes, p. 16.
296. **"H.B. mentions the bypass..."** Steck, Hiking Grand Canyon Loops, p. 260.
297. **"Routes to the three southern..."** Butchart, Grand Canyon Treks: A Guide To The Inner Canyon Routes, (La Siesta Press), p. 35.
298. **"One thing we liked so..."** Tibbetts speaking to authors, January 8, 2004.
298. **"Some hikers have deplored..."** Butchart letter to Myers, 1995.
299. **"If you were a new..."** Doty speaking to Butler, 2004.
299. **"He was a clearing house..."** Thybony speaking to Butler, 2004.
301. **"I didn't hear anything about..."** Butchart letter to Donald Davis, October 27, 1969.
301. **"North Rim–Harvey Buchart, prof..."** Abbey Papers, Journal, June 18, 1969.
303. **"if utilized for a theater..."** Powell, The Exploration of the Colorado River, p. 77.
303. **"I paced the depth and..."** Butchart, "Lees Ferry to Diamond Creek, Impressions (6/8-16/70)," Hiking Logs, Volume 111, p. 551.
305. **"The Redwall aisle both above..."** Butchart, "Sowats, Jumpup, Kanab, and Kwagunt (5/19-20/74)," Hiking Logs, Volume 111, p. 744.

Chapter 22: Spray Paint and Gingersnaps
307. **"After a lecture by the..."** Butchart, "Atoka Route (Summer '56), " Hiking Logs, Volume 1, p. 7d.
308. **"I felt rather peculiar about..."** Butchart letter to Myers, October 23, 1998.
308. **"We camped just below the..."** Packard speaking to Butler, December 7, 2003.
309. **"The fire under my soup..."** Butchart, "94 Mile Canyon, Redwall Near Set (April 25-27, 1977)," Hiking Logs, Volume iv, p. 868.
309. **"I had heard that the..."** Butchart, "Fragment of a log to Cardenas Canyon (date unknown)," Hiking Logs, Volume 1, p. 194.
309. **"This time I carried a..."** Butchart, "Cape Royal to Freya Temple (June 24, 1962)" Hiking Logs of J. Harvey Butchart, Volume 1, p. 176
309. **"If the Park Service would..."** Butchart, "Esplanade above 140 Mile Canyon (Dec. 15-16, 1962)," Hiking Logs, Volume 1, p. 200.
309. **"Butchart typically carried a can..."** George Billingsley speaking to Butler, December 22, 2003.
310. **"We would hike along..."** Kirschvink email to Butler, February 2005.
310. **"Aren't you going to take..."** Cureton speaking to Myers, 2004.
311. **"I planned two interesting trips..."** Butchart, "North Rim (July 1-2, 1968)," Hiking Logs, Volume 111, p. 448.
311. **"I went to the bash..."** Butchart letter to Myers, April 21, 1996.
311. **"You wonder whether this Eden..."** Butchart, "The Lower Gorge Of The Little Colorado," p. 34.
312. **"I have always been..."** Butchart letter to Myers, 1995.
312. **"He was already a legend..."** Baxter speaking to authors, 2004.
313. **"He'd have his meals..."** Thybony speaking to Butler, 2004.
314. **"The two quarts of water..."** Butchart, "Paria Canyon (June 27-29, 1977)," Hiking Logs, Volume iv, p. 875.
314. **"I found plenty of shallow..."** Butchart, "Topocoba Trail to Sinyala Fault and

Matkatamiba Canyon to Supai along the Redwall rim (March 26-30, 1964)," *Hiking Logs, Volume* 1, p. 253.

315. **"One boy I walked with..."** Butchart letter to Myers, December 27, 1994.
315. **"Has anybody ever mentioned what..."** Susan Billingsley speaking to Butler, December 22, 2003.
316. **"I go out alone about..."** Butchart, "Summits Below The Rim," p. 36.
317. **"I made a foolishly long..."** Butchart, "My broken wrist and the Little Colorado River (May 1964)," *Hiking Logs, Volume* 1, p. 257.
317. **"We found that the other..."** Ibid.
318. **"There was a problem in..."** Butchart, "Vishnu Canyon, Sheba, Solomon (June 2-4, 1970)," *Hiking Logs, Volume* 111, p. 550.
318. **"He decided he would teach..."** Susan Billingsley speaking to Butler, December 22, 2003.
319. **"I had carried the rope..."** Butchart, "The Coconino in Saddle Canyon (December 1969)," *Hiking Logs, Volume* 11, p. 526.
319. **"I tied the rope to..."** Butchart, "Fault Route at Mile 30.4, Saddle Canyon (November 1, 1969)," *Hiking Logs, Volume* 11, p. 519.
323. **"I guess I was just..."** Steiger "Dr. Harvey Butchart," p. 32.
324. **"The night he was missing..."** Packard speaking to Butler, December 7, 2003.
324. **"The moon went behind..."** Butchart, "Saddle Canyon to Little Nankoweap (December 20-21, 1969)," *Hiking Logs, Volume* 11, p. 525c.

Chapter 23: Solo Journeys

327. **"Standing at the back..."** Coffey, *Where the Mountain Casts its Shadow*, excerpted from *Outside Magazine*, September 2003. p. 104.
330. **"Yes, I have to confess..."** Butchart letter to Myers, 1995.
330. **"Confessions of a Hiking Widow."** Roma Butchart, unpublished essay, 1984.
332. **"Roma just...she never seemed..."** Thybony speaking to Butler, 2004.
332. **"Looking into Roma's eyes..."** Williams speaking to Butler, 2004.
333. **"She gained quite a reputation..."** Ohlman speaking to Butler, 2004.
336. **"Well, of course," said Roma..."** Anne Madariaga interview with Roma Butchart, 1995.
336. **"Our first vacations in the..."** Butchart, "The Lower Gorge Of The Little Colorado," p. 34.
339. **"My dad wasn't a great..."** Jim Butchart speaking to Myers, 2004.
339. **"Jim hiked with me until..."** Butchart letter to Myers, 1995.
340. **"By the time I was..."** Anne Madariaga speaking to Butler, 2004.
342. **"accusing her of not liking..."** Butchart letter to John Azar, February 27, 1995.
343. **"Roma put up with way..."** Janece Ohlman speaking to Myers, 2004.
344. **"Yes, my wife has been..."** Butchart letter to Myers, 1995.

Chapter 24: The Canyon's Grip

347. **"I've cried in the canyon..."** McGivney, "A Grand Obsession," p. 56.
348. **"Nothing anywhere can rival..."** Rusho, *Everett Ruess: A Vagabond for Beauty*, p. 63.
350. **"Aryan principles..."** Steck speaking to Butler, November 15, 2003.
353. **"Right at the mouth..."** Robert Eschka, unpublished journal, 1983.
353. **"It was a long walk..."** Kruger and Frentz, *The Ultimate Canoe Challenge*, p. 187.

357. **"I came to NAU in..."** Packard speaking to Butler, December 7, 2003.
358. **"We used to do two..."** Walters speaking to Butler, January 13, 2004.
359. **"Goll dang!"** Cureton speaking to Myers, November, 2005.
361. **"Soon I came to a..."** Simmons, *Sun Chief*, p. 126.
361. **"He would carry immense packs..."** Frick speaking to Butler, Feb. 17, 2005.
362. **"I'm obsessed," he told writer..."** McGivney, "A Grand Obsession," p. 47.
363. **"People all have securities, whether..."** Mancuso letter to Butchart, January 23, 1985.
363. **"He almost embarrassed me by..."** Butchart letter to John Azar, April 14, 1996.
364. **"No doubt you, if anyone..."** Mancuso letter to Butchart, April 25, 1984.
365. **"Brehmer had been keeping a..."** Hendricks, Larry. "Searchers find clues in missing woman's journal." *Arizona Daily Sun*, August 23, 2001, p A1.
366. **"Brehmer's sons notified the Coconino..."** Minard, Anne. "Search and rescue team had own safety to consider." *Arizona Daily Sun*, September 2, 2001. p. A1.
367. **"They were having some kind..."** Thybony, Scott. "Salt Trail," fieldnotes, 8/22/01-8/24/01.
368. **"Harvey ~ even as a young..."** Mancuso letter to Butchart, July 7, 1984.
368. **"Anyone who tries to do..."** McGivney, "A Grand Obsession," p. 56.

Chapter 25: Unfinished Business (1976-1988)

373. **"I had no problems with..."** Butchart, "Evans Butte (October 11, 1976)," *Hiking Logs, Volume 111*, p. 851.
373. **"At 69, Butchart claims to..."** Seglund, "Butchart of the Grand Canyon," p. 32.
373. **"I was feeling low because..."** Butchart, "Boucher Creek, Hermit Camp (December 9-12, 1977)," *Hiking Logs, Volume 1v*, p. 890.
374. **"The Time Magazine for that..."** Marley speaking to Butler, 2004.
375. **"I consider that trip to..."** Ohlman speaking to Butler, 2004.
376. **"I needed five and a..."** Butchart, "Phantom and Sturdevant Canyons (February 24-26, 1978)," *Hiking Logs, Volume 1v*, p. 899b.
378. **"Well, it was in July..."** Baxter speaking to authors, 2004.
378. **"I was experimenting..."** Butchart, "209 and 214 Mile Canyons (July 15-18, 1981)," *Hiking Logs, Volume 1v*, p. 984.
383. **"My physical condition..."** Butchart, "North Rim (September 14-15, 1982)," *Hiking Logs, Volume 1v*, p. 1017.
383. **"I was weaker than ever..."** Butchart, "From Burnt Canyon South of Twin Point (March 13-18, 1983)," *Hiking Logs, Volume 1v*, p. 1029.
384. **"I almost elected to try..."** Butchart, "Zion and South of St. George (September 10, 1984)," *Hiking Logs, Volume 1v*, p. 1054.
384. **"One of the things that..."** Quinn interview with Butchart, May 28, 1994.
385. **"When I reached the spring..."** Butchart. "Amos Spring and Zion (May 6-12, 1987)," *Hiking Logs, Volume 1v*, p. 1080.
385. **"In an Arizona Republic newspaper..."** Author unknown, "Canyon hiker bucking for Ripley's," p. 1W-18.
385. **"As a washed up, tired..."** Butchart letter to Bob Packard, December 9, 1989.
385. **"It was a good trip..."** Butchart letter to Dove Menkes, July 30, 1989.
386. **"The thing I remember is..."** Staveley speaking to Butler, 2004.

Chapter 26: Out of the Murk (April 2004)

392. **"Grapevine in the Archean rock..."** Butchart, *Grand Canyon Treks* (La Siesta Press), p. 32.

Chapter 27: The Last Hand Hold (1989-2002)

397. **"Kipling wrote one time, 'Ship..."** Steiger, "Dr. Harvey Butchart," p. 40.

397. **"One of the principal satisfactions..."** Butchart letter to Dove Menkes, September 28, 1976.

397. **"I am finally serious about..."** Butchart letter to Dove Menkes, December 30, 1992.

400. **"He had, obviously..."** Williams speaking to Butler, 2004.

401. **"Since I was a little..."** Carrizosa speaking to Butler, 2005.

Epilogue: It Was A Sporty Climb (2004)

411. **"No farther seek his merits..."** Gray, Thomas. "Elegy Written in a Country Churchyard," 1751.

411. **"I wouldn't want to think..."** Butchart letter to Myers, 1995.

411. **"Usually I don't care..."** Butchart, "Wotan's Throne," p. 8.

413. **"It was nearing 7:30 P.M..."** Butchart, "Fifth Ascent of Wotan (June 1-2, 1962)," *Hiking Logs, Volume 1*, p. 172-173.

Closing Epigraph:

418. **"I would plead guilty..."** Butchart letter to unknown, 1975.

HARVEY BUTCHART CLIMBS IN GRAND CANYON

1.	Shiva Temple	6/5/1957	43.	Burro, Mt.	4/11/1966
2.	Widforss Point	7/4/1957	44.	Horseshoe Mesa	12/4/1966
3.	Powell Plateau	8/17/1957	45.	Diamond Peak	5/14/1967
4.	Comanche Point	12/29/1957	46.	Sumner Butte	5/28/1967
5.	Mt. Huethewali	7/4/1958	47.	Cope Butte	8/9/1967
6.	Cheops Pyramid	4/4/1959	48.	Cogswell Butte	8/18/1967
7.	Chuar Lava Hill*	6/11/1959	49.	Gunther Castle	6/4/1969
8.	Deva Temple	7/18/1959	50.	Elaine Castle*	8/9/1969
9.	Diana Temple	7/30/1960	51.	Pollux Temple	2/7/1970
10.	Whites Butte	1/1/1961	52.	Sheba Temple*	6/3/1970
11.	Escalante Butte	2/18/1961	53.	Solomon Temple*	6/3/1970
12.	Cardenas Butte	3/25/1961	54.	Lyell Butte	7/25/1970
13.	Kibbey Butte	5/31/1961	55.	Siegfried Pyre	10/9/1971
14.	Fossil Mtn.	7/16/1961	56.	O'neill Butte	10/17/1971
15.	Tabernacle*	9/2/1961	57.	Wodo, Mt.	2/13/1971
16.	Juno Temple*	9/3/1961	58.	Coronado Butte	4/4/1971
17.	Wotans Throne	6/1/1962	59.	Alsap Butte	6/15/1972
18.	Saddle Mtn.	6/4/1962	60.	Novinger Butte*	6/15/1972
19.	Freya Castle*	6/24/1962	61.	Ayer Point	8/26/1972
20.	Fishtail Mesa	7/24/1962	62.	Newton Butte	9/16/1972
21.	Woolsey Butte	7/27/1962	63.	Howlands Butte	2/18/1973
22.	Krishna Shrine*	9/5/1962	64.	Vesta Temple	5/18/1973
23.	Rama Shrine*	9/22/1962	65.	Duppa Butte*	5/31/1973
24.	Hubbell Butte*	4/25/1963	66.	Cochise Butte*	6/7/1973
25.	Poston Butte	4/25/1963	67.	Chiavria Point	6/8/1973
26.	Jupiter Temple*	4/26/1963	68.	Swilling Butte*	10/13/1973
27.	Lava Butte*	6/12/1963	69.	Fiske Butte	11/16/1974
28.	Carbon Butte*	6/12/1963	70.	Espejo Butte*	9/6/1975
29.	Barbenceta Butte*	8/27/1963	71.	Colonade	10/12/1975
30.	Nankoweap Mesa*	8/28/1963	72.	Lone Mtn.	3/17/1976
31.	Nankoweap Butte*	8/28/1963	73.	Marion Point	7/16/1976
32.	Newberry Butte*	11/10/1963	74.	Evans Butte	10/11/1976
33.	Dragon	9/1/1964	75.	Vulcans Throne	11/13/1976
34.	Dragon Head*	9/1/1964	76.	Little Dragon	10/8/1977
35.	Steamboat Mtn.*	10/17/1964	77.	Racetrack Knoll	6/3/1978
36.	Bridgers Knoll*	6/4/1965	78.	Red Point*	1/2/1979
37.	Venus Temple*	7/17/1965	79.	Hall Butte	10/12/1980
38.	Apollo Temple	7/17/1965	80.	Hawkins Butte	2/23/1981
39.	King Arthur Castle	8/25/1965	81.	Oza Butte**	c.1949?
40.	Guinevere Castle	8/25/1965	82.	Battleship**	c.1952?
41.	Pattie Butte*	9/19/1965	83.	Unknown Climb ***	
42.	Sinking Ship	9/25/1965			

Half of the climbs were solo; 28 were first recorded ascents.
*   *First recorded ascent.*
**   *No record exists of these actual climb dates. The dates listed are speculation.*
***   *Harvey Butchart claimed 83 summits, however climber Jim Ohlman only found record of 82 climbs in Harvey's logs. This list was complied by Ohlman.*

INDEX

THE AUTHORS

Elias Butler is a freelance writer and large format photographer living in Flagstaff, Arizona.
To view more of his work, please visit
www.eliasbutler.com. This is his first book.

Courtesy Mary Allen

Courtesy Tom Martin

At age 19, Tom Myers began celebrating the
dawning of each New Year by hiking somewhere in Grand Canyon. It is a tradition he
and his wife continue to share with their three
children. He has co-authored two previous
Canyon books, *Over the Edge: Death in Grand
Canyon* (with Michael Ghiglieri) and *Fateful
Journey* (with Chris Becker and Larry Stevens).

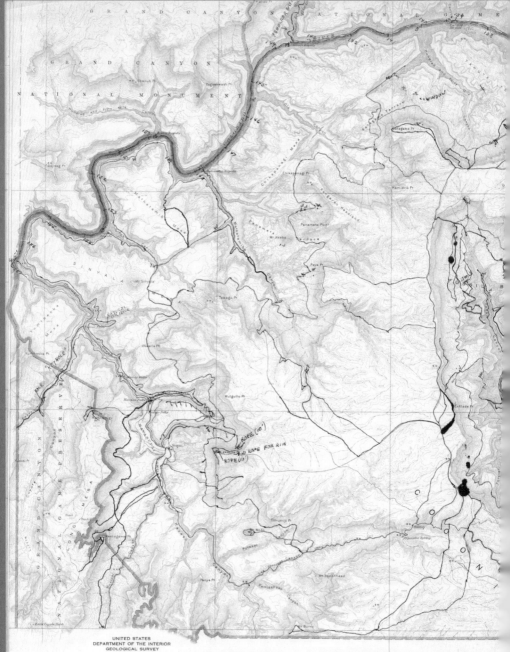

UNITED STATES
DEPARTMENT OF THE INTERIOR
GEOLOGICAL SURVEY
IN COOPERATION WITH THE
NATIONAL PARK SERVICE

TOPOGRAPHIC MAP
OF THE
GRAND CANYON NATIONAL PARK
ARIZONA
(WEST HALF)

Scale 1:48000

Contour interval 50 feet
Datum is mean sea level
Brachymetric indicates that elevations
on this map should be decreased by 4 feet

Topography by Francois E. Matthes and Richard T. Evans
Surveyed in 1902–1923

Polyconic projection   To place on North American datum
move projection lines 675 feet south and 292 feet west
5000-yard grid based upon U. S. zone system F

Edition of 1927
reprinted 1948